Unless Recalled Earlier

The Gerontologist
as an Administrator

The Gerontologist as an Administrator

Jeffrey A. Giordano
and Thomas A. Rich

AUBURN HOUSE
Westport, Connecticut • London

Library of Congress Cataloging-in-Publication Data

Giordano, Jeffrey A. (Jeffrey Anthone), 1942–
    The gerontologist as an administrator / Jeffrey A. Giordano and Thomas A. Rich.
        p.   cm.
    Includes bibliographical references and index.
    ISBN 0–86569–306–4 (alk. paper)
    1. Aged—Services for—Administration.   2. Aged—Services for—Management.   I. Rich,
Thomas A.   II. Title.
    HV1451.G55   2001
    362.6'068—dc21   00–061076

British Library Cataloguing in Publication Data is available.

Library of Congress Catalog Card Number: 00–061076
ISBN: 0–86569–306–4

First published in 2001

Auburn House, 88 Post Road West, Westport, CT 06881
An imprint of Greenwood Publishing Group, Inc.
www.greenwood.com

Printed in the United States of America

The paper used in this book complies with the
Permanent Paper Standard issued by the National
Information Standards Organization (Z39.48–1984).

10 9 8 7 6 5 4 3 2 1

Contents

Tables and Figures

TABLE

FIGURE

Preface

Administration and gerontology are both multidisciplinary areas of study and practice. Most gerontology academic programs offer courses in administration. All students in gerontology require a background in administration of programs for older adults. This text is intended for gerontology students at the undergraduate and graduate levels of study. Current administrators in gerontology will also benefit greatly from this text.

The text integrates administrative theory and practice gleaned from many disciplines, recognizing that older adults are a unique population served by public and private organizations. Effective administrators working in these organizations must be able to integrate knowledge of this population with appropriate administrative practice. The result will be a gerontologist administrator.

TEXT DEVELOPMENT

Gerontology has matured as a discipline, developing distinct areas of study and application. Like many applied fields (for example, business administration, public administration, health administration, and social work administration), gerontology has established an administrative specialty. Educational curricula for all administrative specialties draw upon similar sources for administrative content, integrating it with the particular field. Gerontology administration courses and curricula must emphasize the unique dimensions of working with the older adult population. Research and case studies related to administrative programs for older adults are not abundant, but considerable attention has been generated toward the requirements, demands, and instruction of the gerontologist administrator.

The authors of this text conducted interviews with practicing administrators over a period of two years, in preparation for this endeavor. Information was also obtained at seminars using a formal questionnaire about administrative aspects of programs that serve older adults. Both authors have taught graduate and undergraduate gerontology courses specifically related to administration of programs for older adults. It is worth noting that many students in these courses already hold administrative positions. The authors also have held administrative positions and consulted in administration. Finally, numerous discussions with gerontology faculty revealed the need for a relevant gerontology text for courses in administration.

All of these sources provided a focus for much of the content of this book. Attention is given to the practice of administration in organizations among the three service sectors—public (government), not-for-profit (voluntary), and profit. The result is a book especially designed for future and current administrators in an array of organizations that offer older adult programs. The gerontology student typically wants to work with and help older adults. Dependable, creative work leads to increased responsibility, and suddenly the worker is an administrator. This book is directed toward those who are presently administrators, those who aspire to be administrators, and those who will be offered the opportunity to assume administrative functions.

CONTENT AND SPECIAL FEATURES

Two central themes are presented throughout the text. The first theme emphasizes the importance of knowledge of gerontology for administrative practice in relation to the older adult population. Second, administration is conceptualized as a combination and integration of management and leadership. Information from a multitude of sources was adapted to present administrative practice relevant to programs for older adults. Theoretical information serves as a foundation for practice guidelines, techniques, and methods. Emphasis is placed on the actual practice of administration. Each chapter includes a "learning experience" that requires application of the knowledge gained from the discussion.

The text features an emphasis on contemporary areas of administration, such as ethics, leadership, and the appropriate use of groups and teams for problem-solving and decision-making. Information on groups is integrated into several chapters. The field research on administration of programs for older adults gave direction to the content; consequently, the text includes information on special projects, the use of volunteers, financing and fund-raising, public relations, and staff participation in administrative activities. The text assumes that the reader has basic knowledge of gerontology. For those who lack this background, the reading of either *Aging in a Changing Society* (2nd ed.) by James A. Thorson (2000) or *Social Forces and Aging* by Robert C. Atchley (2000) is recommended.

TEXT CONVENTIONS

Certain terms in administration and gerontology have interchangeable usage in the literature, which can be confusing. The majority of these are clarified in the text. Some conventions and terms that characterize this text are:

- The term "older adult" is consistently used to refer to people over the age of 65, unless it appears in a quotation or in a learning experience.
- The odd-numbered chapters use the feminine pronoun, and the even-numbered chapters the masculine pronoun.
- The word "practice" refers to the practice of administration unless otherwise specified.
- "Clients" and "consumers" are used interchangeably and may refer to individuals, groups, families, organizations, or communities.
- Although the term "staff" refers to a specific set of functions within organizational theory, it is the most common term used in programs for older adults to mean employees. Thus, "staff" and "employees" are used interchangeably.
- "Organization," "agency," and "program" are used interchangeably to refer to clusters of services or a service area for older adults.
- "Programs" are any cluster of services, ranging from indirect coordination, monitoring, and funding to community-based direct delivery of services to older adults and their families.

ACKNOWLEDGMENTS

Our thanks to those whose support and feedback contributed in many different ways to the creation and completion of this book:

Laugene Arnsby, Sarasota, Florida; Maria Daniela Ayala, Bradenton, Florida; Melissa Austin Biasingame, Laurels Nursing and Rehabilitation Center, St. Petersburg, Florida; Marylou Docksey, University of South Florida; Paul A. d'Oronzio, Albany, New York; Nan H. Giordano, Sarasota, Florida; Diane Klein, Fort Worth, Texas; Roger A. Lohman, West Virginia University; Louis Maltaghati, Pines of Sarasota; Janna N. Merrick, University of South Florida; Diane W. Rich, Daphne, Alabama; James A. Thorson, University of Nebraska at Omaha; Jan Wheeler, University of South Florida, New College; Kathleen H. Wilber, University of Southern California.

The Gerontologist
as an Administrator

Chapter 1

Administering Services to Older Adults

Imagine the human service world without administrators. This is a fantasy many service providers have amid the pressures of providing programs for older adults. What would happen? A service provider would emerge to organize the delivery of services, to convert policy into action, to offer vision, and to make decisions. At first, these functions might be shared. Later, the most capable employees or those who enjoyed a different status or perhaps had a knack for bringing compromise to conflict would be seen as leaders. Several leaders would come forward in a sizable organization. An order of authority would follow. These leaders would be called administrators.

Administrators often must choose between the support of staff, the preservation of services, pleasing superiors, or the satisfaction of stakeholders. Rarely can all parties be satisfied. Robert Katz's (1982) reflections on administration, after functioning as an administrator himself, were, "I now know that every important executive action must strike a balance among so many conflicting values, objectives, and criteria that it will always be suboptimal from any single viewpoint. Every decision or choice affecting the whole enterprise has negative consequences for some of the parts" (p. 18). Such are the universal challenges of administration. Administrators at all levels—team leaders, supervisors, department heads, or chief executives—are expected to make important decisions that affect the lives of people immediately and in the future.

Anyone who practices administration is considered an administrator. The term "administrator" is both a title and a general description of a person who engages in administrative activity. Administrative activities occur at many levels of an organization. Administrators should have expertise in the area within which they administer, while possessing knowledge, skill, and abilities in administration.

Gerontology is composed of information on the biological, psychological, and social aspects of aging from all academic disciplines and fields of practice (Hooyman & Kiyak, 1999). According to Atchley (1995), "A gerontologist has a broad knowledge base in academic gerontology, as well as specialized knowledge about various aspects of aging, and does research, provides education or training, and/or applies gerontological knowledge through technical assistance, administration, management, or development of products or programs" (p. 43). Gerontological knowledge assures relevance, produces a deeper understanding of clients, and gives credibility to decision-making.

Gerontology is a science with a body of knowledge. When this science becomes an activity to serve others, it is known as applied gerontology. The gerontologist engaged in administrative practice is an applied gerontologist who combines gerontological knowledge and administrative science. These bodies of conceptual and technical knowledge result in a scientist-practitioner who is a gerontologist administrator. Just as management theorist Mary Parker Follett (1986) argued, at the beginning of the twentieth century, for the appropriate and relevant education of the professional business manager, gerontology seeks to educate and train professional administrators for programs for older adults.

Administration in the field of gerontology is an emerging specialization, and the literature is sparse. Most texts on administration, regardless of the field, rely heavily on a common store of research and information from the social sciences, as will this text. Recently, computer science has provided contributions and mechanisms for modern administration.* Furthermore, selected and adapted information from fields of practice, such as business administration, health administration, social work administration, and human services administration will be drawn upon to educate the gerontologist administrator. This is most consistent with the multidisciplinary nature of gerontology. Aging research, service program information, and information on older clients, as well as published and reported information on staff who choose to work with older adults, will be integrated with theoretical and conceptual information and administrative practices from other fields, to construct this text for the gerontologist administrator.

With the expansion of services to older adults, many administrators have advanced from the direct service ranks with limited administrative training. Other administrators have crossed over from related services of health, mental health, and education or business with limited knowledge of gerontology. A growing number are gerontology-administration graduates.

Administrative jobs for gerontologists exist at several levels (Bluford, 1994). The executive level includes positions such as executive director, chief operations officer, and human resources director. The program level, or middle management, represents department heads or technical coordinators. The supervisory

---

*The text will make occasional reference to relevant computer technology and programs. However, an in-depth treatment is not possible nor, considering the pace of change, desirable. The reader is referred to the journal *Computers in Human Services* (New York: Haworth Press) and the book by J. A. O'Brien, *Introduction to Information Systems: Essentials for the Internetworked Enterprise* (9th ed.) (New York: McGraw-Hill, 1999).

and team leaders focus, assist, and guide staff. A large number of jobs in organizations that have programs for older adults are administrative (Bluford, 1994).

WHAT IS ADMINISTRATION?

Administration in human services and health programs is associated with directing the operations of profit, not-for-profit, and public organizations. Some professions have established specialties such as the Master's in Public Health Administration or Nursing Home Administrator programs. Business administration associated with profit organizations is well established and is epitomized by the coveted Master's of Business Administration (M.B.A.) degree. Historically, the literature speaks to a management theory known as Administrative Management. This concept emphasizes the universality of management as a function that can be applied to all organizations large or small (Gatewood, Taylor, & Ferrell, 1995). This view of administration provides a foundation to extend administration to programs for older adults.

Clarification of terminology as used in this text is necessary, since scholarly presentations often exchange administration and management. Slavin (1980) constructed a theoretical framework for social administration and chose to treat the terms "administrator" and "manager" as interchangeable. Morgan and Hiltner (1992) used the term "administrator" as opposed to "manager" because administrator is the most commonly used term in the literature and by service professions. In a subsequent section of this chapter, a conceptualization is offered as a framework for understanding administration as a combination of management and leadership.

Administration in human services involves translating societal mandates, attaining goals, securing resources and technology, and directing organizational behavior (Ehlers, Austin, & Prothero, 1976). Another definition is that administration is a translation of policy into action requiring decisions, problem resolutions, evaluation, motivation and supervision of employees, as well as routine tasks such as record keeping. Described in a slightly different way, administration is seen "as a process of defining and attaining the objectives of an organization through a system of coordinated and cooperative efforts" (Stein, 1970, p. 7). Other authors emphasize the more expressive aspects of administration, speaking to a process that releases energies so that resources can be applied to organizational goals and objectives. In general, for service organizations, administration is the use of authority, power, and influence to bring about the delivery of services while mediating a network of complex relationships. The administrative process involves setting goals, securing and allocating resources, and coordinating the activities of people while planning for and directing change.

In the past, most authors held that implicit in the definition of administration is leadership. In today's world, leadership is explicit and a major component of administration. Indeed, Skidmore (1995) has stated that the challenge today is "to develop more capable, dynamic leaders who can help to formulate and carry out social policies, plans, and decisions" (p. 4). Abraham Zaleznik (1989) leads the chorus for establishing leadership as a major component of administration.

Contemporary Challenges for Administrators

The primary focus of this text is the administration of community programs for older adults and the roles of the administrators. The administration of these programs has become increasingly complex (Raymond, 1991). Programs for older adults are firmly established in the health and human services system of our country. Community programs are equally well established in the private sector, as seen in the expansion of profit home health services, living facilities and mental health services for older adults. Administration and design of these programs have evolved toward traditional bureaucratic models which limit program effectiveness. Government policy changes have also pushed programs for older adults toward traditional bureaucratic models (Alter, 1988). The movement away from the informal service networks of the 1970s and the 1980s, along with the inclination to avoid institutionalization of older adults, has fostered a proliferation of community programs. Programs such as senior day care, mental health, hospice, home health, and case management continue to grow in today's health and human services environment.

Programs for older adults also experienced the shift in administrative patterns that has had an impact on all service organizations. This changed as the percentage of professionals with higher education increased, which brought the expectation for professionals to be more involved in the planning and implementing of programs. The work force has become more diverse. Sensitivity and appreciation of differences related to age, gender, ethnicity, religion, and race are critical. Adding to the changes is the expanded use of volunteers and contract employees. Increased emphasis on team work characterizes the more participatory nature of administration in organizations today. More than ever before, clients' opinions, feelings, and suggestions contribute to the direction and type of service. In many organizations for older adults, some of the clients are also volunteers. The shift toward traditional models, the professionalism of staff, the diversity of staff, and the involvement of volunteers have all combined to create blended models of organizational structure and design.

Contributing to the challenge are controls exerted by standards from state and federal government, as well as accrediting organizations, like the Joint Commission on Accreditation of Health Organizations (JCAHO). These controls place substantial constraints on administrative decision-making. This is particularly true with regulations in such areas as physical environment, employee relations, and client rights. These regulations and expectations require not only knowledge, but also acquisition of relevant skills such as negotiation, supervision, and effective communications.

Current computer technology has greatly affected the nature of administrative work. Data is readily available and requires less time for collection and analysis. Electronic communication has reduced the amount of time an administrator must spend on mundane tasks. For example, the proofreading and production of reports and documents is considerably less laborious with modern word processing. At the same time, availability of technology has increased the expectation for information, with shorter deadlines, often requiring staff with technical skills and retraining of existing staff.

All of these contemporary changes, including the technology advancements, shift the paradigm of what is necessary to be an effective administrator in organizations that provide programs for older adults. That shift is to a greater emphasis on leadership and time to offer such leadership to the staff, the organization, and the community. Challenges and change are abetted by vision and the ability to gain commitment to the future.

A MODEL OF ADMINISTRATION

Administration and management traditionally have been explained by identifying the functions (sometimes called processes). The notion of static functions has not been found to be useful and is giving way to delineations of roles, skills, and abilities. However, adherence to traditional functions, while limiting, continues to dominate the literature and the classroom. An example from a contemporary textbook demonstrates the wide use of these traditional functions of administration. A current business administration text (Gatewood et al., 1995) classifies management into four different functions of planning, organizing, leading, and controlling as described in Table 1.1. Koontz (1990) organized his text around five functions, adding supervision. Many other authors have adapted this format; for example, Weinbach (1990) and Morgan and Hiltner (1992). The latter authors dropped the supervision function added by Weinbach and Koontz, substituting staffing. This has been a dominant and useful approach to instruction on administration. As the profession of gerontology continues to evolve (Friedsman, 1995), so must the sophistication of instruction for administrators.

Research has not supported these functional classifications either as comprehensive categories of administration or as fully representative of administrative behavior in the workplace. While these functions may be useful to learn how an administrator spends time, they are limiting when the full complexity of administrative activities is contemplated. These classification systems include leadership as one of the functions of management, place leadership under one of those functions, or do not address leadership. A few scholars have dispensed with the traditional functions categorization to provide a more descriptive and integrated presentation of administration (Mintzberg, 1989; Skidmore, 1995).

Management and leadership are integrated concepts with different skills and abilities. Excellent management is not simply management with leadership as a subset of skills and abilities (Brilliant, 1986). Management involves those activities necessary to maintain an organization with a measure of effectiveness and

Table 1.1
Four Functions of Management

PLANNING
- Determining what the organization will accomplish
- Deciding how these goals will be accomplished

ORGANIZING
- Designing jobs for employees
- Grouping jobs into departments
- Developing working relationships among organizational units and employees to carry out the plan

LEADING
- Influencing the activities of others to achieve established goals

CONTROLLING
- Activities an organization undertakes to ensure that tasks lead to achievement of goals and objectives

efficiency. Management emphasizes rationality, control, and systematic selection of goals with associated strategies. Leadership, on the other hand, is the ability to influence people, independently of position and the capability to direct innovative organizational growth. Leadership is more than vision. It is the skill to derive vision from people and motivate them to exceptional accomplishments. Leadership, different from management, may extend beyond the organization, the industry, or professional association to the community (Brilliant, 1986).

The combination of management and leadership may vary from time to time, often depending on the needs of the organization and the characteristics of the person who fills the administrative role. Integration of management and leadership skills and abilities is essential for effective administration of service organizations (Giordano, 1996). The level of administration and the area of function may require a particular mix. The model presented in Figure 1.1 illustrates varying degrees to which administration may combine management and leadership. For example, a supervisory position in a small finance department lends itself to emphasis on management when considering the controls and systematic nature of financial management, whereas a clinical director of mental health services for older adults would require a larger measure of leadership to achieve flexibility in programming. For an executive position of a community-based service agency, administrative effectiveness would require a more extensive mix of leadership and management.

In the last two decades, there has been emphasis on management requirements. This trend is evidenced by calls for human services to be more like "business" with an emphasis on accountability. Leadership abilities are equally important (Austin, 1995; Bargal & Schmid, 1989; Brilliant, 1986; Mintzberg, 1989). Emphasizing the importance of leadership should not minimize the value of management. The vast majority of organizational responsibilities require both

Figure 1.1
Model of Administration as a Combination of Management and Leadership

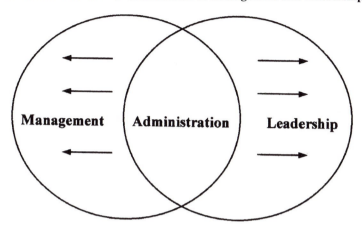

management and leadership to be effective. For example, successful organizational change requires management activities such as measurement of change, selection of a process, and providing structure and procedures. Leadership is needed to overcome resistance to change, to obtain commitment, and to bring about creative problem-solving.

Leaders and Managers

To examine the notion of administration as a combination of the domains of leadership and management, think of an individual in an administrative position. While individuals will bring skills and abilities in both domains, considerable variation in level of skill and ability exists. Figure 1.2 depicts the variations that are possible for a given individual. An effective administrator will possess a high level of both managerial and leadership skills and abilities, which are represented in the lower right quadrant of the figure. An ineffective administrator would be in the upper left quadrant. The other two quadrants represent dominance of one domain over the other. The upper right quadrant would be the leader who lacked management skills. It is all too common to encounter an organization that was built by the vision, inspiration, and dedication of an effective leader who eventually was unable to manage the organization.

Another dimension of leadership and management skills and abilities is the choice an administrator makes in accomplishing a task. A certain mix of leadership and management skills will be optimal for a given situation. Program planning, for example, requires a manager with moderate leadership abilities. Conversely, long-range strategic planning requires a leader who has vision and who is a risk taker. An administrator may hold a position where there is no staff to be supervised. When the person is functioning in that position, there may be

Figure 1.2
Administrative Model that Denotes Variations of Leader and Manager Skills and Abilities

Leader Skills and Abilities

	1	2	3	4	5	6	7	8	9	10

Manager Skills and Abilities (vertical axis: 2, 3, 4, 5, 6, 7, 8, 9, 10)

Low Leader
Low Manager

High Leader
Low Manager

Low Leader
High Manager

High Leadership
High Management

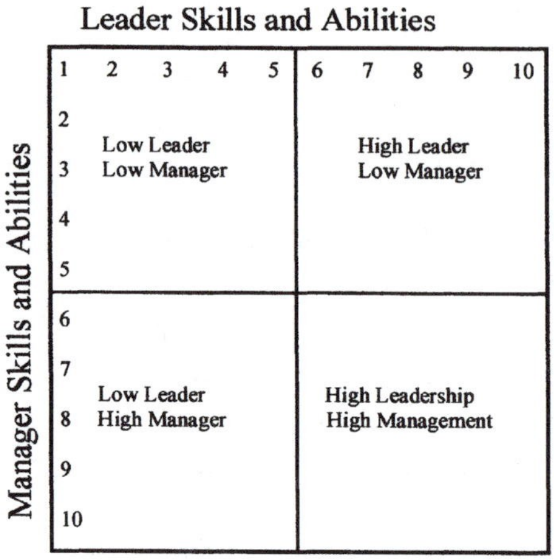

no direct demand for leadership skills and abilities. However, the same person, when asked to function outside of that realm of responsibility, would need to call on leadership skills to participate effectively in the accomplishment of an organizational objective, such as leading a task force on the revision of employee benefits.

The distinction between a manager and a leader has received considerable attention in the current literature. Zaleznik (1977) concludes that a manager is concerned with how decisions are made; a leader is concerned with what decisions are made. Both, of course, are important for effective administration. In a study of 319 individuals in 22 different human services organizations, Glisson (1989) reported a clear distinction between the focus of leaders and managers. He found managers attended to such rational processes as job-task decisions and activities that formally controlled workers; leaders used power to gain commitment to organizational goals and objectives. It is leadership ability that binds followers to commitments that is vitally important for effective program administration.

There is a contention that one person cannot be both a manager and a leader (Zaleznik, 1990). The argument is that personality traits resulting from different life cycle paths produce persons who are either managers or leaders. This is a throwback to the "leaders are born" theory. Even though each person brings to an administrative position talents and potentialities from socialization and education, some individuals will possess a relative balance of leadership and management skills and abilities; others will need to develop one or the other domain to be effective.

OLDER ADULT SERVICE ORGANIZATIONS

Public, profit, and not-for-profit organizations are the three sectors that contribute to the efforts to meet the needs of older adults. Various combinations of these sectors may be represented in a given organization. Traditionally, great care was taken to distinguish between not-for-profit, profit, and public organizations. Such sharp distinctions now only occasionally apply. Most not-for-profit agencies have multiple funding sources. It is rare to find a not-for-profit service organization that has no portion of its funding from government. Many organizations that serve older adults could not exist without the income of Medicare or Medicaid.

In addition, some not-for-profit organizations have found it necessary to establish profit companion organizations. Some profit corporations have found it useful to establish a related (parallel) not-for-profit organization. One large nursing home chain recently purchased a group of nursing homes through an affiliated not-for-profit organization designed by the corporation. The not-for-profit organization then leased the nursing homes to the profit corporation to be managed. There is increasing complexity as organizations seek a variety of economic strategies to fund services. The atmosphere has ripened for value conflicts and ethical concerns, placing even greater challenges on administration.

Three Sectors of Older Adult Programs

Organizations with an economic impact on society have been traditionally divided into two sectors: public, meaning government; and private, for-profit businesses of all types (McConnell & Brue, 1996; Olson, 1982). More recently, the private sector has been divided into a not-for-profit sector and a profit sector. Not-for-profit organizations are tax exempt under U.S. law and employ more civilians than the U.S. federal government and the 50 state governments combined (O'Neill, 1989). There are over 25 different types (Duca, 1996). For human and health service organizations, it is common to refer to three sectors.

A closer examination of the three sectors—profit (private business), not-for-profit (voluntary), and public (government) service organizations—highlights the differences and the challenges for administrators. An example of a profit organization is a case management service covering three counties that provides in-home and community assistance, like home care for older adults, for a contractual fee. An example of a not-for-profit program is a senior center that provides meals, day care, and activities for older adults. A public program can be as extensive as the Social Security Administration, with local offices or a department within a larger state agency that is dedicated to protective services for older adults.

Profit organizations value efficiency where decision-making is driven by efforts to accomplish goals with minimum resources (Gatewood et al., 1995). Social responsibility is optional. Client services can be highly selective, and professional staff requirements may allow for greater flexibility in staffing. In these organizations, little time is dedicated to fund-raising, like grant writing or events. Considerable time is dedicated to marketing, often including the administrator's time. Resources to attract experienced, highly trained professionals and to engage in program innovation or expansion will depend greatly on investment capital and profit.

Not-for-profit organizations value effectiveness over efficiency. That is, the mission that guides these organizations is the commitment to quality services for those in need, with a positive result for society. Not-for-profit organizations present unique circumstances for administrators, the difficulty of which is frequently underrated (Anthony & Herzlinger, 1975; Drucker, 1989). Not-for-profit organizations typically have multiple funding sources as well as a range of professionals and paraprofessionals, and are governed by a voluntary board of trustees. Payment by clients, if it exists, is often a secondary source of funding. Administrators, depending on the level of administration, will spend a measure of time with fund-raising activities. Those that provide resources to the organization may intrude upon the internal operations of the organization, and influence can be exerted by external forces, such as client associations, professional organizations, the public, and the media. Client selection is based on established criteria rather than on the likelihood of success or financial resources.

Public agencies are funded by federal, state, and local taxes; have a hierarchical reporting structure to higher levels of government; have origins based in law; and are more likely to provide coordination, funding, planning, professional education, and other indirect services. Administrators may become involved in lobbying efforts to obtain more financial resources or changes in policy that allow for expansion or improvement of services. Typically, these organizations offer the stability of regular employees who remain with the organization for extended periods of time (Bevilacqua, 1995). The exceptions are the top officials, who often are subject to political appointment. Many of these organizations are involved in developing and enforcing standards for profit and not-for-profit organizations.

A feature of public organizations for older adults is that when these organizations are funding programs, they must provide equitable services (although this may not be achieved) to all of those in need. Public service programs are often the last resort for older adults who have nowhere else to turn. Lastly, government programs are the most highly subject to pressures and attention from the public and the media. They are frequently politicized and often misrepresented; administrators are expected to explain to the public the problems, alleged and real, or deficiencies in programs.

Understanding Older Adult Service Organizations

Organizations from all three sectors share certain similarities when they deliver either indirect or direct services. Service organizations have features that distinguish them from those organizations that are predominantly oriented toward sales and distribution of products. More specifically, organizations that provide programs for older adults are part of the larger network of human and health services and have a set of common characteristics:

- Service objectives are difficult to measure because the process of offering the services is as important as the outcome.
- The quality of service may be intangible and difficult to ascertain because of the existence of multiple service objectives.
- There may be employees who are committed to professional organizations or causes that compete with loyalty to the organization.
- The administrator's authority is shared with professional staff or, as in governmental programs, is limited by the structure of the organization.
- The professional staff, with high levels of education and expertise, hold informal yet influential positions in the organization.
- Determination of whether services are to be provided may be placed in the hands of others than the client, such as individuals with a power of attorney, guardians, a health care surrogate, physicians, insurance companies, health maintainance organizations (HMOs), and managed care.
- Motivation and participation in programs is highly subject to the individual's attitude about such services.
- Services may be indirect, such as monitoring, coordinating, funding of programs, or regulating programs.

Elements of Service Organizations

The four elements common to all service organizations, clients, practitioners, the organization (agency), and stakeholders influence the organizational structure and administration. Administrators must be aware of the relationship among these elements, the degree of influence of each cluster of elements, and the level of commitment to success, as well as the expectations of the organization held by these individuals and groups. In older adult programs the external expectations and influences are strong. While each element requires understanding and attention, certain segments within an element will require more direct efforts from time to time; for example, recruitment of staff in a new organization. One skill of an effective administrator is the ability to determine where to concentrate efforts, when, and for how long. A basic definition and description of the four universal elements is presented:

1. The clients, also referred to as consumers or patients, often pay no direct fee (insurance payments), or a reduced or indirect fee for services received. Many older adults become involved with a human services system for the first time. While some clients seek services, others are recruited, and some are referred. The older adult may lack motivation for services, as is often the situation with adult protective services and long-term care. Clients who are motivated

learn the requirements for obtaining services and the norms for remaining in the service system. Frequently, this is learned from other clients. Other clients or their families bear the burden of fees, sometimes until resources are depleted. With older adults, family members often become "clients," even though they often cannot be officially designated. This is particularly true for adult children of older clients.

2. Practitioners in organizations that serve older adults are from many different disciplines. Some are members of professions; others are at various levels of professionalism. Many practitioners have crossed over from other areas of service with limited knowledge of aging, while others have had specific training in a given discipline such as nursing or social work, which may be supplemented by education and experience in the field of aging. Beginning in the late 1960s, more professionals trained in gerontology have taken positions in these organizations. Conflicts and tensions between the different practitioners can occur. Practitioners with large caseloads or a wide range of responsibilities are also common in organizations that serve older adults. Many practitioners belong to professions that have professional associations that provide guidance and standards as to appropriate behavior.

3. The influence of the organization can be understood by dividing it into the governance segment—the board of directors or its equivalent—and the administrative staffing structure. The boards of directors in not-for-profit organizations that serve older adults, unlike those in profit organizations, play a major role (Drucker, 1989; Gatewood et al., 1995). Board members generally come from a broad cross-section of the community, representing many different interests. Boards are responsible for overseeing the program, establishing policy, and selecting the chief administrative officer. The governing structure for public agencies is frequently far removed, such as the relationship of Area Agencies on Aging to the Department of Health and Human Resources, as mandated by the Older Americans Act. Direct involvement in service delivery, although possible through formal and informal inquiry, is less likely than with independent, not-for-profit organizations. The administrative structures for public agencies are typically hierarchical, are well established, and have limited authority.

In profit organizations, like nursing home chains, home health agencies, or hospitals, the governance structures are the least influential. The boards are rarely involved in programs and services. The administrative structures vary greatly, with top administrators changing frequently in larger organizations. In smaller, entrepreneurial organizations, such as home health agencies, the administrative structure may be streamlined and simple, where administrative responsibilities also include services to clients.

Ideally, the administrative design of an organization would be that which best serves the clients and fully utilizes practitioner resources. Many community-based organizations that serve older adults are a product of evolving resource changes and unplanned growth; still other organizations are a reflection of a dominant administrator, founder, or owner.

4. A stakeholder is a person or group who has an impact on the organization through expectations or influence (Blair & Fottler, 1990; Mintzberg, 1979). To be a stakeholder, one must have interaction with the organization. Depending on the interaction, stakeholders can be classified into three tiers. The first tier, where there is most likely to be frequent interaction, includes clients, volunteers, employees, board members, and family members. The second tier is composed of funding sources and regulatory agencies, benefactors, and vendors. In the third tier of influence, interaction is intermittent and media involvement is typical. This level is composed of the public and interest groups, such as client organizations or organizations which represent older adults, such as the American Association of Retired Persons (AARP).

The gerontologist administrator needs to identify all stakeholders, to informally assess their level of involvement, and to formally engage in systematic study by collecting information. For example, some day care programs for older adults conduct annual consumer surveys of the clients' family members. The expanded group of stakeholders and the often intense level of involvement represent one of the many unique features of programs for older adults.

Government Organizations and Aging Services

The administrator of older adult services will often work within the complexity of organizations that have been established by federal and state government. Government systems overlap and interlock with community-based, direct service programs. The gerontologist administrator needs to be cognizant of the system's structure and design. The mission of most governmental entities is to implement, coordinate, and plan services. Funding is channeled through various levels of government to a direct service organization. For example, for the approximately 20,000 nutrition sites receiving support from the federal government, the funds are channeled through the Area Agencies on Aging. On occasion, governmental agencies, originally set up to operate indirect services, may provide or pilot service programs. Funds are also obtained by direct payment of a government program for a unit of service to the individual.

The heavily amended Older Americans Act of 1965 was amended in 1973 to create a network of organizations to bring services exclusively to older adults. This amendment, known as the Comprehensive Service Amendment, also emphasized coordination and planning of services (Atchley, 2000). The administrative components of this network are depicted in Figure 1.3. Health and Human Services and the Administration on Aging (AOA) are administratively linked to the president's office, and receive oversight by Congress. State Offices of Aging, also called Commissions on Aging, are created by and partially supported by state legislatures. Area Agencies on Aging (AAA), while part of the network, are independently incorporated, not-for-profit organizations with boards of directors. They have a contractual arrangement with the AOA. The relationship to the State Office of Aging varies from state to state. Many community service–

Figure 1.3
Components of the Aging Network

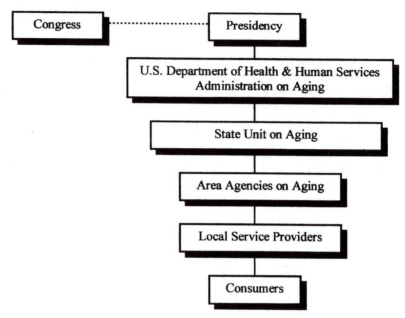

Source: Adapted from Torres-Gil (1992).

based projects, programs, and organizations receive funding through, and are monitored by, the AAA.

Other government organizations that fund services, not necessarily exclusive to older adults, emanate from the federal government. The Social Security Act authorized Medicare, Title XVIII; Medicaid, Title XIX; and Social Services, Title XX. Medicare, which is for older adults, the blind, and disabled, is administered by the federal government through contracts with private insurance companies, and payment of funds is retroactive to the provision of health services to individuals. Medicaid is for all people who qualify under the federal poverty guidelines. It is funded by the federal government, includes contributions by the state, is state administered, and often contracts the processing of claims and payments to a profit organization called an intermediary.

Social Services provides federal funds channeled through the state into highly bureaucratic welfare departments (that have such names as Department of Family Services or Department of Securities and Pensions) which have regional offices where direct services are delivered; for example, the adult protective services. Community-based, non-institutional long-term care programs like home health are funded through Medicare and Medicaid (Capitman, 1986).

Other government agencies that sponsor, fund, or direct resources to older adults are more broadly based. Generally, these programs are a small component of a much larger array of services. Community mental health service centers receive funds for aging and mental health services from a variety of governmental sources. Local police departments receive federal funds through criminal justice channels. Local community colleges receive support and funding for educational programs pertinent to older adults and professionals who serve older adults through educational channels of state and federal government. These pathways are too numerous to be elaborated on here; however, cognizance of such resources and the necessity of interaction with these resources is important for the gerontologist administrator.

GUIDING PRINCIPLES FOR THE GERONTOLOGIST ADMINISTRATOR

The constellation of programs for older adults, with its mix of public, not-for-profit, and profit organizations, requires ethical administrators with gerontological knowledge and a tailored set of administrative skills and abilities. The notions set forth in this chapter, combined with practice experience, allow for a number of guiding principles to be formulated for the gerontologist administrator. The list of guiding principles presented will serve as a checklist for expected behavior and as a road map for learning how to be a more effective gerontologist administrator:

- Maintain a clear focus on the mission so that the organization serves its basic purpose (Mintzberg, 1980). This is accomplished by assuring that the continuous change process is oriented to the older adult client's needs. The change process should be driven by information from evaluation and feedback.

- Adopt a client orientation that involves and recognizes the older adult in multiple roles related to the organization (volunteer, advocate, etc.). For agencies that serve older adults, it must be remembered that there are clients who will be receiving services and unofficial "clients" such as adult children.

- Be an advocate for older clients and older adults in general. Such advocacy goes beyond one's own organization to include policy and legislation in the greater community.

- Stay in tune with the events of the larger environment, that is, the local community and the state and the federal governments, as well as regulatory bodies. The higher the level in the organization, the more time and energy is directed toward these external influences (stakeholders).

- Remember that every leadership position in an organization means representation of others.

- Define and redefine roles and expectations of staff using performance evaluations, informal feedback, job descriptions, and supporting supervisory relationships.

- Administrators are expected to perform according to ethical standards.

- Frequent adjustment of the leadership/management mix to fit the situation is required. By examining the organization's elements and understanding its design and the expectations of stakeholders, adjustments can be made in focus, effort, and approaches by the administration.

- Focus on both effectiveness and efficiency (Ginsberg, 1995). Effectiveness in meeting goals and objectives cannot be accomplished at the cost of being inefficient.
- Seek training and development opportunities to achieve management and leadership skills and abilities.
- Maintain a vision of the future and be willing to make risk-taking decisions to exert control and provide focus for the organization (Drucker, 1982; Giordano, 1996).

The gerontologist administrator, trained either formally or on the job, will need to engage in lifelong education to master the complexities of the position. This can be accomplished, in part, by membership in national professional associations related to gerontology. These organizations are presented in the Appendix at the end of this book. Attendance at conferences and workshops, exposure to colleagues, and reading academic and professional publications will contribute to the administrator's continued development.

SUMMARY

Emphasis is placed on the need for administrators of programs for older adults to have expertise in the field of gerontology. The gerontologist administrator is a scientist practitioner within the broader discipline of gerontology and aging services. These practitioners integrate knowledge about older adults and administration to assure relevance of decision-making and problem-solving. Gerontologists have recently begun to identify and develop the concepts, models, and skills germane to the application of administration of older adult programs.

Administration of programs for older adults draws upon many sources and resources of information to deliver services. It involves a wide network of complex relationships with those who have varying levels of interest and involvement with older adult programs. These programs are in a context of expanding community services, which includes increasing professionalization, diversity of staff, and responses to changing external standards and guidelines.

Administration has been conceptualized as a combination of both management and leadership skills and abilities. This conceptualization places leadership in an equally paramount role with management. The effective administrator will possess a high level of managerial and leadership skills and abilities. Administrators must adjust the mix of these skills and abilities to fit the demands and expectations of the position held within the organization.

The gerontologist administrator needs to understand the nature and characteristics of the various sectors where programs are offered. Each sector has distinguishing features offering different challenges, although service organizations share certain common characteristics. Every service organization has four elements: practitioners, clients, the organization itself, and stakeholders. Each group offers expectations and involvement of various levels with services. Organizations that provide programs for older adults have a large group of stakeholders, many of whom have multiple levels of involvement with the organization.

Principles for the gerontologist administrator are presented as a guide for administrators and as a way to chart the remainder of this text. Inherent in these principles is the model of administration that gives equal value to management and leadership. Each of these domains of administration will be elaborated upon in the next two chapters. The classical theories of management and leadership will be addressed along with current concepts and applications. This chapter and the two following chapters will build the foundation for administering programs to older adults. Subsequent chapters will elaborate upon the essential knowledge, skills, and abilities necessary for the effective gerontologist administrator.

LEARNING EXPERIENCE

No Time for Marketing: An Administrative Decision

For further exploration of the issues related to the distinction between management and leadership, examine the following case and related approaches.

Jill is the assistant administrator of a day care center that has been in existence for over two years. As assistant administrator, she is more or less in charge of intake and "all other duties assigned by the administrator." The administrator was recently asked to resign. Jill anticipates being asked to take the administrative position, but no one has formally discussed this possibility with her yet. It is rumored that the position of assistant administrator will be eliminated in the next fiscal year.

The day care center has six staff and two part-time volunteers. The center also has a gerontology intern 20 hours a week. The center is part of a multipurpose complex that includes a long-term care center and an assisted living facility (ALF). Both of these facilities have administrators. The three administrators report to the chief executive officer (CEO), who has an accounting and financial background. The day care center, which is attractive and roomy, has the capacity to serve 50 older adults each day; however, over the past year, the number of people served per day has ranged between 20 and 36. These low numbers have caused concern for the board of directors and the CEO.

The AAA is planning an event for the spring of this year, called "Aging and Adult Children Weekend," which will be held at St. Petersburg Island Park. This outdoor event will feature live big bands with music from the Dorsey Brothers, Count Basie, and other old-time swing and jazz bands. This is an excellent opportunity for marketing the services of the day care center. Jill eagerly contacts the "central office" to solicit help from the marketing director, who agrees fully with the opportunity. He pledges his assistance.

The CEO calls Jill several hours later to explain that the marketing director will not be available to assist with the project because the census is down in long-term care, and the marketing director will have to spend all of his time helping to increase the census. The CEO, seeking to be motivating, states, "I am sure you will find some way to get a booth together for that weekend." In addition, the CEO says, "This is your opportunity to increase your census." The real message is: this is your opportunity to assure your appointment as the administrator. Neither Jill nor any of her staff has experience in marketing; the advertising budget is overspent; however, the center has plenty of brochures (about 1,000) in boxes.

Approaches

Jill resolved that it was important to take advantage of this opportunity to market the day care center. She decided to appoint a special team to accomplish the project. Which of the following approaches would you select?

Management Approach

Jill appoints a team and designates one member who is task-oriented as leader. She calls a meeting to explain the task and what is expected of the team members. Jill assures the team that she will be willing to help. She acknowledges that this represents additional work, but the opportunity is important to the future of the day care center. It is essential for the project to be successful.

Comments: _____

_____

Leadership Approach

Jill looks for a key person with interpersonal skills to appoint as a team leader. She then works with the team leader to select other members of the team. Jill's main function at this point is to facilitate an expanded pool of possible team members. Once the team is formulated, she meets with them to provide a charge to frame the expected outcome. Jill explains that she is willing to help, but only when absolutely necessary. She intends to offer only a minimum level of supervision, to remain supportive, and to use verbal cues to motivate.

Comments: _____

_____

Analysis

Both approaches are appropriate and will likely result in a project. However, the leadership approach is more effective and more likely to result in a project that will be successful. Review the materials that distinguish between management and leadership. This is a project for which there are no dedicated funds. Staff are expected to go beyond their basic job responsibilities and to exhibit a commitment to the future of the organization. The leadership approach is less controlled than the management approach and is thereby riskier; however, it sets the conditions for creativity, commitment, personal growth, and self-satisfaction.

REFERENCES

Alter, C. F. (1988). The changing structure of elderly services delivery systems. *The Gerontologist, 28*(1), 91–98.

Anthony, R. N., & Herzlinger, R. E. (1975). *Management control in nonprofit organizations*. Homewood, IL: Richard D. Irwin.

Atchley, R. C. (1995). Gerontology and business: Getting the right people for the job. *Generations, 19*(2), 43–45.

Atchley, R. C. (2000). *Social forces and aging: An introduction to social gerontology* (9th ed.). Belmont, CA: Wadsworth Thomson Learning.

Austin, D. M. (1995). Management overview. In R. L. Edwards & J. G. Hopps (Eds.), *Encyclopedia of social work* (Vol. 2, 19th ed., pp. 1642–1658). Washington, DC: National Association of Social Workers.

Bargal, D., & Schmid, H. (1989). Recent themes in theory and research on leadership and their implications for management of the human services. In Y. Hasenfeld (Ed.), *Administrative leadership in the social services: The next challenge* (pp. 37–54). New York: Haworth.

Bevilacqua, J. (1995). The imperative of professional leadership in public service management. In L. Ginsberg & P. R. Keys, (Eds.), *New management in human services* (2nd ed., pp. 283–289). Washington, DC: National Association of Social Workers.

Blair, J. D., & Fottler, M. D. (1990). *Challenges in health care management: Strategic perspectives for managing key stakeholders*. San Francisco: Jossey-Bass.

Bluford, V. (1994). Working with older people. *Occupational Outlook Quarterly, 38*, 28–31.

Brilliant, E. L. (1986). Social work leadership: A missing ingredient? *Social Work, 31* (5), 325–331.

Capitman, J. A. (1996). Community based long-term care models, target groups, and impacts on service use. *The Gerontologist, 26*(4), 389–397.

Computers in human services [Journal]. New York: Haworth.

Drucker, P. F. (1982). *The practice of management*. New York: Harper & Row.

Drucker, P. F. (1989, July–August). What business can learn from nonprofits. *Harvard Business Review*, pp. 88–93.

Duca, D. J. (1996). *Nonprofit boards: Roles, responsibilities, and performance*. New York: John Wiley.

Ehlers, W. H., Austin, M. J., & Prothero, J. C. (Eds.). (1976). *Administration for the human services*. New York: Harper & Row.

Follett, M. P. (1986). Management as a profession. In M. T. Matteson & J. M. Ivancevich (Eds.), *Management classics* (3rd ed., pp. 7–17). Plano, TX: Business Publications.

Friedsman, H. J. (1995). Professional education and the invention of social gerontology. *Generations, 19,* 46–50.

Gatewood, R. D., Taylor, R. R., & Ferrell, O. C. (1995). *Management: Comprehension, analysis, and application.* Chicago: Austen.

Ginsberg, L. (1995). Concepts of new management. In L. Ginsberg & P. R. Keys (Eds.), *New management in human services* (2nd ed., pp. 1–37). Washington, DC: National Association of Social Workers.

Giordano, J. A. (1996, October). *Management skills.* Intensive presented at Professional Proficiency: It Takes a Whole Network, a regional training conference, Area Agencies on Aging, Tampa, FL.

Glisson, C. (1989). The effect of leadership on workers in human service organizations. *Administration in Social Work, 13*(3/4), 99–116.

Hooyman, N. R., & Kiyak, H. A. (1999). *Social gerontology: A multidisciplinary perspective* (5th ed.). Boston: Allyn & Bacon.

Katz, R. L. (1982). Skills of an effective administrator. In D. A. Nadler, M. L. Tushman, & N. G. Hatvany (Eds.), *Managing organizations: Readings and cases* (pp. 7–19). Boston: Little, Brown.

Koontz, H. (1990). *Essentials of management* (5th ed.). New York: McGraw-Hill.

McConnell, C. R., & Brue, S. L. (1996). *Economics: Principles, problems, and policies* (13th ed.). New York: McGraw-Hill.

Mintzberg, H. (1979). *The structure of organizations.* Englewood Cliffs, NJ: Prentice-Hall.

Mintzberg, H. (1980). *The nature of managerial work.* Englewood Cliffs, NJ: Prentice-Hall.

Mintzberg, H. (1989). *Mintzberg on management: Inside our strange world of organizations.* New York: Free Press.

Morgan, E. E., Jr., & Hiltner, J. (1992). *Managing aging and human service agencies.* New York: Springer.

O'Brien, J. A. (1999). *Introduction to information systems: Essentials for the internetworked enterprise* (9th ed.). New York: McGraw-Hill.

Olson, L. K. (1982). *The political economy of aging: The state, private power, and social welfare.* New York: Columbia University.

O'Neill, M. (1989). *The third America.* San Francisco: Jossey-Bass.

Raymond, F. B. (1991). Management of services for the elderly. In P.K.H. Kim (Ed.), *Serving the elderly: Skills for practice* (pp. 233–258). New York: Aldine De Gruyter.

Skidmore, R. A. (1995). *Social work administration: Dynamic management and human relationships* (3rd ed.). Boston: Allyn & Bacon.

Slavin, S. (1980). A theoretical framework for social administration. In F. D. Perlmutter & S. Slavin (Eds.), *Leadership in social administration: Perspectives for the 1980s* (pp. 3–21). Philadelphia: Temple University.

Stein, H. (1970). Social work administration. In H. Schatz (Ed.), *Social work administration: A resource book* (p. 7). New York: New York Council on Social Work Education.

Torres-Gil, F. (1992). *The new aging: Politics and change in America.* Westport, CT: Auburn House.

Weinbach, R. (1990). *The social worker as manager: Theory and practice.* New York: Longman.

Zaleznik, A. (1977). Managers and leaders: Are they different? *Harvard Business Review,* *55*(3), 67–78.

Zaleznik, A. (1989). *The managerial mystique: Restoring leadership in business.* New York: Harper & Row.

Zaleznik, A. (1990). The leadership gap. *Academy of Management Executives, 4*(1), 7–22.

Chapter 2

Leadership Theory and Practice

Administration is a combination of leadership and management. These two theoretical and behavioral concepts of administration are intermingled with one another, but have independent features that have been identified in the literature and in practice. It is deemed constructive to differentiate leadership from management (Bennis & Nanus, 1985; Fiedler & Chemers, 1974; Gatewood, Taylor, & Ferrell, 1995; Legnini, 1994; Zaleznik, 1989, 1990). In Chapter 3, we will discuss management theory and practice.

Management involves activities necessary to maintain an organization with a measure of efficiency and effectiveness with authority related to organizational position. In contrast, leadership is the skill of influencing people and the ability to direct innovative organizational growth. Leadership is exercised in relation to people, even when the leader is not in an administrative position. In an administrative position, the leader has additional authority and responsibility. Independent of administrative position, a person may have influence because of vision, charisma, innovations, advocacy, or knowledge. Leadership, in contrast to management, is more expressive, people focused, creative, and compassionate.

The notions about leadership exist amid a public perception that service organizations need more management. However, the observations of many students of organization hold the view that management is overemphasized and better leadership is needed (Gatewood et al., 1995; Glisson, 1989; Oakley & Krug, 1991; Zaleznik, 1989). With management, efforts are often directed toward oneself or toward tasks, such as time management, organizing the work, or goal development. For leadership, most efforts are directed toward other people. A prerequisite of leadership is that there are followers. A manager can be in charge of an entire organization and have no followers. Leaders use re-

Table 2.1
Traditional Leadership Theory Categories

	Traits	Behavioral	Situational
Assumptions	• Leaders are born; cannot be learned • Physical and personality traits • Common denominators exist for leaders	• Leader can be strong or weak • Can identify good leader behavior • Leadership can be learned • Observable behaviors can be identified • There is one best way	• Depends on situation • Depends on the individual • Varies with staff experience and tasks • There is not one best way
Elements of Leadership	• Attractive physical appeal • High verbal ability • Intelligence • Initiative • Self-assurance	• Use of authority • Level of task orientation • Treatment of staff • Relationship orientation	• Use of different abilities and styles • Flexibility • Leader to make adjustment in behavior for effectiveness • Leaders assess situations

Sources: Adapted from Fiedler (1967); Gatewood, Taylor, & Ferrell (1995); Hoy & Miskel (1978);
   Lewis, Lewis, & Souflée (1991); Weinbach (1998).

lationships, influence, creation of vision, and motivation to challenge others to
accomplish more than thought possible.

The leader in an organizational setting is not necessarily a charismatic hero
who commands respect and awe. Indeed, the perceptions of leadership and who
can lead have changed, broadening considerably over the years. As background,
a brief overview of traditional and contemporary leadership theory will be presented. Leadership style can take several forms. Following the discussion of
leadership theory, three distinct styles will be considered. A practice model of
leadership tailored for the gerontologist administrator provides four goals and
nine strategies. Finally, consideration will be given to leadership limitations and
problems.

LEADERSHIP THEORY

Current leadership literature and practice are linked to traditional theories,
most of which emerge from a long history of research. The traditional theories
have been organized into three categories in Table 2.1 to contrast the assumptions and the elements. All these concepts continue to influence the practice of
organizational leadership. The first category, often called the "great man" theory,
is based on the study of people who were identified as effective leaders. However, among the various studies the lists did not always agree (Weinbach, 1998).
Further, the list of traits was not limited to leaders; that is, many other individuals possessed those traits and did not have the opportunity to exhibit leadership
qualities, or were not leaders. Two personal characteristics did appear on many
lists: intelligence and the inclination to be highly verbal.

Most of the behavioral theories categorize leadership behavior as either directed to tasks (production) or directed toward relationships (people). For this conceptualization, the most effective leaders strike a balance between these two foci. Thus, there is one best way to lead. Associated with behavioral theories are different applications of authority; specifically, autocratic versus democratic authority. Years of research could not substantiate consistent effectiveness of one application of authority over the other (Gatewood et al., 1995; Robbins, 1995; Weinbach, 1998).

Both the trait and behavioral theories fail to recognize the organizational situation and the circumstances of the followers that are emphasized by situational leadership theory. Through a series of studies, Fred Fiedler (1967) discovered that successful leadership is a match between certain styles and the organizational situation. Additionally, situational theory postulates that leadership style and approach should depend upon the followers' competence and level of development (Blanchard, Zigarmi, & Zigarmi, 1985). Situational leadership theory has continued to evolve, combining certain leadership characteristics with the ability of the leader to adapt to different circumstances. The conclusion offered by situational leadership theorists is that there is no one best way to lead. This suggests that, for the administrator, knowledge and assessment skills of organizations and understanding of human behavior are essential for effective leadership. Contemporary theories expand the situational perspective on leadership.

Contemporary Leadership Theories

Situational leadership theory, particularly contingency theory, continues to influence current thinking about leadership in organizations. The trend has been to identify different styles that can be matched with employee and organizational characteristics. Contemporary research on leadership also provides a clearer picture of the distinctive features of leadership compared to management. Leaders can be followers, forming concerned relationships and using influence to motivate employees independent from the management responsibilities or position (Burke, 1982; Zaleznik, 1990).

In path goal theory, it is the leader's responsibility to help followers to overcome obstacles that prevent the attainment of goals and to perform effectively (Robbins, 1995). The activities of the leader are classified into four leadership behaviors (House & Mitchell, 1978):

- *Directive*. This style provides guidance for accomplishing work activities, holding staff to standards, and interpreting job requirements.
- *Supportive*. The leader shows consideration for the employee's well-being, focuses attention on the employee, and seeks to make the work atmosphere more pleasant.
- *Participative*. The leader involves the staff person in decisions whenever possible, consults with the person, and seriously considers his contributions.

• *Achievement Oriented.* This is the expectation of performance, frequently beyond what the staff member thinks he can accomplish, and efforts to assist the staff member in improving performance, while maintaining confidence in his ability.

The leader draws upon these styles to influence followers, depending on the characteristics of the employee and the characteristics of the situation. The leader's behavior is successful to the extent it increases followers' goal attainment and clarifies the path of the adopted goals and desired rewards (House & Mitchell, 1978). This theory shows how identified leader behaviors, used selectively depending on the situation, can explain the motivations of followers.

Participative theory establishes eight situational characteristics, such as how important the technical quality of the decision is in relation to the level of the employee's participation in the decision (Gatewood et al., 1995). Five decision styles are identified by this theory. For example, one decision style is the manager asking for information from the staff, but making the decision independently. These styles range from a completely independent decision by the leader to complete delegation of the decision to an individual or group. The leader selects the decision style in relation to the level of employees' involvement that fits with the situation. Again, the theme is leader flexibility and ability to assess the situation to match an appropriate behavior.

The leader–member exchange theory depicts leader–follower relations common to some organizations where close emotional relations are found between leaders and followers. These relations are best described as having strong mutual commitment, loyalty, and positive mutual attitudes toward one another (Gatewood et al., 1995). This approach to leadership forms bonds with selective groups of employees. Those who are part of the group are motivated, while those who are not may lack motivation. For example, an administrator of a public paratransportation service that served older adults actively solicited membership of certain employees in a community service club. Consequently, the social contact and shared experiences of this select group produced a unique and exclusive relationship with the leader. Other employees, because of the nature of their jobs (for example, drivers who could not attend day meetings), could not join the social club. A situation arose with the public relations director, who engaged in a flagrant violation of policy and was not disciplined. He was a member of the select group. This created resentment and hostility toward the leader. This leadership approach in an organization where the leader may also be a manager will result in a compromise of authority and morale problems.

LEADERSHIP STYLE

The contemporary leadership theories depict a variety of leadership styles emphasizing the importance of using different styles with different situations. Leadership styles in the practice of administration can be blended, used selectively, or used exclusively, regardless of the situation. The latter is like a re-

Table 2.2
Behaviors Associated with Charismatic Leaders in Organizations

- **Project power and confidence.** When speaking to a group or to individuals, the manner, tone, and body posture convey self-assurance. People perceive the leader is speaking directly to them.
- **Communication of vision.** Persistent presentation of a goal (or goals) that is important and relevant to people so they adopt the goal for themselves.
- **High performance expectations.** Expression of confidence to accomplish tasks. Often work is cast as a challenge, competition, or a dramatic change.
- **Sensitivity to followers' needs.** This is accomplished by listening, showing concern, and acceptance. This requires the ability to assess emotions, moods, and interests of individuals and groups.

Source: Adapted from Robbins (1995).

pairman who has only a hammer and, thus, must use the hammer for all jobs. Many of the styles depicted in the literature have a specific application to either a set of organizational characteristics or employee characteristics. Some styles of leadership incorporate generalized attitudes toward staff. It is more constructive to think of style in a broader context as overall influence on the leader's behavior. Three broad styles that influence leaders' behavior are identified for examination: charismatic, transactional, and transformational.

Charismatic Style

The common view of the leader is that of a charismatic person who is a convincing and emotional speaker, conveys enthusiasm, is inspirational, and produces devotion and, often, unquestionable obedience. Often, charismatic leaders are heroic risk takers who can produce a highly charged and motivated environment. Charismatic leaders are often found in the greater community, like Francis Everett Townsen, who, during the depression, led an effort to establish a national old-age pension that contributed to the eventual passage of the Social Security Act; or Maggie Kuhn, who founded the Gray Panthers and led advocacy efforts for older adults. In organizations, charismatic leaders promote innovative strategies and change efforts. They have the ability to improve employee performance, convey the importance of tasks and goals, and achieve satisfaction among followers. Behaviors associated with charismatic leaders in organizations are listed in Table 2.2.

Charismatic leaders are typically intuitive, have the ability to alter behavior when necessary, and are capable of forming very personal relationships with individuals. There is a tendency for charismatic leaders to have followers and also a group of opponents. Charismatic leadership style is appropriate for various stages and situations of an organization (Perlmutter, 1995). Often, when a new program is beginning or needs to take a dramatic change in orientation, charismatic leadership is most functional and useful. However, charismatic leaders often have difficulty with organizations that are stable or seeking systematic maintenance and growth. Elements of the charismatic style can be woven into other styles and approaches to leadership.

Transactional Style

This is an exchange approach where the needs of the follower are met by the leader if performance is adequate. The transactional leader achieves productivity by rewarding performance with recognition, praise, pay increases, and opportunities for advancement (Bass, 1985; Gatewood et al., 1995). Higher levels of performance receive concomitant rewards. When the administrator is a transactional leader, the focus is on compromise, mutual agreement, and control (Bass, 1985; Zaleznik, 1990). The follower's level of effort is connected to the anticipated rewards and the leader's integrity in producing them. That is, efforts are related to the confidence felt in the leader. This confidence is built as the leader communicates individual consideration for the employee and demonstrates the ability to provide rewards (Bargal & Schmid, 1989; Bass, 1985). This could include, for example, the strong support by the leader for a staff member's continued professional development. For some organizational settings, the leader's use of this style is determined by the leader's formal position and the extent of control over rewards.

Transformational Leadership

Transformational leadership incorporates the recognition and satisfaction of followers' needs of transactional leadership, but focuses on needs of fulfillment, purpose, and self-awareness (Bass, 1985; Gatewood et al., 1995). This style seeks to produce motivation that transcends self-interest. Appeals by these leaders are to ideas, values, social justice, fairness, or in-group solidarity. While transactional leadership would be typical of network marketing that appeals to interest in personal wealth, transformational leadership is exemplified by Martin Luther King's famous speech, "I have a dream." Transformational leadership uses intellectual stimulation and imagination to energize followers (Bargal & Schmid, 1989), while transactional leadership uses appeals to personal gain, fear, and power, especially in highly politicized organizations. Bass (1985) summarizes transformational style as follows:

• Raising level of awareness and consciousness.
• Transcending self-interest.
• Appealing to higher levels of need.

Transformational leadership has a measure of charisma, as leaders characteristically exude self-confidence, conviction, competence, and intellectual prow-

Figure 2.1
The Practice Model of Leadership

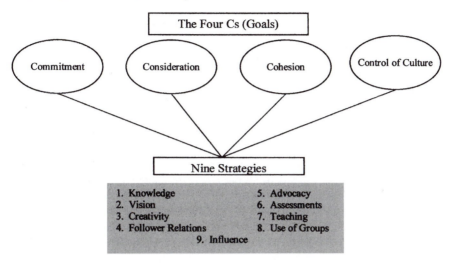

ess. They can inspire followers to achieve or perform at higher levels than the followers thought possible and to overcome obstacles with creative problem-solving. This style can exist at all levels of organizations and with a broad range of organizations. In programs for older adults, where rewards and recognition frequently do not match the demand of the work, a transformational leadership style is most appropriate for effective administration.

A PRACTICE MODEL OF LEADERSHIP

The gerontologist administrator should remain aware that different circumstances will require different leadership skills, and he must be capable of adapting (Raymond, 1991). The circumstances and kinds of organizations that offer programs for older adults allow for a focus on leadership concepts and behaviors that are most relevant. Conducting workshops and seminars for gerontologist administrators has also contributed to the development of concentrated concepts and strategies for leading. Drawing on the existing theories and models of leadership, as well as some published leadership practice applications (see for example Blanchard et al., 1985; Lynch & Kordis, 1988; Oakley & Krug, 1991), a general practice model for the gerontologist administrator is summarized in Figure 2.1. The model is composed of four goals and nine strategies. The four goals are commitment, cohesion, consideration, and control of culture; called the four Cs of leadership. The strategies are knowledge, vision, creativity, follower relations, advocacy, assessments, teaching, use of groups, and influence.

Acknowledging that certain personal characteristics—intelligence, verbal skills, and persistence—are common for leaders and that motivation to lead is present, this practice model will be instructive and useful for the gerontologist administrator. Further, this model is primarily for leadership in organizations, but is not necessarily limited to those who hold an administrative position.

Four Goals for Leadership

- *Commitment.* It is the responsibility of the leader to create commitment that overrides personal interest (Bennis & Nanus, 1985; Zaleznik, 1989). Obtaining behavior from followers that demonstrates commitment is expected of leaders. The commitment is to the clients, the vision, the values, and the purpose of the organization. The expected commitment is not just global, but is also necessary for specific decisions, efforts at change, agreed-upon technologies, and innovations.

- *Cohesion.* Build cohesion in groups, teams, and in the entire organization. A sense of togetherness is achieved by encouraging and mandating cooperation, explaining the interrelatedness of system components, and connecting tasks to the shared purpose of the organization. In this vein, cohesion relates to commitment to the shared purpose and goals. Achieving consensus builds cohesion, while compromise and so-called democratic practices will not.

- *Consideration.* Demonstrate consideration for staff by expressing concern, by showing understanding, and by accepting expressions of feelings and opinions. Successful leaders encourage feedback and engage in self-disclosure (Burke, 1982). Consideration also requires giving support when it is needed (Blanchard et al., 1985). Consideration is more sophisticated than simply a person or relationship orientation to leadership. It means dealing with conflicts, clashes of authority, and differences, while recognizing individual goals and needs (Zaleznik, 1990).

- *Control of Culture.* This goal can be easily misunderstood, as control is not directed at individuals. Control here is of the organization's culture. Often the leader helps to create that culture. Much of the culture is embedded in the informal organization. This structure includes the personal relationships, shared attitudes, and behavioral norms that are not consciously governed by authorities in the formal structure (Barnard, 1978). The focus of the culture should be on the older adult and the programs (Raymond, 1991). Control also pertains to the attitudes, work ethics, and social relationships necessary for a climate of excellence and efficiency. As managers attend to the formal and informal structure, leaders must develop change and influence the organizational culture. Schein (1987), commenting on leadership and organizational cultures, states, "There is a possibility—under-emphasized in leadership literature—that the only thing of real importance that leaders do is to create and manage culture and that the unique talent of leaders is their ability to work with culture" (p. 381).

Achievement of any one of these goals will afford some measure of leadership; obviously, achievement of all the goals will produce excellent leadership. To achieve the goals requires certain behaviors and activities. Thus, we have identified nine strategies for the gerontologist administrator.

The Nine Strategies of the Practice Model of Leadership

The successful use of these strategies will require knowledge, skills, and abilities discussed in this textbook, combined with what the leader brings to the situation from life experience and work experience. Some of these skills and abilities are relevant for management as well, for in the practice of administration, leadership and management are blended. Yet, leadership is distinguished from management, as it is "based on a compact that binds those who lead and those who follow into the same moral, intellectual, and emotional commitment" (Zaleznik, 1990, p. 12). Often, it is the followers who determine if one is a leader. Thoughtful application of the following strategies will enhance the perception of the gerontologist administrator as a leader.

Demonstration of Knowledge

The leadership literature is replete with discussions of knowledge. Knowledge means expertise in a certain area and ability to access information (Brilliant, 1986). Most literature relates to broad notions of leadership as opposed to leadership in an organization that serves older adults. The problem in the field of aging (applied gerontology) is that many administrative positions are occupied by persons without a background in gerontology. In a discussion of leadership, Zaleznik (1990) indicated that to hold expertise in a relevant area of endeavor is to show substance over style. Thus, knowledge of older adults, aging policy, and programs is essential. Certainly, administrative knowledge discussed in this textbook is equally important. Some of these major areas of knowledge are organizational design, management theory and practice, ethics, and group dynamics.

For leaders, however, it is not adequate to have the knowledge; it must be demonstrated. If the knowledge is not communicated, followers will assume it is not present. Therefore, the leader, through interpersonal interaction, presentations, and written communications, must display relevant knowledge. A pertinent example from the world of computer software technology is the frequent presentations by Bill Gates to his employees demonstrating his in-depth knowledge of the field (see, for example, Gates, 1998). Knowledge can also be displayed symbolically, such as by having a degree or certificate in gerontology posted on the office wall.

Vision

Vision is created by the ability to articulate and conceptualize "the big picture" that supersedes the mundaneness of daily efforts. Clearly, it is the creation of vision that identifies a leader (Bargal & Schmid, 1989; Bennis & Nanus, 1985). The communication of innovative ideas related to organizations, programs, projects, and change efforts that form a mental image of a positive outcome in the follower's mind is the creation of vision. Followers can be motivated by a dream, especially if it also includes new opportunities.

An element of risk taking generally occurs with attempts to reduce followers' uncertainty about innovation and change (Kindler, 1999). For the gerontologist administrator, the ability to create vision has two aspects. The first aspect is to possess and communicate the vision when appropriate. Timing is always a factor. The second aspect is to possess the willingness to draw upon the vision of followers that can be reinforced and articulated (Oakley & Krug, 1991).

Creativity

Creativity is closely akin to vision and can be employed in most administrative situations, but always carries a measure of risk and choice. Consider the issue of a staff member wasting time, which can be approached using a standard and useful problem-solving method (described in Chapter 3), or a creative approach as described in the learning experience at the end of this chapter. Being creative as a leader is part of the strategy, while encouraging, supporting, and teaching creativity is equally as powerful. Further, when a creative endeavor fails, it should not be condemned, but considered "a learning experience." Neither the leader's nor the follower's self-worth is contingent upon the success of the creative project. In a creative organizational atmosphere, "If you haven't failed, you haven't tried."

Creativity also translates into innovation, a necessary ingredient to remain current and competitive (Sifonis & Goldberg, 1996). Innovation leads to the possibility of greater effectiveness and increased satisfaction. To be innovative frequently requires identifying and challenging limiting assumptions (Kindler, 1999). Leaders use and encourage creativity in organizations "by brainstorming in team settings, by reviewing new ideas quickly, by providing rewards for successful innovations, by making a point of evaluating ideas positively, and perhaps most important, by not demanding new ideas on tight deadlines" (Sifonis & Goldberg, 1996, p. 180). Thus, the leader facilitates creativity by providing time and creating opportunities to engage in those activities. There must also be the belief that time spent in creative activities is good time, not wasted time, and part of the job.

Follower Relations

Leadership requires followers, and many followers are potential leaders. A reciprocal relationship exists between leader and follower that is mutually reinforcing (Bargal & Schmid, 1989; Zaleznik, 1989). There are two sides to this strategy: the relationship with the follower and the ability to be a follower. Sociologist Amitai Etzioni said, "The concept of leadership is fifty percent followership" (Kidder, 1989, p. 72).

Relations with followers are enhanced by teamwork, participation in decision-making, mutual goal setting, and challenging assignments that stretch beyond the job requirements. These kinds of cooperative collaborative relationships empower followers. An example of the latter is involving human behavior professional staff in marketing. The effective leader will use delegation of tasks and authority to competent staff who can work without close supervision (Blanchard et al., 1985).

The ability to be a leader involves accepting challenges from followers, accepting criticism, and taking risks. Followers are more likely to challenge when there is no threat of repercussions (Sifonis & Goldberg, 1996). Criticism will be welcomed as feedback, and changes of behavior will be seriously considered. Taking risks with ideas and people means following the innovative, creative suggestions of staff or thrusting staff into leadership situations. In most instances, the risk is shared by the leader and the follower.

Advocacy

Leadership theories and models often fail to identify certain obvious behaviors of leaders. None is so evident as advocacy. Recognized leaders in the community without formal position are commonly advocates of a cause or a solution to a problem. Betty Friedan's advocacy of women's rights is a classic example. Advocacy breeds controversy and criticism, such as when Jane Fonda advocated the end of the Vietnam War; however, she was still recognized as a leader.

Gerontologist administrators, especially those in highly visible positions, would be expected to be advocates for older adults. Jeannette C. Takanura, the Assistant Secretary for Aging of the U.S. Department of Health and Human Services and head of the Administration on Aging, spoke in 1998 on global aging. In her remarks, she stressed the "need to create many venues for sustained discussions and exchanges involving persons of all ages drawn from both the public and private sector" (Administration on Aging, 1998, p. 1). Certainly, individuals in positions such as the Assistant Secretary for Aging, State Office of Aging Director, or the CEO of a network of profit home health organizations would be expected to demonstrate leadership through advocacy.

High-level administrators in service organizations spend considerable time as advocates and with related activities (Ezell, 1991). For those gerontologist administrators who accept a position, there is an obligation to be an advocate for change that will benefit older adults and society. Further, the gerontologist administrator must recognize that staff of programs for older adults are highly dedicated and committed to improving the quality of life of older adults. Thus, advocacy by the administrator is often congruent with many of the goals and values of followers (Kindler, 1999). Gerontologist administrators as advocates rely on knowledge of older adults, policy, and community attitudes; for example, the administrator might see the need to speak out for additional services for the large number of very old, widowed women who are living alone.

Often, one thinks of civil disobedience as associated with advocacy. In the case of the gerontologist administrator, the methods are less dramatic. First, leadership is demonstrated to staff by displaying advocacy for older adults, then through public speaking, networking, and lobbying of city, county, state, and national governmental bodies. Advocacy can also be displayed by joining relevant organizations that advocate for the elderly. Additionally, maintaining an expectation of staff to be advocates is a critical component of leadership.

Assessments

Information can be gleaned from formal or informal assessments. Formal assessments, such as organizational analysis, morale studies, and attitudes toward management surveys, all provide valuable information. Individual assessment instruments of various leadership and management styles, values, and motivations also provide valuable information, particularly when discussed in a seminar format. Most assessment information will come from a less formal process, by way of observations, organizational reports, and interpersonal interactions. Leaders need to rely on the perceptions of other trusted leaders and staff in making assessments (Sifonis & Goldberg, 1996). While relying on others presents an element of risk, the leader must use assessment skills to determine the others' competency, integrity, and loyalty.

Leader assessment occurs in three distinct areas: self-awareness, forces in the individual, and organizational dynamics (Tannenbaum & Schmidt, 1986). Self-awareness requires insight into how one's own values, attitudes, strengths and weaknesses, and personality characteristics will influence one's behavior. Formal and intuitive knowledge of human behavior allows the leader to assess the forces that are operating within individual followers. An individual's motivation, stage of life, competencies, and capabilities all contribute to the assessment process (Blanchard et al., 1985). Last, and most complex, is assessment of organizational dynamics. This requires the ability to view the entire system and to see how the subsystems relate to one another, including the functioning of departments, teams, and groups within the organization. Adjustment and selection of strategies are dependent on information from these three areas.

For the informal assessments, a multitude of skills can be employed by the leader. Three skills have been selected as the most essential. First, observational skills, which include one's own behavior in different situations, watching staff perform duties, and paying attention to what drives the organization. This is why great emphasis is placed on "walking around" the organization. The second skill is listening to others in such a way that they are able to give you their observations, information, and perceptions (Alderson & McDonnell, 1994; Oakley & Krug, 1991). Details on effective listening will be elaborated upon later in this text. The third skill is the use of open-ended questions: questions that are phrased so that respondents have great latitude in answering. The leader wants the respondents' perceptions to be uninhibited and candid.

Teaching

Leadership involves teaching, even if it is not conscious, aware, or deliberate. Since leaders are highly visible, their behaviors are closely observed and often emulated. It is desirable for leaders to develop the ability to communicate knowledge and skill to other leaders and followers. Successful organizations from all sectors are characterized by leaders committed to teaching (Cohen & Tichy, 1998). Two aspects of teaching that are most important for leadership have been selected: the leader as a model and leadership development.

Leaders epitomize how they want others to behave, and they encourage them to do it (Gatewood et al., 1995). Leaders need to remain cognizant that their behavior is constantly scrutinized, observed, and often replicated. Even mannerisms and manner of dress will influence other individuals. Often the influences are not even conscious. Thus, almost all behavior of the leader, including behaviors that may be only attributed to the leader, even exaggerated, will compose the behavioral model for others. This will vary in accordance with the perception of the leader as being powerful, influential, or effective. The impact of the teaching and learning will also depend upon the level of identification that followers have with the leader.

The successful leader will have the desire for and see the necessity of developing leadership in the organization. Using the assessment skills discussed previously, the leader can identify selected individuals on whom to concentrate development. Recognizing that many large organizations have leadership development programs, this discussion of teaching specifically relates to the leader identifying individuals and focusing attention through regular work activities. Leadership development is frequently very satisfying and reciprocal for the leader (Cohen & Tichy, 1998). A basic formula can be constructed for leadership development, which begins with providing the potential leader with a challenge. The formula is as follows:

Challenge + Support + Recognition = New Leader

Once a challenge has been provided, such as a specific task (frequently outside the potential leader's job description), the leader should support and encourage support of the potential leader in his efforts to meet the challenge, providing recognition during the process and at the end of the task. Leadership development using this method will require a number of tasks over a period of time.

Use of Groups

Current administration practices emphasize the use of groups, teamwork, and broad participation of staff. Much of what occurs and is decided in service organizations is a group process. Leadership extends beyond management, where groups, in addition to receiving tasks, are given greater responsibility (Oakley & Krug, 1991). Techniques to increase participation in group process are extensively used by effective leaders.

The nominal group process is one such technique (Ford, 1975). It has three steps. First, after presenting a particular problem or decision, group members sitting in full view of each other and without discussion write down their thoughts about the problem. This is followed by a sharing of ideas that are written on a flipchart in the front of the room in full view of everyone, still with no discussion. Second, the group leader facilitates a discussion of all of the ideas written on the flipchart to gain clarification and amplification. The third step is nominal voting, where the group sets priorities or ratings on each of the remaining items that offer a solution to the problem. The outcome of this process produces a top-ranked solution that the group can now discuss in terms of implementation. Several variations on this process can be used. The major theme is that greater participation is achieved by focusing group discussion on the anonymous ideas so that more ideas can be generated and a course of action decided on with guided discussion, to avoid digressions.

Work groups that have been led, rather than managed, have greater levels of staff participation, commitment, and satisfaction (Elloy & Randolph, 1997). The leader needs to ensure that the group activity is productive and useful. Groups are not always the appropriate forum for solving problems and making decisions. Many groups need to be open to conflict and disagreement, but devoid of competition (Sifonis & Goldberg, 1996). In effective decision or problem groups, work roles are often blurred, and there is ample opportunity for leadership to be shared. Leaders should be facilitative of others to lead groups. To avoid problems, the leaders must remain accessible to the group. Cohesion is developed and commitment is achieved by a successful group process.

Influence

Most definitions of leadership, for example, Gatewood's "the process of influencing the activities of an individual or a group toward the achievement of a goal," incorporate or suggest influence (1995, p. 492). Although influence is a way of defining leadership, it is often neglected in leadership models in favor of power. In this conceptualization for the gerontologist administrator in the health and human services environment, we have opted for the strategy of influence, because it creates fewer problems and barriers than power. Power accumulation in service organizations is for leadership of the past. It creates separateness and unnecessary competition (Oakley & Krug, 1991).

More specifically, acknowledging that power is one of the means of influencing others, we have chosen other means of exerting influence. This choice is also based on the observation that power has come to mean, and is portrayed in the media as, being ruthless and reckless, with disregard for others, the very antithesis of good leadership. Influence is the ability to affect the behavior of others to the extent that it will override personal interests, choices, and perceived self-limitations.

Foremost, influence comes with building social networks among followers (Gatewood et al., 1995). Interrelated is credibility and trust. Credibility results from "walking the talk," that is, behavior that is consistent with verbalized intentions. Trust, in this context, means reliability and predictability (Bennis & Nanus, 1985). We have previously identified knowledge as a strategy for leadership, and there should be little question that superior knowledge brings major influence. Further, influence will flourish when the leader can continuously and consistently demonstrate credibility by achieving goals. Such credibility at times can be achieved even when the leader is not necessarily liked by the followers.

While followers will be influenced by perceived competency and achievement, they wish to be influential as well. A leader is more likely to influence others who have a sense that they can influence the leader—a process of exchange (Bargal & Schmid, 1989). Activities that influence the influential will often transverse several levels of the organization, involving a series of leaders. Influence, more gentle and subtle than power, builds strong organizations and produces new leaders.

Limitations and Problems of Leadership

To consider the problems with leadership fully, we must first continue the discussion on power. An examination of some organizational limits on leadership and leaders without substance will also be discussed. This will require further contrasting of the two domains of administration: management and leadership.

There is a great debate on the use and misuse of power by leaders in organizations. There are those who lament the new thoughts on leadership, saying "We are going forward, but we are doing so without affording power a place in the new vision" (Bennis & Nanus, 1985, p. 16). There is the hedging on the issue, where leadership is defined as compassionate or proper use of power (Kotter, 1986). Perhaps the other extreme is that power is what is used when leadership is flawed or failing: more precisely, both the power that comes with a position and the power that is associated with coercion are perceived as problematic for leadership. These kinds of power, misused, produce a number of problems:

- *Politicalization of the Organization.* An organization becomes more politicized where power is sought for itself, and manipulation and competition characterize the organizational environment (Zaleznik, 1990).

- *Overreliance on Position.* When this source of power is used, it will serve to further unequalize relationships, replace other means of motivation, and foster power in the informal structure of the organization.

- *Success Measurement.* In some instances, in the competition for accumulation of power rather than goal achievement, power becomes the criterion for success (Oakley & Krug, 1991).

- *Counteracts Empowerment of Staff.* The use of power supports the central aspects of the traditional bureaucracy, which is most resistant to sharing power and authority (Oakley & Krug, 1991).

- *Compliance over Commitment.* Legitimate position power produces compliance, which is doing what is required. This may at times be necessary. However, the desired condition of commitment, which cannot be commanded, comes with a desire to please or influence the leader (Gatewood et al., 1995).

- *Resistance.* A typical response to the use of power, especially coercive power, is staff resistance. A classic example of resistance occurred when a CEO visited a satellite center of a comprehensive older adult service organization. He noticed a decline in attendance of a day care program and several other smaller programs, and attempted to motivate the employees to engage in outreach and marketing by telling them that if they didn't they might not have a job. The response of most of the employees over the next couple of weeks was to take longer breaks and lunch hours. This brought more emphasis on compliance by the local administrator.

Limitations on leadership are present in most organizations. Mandates for change or new programs may come from corporate headquarters, the board, or superior agencies, requiring deadlines and certain conditions. Mandates of this nature counteract the use of leadership and force a more management-oriented approach. The more traditional the organizational structure, the greater the emphasis will be on position power and the traditional chain of command. This structure constrains leadership efforts to produce greater cohesion and commitment.

Administrative transitions where the administrators are promoted or leave bring problems for replacements. While filling the management aspects of the position may not prove that difficult, replacing the leadership is more complicated. This is the case especially when the leadership rests on personal characteristics and constructive relationships with followers. Both domains—management and at least the potential for leadership—must be considered when seeking a replacement. Emphasis on only management abilities will not be sufficient. This applies to all levels of administration.

Last, an environment of flawed leadership and misuse of power has plagued the last part of the twentieth century. Service organizations are not immune from this perception. While a number of misguided practices can be identified, the most frequent is choosing the charismatic leader with no substance. We call this "the leader without a clue." These articulate communicators and cunning individuals do irreparable harm, stay short periods of time, and leave crippled organizations in need of repair. The selection of a gerontologist administrator should be a non-political, thorough, and highly participatory process. Procedures to assess management and leadership skills and abilities should be utilized by administrators, skilled human resources personnel, board members, corporate executives, or external consultants.

SUMMARY

Leadership, in contrast to management, is the ability to influence followers and communicate vision using charismatic qualities, personal attributes, and creativity. Leadership activities are directed toward other people. Traditionally, leadership was conceptualized as a cluster of personality traits, contrasting behaviors directed either toward tasks or people, or a wide variety of behaviors that can be selected from to apply to a given situation. The latter conceptualization, called "situational leadership," holds that there is "no one best way" to lead.

Contemporary leadership theories build upon situational leadership thinking. In the path goal theory, leaders have the responsibility to help followers overcome obstacles that prevent attainment of goals. A leader does this by being direct, giving support, and being participation and achievement oriented. Another theory, called participation theory, presents varying levels of participation and responsibility that can be delegated to followers. A final contemporary theory holds that a leader with close emotional relations with followers tends to develop a small group following.

In addition to leadership theories, various styles have been integrated with theory. Three broadly conceived styles are: charismatic, transactional, and transformational. Charismatic leaders are often seen as heroes, are usually highly verbal, and convey enthusiasm. Transactional leaders use rewards of performance, like recognition and praise, to gain followers and achieve greater influence. Transformational leaders motivate individuals beyond their self-interest by appealing to ideas, values, social justice, and fairness, as well as group solidarity. While elements of all three leadership styles can be used by gerontologist administrators, the transformational leadership style would make the most constructive contribution to administration in organizations that serve older adults.

A practice model of leadership for the gerontologist administrator is offered. This model is composed of four goals and nine strategies. The four goals are commitment, cohesion, consideration, and control of culture. These goals are directed at gaining commitment to purpose and visions, building teams and relationships within groups, demonstrating concern and understanding for followers, and influencing the culture of the organization to support goals and objectives.

There are nine strategies. First is knowledge, which places particular emphasis on knowledge of older adults' behavior, policies, and programs. The second is the communication of innovative ideas so the vision can form a desirable mental image for followers. The third strategy is creativity, which is closely aligned with vision. It involves taking risks with new programs, new approaches, and people assignments, as well as encouraging creativity in followers. Fourth, the relationship with followers is reciprocal as the leader at times will be a follower. Fifth, for organizations that serve older adults, the leader must be seen as an advocate of programs and policies that will improve the quality of life for older adults. Sixth, information gleaned from formal assessment procedures and informal information about oneself, individuals, and the organization allows the leader to adjust behavior and select strategies. Seventh, the leader is a teacher, directly through supervision, coaching, and interpersonal interaction, and indirectly as a model performing behaviors that will be emulated by followers.

Eighth, using groups and fostering team work that produces broad participation of staff is a way in which leaders achieve goals. Certain formal, structured group activities, such as the nominal group process, can be applied to appropriate group decision-making and problem-solving situations. There are many such tools in the literature on administration. Ninth, influence is seen as being more productive than the use of power for the gerontologist administrator. Influence comes from exercising strategies, such as accumulation of knowledge and creating vision, and from credibility by keeping commitments.

Perhaps one of the greatest limitations on leadership today is not only the misuse of power but the mere exercise of power because it is highly suspect. Even the innocent use of power may bring negative responses, particularly as it relates to empowering staff and achieving commitment. Many leaders, also, do not have as much latitude in decision-making and creative areas because of mandates from superiors in the organizational structure. More traditional organizational structures place constraints on leadership.

In administrative transition, attention must be paid to selecting a leader as well as a manager. The selection of the leader is perhaps the more difficult process, as the qualities and attributes are not as highly visible or demonstrable in a short period of time, with the notable exception of verbal ability. Interaction opportunities for prospective leaders with staff and other leaders is a valuable practice for selecting the right leader to fit the situation.

LEARNING EXPERIENCE

Creative Problem-Solving: Forced Fit

Creative problem-solving means using techniques, tools, and methods different from the standard, sequential problem-solving model. The technique can be used by anyone as a solitary process and with groups, but if the problem is a person's behavior, it is not to be used with the person present. Those who seek to lead must be willing to risk different approaches to issues and to share those approaches with followers. The creative technique used in this learning experience promotes forming combinations and making associations by using divergent thinking. It may bring some discomfort to those who are unfamiliar with this approach. Its usefulness will be evident if the procedure is followed.

"Forced fit" generates options by linking apparent dissimilar objects and ideas (Schoonover, 1996). That is, this technique makes connections between the problem and something unrelated. It uses metaphors that may be funny or illogical. By forced association, the issue is expanded and old barriers are overcome, often bringing a sudden burst of insight that can lead to a solution. Five steps have been adapted from Schoonover (1996) that outline this approach:

- Step 1. State the problem and be specific.

- Step 2. Give the problem an unusual twist by focusing on an apparent irrelevant object, or adopt an unusual perspective.

- Step 3. List a few attributes of the item under concern and a few attributes of the identified object. Write them down.
- Step 4. Select one of the attributes from the chosen object and apply it to the problem, generating a new idea (an insight) that goes beyond your first understanding of the problem.
- Step 5. Formulate a new action to apply to the problem.

The process can be repeated using one or all of the attributes. A "forced fit" process can use ideas, puns, or analogies. It can be used individually or in groups, repeatedly, with the same issue or problem, or with different elements of the problem. An example is provided, followed by an opportunity to test the use of forced fit.

Example of Forced Fit

Problem: The marketing director, Bill, wastes time chit-chatting with the staff. How can I get him to stop?

Object association: A Cadillac is the irrelevant object (seen from the office while staring out the window).

Attributes of Bill's Behavior

1. good marketing
2. gift of gab
3. overbearing
4. proud professional

Attributes of a Cadillac

1. attractive
2. big auto
3. expensive
4. low gas mileage
5. used to be considered the "best"

Insight: Maybe Bill used to be better at marketing or received more feedback. Now, in this setting, he is not being reinforced, so he actively seeks feedback from others. The chit-chatting allows him to tell his stories and receive praise.

New action: Speak with the CEO about ways to give Bill more or different recognition and feedback.

Time to try "forced fit" problem-solving. (Make up information as needed.)

The problem: You have been asked by the CEO to participate in the long-range strategic planning process. This is recognition of leadership activities that have gone beyond your position as a supervisor. You know very little about strategic plans, have never read one, and generally have had a negative attitude. Now you are concerned about being able to make a significant contribution to the planning process that is consistent with your recognized leadership. To make things more difficult, the session is this Saturday and this is Thursday afternoon.

Associate the problem with an irrelevant object: _____

Attributes of a Strategic Plan   **Attributes of the Object**

1. _____   1. _____

2. _____   2. _____

3. _____   3. _____

4. _____   4. _____

5. _____   5. _____

Think about the different attributes. What comes to mind? _____

_____

_____

Action to be taken: _____

_____

Try it again, using one of the other attributes of the unrelated object.

REFERENCES

Administration on Aging. (1998). Assistant Secretary for Aging stresses need to prepare for global aging. *Administration on Aging Update, 3*(6) [On-line serial]. Available FTP: Hostname: aoa.dhhs.gov Directory:update/default.htm

Alderson, W. T., & McDonnell, N. A. (1994). *Theory of management.* Atlanta, GA: Thomas Nelson.

Bargal, D., & Schmid, H. (1989). Recent themes in theory and research on leadership and their implications for management of the human services. In Y. Hasenfeld (Ed.), *Administrative leadership in the social services: The next challenge* (pp. 37–54). New York: Haworth.

Barnard, C. (1978). Informal organizations and their relation to formal organizations. In W. E. Natemeyer (Ed.), *Classics of organizational theory* (pp. 239–243). Oak Park, IL: Moore.

Bass, B. (1985). *Leadership and performance beyond expectations.* New York: Free Press; Macmillan.

Bennis, W., & Nanus, B. (1985). *Leaders: The strategies for taking charge.* New York: Harper & Row.

Blanchard, K., Zigarmi, P., & Zigarmi, D. (1985). *Leadership and the one minute manager.* New York: William Morrow.

Brilliant, E. L. (1986). Social work leadership: A missing ingredient? *Social Work, 31*(5), 325–331.

Burke, W. W. (1982). Leaders: Their behavior and development. In D. A. Nadler, M. L. Tushman, & N. G. Hatvany (Eds.), *Managing organizations: Readings and cases* (pp. 237–245). Boston: Little, Brown.

Cohen, E., & Tichy, N. (1998). Teaching: The heart of leadership. *The Healthcare Forum Journal, 41*(2), 20–22, 24, 75.

Elloy, D. F., & Randolph, A. (1997). The effect of superleader behavior on autonomous work groups in a government operated railway service. *Public Personnel Management, 26*(2), 257–270.

Ezell, M. (1991). Administrators as advocates. *Administration in Social Work, 15*(4), 1–18.

Fiedler, F. E. (1967). *A theory of leadership effectiveness.* St. Louis, MO: McGraw-Hill.

Fiedler, F. E., & Chemers, M. M. (1974). *Leadership and effective management.* Glenview, IL: Scott, Foresman.

Ford, D. L. (1975). Nominal group technique: An applied group problem-solving activity. In J. E. Jones & J. W. Pfeiffer (Eds.), *The 1975 annual handbook for group facilitators* (pp. 35–37). La Jolla, CA: University Associates.

Gates, B. (1998, April 21). *Bill Gates outlines Windows principles.* [On-line]. Available: www.microsoft.com/ntworkstation/news/newsarchive/Apr98/BillGkeynote.asp

Gatewood, R. D., Taylor, R. R., & Ferrell, O. C. (1995). *Management: Comprehension, analysis, and application.* Chicago: Austen.

Glisson, C. (1989). The effect of leadership on workers in human service organizations. *Administration in Social Work, 13*(3/4), 99–116.

House, R. J., & Mitchell, T. R. (1978). Path-goal theory of leadership. In W. E. Natemeyer (Ed.), *Classics of organizational theory* (pp. 226–236). Oak Park, IL: Moore.

Hoy, W. K., & Miskel, C. G. (1978). *Educational administration: Theory, research, and practice.* New York: Random House.

Kidder, R. M. (1989). *Agenda for the 21st century.* Cambridge, MA: Massachusetts Institute of Technology.

Kindler, H. S. (1999). Risk taking for leaders. In E. Birch (Ed.), *The 1999 Annual* (pp. 169–178). San Francisco: Jossey-Bass/Pfeiffer.

Kotter, J. P. (1986). Why power and influence issues are at the very core of executive work. In S. Srivastva (Ed.), *Executive power* (pp. 20–32). San Francisco: Jossey-Bass.

Legnini, M. (1994). Developing leaders vs. training administrators in the health services. *American Journal of Public Health, 84*(10), 1569–1572.

Lewis, J. A., Lewis, M. D., & Souflée, F. (1991). *Management of human service programs* (2nd ed.). Pacific Grove, CA: Brooks/Cole.

Lynch, D., & Kordis, P. L. (1988). *Strategy of the dolphin: Scoring a win in a chaotic world.* New York: William Morrow.

Oakley, E., & Krug, D. (1991). *Enlightened leadership: Getting to the heart of change.* New York: Simon & Schuster.

Perlmutter, F. D. (1995). Administering alternative social programs. In L. Ginsberg & P. R. Keys (Eds.), *New management in human services* (pp. 203–218). Washington, DC: National Association of Social Workers.

Raymond, F. B. (1991). Management of services for the elderly. In P.K.H. Kim (Ed.), *Serving the elderly: Skills for practice* (pp. 233–258). New York: Aldine De Gruyter.

Robbins, S. P. (1995). *Supervision today!* Englewood Cliffs, NJ: Prentice-Hall.

Schein, E. H. (1987). Defining organizational culture. In J. M. Shafritz & J. S. Ott (Eds.), *Classics of organization theory* (2nd ed., pp. 381–395). Chicago: Dorsey.

Schoonover, P. (1996). Forced fit: Like a glove. *Think: The magazine on critical and creative thinking, 7*(2), 18–21.

Sifonis, J. G., & Goldberg, B. (1996). *Corporation on a tightrope: Balancing leadership, governance, and technology in an age of complexity*. New York: Oxford University.

Tannenbaum, R., & Schmidt, W. (1986). How to choose a leadership pattern. In M. T. Matteson & J. M. Ivancevich (Eds.), *Management classics* (3rd ed., pp. 325–341). Plano, TX: Business Publications.

Weinbach, R. (1998). *The social worker as manager: A practical guide to success* (3rd ed.). Needham Heights, MA: Allyn & Bacon.

Zaleznik, A. (1989). *The managerial mystique: Restoring leadership in business*. New York: Harper & Row.

Zaleznik, A. (1990). The leadership gap. *Academy of Management Executives, 4*(1), 7–22.

Chapter 3

Management Theory and Practice

Effective administration is composed of a high level of management and leadership skills and abilities. Together, the two components compose our conceptualization of administration, particularly as administration relates to service organizations that provide programs for older adults. The mix of management and leadership will vary depending on the situation, the nature of the service, and, to some extent, the external environment. Accomplishing the goals of a service organization will require both sets of skills, fully integrated. This chapter will focus on the management component of administration by providing a theoretical foundation for management practice, examining approaches to management, and offering selected techniques and methods of management.

The primary goal of the gerontologist manager is *service effectiveness*, that is, quality services that produce change in people, organizations, or systems. However, a manager will be judged not only on effectiveness but also on the manner in which she accomplishes tasks, including ethical considerations (Patti, 1987). The manager will be expected to use resources efficiently to accomplish the goals of the organization. Good management is not merely the performance of the traditional functions of planning, organizing, controlling, and administering, but rather a synergy of processes to accomplish tasks and meet goals. This process, involving human and physical resources, relies heavily on interpersonal skills and technology to transform the mission of the organization into relevant work activities.

Management processes and tasks are performed primarily by those who hold administrative positions, such as a supervisor of clinical services for older adults in a Family Service Agency or the administrator of a congregate meals program. The administration context is of utmost importance. Generally, the gerontologist manager must acknowledge the management activities engaged in by direct service professionals and other staff. In many organizations, management activities, depending on the setting, are shared with service professionals with backgrounds in health care, planning, social work, psychology, and gerontology. Management authority must be integrated with the multiple knowledge base and expertise of the professional staff of the organization (Longest, 1976). Thus, the definition of the management component for the gerontologist administrator needs to consider these contingencies.

DEFINITION OF MANAGEMENT

Considerable diversity exists in the nature, scope, and meaning of management. In its simplest form, effective management is the ability to get things done (Drucker, 1985). Weinbach (1990) considers management to be specific functions performed by persons within the work setting that are intended to promote productivity and organizational goal attainment. Longest (1976), writing about management in the health care setting, defines management as "a process with both interpersonal and technical aspects through which the objectives of an organization or that part of it being managed are accomplished by using human and physical resources and technology" (p. 138). Other authors have opted for simpler definitions. In a textbook on management in the field of gerontology, the definition offered is "the ability to get things done through people" (Morgan & Hiltner, 1992, p. 13). A straightforward, general definition is offered by Gatewood, Taylor, and Ferrell (1995), who allow that management is "a set of activities designed to achieve an organization's objective by using its resources effectively and efficiently" (p. 4).

The latter definition presents two key elements for the gerontologist administrator: effectiveness and efficiency. To achieve both, certain common ingredients must be present. Management should be goal oriented and consistent with the mission and purpose of the organization. Management should be a cooperative, planned venture where goals and objectives are reached through people with a task orientation. Additionally, the caliber of programs for older adults must also be attended to by management. Therefore, management in this text is defined as a rational process of control and the systematic selection of goals with associated strategies, involving those activities necessary to offer quality programs in an effective and efficient manner.

Modern management is based on an extensive body of knowledge. Part of this knowledge is practice knowledge that includes specific techniques, methods, and tools for effective and efficient management acquired from experience. Another source of knowledge is derived from management theories. The next section summarizes historical management theories, modern management concepts, and selected approaches to management. These notions constitute an important foundation for the skills and abilities of the gerontologist administrator.

MANAGEMENT THEORIES

Management theory may attend to principles, structure, the interaction between individuals and the group, or the behavior of individuals in organizations. There are no rules to guide management theorists. It is useful to distinguish between management theories, which are primarily conceptual and relate to behaviors in an organization, and organizational theories, which pertain to structure and design. The structure, environment, culture, and distributions of tasks and functions in an organization will be presented in Chapter 6. Management concepts, styles, and behaviors are featured in this chapter. It will be constructive to examine the rich history of management theory.

Historical Management Theories

A myriad of theories are classified and described in detail by a number of authors (George, 1972; Natemeyer, 1978; Wren, 1979). A summary of historical management theories is presented in Table 3.1, which also identifies major theorists associated with the three major schools of thought. From varied backgrounds, the theorists range from Henri Fayol, who was an engineer, to Elton Mayo, a recognized social philosopher, to Douglas McGregor, a professor of management at the Massachusetts Institute of Technology (MIT). The *Classic School* emphasizes rational principles of management. The *Human Relations School* focuses on individuals, particularly on their motivation and productivity. The *Social Science School* emphasizes the social psychological aspects of organizations and the sociological nature of the work environment. Particular attention should be given to the role of the manager in Table 3.1. The thoughts about management behavior evolved from authoritarian to humanitarian (more consideration for the individual) and later to the notion of the manager as a facilitator.

The historical theories presented are a product of their times and reflect manufacturing organizations rather than service organizations. These historical theories and associated principles remain valuable for the contemporary gerontologist manager because they serve as a foundation for modern management, and many practices derived from these works have stood the test of time. An examination of Fayol's General Principles of Management (see Table 3.2) reveals that many of these prescriptions are utilized today.

Many elements of bureaucratic management, although the notion of bureaucracy is frequently maligned, have persisted. The use of the principle of hierarchy (chain-of-command) and the need for rules to regulate conduct (policies) are an integral part of modern organizations that serve older adults (Etzioni, 1964). McGregor's dichotomization of the conceptualization of managers' beliefs about workers—into "Theory X," where the worker lacks ambition, dislikes responsibility, is selfish and gullible, versus "Theory Y," where the worker is motivated

Table 3.1
Historical Summary of Management Theories

	Classical
Theorist	Frederick Taylor (scientific information) Henri Fayol (administrative management) Max Weber (bureaucracy)
Contributions	– There exists a hierarchy of positions and authority in all organizations – Impersonal, logical, and rational rules which should be followed – A division of labor based on technical qualifications – The necessity of scientifically selecting, training, and developing workers – Chain of command
Limitations	– Concept lacked sensitivity to human needs – People proved to not always be rational and motivated by economic interests – Highly structured and formal principles; situational context ignored – Emphasis on structure and documentation distract from focus on purpose and goals
Role of Manager	– Use authority to increase work productivity – Discover the "one best way" to perform tasks – Create harmony and reduce conflict – Distribute work among the employees

Human Relations	Social Science
Elton Mayo (human interaction) Mary Parker Follett (human behavior) Douglas McGregor (individual centered) Abraham Maslow (humanistic approach)	Rensis Likert (organizationally centered) Fred Emory and Erick Trist (group centered) Joan Woodward (fit with technology) Chester Barnard (cooperative systems)
– Management should focus on people – The notion that assumptions about human motivation impact management effectiveness – Focus on basic innate human needs – Work as a source of human fulfillment – Recognition of the informal organization	– Focus on organizational framework – Employee involvement in major decision making – Focus on group interaction and teamwork – Social science-based professional bureaucracy – Need to adjust management approach to changing environment – Focus on organizational purpose and goals – Importance of communications related to authority
– Ignores or minimizes organizational structure and design – Commonly misinterpreted as tending only to individual desires and prerogatives – Overemphasizes the importance of psychological factors	– Misconception that employee involvement is a "democratic" approach – Varying levels of employee sophistication limit contributions and ability to gain from the group process – Time-consuming processes – Cooperation and participation of employees is highly dependent on sphere of interest – Lax recognition of marked individual differences in employees' ability, motivation, and level of integrity
– Motivate employees by showing concerns and addressing psychological aspects – Offer cooperative, pleasant work environment – Treat workers with respect – Provide opportunities for meaningful involvement and success	– Utilize knowledge of group dynamics and human behavior to manage – Facilitate involvement and cooperation using group and teams – Articulate and support purpose and goals of the organization – Rely more on leadership than on authority

Table 3.2
Fayol's General Principles of Management

Division of Work	The object of division of work is to produce more and better work with the same effort. It reduces the number of things one has to pay attention to and is applicable to all work involving a considerable number of people.
Authority and Responsibility	Authority is the right to give orders and the power to exact obedience. A manager must have both personal and official authority. Responsibility is the natural consequence of authority and accepting responsibility requires courage. Fear of responsibility must be reduced in both managers and subordinates.
Discipline	Discipline is basically respect for agreements between the firm and its employees. It is absolutely necessary for the smooth running of a business, and it requires good leaders at all levels, clear and fair agreements between the firm and its employees, and penalties for disobedience fairly applied.
Unity of Command	An employee should receive orders from one superior only. If it is violated, authority is undermined, and discipline, order, and stability are threatened.
Unity of Direction	Activities with the same purpose should have one plan with one person in charge.
Remuneration of Personnel	Pay should be fair and as satisfying as possible to both employees and the firm. A method of payment should encourage and reward good performance, it should not lead to overpayment, and it may include rewards other than just money.

Centralization	Everything that increases the importance of subordinates' roles is decentralization; everything that reduces it is centralization. Every organization will naturally have some degree of centralization; however, the exact degree must vary according to different cases, with an objective of optimum utilization of all talents/skills of personnel.
Scalar Chain	The Scalar Chain is the chain of authority ranging from the top to the bottom of the organization. This is the route by which all communication should flow except in cases requiring quick action. In this case communication between peers is appropriate as long as all managers in the chain are kept informed.
Order	All material things should have a well-chosen place and be kept in that place. All people should be carefully selected and placed in well-organized positions—the right person in the right place.
Equity	In order to ensure devotion and loyalty from employees they must be treated with kindness and justice.
Stability of Tenure of Personnel	Managerial personnel must be given enough time to get to know their jobs and to succeed in doing the job well. Turnover is expensive and has negative effects on the firm.
Initiative	Managers should encourage all members of the organization to develop and implement plans. The manager who encourages initiative on the part of employees and allows the exercise of initiative is a superior manager.
Esprit de Corps	Managers should try hard to create harmony and unity among the employees of a firm. Toward this end, managers should encourage the use of oral communication between employees as opposed to written communication, and managers must take care not to create jealousy between workers.

Source: Adapted from Fayol (1949).

to work, accepts responsibility, and can fulfill higher order of needs at work—continues to be instructional in understanding management approaches. The *Social Science School* of management has dramatically influenced contemporary approaches to management which will be explored next.

Contemporary Management Concepts and Approaches

Contemporary management concepts emanate from the management theories of the past and are less centered upon a given theorist. Even open systems theory, a subset of general systems theory that describes an organization as interdependent and interrelated parts, has a conceptual connection to social science management theories. An examination of Open Systems Theory, the Contingency Model, Participatory Management and what has been called the Japanese Management approach will prove fruitful for the gerontologist manager. These constructs suggest behaviors for the individual in modern older adult service organizations that will lead to effective and efficient management.

Open Systems Theory

Open systems theory focuses primarily on a way to conceptualize an organization. This theory will be examined again from an organizational perspective in Chapter 6. For the present, attention is given to open systems as an approach to management. This conceptualization emphasizes interaction with the external environment and is most appropriate for understanding organizations that serve older adults. Closed systems have limited interaction with the surrounding environment. Systems thinking characterizes organizations as composed of interdependent components in relationship to one another. According to open systems theory, organizations are contrived—that is, they do not exist naturally in the environment. These systems input energy and resources; they have a process called "throughput" that eventually results in some change and improvement in the client, referred to as the "output." Figure 3.1, adapted from a formulation of open systems by Katz and Kahn (1978), summarizes key features of an open systems model.

For the gerontologist manager utilizing this theory, it is important to think of an organization as subsystems and to focus on the relationship between those subsystems (Kast & Rosenzwig, 1986). Further, any change or impact on a subsystem will affect all other subsystems. For example, the dismissal of an individual from one unit may not seem, on the surface, to impact other units, but it may change the informal system of communication and power.

Contingency Model of Management

The first cousin to the open systems theory is the contingency model of management. A basic contingency tenet is that different management approaches and behaviors are necessary for particular organizational situations or organizational purposes. Indeed, even within an organization, departments or units

Figure 3.1
Open-System Model of an Organization

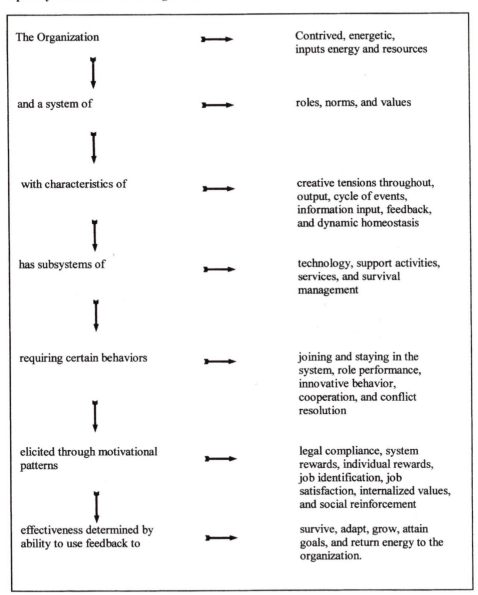

The Organization	Contrived, energetic, inputs energy and resources
and a system of	roles, norms, and values
with characteristics of	creative tensions throughout, output, cycle of events, information input, feedback, and dynamic homeostasis
has subsystems of	technology, support activities, services, and survival management
requiring certain behaviors	joining and staying in the system, role performance, innovative behavior, cooperation, and conflict resolution
elicited through motivational patterns	legal compliance, system rewards, individual rewards, job identification, job satisfaction, internalized values, and social reinforcement
effectiveness determined by ability to use feedback to	survive, adapt, grow, attain goals, and return energy to the organization.

Source: Adapted from Katz & Kahn (1978).

might require different approaches to management. For example, the geriatric unit in a hospital could require a highly structured, more classical approach because of external regulatory requirements, while the gerontology department in that same hospital, which allows for greater freedom of programs and is dedicated to patient education and health prevention, may have a stronger human relations orientation. This is in stark contrast to the cornerstone of those historical management theories that hold there is "one best way" to management.

Contradictory research emerged amidst the trend in management to shift focus toward the individual and the use of group participation in management. Morse and Lorsch (1970) found that organizations with rigid, formal structures can be effective and productive, supporting an adaption of approaches to different situations.

Another underlying assumption of the contingency model is that many modern complex organizations are constantly changing, and are less predictable than organizations of the past (Netting, Kettner, & McMurtry, 1993; Patti, 1987). Therefore, many organizations are not suited to a structured, one-dimensional approach to management. This is especially the case for organizations serving older adults, which often require adjustment to new needs and changes in funding formulas.

In the contingency model, the manager must assess the situation at hand and select from a range of management tools and techniques to discover what is most appropriate for her situation. This should not be misunderstood as a "whatever works" approach, but rather as a thoughtful assessment and selection of activities to "fit" the characteristics of the organization, its particular technology, the clients, and the surrounding environment. The management approach might also vary, depending on the stage of the organization. An organization in its beginning stages may require a more flexible approach to management. Later, management may need to adjust selectively to be more structured as subsystems achieve greater identity through clustering of functions and tasks.

Management Behaviors

Open systems theory and the contingency model provide a useful perspective for management behaviors. Developments of these concepts in the literature have been directed more to ways of thinking about an organization than to offer practice principles for managers, like those of Fayol. There is a continual quest to identify management practices associated with these concepts. Considering the features of organizations that serve older adults, while thinking about those organizations as open systems as well as considering the contingency model, a cluster of management behaviors can be elucidated.

Gerontologist managers using open systems conceptualizations need to strive to think at four levels simultaneously: (1) the external environment; (2) the total organization; (3) the subsystems within the organization; (4) the individual's roles within the subsystems (Kast & Rosenzwig, 1986). Managers must also focus on the relationship between these four levels. More specific management behaviors suggested by open systems theory and the contingency model are:

- Focus on problem identification by examining key variables (Netting et al., 1993).
- Give consistent attention to importing energy, such as human and financial resources from the environment.
- Develop a margin of organizational safety beyond maintaining the organization (Katz & Kahn, 1978). This means to continue to grow and expand the organization in new ways while remaining consistent with the mission of the organization.
- Strive to achieve flexibility with emphasis on constant evaluation and adjustment to achieve quality services (Zastrow & Kirst-Ashman, 1997).
- Vary supervisory and management methods to fit with high-motivated and low-motivated individuals.
- Solve problems in a timely fashion, recognizing the changing nature of organizations.
- Impose a structure in relation to the assessed stability of the organization. An organization in an unstable environment, for example, may need more structure.

Participatory Management

The participatory management approach rests on the belief that employees are more cooperative, productive, satisfied, and committed to organizational goals when they are given a role in problem-solving and decision-making (Albanese, 1975; Champion, 1975; Sonnenberg, 1994; Weinbach, 1998). Emerging from Elton Mayo's Hawthorne studies and the social science theories of management (see Table 3.1), participatory management is widely used today, sometimes selectively, by managers in service organizations from all sectors. Indeed, participatory management is a means to soften and professionalize the bureaucracy. This is especially important for the gerontologist manager who must deal with maturing agencies that have become more bureaucratic. Over the years, government policies have pushed services to older adults toward more traditional structures (Alter, 1988).

Early research by Coch and French, reported by Wren (1979), documents the effectiveness of the participatory approach over non-participation or representative participation in causing change. Later research sought to examine the utility of participatory management when used for decision-making by involving subordinates. Greiner (1973) found that effective leadership was associated with a participatory style. Research on employee satisfaction reported that participation in the development of policy and program planning by employees working at health and social service organizations caused high worker satisfaction (Hage & Aiken, 1970).

Of utmost importance is the relationship between participatory management and service to clients. A study of employees participating in management decisions at a community mental health center found a positive association between participation and effectiveness with clients (Patti, 1987). Support for the "democratic voting" aspect of participatory management was not found in the literature, and while a politically appealing notion, it is not a useful component of this approach.

Participatory management has emerged as a broad-based approach to administration that involves an open exchange of ideas among all levels of employees; delegation of responsibility and authority; the broad elicitation of input, both from individuals and groups, about management decisions; and a considerable degree of discretion on how decisions can be administered by staff. It involves building voluntary consensus and commitment among staff (Patti, 1987). This approach requires the manager to use leadership skills as well as interpersonal and group facilitation skills.

Perhaps the best way to gain a clear, in-depth understanding of participatory management is to contrast it with the popular benevolent authority figure approach. The benevolent manager will usually follow one of three strategies: (1) the decision is made and announced; (2) there is an attempt to convince, or sell to, the employees that the change or decision is beneficial; and (3) ideas and notions are presented and questions are entertained with no commitment to a participatory process. When the participatory management approach is practiced effectively, strategies range from the manager soliciting suggestions that are *seriously* considered before a decision is made to the manager defining certain limits while asking an individual or groups to solve the problem or make a decision.

For effective participatory management, the manager does not relinquish ultimate authority; nor does the manager submit all decisions and problems to be solved through the participatory process. There are times when the manager may be the only person with certain confidential information and must independently choose a course of action. In other instances, the manager may find it necessary to bypass the participatory process because it is contrary to established goals or counterindicated by limited resources. Consequently, this approach requires a measure of trust and honesty between the gerontologist manager and the staff (Weinbach, 1998).

In contemporary organizations that serve older adults, the broadly based, well-trained gerontological manager should be aware that the participatory approach is more effective in some areas than others. It is most effective in development and implementation of policy, when planning, and when engaging in organizational change. This approach is essential for many dimensions of a modern day service organization, such as quality assurance or improvement, ethics committees, and safety committees. The gerontological manager should use participatory methods for those situations where the outcome is not fixed and subject to variation, in situations where the outcome can potentially be implemented, and in situations where there is a perceived interest by the staff in the task at hand.

In contrast, broad participation is not effective in the evaluation of staff, in decisions about resources for other units, or for involvement in decision-making in areas where the staff members have little investment or interest. Further, the use of participatory management by simply involving "whoever is handy" is a dangerous endeavor that fosters competition and power struggles. For example, one manager, a smoker, took pride in frequently consulting those on the "smokers' porch" about agency decisions. By the same token, the invoking of participatory strategies as a manipulative approach, attempting to disguise an authoritative style, rarely achieves the benefits of participatory management.

It is important to remain aware of other limitations of the participatory management process. Paramount among those limitations is that a participatory process, especially when it involves groups, can be time-consuming. Thus, when the nature of a problem or a decision has serious time limitations, the use of participatory methods may need to be modified or limited (Weinbach, 1998). Some managers have chosen to use this approach in an attempt to relinquish decision-making about items that could be controversial or politically unpopular, thereby seeking to unload the responsibility. Overuse and misuse of this process is often perceived by staff as a weakness: the manager is seen as someone who cannot make a timely decision. The gerontologist will need to call upon leadership skills to use this management approach effectively.

Gerontologist administrators' remarks in workshops, classrooms, and the survey noted in the preface report effective use of the participatory management approach. Most of these administrators are more comfortable with individual strategies than with the use of group strategies. Perhaps some additional training in group dynamics would allow for expansion of this approach. In Chapter 5, on communication, we offer knowledge and resources for working with groups. Professionals and volunteers in programs for older adults expect to be involved in decisions and with problems that affect the services and the work environment. In these settings, relinquishing some control of management to others with resources and expertise is an essential tenet of effective administration.

Japanese Management Approach

A cluster of values and management practices closely aligned with the participatory management approach have come to be known as Japanese management. Actually, this approach extends and formalizes participatory management. In addition to collective decision-making, collective responsibility, and emphasis on cooperation instead of competition, it advocates organizational loyalty, informal control, and concern for the quality of the work life. Perhaps the most far-reaching aspect of Japanese management is the emphasis placed on the quality of the work itself.

This approach to management was brought to Japan by statistician W. Edwards Deming following World War II (Gatewood et al., 1995) and introduced to Japanese manufacturers. Years later, authors Ouchi and Jaeger (1978) collected the principles and practices into a trade book, *Theory Z*. This is not a theory but an approach that extends McGregor's "Theory Y," which characterizes a management attitude that incorporates worker responsibility and expects motivation to work. These notions are in contrast to the typical traditional bureaucracy of government, manufacturing, and many service agencies in the United States that emphasize exclusive controls, individual decision-making, and selective concerns for organizational goals. Japanese management concepts and practices are commonly associated with manufacturing. Lesser known, however, is that Japanese management practices are prevalent in human service agencies in Japan.

Research has demonstrated the applicability and effectiveness of selective practices of Japanese management to American human services (Keys, 1995). The most common practice associated with this approach is "quality circles." These are teams of 10–20 employees who are given a certain amount of authority and autonomy, which meet frequently, research topics of concern, and forward data-supported suggestions to upper management.

This management approach also subscribes to flexible job descriptions and encourages responses to problems that reach across organizational lines and departments as well as cross-training for other positions. Cross-training will require some job reassignment for selected periods of time so that individuals can be competent at several different positions. This is an especially important practice for small agencies that serve older adults.

Decision-making is frequently facilitated by the use of a written memo, not with a decision already announced, but with a prescription of a decision under consideration with supporting information. This is a "trial balloon decision" allowing employees at various levels who are affected by the decision to reflect upon and provide feedback to management before a decision is finally made.

Emphasis on training is common among human service agencies serving older adults. Japanese human service agencies are much more comprehensive. Training starts with formal public recognition, with an introduction of a new employee and her background, and includes meeting other employees on the job and in social events. All of these activities are directed toward socializing the person to the organization's values and goals.

Practices associated with Japanese management known as Total Quality Management (TQM) are popular in both manufacturing and the human services. TQM is a customer (client)-centered philosophy of management that focuses attention on quality-related goals and the planning and implementing of services. Because of the importance of this technique to organizations that serve older adults, and its usefulness to the gerontologist manager, it will be presented in greater detail in a following section.

The Japanese management approach presents two difficult areas for the gerontologist manager. First, the expectation of loyalty and commitment to the organization over and above one's loyalty and commitment to a profession is not consistent with the American culture of human services, nor would this expectation meet with a high level of acceptance by college-educated professionals. Second, as with participatory management, many of the methods (such as the extensive use of groups) associated with Japanese management are time-consuming. Crisis management is a common phenomenon in service programs, and often time is not available for fully utilizing the Japanese management technology. Neither of these limitations should preclude the selective use of these techniques or the incorporation of their values into an overall approach to management. The adaption and appropriate integration of these techniques will increase the effectiveness of the gerontologist manager by reducing crises, increasing commitments, and improving cooperativeness.

TECHNIQUES AND METHODS FOR THE GERONTOLOGIST MANAGER

Considering the unique features of organizations that serve older adults—the extensive use of volunteers, the diversity of professionals, and the involvement of older adults themselves—it becomes clear that the participatory management and the Japanese management techniques can be applied in combination with leadership to administer an organization effectively. Therefore, a selection of techniques that are consistent with a participatory management approach and thought to be useful for services to older adults will be presented. Often the use of these techniques is left to the manager to incorporate into an overall approach. The focus will be on TQM, problem-solving, time management, and valuing diversity.

Total Quality Management (TQM)

TQM is a participatory, decentralized approach to quality and productivity improvements. The use of the TQM approach to management specifically relates to improvement in customer satisfaction, employee relations, and motivation of staff, as well as to reduction of cost of operation. One of the recognized fathers of TQM, William Deming (1986), maintains that 85 percent of all problems stem from faulty systems. TQM focuses energies on improving the system and the organizational processes. Four fundamental beliefs underline TQM: to be customer focused, to seek continuous improvement, to prevent defects, and to recognize that quality responsibility is universal (Berk & Berk, 1993). The elements of TQM that emanate from these beliefs are summarized in Table 3.3.

TQM had its origins in the product manufacturing industries, which required a substantial shift in values and management philosophy in order to embrace TQM. Such is not entirely the case for service organizations. TQM is most consistent with the client focus, process orientation, and participatory nature of many professional service organizations. Research reports have documented the success of TQM with public as well as health and human service organizations (Martin, 1993).

TQM is established by following some basic steps and utilizing certain related tools to achieve the desired outcome. It should be noted that the basic steps and orientation are not problem-focused, as TQM holds it is not necessary to have

Table 3.3
Elements of TQM

- Employee involvement and empowerment using teamwork
- A sustained management commitment to quality
- Focusing on customer requirements and expectations
- Preventing defects rather than detecting them
- Alignment of internal processes with customer satisfaction
- Facilitating a long-term approach to improvement
- Quality measurement
- Expecting management by fact and data
- Pursuing root cause that leads to corrective action
- A commitment to continuous improvement and training
- Looking outside the organization for opportunities to form partnerships

Sources: Based on information from Berk & Berk (1993); George & Weimerskirch (1994).

a problem to make improvements. The steps are as follows: (1) identify expectations; (2) measure and describe current situation; (3) seek out root causes; (4) examine and select solutions; (5) pilot test the solution; (6) based on evaluation of the pilot test, implement the change; and (7) monitor the change.

To apply this method the first tool is the use of *quality teams*. This should not be confused with quality circles, as the success of quality circles has been minimal in the United States. Quality teams have a more directed approach in which the team is focusing on a specific area for improvement. Organizations may have several teams, each with a different focus (Berk & Berk, 1993).

Visual tools are used frequently with TQM. Among those are cause-and-effect diagrams on which all the possible causes are entered on the left side of the chart, leading to the issue at hand on the right side of the chart. Another visual tool is a flow chart that might, for example, track the communication path of a particular memorandum from the manager. Check sheets are also used to track problem frequencies or potential causes of a problem.

One can surmise that some staff might not be prepared to utilize this management approach with its values and required commitment to quality. One aspect of staff preparedness is a perceived threat to job security. Knowledge of the method and its particulars will reveal that increased efficiency will not usually result in loss of jobs. The effective gerontologist manager will need to assess the preparedness of staff before implementing this approach. It is conceivable that staff may need considerable training before being able to use TQM tools effectively. A useful guide for such training, which can be accomplished in-house, is the book *Total Quality Management in Human Service Organizations* (Martin, 1993). This book includes an extremely useful "Quality Management

Table 3.4
Traditional Problem-Solving Technique

Steps	Tasks
1. Identify the problem	Preliminary data including barriers
2. Analysis and redefinition	Historical aspects; who is impacted most; causes; refine problem
3. Formulate objectives	Base upon existing information; state acceptable, measurable results
4. Collect information and data	Use existing information—personnel reports, records, financial statements, evaluations, etc.
5. Develop and evaluate alternatives	List strategies and solutions, making judgment after listing
6. Select alternatives	Prioritize using objectives and barriers
7. Construct a plan of action	Produce a sequence of steps, with needed resources
8. Evaluation and follow-up	Continuous assessment of outcome; make adjustments or select another alternative

Readiness" test that can be given to employees to help assess the likelihood of success in the use of TQM.

Problem-Solving Techniques

Problem-solving differs from decision-making because decision-making is a choice between known alternatives, whereas problem-solving is a process by which alternatives are generated (Umiker, 1988). Decision-making is a primary responsibility of daily management. The problem-solving process is used to reach a point where a decision can be made. Managers may use an independent problem-solving process whereby input for steps in the process is provided by staff members or as a group process. The traditional problem-solving technique is summarized in Table 3.4.

A systematic problem-solving technique is essential to avoid the most common and unfortunate mistake of quickly seizing upon an apparent solution to the problem. This is a mistake because the problem will at this stage be poorly defined; therefore, the solution is not likely to be relevant. Furthermore, quick solutions without proper analysis fail to create the investment in the eventual selected alternative either for the individual or for the group. The thinking through of a problem step by step should become an automatic skill for the gerontologist manager.

Using the traditional problem-solving technique, step one is relatively automatic. Following step two is essential, for this is where what was perceived as the problem is almost always changed and clarified. The objectives allow for constant assessment of the progress of the problem-solving process. Today, data is readily available, as computer-assisted software programs can generate data and help to list and suggest alternatives.

Data also may determine the extent and nature of the alternatives. For example, in a health care center providing geriatric services, one segment of the client population with a particular condition demanded staff changes that would require a specialist. This demand took the form of letters to the board of directors and picketing of the center. Upon analysis of the clients afflicted with this condition, it was revealed that less than 1 percent of the 3,000 older adults served had this condition. Thus, the alternatives in response to this need would have to be guided, at least in part, by this finding.

Once alternatives are formulated, the most critical step is to prioritize them. This begins the decision-making process. When a plan of action is formulated, those responsible for aspects of the plan should be clearly identified, time limits placed, and a mechanism for reporting the outcome established. The length of time to follow this traditional problem-solving technique is dependent on the size and severity of the problem. This systematic model can be used briefly or can be extended as necessary.

Another more complex, useful, systematic problem-solving technique for the individual or a group is Force Field Analysis. This is a framework devised by Kurt Lewin that leads to planned change for a wide range of problems (Pfeiffer & Jones, 1973; Spier, 1973). This technique begins by analyzing a given problem, selecting an aspect, and formulating a concise problem statement (see example in Table 3.5). Lewin maintains that problems are held in a state of equilibrium by driving and restraining forces. Thus, the procedure is first to list items that are driving toward change for the stated problem, then to list forces that are perceived to represent restraints that act as a barrier to solving the given problem.

Once identified, a systematic assessment of each force is made to determine whether that force is mild, moderate, or major. Next, action can be taken to solve the problem using a variety of strategies. These strategies include: (1) strengthening the driving force; (2) adding a driving force; (3) reducing a restraining force; (4) removing a restraining force; or (5) changing the direction of either a restraining or a driving force. With this technique, any movement would disrupt the equilibrium and provide an opportunity for change and a solution to the problem. This is a powerfully effective problem-solving technique, which one of the authors has used on numerous occasions with staff and administrators at all levels. It always results in insights and options to solve problems, as well as energy to engage in positive change.

Table 3.5
Force Field Analysis Problem-Solving Approach

General problem statement:	The impact of the day care program on the male participants
	is minimal with little change in individuals

Concise problem:	The elderly men in the program have poor attendance

Forces driving toward change:

mild	One of the seven men who attends shows improvement
mild	The men typically have greater health limitations
moderate	There are no transportation problems
major	All of the men qualify for Medicare waiver
major	Several men have made formal complaints that the program is
	not responsive to their needs
moderate	Male clients have increased over the past year

Restraining forces:

moderate	The program is 5-to-1 female to male
moderate	All of the staff are women
major	Most of the activities are female oriented
moderate	All of the volunteers are female
mild	Program changes could serve to reduce female attendance
moderate	Administration is not concerned with this issue
major	The program registered nurse is not responsive to the male
	clients—several complaints have been lodged

Source: Format adapted from Pfeiffer & Jones (1973).

Time Management and Delegation

The effective gerontologist manager must consciously manage time. This is especially true for the administrator who wishes to offer the organization leadership qualities and at the same time complete management tasks. The approaches of participatory management and Japanese management are known to be more time-consuming than authoritative and directive approaches. Experience shows that these participatory approaches actually save time because they bring about improved decision-making and reduction of mistakes (Martin, 1993). It is essential that the gerontologist manager make efficient use of time so that effective approaches and techniques of management are not discarded because of lack of available time.

There are many challenges to the manager's time, including lengthy meetings, interruptions, and involvement in accomplishing the tasks of subordinates. Tardiness and excessive absences on the part of subordinates contribute to time

Table 3.6
Time Management Hints for Administrators

1. Establish short-term (three month) objectives and prioritize.

2. Work from a written, daily "things to do" (TTD) list; must be prioritized daily.

3. Practice interruption control by scheduling your time.

4. Commit to reduction of paperwork by moving paper forward, using informal interoffice memos and e-mail.

5. Reduce telephone time by having calls screened and using the fax.

6. Master procrastination by attending to top priorities and segmenting large projects.

7. Place limits on information gathering and processing of problems in relation to the problem and decide whatever you can as soon as possible.

8. Delegate tasks and the appropriate authority.

Sources: Adapted from Davidson (1978); Lakein (1974); Umiker (1988).

pressure. Poorly planned meetings that lack agendas and stray from the focus waste time. Procrastination, particularly when it is related to personnel problems and completing performance evaluations, can become a serious time waster (Umiker, 1988). Perhaps one of the most misleading practices of managers is the highly touted "open door" policy, which actually fosters interruptions, disrupts schedules, and provides excuses for procrastination.

Many time management experts have established principles for effective time management. A compilation of time management principles appears in Table 3.6. It will prove useful to elaborate on several of those principles. The effective use of a daily "things to do" (TTD) list can only be achieved by using a priority system. Any priority system will work. Alexander Lakein (1974) recommends the "ABC" method, with "A" being the top priority. Using this method, some of the priorities marked "C" may be delegated or not be accomplished. Most importantly, the effect is that one's time is dedicated to the top priorities.

One of the most powerful tools is scheduling supervision time. Supervision time should be scheduled not only with subordinates, but also with superiors (Umiker, 1988). Adhering to a schedule and judicious rescheduling are important for effective time management. To accomplish this, the manager may need to excuse herself from a meeting once the meeting turns to agenda items where management involvement is not essential, to limit personal discussions on the job, and to curtail unnecessarily lengthy conversations.

For the gerontologist manager, delegation is essential to conserve time. Some managers are reluctant to delegate because they are relinquishing authority. Authority can be delegated in different degrees. It is understandable that subordinates can be trusted with varying levels of authority, depending on the task and on the work relationship. A guide for delegating tasks and authority is provided

Table 3.7
Degrees of Delegation and Authority

1. **Take action** — No further contact will be necessary.

2. **Take action** — Let me know what you did.

3. **Examine the problem** — Let me know what you intend to do, and do that unless I direct otherwise.

4. **Examine the problem** — Let me know what you intend to do, but don't take action until I approve.

5. **Analyze the problem** — Let me know alternative actions, including the pros and cons of each, and recommend an action for my approval.

6. **Analyze the problem** — Record all the facts, and I'll decide what to do.

in Table 3.7. It is useful to remember that delegation is not only for subordinates but can also be used with superiors and peers. Obtaining the cooperation of another agency executive in the aging network, for example, might be most effectively accomplished if the middle manager delegated this to the chief executive of her organization.

Valuing Diversity

It is commonly recognized that in the current work environment, management skill and abilities must be applicable to people of diverse backgrounds. This notion suggests a problem-oriented approach to diversity that is limited. As a manager seeks to mold her own behavior to become effective, a more useful perspective is to value diversity (Jamieson & O'Mara, 1991). Valuing diversity requires a desire to utilize the talents, energies, and approaches of a wider variety of employees than has existed in the past.

Diversity incorporates a broad view of the workplace that includes ethnic background, gender, race, older workers, and workers with varying lifestyles, as well as the use of contract employees, part-time employees, and volunteers. To value diversity, the manager must possess the ability to engage diversity. This means developing diversity awareness and tolerance of ambiguity. Diversity awareness begins with self-examination of values, biases, and prejudices. It is furthered by knowledge of one's own cultural heritage and preferably a positive feeling about that heritage (Nixon & Spearman, 1991). Individuals who are clear and positive about their own cultural identity possess fewer fears and are less threatened by those who are different (Pinderhughes, 1989). Awareness and appreciation of one's own background serves to prevent the fallacy of "sameness" that leads to the expectation that others will think and perform as the manager does.

Tolerance of ambiguity has always been an essential quality for managers in service organizations. Generally, this tolerance was in relation to the diversity of the client and the nature of the technology of human services. Such tolerance is also essential when interacting with and directing employees. This requires the ability to view things simultaneously from many points of view. It has been found that the most effective managers do not view conflicts of points of view as opposites (Havassy, 1990).

The responsibilities of the manager extend far beyond the affirmative action requirements of hiring people of diverse backgrounds. A responsible manager must create an organizational culture that accepts and utilizes diversity. One approach that fosters such a culture is participatory management supplemented by the use of team work and the Japanese management practices mentioned in this chapter. Participatory management stresses the importance of cooperation over competition while placing emphasis on the needs of the group and allowing the group's goals a higher priority than personal goals. This approach to management seeks to empower employees by creating opportunities for leadership, involvement, and commitment to organizational goals.

Building an organizational culture that values diversity starts with the attitude of the manager. This may require training beyond a college education. The value of this training for the manager should bring about the manager's commitment to diversity training for supervisees. This training helps individuals recognize differences in communication styles, problem-solving, and professional experiences that are influenced by differences in age, gender, or ethnic background. Training is also available to demonstrate how alternative work arrangements can be mutually beneficial to the individual and the organization. Diversity training is widely used in industrial organizations (Jamieson & O'Mara, 1991), and it is becoming more common in professional service organizations. There are a wide variety of approaches to diversity training. Training models and programs are readily available (Caudron, 1994; Pearlman, 1996; Tan, Morris, & Romero, 1996).

SUMMARY

Management tasks represent one dimension of administration, with the other identified as leadership. The manager is viewed as a facilitator, a coordinator, and the creator of a work environment conducive to the accomplishment of tasks and goals. Management is presented as a rational and systematic process directed at producing effectiveness and efficiency in operating quality programs.

Management theory has a rich history; many concepts and practices have persisted over time. Contemporary management concepts emanating from open systems theory, contingency model, participatory management, and the Japanese management approach offer many common practices for management of older adult programs. These modern approaches emphasize staff involvement, use of groups, shared problem-solving, continued growth and change, flexibility, and adaption. These approaches are appropriate for older adult programs in all sectors.

Additionally, specific techniques highly consistent with modern approaches and rooted in management theory have been identified. Total Quality Management (TQM), a comprehensive set of techniques, is directed at customer satisfaction, employee relations, motivation of staff, and cost effectiveness. The time-tested systematic problem-solving techniques can be used by individuals or groups and accelerated by use of computer software technology.

The practice of effective time management, including the judicious application of delegation, is essential for the gerontologist manager. The more progressive management approaches and techniques require effective usage of time. Awareness and adaption to utilize the talents and skills of staff from different backgrounds require self-awareness and valuing diversity. The effective gerontologist manager will ensure opportunities for involvement, career growth, and commitment to program goals for all.

Many variations and approaches to management can be effective. No matter how effective a manager, however, administrative effectiveness requires the additional dimension of leadership. Service organizations will not succeed by emphasizing management alone. Leadership is not just a role for managers, as some theorists postulate. Leadership is an equally important component with another group of approaches and set of skills and techniques. It is the best combination of management and leadership, in conjunction with a working knowledge of the aging population, that produces the most capable gerontologist administrator.

LEARNING EXPERIENCE

The Advocates

The Enrichment Center began 20 years ago as a congregate meal program and has grown into a comprehensive agency that provides a multitude of services to older adults in three communities. With 85 staff members and 25 volunteers, the agency offers two types of day care. One is specifically for those with Alzheimer's; the other, a general daily activities program. These programs include congregate dining as well as an outreach case management program. The Enrichment Center enjoys multiple funding, including productive fund-raising activities engaged in by the volunteer Board of Directors. This is a not-for-profit, private corporation. It currently has five government grants to assist with the funding. The 32-member board is informally divided into two major subgroups:

Professional and Business. Approximately half of the board members are individuals who hold professional degrees and positions in the community or are small-business owners. One or two of these members have been on the board for over 10 years. This group has sought to professionalize the agency as it has grown larger and has pressed for expanded quality services.

The Founders. Most members of this group have been on the board for more than 15 years, and the majority are retired. Many of this group helped to run the organization in the early days, and others are either relatives or friends of those who began the organization. This group has strongly advocated the use of volunteers to supplement the professional staff. Members of this group have been the most successful with the board's fund-raising activities.

The Executive Director is middle-aged and holds a Master's in Social Work. She has no formal training in gerontology, but formerly had worked with the State Human Services Department in the Adult Protective Services Program. She replaced a minister who left the church to direct this program. The minister was the director for over 18 years. The new Executive Director has made few changes in the basic organizational structure but, at the board's urging, has expanded the outreach program over the past year. Consequently, there has been an increase in staff of about 10 percent. The number of volunteers has remained consistent for the past four or five years.

Approximately five years ago, a group of volunteers brought a proposal to the Board of Directors, with the support of the Executive Director. They proposed that a subgroup of volunteers function as advocates for the clients. The intent was for every client to be assigned a volunteer advocate. These advocates would work with the community to assure that poor older adults were receiving appropriate social, legal, and medical services, and would help to guard against exploitation. After a slow start, the advocacy program became quite active, achieving success in the second year. It expanded to approximately 15 volunteers.

At times, this advocacy program ruffled some feathers in the community, which had to be smoothed by the Executive Director. It is rumored that the former Executive Director resigned in part because he grew weary of smoothing feathers and was distracted from the administration of the center. More recently, the advocacy volunteers have turned their attention to the programs within the Enrichment Center. These volunteers have challenged staff members about program content, lodged complaints about professional staff members to the Executive Director, and called board members about their concerns. The head of this group is a retired nun known as "Sister Ann." She is the sibling of one of the founding board members.

Approximately half of the advocate volunteers have quit over the past year, as the adocate's attention has turned to examining the internal workings of the Enrichment Center. The Human Resources Director has reported that, based on information from exit interviews, three key professional staff members have resigned during the past year because of "interference" by the advocate volunteers. Other members of the executive team report occasional conflicts between supervisors and the advocate volunteers.

The executive team, which is composed of the Executive Director, the Human Resources Director, the Chief Financial Officer, the Program Director, and the Assistant Executive Director, meet weekly. During the most recent weekly meeting, while the Executive Director was out of town at the Southern Gerontological Society Conference, the issues regarding the advocate volunteers were the main subject of discussion. This group resolved to request direct action by the Executive Director to deal with the advocate volunteers. More specifically, the group asked the Executive Director to dissolve that program.

If You Were the Executive Director:

1. Based on the characteristics of this situation and what you've learned from this chapter, what would be your response to the executive team?

2. Is this an area where you would make the decision, or would you delegate it to someone else?

3. How would you approach the board, if you chose to do so, about this problem?

4. Which management approach do you think would be most effective in resolving this problem?

5. What problem-solving technique would you use to deal with this problem?

6. What priority would you give this problem compared to such other issues as completing the state grant, interviewing prospective new staff members, or continuing to assist with the expansion of the outreach program?

REFERENCES

Albanese, R. (1975). *Management: Toward accountability for performance*. Homewood, IL: Richard D. Irwin.

Alter, C. F. (1988). The changing structure of elderly services delivery systems. *The Gerontologist, 28*(1), 91–98.

Berk, J., & Berk, S. (1993). *Total quality management: Implementing continuous improvement*. New York: Sterling.

Caudron, S. (1994). Diversity ignites effective work teams. *Personnel Journal, 73*(9), 54–63.

Champion, D. (1975). *The sociology of organizations*. New York: McGraw-Hill.

Davidson, J. (1978). *Effective time management*. New York: Human Sciences.

Deming, W. E. (1986). *Out of the crisis*. Cambridge, MA: Massachusetts Institute of Technology.

Drucker, P. (1985). *The effective executive*. New York: Harper & Row.

Etzioni, A. (1964). *Modern organizations*. Englewood Cliffs, NJ: Prentice-Hall.

Fayol, H. (1949). *General and industrial management*. London: Sir Isaac Pitman.

Gatewood, R. D., Taylor, R. R., & Ferrell, O. C. (1995). *Management: Comprehension, analysis, and application*. Chicago: Austen.

George, C. (1972). *The history of management thought*. Englewood Cliffs, NJ: Prentice-Hall.

George, S., & Weimerskirch, A. (1994). *Total quality management: Strategies and techniques proven at today's most successful companies*. New York: John Wiley.

Greiner, L. (1973). What managers think of participative leadership. *Harvard Business Review, 51*(2), 111–117.

Hage, J., & Aiken, M. (1970). Organizational alienation: A comparative analysis. In O. Grusky & G. Miller (Eds.), *The sociology of organizations* (pp. 517–526). New York: Free Press.

Havassy, H. M. (1990). Effective second story bureaucrats: Mastering the paradox of diversity. *Journal of the National Association of Social Workers, 35*(2), 103–109.

Jamieson, D., & O'Mara, J. (1991). *Managing work force 2000.* San Francisco: Jossey-Bass.

Kast, F. E., & Rosenzwig, J. E. (1986). General systems theory: Applications for organizations and management. In M. T. Matteson & J. M. Ivancevich (Eds.), *Management classics* (3rd ed., pp. 44–62). Plano, TX: Business Publications.

Katz, D., & Kahn, R. (1978). *The social psychology of organizations* (2nd ed.). New York: John Wiley.

Keys, P. R. (1995). Japanese quality management techniques. In L. Ginsberg & P. R. Keys (Eds.), *New management in human services* (2nd ed., pp. 162–170). Washington, DC: National Association of Social Workers.

Lakein, A. (1974). *How to get control of your time and your life.* New York: New American Library.

Longest, B. B. (1976). *Management practices for the health professional.* Reston, VA: Reston Publishing.

Martin, L. (1993). *Total quality management in human service organizations.* Newbury Park, CA: Sage.

Morgan, E. E., Jr., & Hiltner, J. (1992). *Managing aging and human service agencies.* New York: Springer.

Morse, J. J., & Lorsch, J. W. (1970). Beyond theory Y. *Harvard Business Review, 48*(3), 61–68.

Natemeyer, W. E. (Ed.). (1978). *Classics of organizational behavior.* Oak Park, IL: Moore.

Netting, E. F., Kettner, P. M., & McMurtry, S. L. (1993). *Social work macro practice.* New York: Longman.

Nixon, R., & Spearman, M. (1991). Building a pluralistic workplace. In R. L. Edwards & J. A. Yankey (Eds.), *Skills for effective human services management* (pp. 155–170). Washington, DC: National Association of Social Workers.

Ouchi, W., & Jaeger, A. (1978). Theory Z organizations: Stability in the midst of mobility. *Academy of Management Review, 3*, 305–314.

Patti, R. J. (1987). Managing for service effectiveness in social welfare: Toward a performance model. *Administration in Social Work, 11*(3/4), 7–22.

Pearlman, S. (1996). Dignity and respect for all. *CA Magazine, 129*(8), 29–32.

Pfeiffer, J., & Jones, J. (1973). Force-field analysis inventory. In J. Pfeiffer & J. Jones (Eds.), *A handbook of structural experiences for human relations training* (Vol. II, pp. 79–84). La Jolla, CA: University Associates.

Pinderhughes, E. (1989). *Race, ethnicity, and power.* New York: Free Press.

Sonnenberg, F. (1994). *Managing with a conscience: How to improve performance through integrity, trust, and commitment.* New York: McGraw-Hill.

Spier, M. (1973). Kurt Lewin's force field analysis. In J. Jones & J. Pfeiffer (Eds.), *Annual handbook for group facilitators* (pp. 111–113). La Jolla, CA: University Associates.

Tan, D., Morris, L., & Romero, J. (1996). Changes in attitude after diversity training. *Training and Development Journal, 50*(9), 54–55.

Umiker, W. (1988). *Management skills for the new health care supervisor.* Gaithersburg, MD: Aspen.

Weinbach, R. (1990). *The social worker as manager: Theory and practice*. New York: Longman.

Weinbach, R. (1998). *The social worker as manager: A practical guide to success* (3rd ed.). Needham Heights, MA: Allyn & Bacon.

Wren, D. (1979). *The evolution of management thought*. New York: John Wiley.

Zastrow, C., & Kirst-Ashman, K. (1997). *Understanding human behavior and the social environment* (4th ed.). Chicago: Nelson-Hall.

Chapter 4

The Ethics of Administration

Administrative ethics are the rules and codes of conduct that guide behavior in an organization. They reflect personal values, morals, and professional standards that help define administrative behavior (Gatewood, Taylor, & Ferrell, 1995). Administrative ethics extend far beyond legal constraints. They involve cooperative relationships, trust, perceptions of morality, and leadership. Knowledge of ethical issues of administration, services, and related societal influences is the first step to ethical administration. Many professions have developed guidelines for the professional–client relationship, but have been slow to develop comprehensive guides for administration. For example, the code of ethics of the American Society for Public Administration (1994), presented later in this chapter, was first adopted as a set of moral principles in 1981; three years later, in 1984, the code of ethics was approved.

This chapter concentrates on administration of programs for older adults, with a focus on ethical issues. The ethics of administration are related to the external culture. Societal considerations and issues provide the broader environment for administrative behavior in organizations. At the macro level, the culture, which may vary by region, imposes certain values and expected behaviors. In the United States, policies regarding the hiring of relatives vary from totally forbidden to encouragement to hire. In other cultures, such as Mexico and Japan, the hiring of relatives is an accepted practice. Recognition that such cultural issues can change over time is important. Additionally, theoretical notions based on religion, common sense, and social contract offer the foundation for resolution of ethical problems. Humanism, which centers on human interest and values, and utilitarianism, which professes the greatest good for the greatest number, profoundly influence the service professions and programs of service. From these theories, principles and rules follow.

A myriad of vital concerns exist for programs that serve older adults. An overview of some of these issues will help to place administrative ethical concerns and behaviors in context. Moody (1992), for example, discusses two topics: patient autonomy in long-term care and justice between generations. Recognition of these ethical issues as an example of a broader problem is important. Community service programs must be designed to maximize client autonomy while providing a stable continuum of care. Justice between generations arises with competition for funding in the community. The perception exists that children's programs and older adult programs compete for resources.

Larue (1992) presents geroethics as "the consideration of the ethical principles with regard to the particular segment of the population: the elders" (p. 16). Areas of concern discussed by Larue include elder abuse, the right to know about medical treatment, and elder isolation. These issues highlight the tenuous, critical interactions and dependencies among families, older adults, and human services.

ETHICAL ISSUES RELATED TO OLDER ADULTS

Many questions frequently have no clear, concise answers based on precedent and reflect value complexities or conflicts within our society. These ethical dilemmas often have several "right" answers, depending on the perspective. Moody (1982) presents this dilemma in relation to family caregiving.

A policy perspective might encourage family care-giving and keeping the frail elderly at home, justified either by an appeal to autonomy or cost effectiveness, or both. A practice perspective might confront the same problem by a case management to draw on informal support systems, perhaps encountering value dilemmas associated with distribution of the burden of care on different family members. Finally, an individual perspective might stress my own personal belief in filial responsibility and intergenerational obligations: a duty of gratitude toward my parents. (p. 104)

In lieu of a discussion, a listing of issues is provided. To exemplify these issues, three areas—health care, community care, and mental health care—were selected to present ethical questions and discussion.

Health Care Issues

1. When is placement in a nursing home appropriate, and who makes that decision? This is a complex issue involving the person's capacity for independent living, home services available, caregiver stress, and finances.

2. What are the issues in assisted suicide? The right to die movement has affected all health care institutions.

3. Should health care be rationed? The withholding of scarce medical care on the basis of age has been proposed. Health maintenance organizations and managed care seek to limit health care based upon cost rather than need.

4. Right to die decisions. Who decides: the person, the family, the medical practitioner? Is a living will valid? Is there adequate education regarding advance directives?

Community Care Issues

1. What is the family responsibility for older family members?

2. Are community agencies obliged to provide home services to maintain the independence of older adults?

3. Who is responsible for providing adequate transportation systems for older adults in rural and urban areas?

4. Guardianship programs are needed as some older adults need care and protection. People are frequently unaware that some abuse is by family.

Mental Health Issues

1. Mental health clinics for differential diagnosis of dementia, depression, and other conditions are needed. Who is responsible for meeting these needs?

2. Are day care centers available, and do they provide effective care and caregiver relief? Care may range from activities consistent with enhanced functioning to warehousing.

3. Do older adults have the same opportunities for mental health care as other age groups? In the past, older adults have been less likely to receive counseling and more likely to receive medication only. Mislabeling clients to meet diagnostic requirements for reimbursement is a common practice.

4. Who should have access to mental health records: the client, adult children, or those with power of attorney?

The views from human services, businesses, philosophy, and medicine reveal the multidisciplinary nature of these issues. Awareness of these issues is important for the administrator. While some scholars have suggested that ethical administration may not be possible (Lewis, 1987), this presentation holds that ethical administration is not only possible but necessary for effective administration. In the remainder of this chapter, we will focus on administrative practice related to ethical considerations that confront the gerontologist administrator.

KNOWLEDGE AND ETHICAL ADMINISTRATION

The entry point for many staff is at the direct service level. The new employee begins to apply direct service skills and encounters ethical questions. Supervisors must teach and provide role models for the new employee. With experience and promotion, the employee's emphasis shifts to program development, requiring different knowledge and broader questions about efficient and ethical programs. Ultimately, the chief executive is responsible for overall competencies reflecting knowledge and ethical behavior. Many ethical issues involve staff relations and management decisions, as well as staff–client relationships. Service providers for older adults many times make decisions based on their own preferences,

Figure 4.1
Knowledge Required for Administration in Gerontology

attitudes, and beliefs, often with little awareness (Golden & Sonneborn, 1998). Continuing education becomes both a personal and an organizational responsibility.

The model for the effective gerontologist administrator requires a level of appropriate education integrating administrative practices, gerontological knowledge, and ethical awareness of standards of behavior (see Figure 4.1). A lack of competency in any of the three areas may lead to faulty administrative action and behavior. Gerontologist administrators face an increasingly complex task assuring the consideration of ethical issues in all aspects of their work. Ethical administration requires consideration of ethics, gerontological knowledge, program planning, research, and program implementation and evaluation. The first chapter in this text offered guiding principles for gerontologist administrators to be effective and for continued development. These principles also require understanding and application of ethical principles.

Ethical Principles

Ethical knowledge, program concerns, and behaviors of the gerontologist administrator can be guided by an additional set of principles:

1. Programs must be planned based on knowledge of older adult needs and evaluated for effectiveness. A well-designed evaluation program provides information for im-

provement or termination. Competent, independent evaluators can provide assurance that the program serves the client, not the organization's needs.

2. Administrators and staff must recognize the client in multiple roles. A client may also be a volunteer, an advocate, a board member, a spouse's caregiver, or have other work roles and responsibilities. An effective administrator avoids ageist assumptions and recognizes individual differences and competencies in older adults.

3. Administrators should initiate, encourage, and support enlightened ethical policies for adults by government at all levels. This can be accomplished by initiating internal policy changes, serving on boards, and working directly with government and industry officials who have an interest in older adults.

4. Administrators must be knowledgeable about clinical standards governing different disciplines in their organizations, such as medicine, social work, psychology, nursing, and rehabilitation.

5. Evaluation feedback from clients is important. Client satisfaction studies are useful to evaluate staff performance. Ageist and unethical behavior may be identified and training programs devised.

6. The administrator who is a chief executive is responsible for keeping abreast of changes needed in programs, differences in older adults, and evolving societal standards. Program adjustments must be made in a timely manner.

ORGANIZATIONAL CULTURE AND ADMINISTRATION

The organizational culture exerts a great influence on the behavior of administrators and staff. Ethical and unethical behaviors are related to the organizational environment. Administrators are models of behavior who influence the environment and can foster an ethical climate (Levy, 1985). A positive organizational culture includes an atmosphere free of ageism, a proactive training program for professional staff on gerontological knowledge, a commitment to effective service, and openness to change. The gerontologist administrator must guard against and eliminate conditions that breed unethical behavior. Listed are some of those conditions:

- *Lack of Confidentiality*. Failure to provide confidentiality for client and staff personal matters violates rights to privacy and is a breach of trust.
- *Competitiveness*. Competition is built into most work situations as resources and rewards are limited. When the administrator chooses to heighten the competition, the likelihood of unethical behavior increases.
- *Rewards for Unethical Behavior*. When unethical behavior goes unpunished or unchecked or even rewarded, informal norms supporting unethical behavior are established for the organization.
- *Emphasis on the Bottom Line*. Excessive emphasis on outcome, whether profit, earned income, or number of clients, can imply that the end justifies the means.
- *Flawed Leadership*. Leaders inclined toward dishonesty, deception, manipulation, and abuse of power foster an unethical environment.

- *Concentrated Power.* Organizations where power and authority rest with one or a few individuals are more inclined to experience unethical behaviors.
- *Handling of Whistle Blowers.* The manner in which an organization deals with individuals who have reported an unethical or questionable practice and the attitude of the administration toward these individuals contribute to the organization's atmosphere.

ADMINISTRATIVE BEHAVIOR

Administrative positions bring power, influence, and opportunity, which when misused may result in abuse of employees and clients. Many laws and organizational policies are unclear and require the use of personal judgment. Consequently, professional organizations like the American College of Health Care Executives have developed a code of ethics (Kovner & Neuhauser, 1997). Many codes and administrative practices may be guided by religious doctrine or principles. A closer examination of an ethical code will serve to illustrate the usefulness of such documents. The American Society for Public Administration's code of ethics is presented in Table 4.1. A close examination of this code of ethics reveals that a number of important areas deserving attention are not directly addressed, such as dual relationships and advertising. These areas, critical for the gerontologist administrator as well as work relationships, communications and reports, human resources, and decision-making, will be discussed in this chapter.

Work Relationships

The relationships an administrator has with co-workers (superiors, subordinates, and peers) are the heart of administrative behavior. These relationships require the use of good judgment, control, and an acute awareness of the complexities that can emerge. While this discussion is focused on co-workers, the issues also apply for those administrators who continue to have contact with clients.

Two dimensions of administrative relationships as related to ethical considerations will be explored: administrative expectations and dual relationships. Very high expectations, often called "pressure," may lead to unethical behavior. Especially problematic are those result-oriented expectations without direction or attention to the methods employed. The unethical behavior could range from misleading individuals or groups to a serious breach of organizational policy. By the same token, excessive expectations of loyalty are likely to breed unethical behavior (Levy, 1985). When expected, such blind loyalty is frequently couched in the context of sanctions or retribution for a lack of loyalty.

Dual relationships are relationships with co-workers, such as close personal friendships, intimate romantic relationships, or business relationships outside of the organization. All of these relationships have great potential for unethical

Table 4.1
American Society for Public Administration Code of Ethics

The American Society for Public Administration (ASPA) exists to advance the science, processes, and art of public administration. The society affirms its responsibility to develop the spirit of professionalism within its membership and to increase public awareness of ethical principles in public service by its example.

I Serve the Public Interest
Serve the public, beyond serving oneself.

ASPA members are committed to:
1. Exercise discretionary authority to promote the public interest.
2. Oppose all forms of discrimination and harassment, and promote affirmative action.
3. Recognize and support the public's right to know the public's business.
4. Involve citizens in policy decision making.
5. Exercise compassion, benevolence, fairness and optimism.
6. Respond to the public in ways that are complete, clear, and easy to understand.
7. Assist citizens in their dealings with government.
8. Be prepared to make decisions that may not be popular.

II Respect the Constitution and the Law
Respect, support, and study government constitutions and laws that define responsibilities of public agencies, employees, and all citizens.

ASPA members are committed to:
1. Understand and apply legislation and regulations relevant to their professional role.
2. Work to improve and change laws and policies that are counter-productive or obsolete.
3. Eliminate unlawful discrimination.
4. Prevent all forms of mismanagement of public funds by establishing and maintaining strong fiscal and management controls, and by supporting audits and investigative activities.
5. Respect and protect privileged information.
6. Encourage and facilitate legitimate dissent activities in government and protect the whistle blowing rights of public employees.

III Demonstrate Personal Integrity
Demonstrate the highest standards in all activities to inspire public confidence and trust in public service.

ASPA members are committed to:
1. Maintain truthfulness and honesty and to not compromise them for advancement, honor, or personal gain.

2. Ensure that others receive credit for their work and contributions.
3. Zealously guard against conflict of interest or its appearance: e.g., nepotism, improper outside employment, misuse of public resources or acceptance of gifts.
4. Respect superiors, subordinates, colleagues, and the public.
5. Take responsibility for their own errors.
6. Conduct official acts without partisanship.

IV Promote Ethical Organizations
Strengthen organizational capabilities to apply ethics, efficiency, and effectiveness in serving the public.

ASPA members are committed to:
1. Enhance organizational capacity for open communication, creativity, and dedication.
2. Subordinate institutional loyalties to the public good.
3. Establish procedures that promote ethical behavior and hold individuals and organizations accountable for their conduct.
4. Provide organization members with an administrative means for dissent, assurance of due process, and safeguards against reprisal.
5. Promote merit principles that protect against arbitrary and capricious actions.
6. Promote organizational accountability through appropriate controls and procedures.
7. Encourage organizations to adopt, distribute, and periodically review a code of ethics as a living document.

V Strive for Professional Excellence
Strengthen individual capabilities and encourage the professional development of others.

ASPA members are committed to:
1. Provide support and encouragement to upgrade competence.
2. Accept as a personal duty the responsibility to keep up to date on emerging issues and potential problems.
3. Encourage others, throughout their careers, to participate in professional activities and associations.
4. Allocate time to meet with students and provide a bridge between classroom studies and the realities of public service.

Source: Provided by the American Society for Public Administration (1994).

behavior and serious conflicts of interest. However, it is unrealistic to expect that such relationships will be avoided, and it is impossible for them to be eliminated (Ryder & Hepworth, 1990). While it may be useful to have organizational policies that place limits on dual relationships, it is impractical to cover all circumstances. Beyond policy control, the administrator must exert personal and supervisory control that prevents conflicts of interest or unethical behaviors. In fact, recognition of such relationships, which may include open discussions, and the expectation of self-regulation would be conducive to ethical behavior. For example, an executive might remove himself from an executive team discussion, depending on the topic, of an organizational unit managed by a close friend.

Communications and Reporting

Communications with co-workers, stakeholders, and the community demand honest and ethical information. Perhaps the most widely recognized area for potential unethical behavior is marketing activities (Schick & Schick, 1989). Stiff competition, compounded by complex and changing government reimbursement systems in such areas as home health, hospital care, nursing homes, mental health services, and day care have often produced exaggerated program descriptions and false promises. Many of the ethical issues related to marketing remain unresolved; often, marketing activities are conducted by individuals who are neither guided by a professional code of ethics nor have knowledge of the clients.

Unfortunately, misrepresentations about available services and the extent of service are common today. For example, an adult day care organization decided to target Alzheimer's patients and had a professional organization produce a brochure about an Alzheimer's day care center. This brochure outlined specifics about a dedicated program for those suffering from Alzheimer's. In actuality, Alzheimer's patients were simply integrated into existing day care activities. Only occasionally were separate activities, out of practical necessity, instituted for Alzheimer's patients.

Results from grant-funded activities frequently include evaluative components, and administrative scrutiny of reports is required. It is also useful to have someone with evaluation experience, who is not directly impacted by the funding, review the report. Opportunities to skew data to ensure continued funding are always available. For instance, one researcher simply doubled the number of elderly mental health patients served to give the findings more impact. This researcher rationalized this by stating that the same results would be obtained even with the larger numbers.

Many other unethical behaviors of administrators have been identified, such as fabricating or postdating a memo to justify an administrative decision or destroying records that might reveal violations of policy or law. Another area is related to client files that document service activities. In a nursing home facility, an administrator ordered a newly hired professional social worker to document and backdate files for the period of time that the home did not have a social worker employed. The new social worker refused, but the administrator persisted, and the social worker resigned.

Human Resources Issues

Gerontologist administrators at all levels are involved with the increasingly complex process of hiring, promoting, motivating, and dismissing employees. These areas represent a host of ethical challenges. Currently, for programs for older adults, there is greater emphasis on the screening of employees, including police background checks, drug screening, and the controversial credit screening. Legally mandated screenings have become extensive for some health care personnel. Ethical issues are complicated by concerns for the client and by the extent to which management seeks to screen prospective employees (Levy, 1985). Equal employment opportunity is more than a philosophical statement, and it must be remembered that this includes equal opportunities for older adults as well. Ethical issues arise in negotiations with the unions that seek to represent employees with little regard for the client, placing pressure on the administrator to make compromises that could affect quality and quantity of service.

A major aspect of supervision is performance appraisals, which will be discussed more extensively later in the text. Performance appraisal systems that lack objective criteria and rely more on relationships provide an opportunity for unethical judgments. An ethical appraisal system should involve frequent objective communications about performance by the administrator and the staff person (Blanchard & Peale, 1988). Many of the same issues arise around promotion issues and the extent to which they are based on objective criteria. The case study at the end of this chapter, "Joan's Dilemma," illustrates questionable ethical behavior in promoting employees. This case study presents a wide range of issues, demonstrating how strategies that incorporate competition as a way to motivate employees can foster unethical behavior.

Highly charged and difficult decisions surround the handling of impaired and recovering professionals. Concerns for the care of the clients again are balanced with concern for the staff person. Further, confidentiality in this area, as with all personnel matters, is essential to ensure fairness, trust, and a cooperative work environment.

Decision-Making

Much of the daily activity of an administrator is to make decisions. These decisions can be made independently, in collaboration with colleagues, or in a group. Some decisions are mandated by extensive federal, state, and local government regulations. A beginning step is to recognize and learn about the problems and decisions that are relevant for an organization, department, or team.

As a guiding principle, broad participation in decision-making that brings about input and feedback decreases the likelihood of unethical decisions. Ethical decisions by administrators are more likely when the previously agreed-upon decision-making procedure is not compromised or bypassed (Blanchard & Peale, 1988).

The gerontologist administrator must be a professional who is capable of putting aside personal feelings, opinions, and biases. Decisions should be governed, even without a formal code of ethics, by fairness, honesty, respect, consistency, and openness. Adherence to organizational policies and willingness to refer to those policies are yet other ways to ensure ethical decisions. All administrative decisions are best made by maintaining a focus on the client's needs (Manning, 1997).

Guides that offer ethical principles for decision-making have been offered by a number of scholars (Beauchamp & Childress, 1989; Gewirth, 1978; Loewenberg & Dolgoff, 1992). These principles emphasize decisions that cause the least harm, promote respect and protection of people's rights, consider obligations to the welfare of others, and that are truthful. Reliance on shared principles decreases the use of personal values and biases and is more likely to receive support for decisions.

Many decisions in modern organizations are made by group involvement. Indeed, modern management approaches such as quality circles and participatory management promote group decision-making. As a rule, it is thought that ethical decisions are more likely to be made in a group; however, certain group conditions may prove otherwise. When a group's desire for unanimity or loyalty to the apparent group position precludes alternative courses of action or when individuals fear rejection or exclusion from the group, flawed decision-making can occur. In this "groupthink" situation, the group develops an illusion of unanimity (Janis, 1982).

Groupthink occurs in strong, cohesive groups where criticism and differences of opinion are not tolerated. This desire for conformity, when the members suppress or minimize their own positions, can result in unethical decisions. Such an atmosphere may be further characterized by the "illusion" of morality, where group members come to believe that whatever they agree upon is ethically and morally correct when it may not be (Janis, 1982). Such decisions are evidenced by routine statements of agreement, often without clarification, such as "right, sounds good to me, don't you agree?" Another indicator of groupthink occurs when group leaders negatively stereotype outside opposition. For example, "We have a few adult children who will take issue with this decision, but they take issue with everything." To avoid potential unethical decisions by groups, consider the following:

• Encourage group members to express reservations.

• Appoint or encourage a "devil's advocate" to challenge group decisions.

• The group leader withholds his position or opinion until a full discussion has occurred.

- For data-based decisions, have data evaluated by an uninvolved source.
- Consider bouncing a tentative decision off individuals outside the organization.
- Break the group into subgroups for discussion of issues, having groups take pro and con positions.
- Create group conditions that tolerate conflict and disagreement.
- Be cautious or suspicious about decisions too easily reached.
- Diversify groups by appointing members from different backgrounds.

IMPROVING ETHICAL BEHAVIOR

Administrative ethics are composed of personal values, morals, and organizational standards. We have discussed the use of professional ethical codes to help guide and improve behavior, the importance of being aware of ethical issues, and the need to have gerontological knowledge. To improve one's own ethical behavior and that of those in the organization, it is important to enforce standards of behavior. Many such standards are reflected in specific organizational policies. Additionally, the presence of an ethical policy of expected behavior and the inclusion of ethical standards in professional contracts reinforce ethical behavior.

A philosophical guide composed of four principles of ethical behavior in relation to clients has been offered by Beauchamp and Childress (1989):

1. The Principle of Respect for Autonomy. This refers to self-determinations.
2. The Principle of Non-malfeasance. One ought to do no harm.
3. The Principle of Beneficence. In addition to doing no harm, one must actively pursue the welfare of others.
4. The Principle of Justice. This means fairness.

The application of these rules to ethical dilemmas with clients is intended to facilitate resolutions that are fair and consistent. Further, these principles can contribute to policies in the work environment that are influenced by ethical considerations.

Ethical behaviors are usually judged by intentions rather than by consequences (Lewis, 1987). Thus, the behavior of an administrator is linked to the way he thinks about himself and to related behaviors. Blanchard and Peale (1988) have offered an ethical check (see Table 4.2) for the individual in an administrative position. We have formulated a list of practical ethical guidelines for the gerontologist administrator:

- Keep in mind that your behavior is a reflection of your character.
- Think of the general good of your actions.
- Think as a member of a profession and as a representative of that profession.

Table 4.2
The "Ethics Check" Questions

1. *Is it legal?*
   Will I be violating either civil law or company policy?

2. *Is it balanced?*
   Is it fair to all concerned in the short term as well as the long term?
   Does it promote win-win relationships?

3. *How will it make me feel about myself?*
   Will it make me proud?
   Would I feel good if my decision was published in the newspaper?
   Would I feel good if my family knew about it?

Source: Adapted from Blanchard & Peale (1998).

- Realize that ethics goes beyond legal compliance.
- Know that there are moral rules without exceptions, called categorical imperatives.
- Consider the person you are and whether your behavior will make you feel good about yourself.
- Avoid "when in Rome" ethical error. Don't violate your own moral values.
- Concluding that a particular phenomenon is a "gray area" is not justification for unethical behavior.

Ethics Committees

Ethical issues often are complex and may require considerable deliberation. Ethics committees have emerged to provide continuing programs of education and a forum for open discussion, and to assist with development of and compliance with regulations and policies. Ethics committees have grown in private industries as one-third of the Fortune 1000 companies have established committees (Gatewood et al., 1995). The use of such committees by organizations that serve older adults has also grown. There are numerous models, many of which are offered in long-term care settings (Blackmon, Mdir, Craig, Jackson, Urguhart, & Noel, 1997) and hospitals.

Ethics committees are usually small and have representatives from different work areas as well as community membership. Community membership often includes professionals from social work, law, and the clergy. Ethics committees may not meet routinely. When an ethical question arises in the organization, the committee reviews and recommends solutions. Ethics committees do not make decisions. The committee exists primarily to provide an open forum of frank discussion of the issues in order to gain multiple perspectives. Open, honest debate is a cornerstone of an effective ethics committee.

These committees function best with structure, the adoption of a mission statement, and a strong commitment to confidentiality. Such committees are not exclusively for administrative ethics and matters; they are useful for the full range of ethical questions that confront those who provide services to older adults and for the older adults themselves and their families.

Having ethical policies, committees, and guides in an organization will not ensure ethical behavior, for these are sometimes only for appearance (Dreilinger, 1998). Indeed, actual behavior that differs greatly from these expectations showcases the discrepancy and may increase unethical behavior. Administration must model ethical behavior, expect ethical behavior, and hold staff accountable for unethical and inappropriate behavior. This will require taking a risk and it may bring criticism. The administrator who is a leader "does what is right" for the greater good.

SUMMARY

Ethical issues of administration are related to broader issues in society and issues directly related to programs for older adults. Many of these areas are ethical dilemmas that depend upon one's perspective. The gerontologist administrator must have an awareness of the program-related ethical issues, which starts with a broad gerontological knowledge and appropriate administrative practices. A proffering of general principles for the gerontologist administrator related to programs for older adults provides beginning guidelines.

Ethical issues permeate all aspects of daily administration. The gerontologist administrator currently does not have a formal code of ethics. In the past several years, more attention has been focused on the specialization of administration of services for older adults (Atchley, 1995, 1996). Perhaps an ethical code for the gerontologist administrator will follow the establishment of administration as a specialization within the field of gerontology. In addition to following a professional or personal code, not taking action when required or not confronting unethical conduct serves to foster unethical behavior. Ultimately, for gerontologist administrators, decisions about complex ethical issues and situations depend on one's personal ethical code and the ability to adhere to it. The personal attribute of trustworthiness is highly associated with ethical behavior (Lewis, 1987).

Responsibility for the overall organizational environment rests with its administrators. This must be an environment where individuals can speak freely about questionable behaviors or practices, where there are appropriate models of ethical behavior, and where unethical activities are not tolerated. Such an environment is free of unnecessary competition and fosters trust among individuals. Further, administrators must avoid opposing the interests of the organization which they represent.

Administrators should not assume or accept responsibilities for which they are not qualified. Those who manage programs for older adults will always have the responsibility of being knowledgeable about clients and having awareness of the ethical issues that impact older adult clients and staff. Decisions must be balanced by consideration for employees, the community at large, and responsibilities to stakeholders. Gerontologist administrators must continue to increase their knowledge about older adults, strive to improve ethical behavior, and demand ethical behavior from co-workers.

Administrators must guard against abusing the power of the position to their own advantage or to take advantage of others (Congress, 1997). This can be accomplished in part by collaboration with others, appropriate use of groups including ethics committees, and frequent use of "ethics checks." Use of groups must include specific measures to ensure full, open discussion that will lead to ethical decisions. Administrative behaviors and actions of employees have moral and ethical connections to broader issues in society.

LEARNING EXPERIENCE

Joan's Dilemma

The location is a large community mental health center in a metropolitan area. The mental health center has a gerontological mental health unit that provides a range of mental health services on an outpatient basis to older adults in the community. The unit also offers mental health overlay services to long-term care and other residential care facilities where older adults reside. Joan is the supervisor of the mental health unit. She has worked for the mental health center for seven years. The unit has two licensed professional therapists, a psychiatric nurse, and four bachelor's-level mental health workers, as well as two support staff.

Scene One

Joan conducted a regular supervisory session with the two licensed mental health practitioners, Bill and Harry. During the first hour, they discussed various cases, and she provided clinical guidance. Following the clinical portion of the supervision, they engaged in a discussion of administrative matters. At the end of this discussion, Joan announced that she would be promoted to a newly created position of Assistant to the Executive Director. Bill asked, "You already know you'll be promoted to the position?"

Joan responded, "It's a done deal. Once the budget is approved, the announcement will be made."

Both Bill and Harry silently wondered whether it wasn't required to advertise for such a position. Of course, both also figured this could mean that one of them could be promoted to the supervisory position in the gerontological mental health unit.

Joan said, "I have several months to decide which of you will take my position. It will be my decision. My decision will be based on what's best for the organization. I want to be fair in this choice, but only one of you can be promoted."

Bill and Harry remained silent. The session ended.

Scene Two

Bill scheduled a meeting with Joan for the following Monday. He knew that in general he had been favored by Joan in the past. After some chitchat, he revealed to her that even though his employment agreement prohibited it, he has had a small private practice in which he has provided mental health services to a long-term care facility. He assured her that he did this after work hours and on weekends. She had been aware of this, but never confronted him. He had been an excellent therapist and a good supervisor. She hadn't wanted to jeopardize their relationship. She didn't reveal her prior knowledge.

Just before he left the meeting, he said, "I suspect that if I am promoted to supervisor I will no longer be able to continue mental health services to the long-term care facility. What I'd like to do, if I'm promoted, is switch that contract to the mental health center, and then our unit can provide the mental health services."

Joan asked, "How large a center is it?"

Bill replied, "Two hundred twenty beds, and I have 24 patients." Joan let out a low volume whistle as Bill smiled, and the session ended.

Scene Three

Harry scheduled a meeting with Joan for Tuesday. Harry and Joan had a romance that ended eight years ago, before either of them were married. Harry was already working in the gerontological mental health unit when Joan took the position of supervisor. Their romance didn't end amicably. For several years, they avoided one another and did not speak. The passage of time has allowed them to work comfortably together. Following some administrative details which were mostly irrelevant and an excuse for the meeting, Harry hesitantly said, "I need to ask you something sensitive."

Joan nodded and said, "Shoot."

Harry continued, "I hope our past won't affect your decision about the supervisor's position. I really feel that I am best qualified and will do a good job."

"No, not at all. Like I said, I need to make a decision that will be best for the organization. It's up to you and Bill to show me which one of you will help this place grow and develop further."

Harry said, "Thanks, enough said. By the way, have you run into Robert Chandler lately?"

Joan replied, "No." Robert Chandler is Harry's cousin and a powerful member of the Board of Directors. Joan resented the reference to Mr. Chandler.

As Harry stood to leave, he announced to Joan that he had located someone in the community who would be a perfect replacement for him, should he be promoted. His parting comment was, "Sure would make life easier if we had someone to fill my old position right away."

Scene Four

Joan had lunch with an old friend at a restaurant close to the mental health center. During the lunch, she reminded the friend that one of her former boy-friends, Harry, works with her at the mental health center. The girlfriend smiled and said, "You told me this before."

"Yeah," said Joan, "but what I haven't told you is I still sometimes find him attractive."

"Oh. I thought that was over a long time ago."

Joan reflected, "Yes it was, and it means nothing."

The subject changed, and they finished their lunch.

Answer the Following Questions:

1. What factors foster an unethical environment?
2. How many actual or potential ethics violations can you identify?
3. Should the supervisor make the decision about the promotion? Explain your answer.
4. What is the "ethical dilemma" directly pertaining to older clients?
5. Identify possible violations of law or policy.
6. If you were the supervisor, how would you determine who is the best person for the job?
7. If you were one of the therapists and wanted the position, given the circumstances, what would you do to get promoted?

REFERENCES

American Society for Public Administration. (1994). *Code of Ethics.* Washington, DC: Author.

Atchley, R. (1996). Are we preparing gerontology students for the real world? *AGHE Exchange, 20*(2), 1–9.

Atchley, R. C. (1995). Gerontology and business: Getting the right people for the job. *Generations, 19*(2), 43–45.

Beauchamp, T. L., & Childress, J. F. (1989). *Principles of biomedical ethics.* New York: Oxford University.

Blackmon, T., Mdir, M., Craig, T., Jackson, D., Urquhart, P., & Noel, M. (1997). Case study: Utilization of a bioethics consultation team in the nursing home setting. *Nursing Home Medicine, 5*(1), 21–23.

Blanchard, K., & Peale, N. (1988). *The power of ethical management.* New York: William Morrow.

Congress, E. (1997). Is the code of ethics as applicable to agency executives as it is to direct service providers? In E. Gambrill & R. Pruger (Eds.), *Controversial issues in social work ethics, values, and obligations* (pp. 138–142). Boston: Allyn & Bacon.

Dreilinger, C. (1998). Get real (and ethics will follow). *Workforce, 77*(8), 101–102.

Gatewood, R. D., Taylor, R. R., & Ferrell, O. C. (1995). *Management: Comprehension, analysis, and application.* Chicago: Austen.

Gewirth, A. (1978). *Reason and morality.* Chicago: University of Chicago.

Golden, R. L., & Sonneborn, S. (1998). Ethics in clinical practice with older adults: Recognizing biases and respecting boundaries. *Generations, 22*(3), 82–86.

Janis, I. (1982). *Groupthink.* Boston: Houghton Mifflin.

Kovner, A., & Neuhauser, D. (1997). *Health services management: Readings and commentary* (6th ed.). Chicago: Health Administration.

Larue, G. (1992). *Geroethics: A new vision of growing old in America.* Buffalo, NY: Prometheus.

Levy, C. (1985). The ethics of management. In S. Slavin (Ed.), *Managing finances, personnel, and information in human services. Vol. 11 of Social administration: The management of the social services* (2nd ed., pp. 283–293). New York: Hawthorn.

Lewis, H. (1987). Ethics and the managing of service effectiveness in social welfare. *Administration in Social Work, 11*(3/4), 271–284.

Loewenberg, F. M., & Dolgoff, R. (1992). *Ethical decisions for social work practice.* Itasca, IL: F. E. Peacock.

Manning, S. (1997). The social worker as moral citizen: Ethics in action. *Social Work, 42*(3), 223–230.

Moody, H. (1982). Ethical dilemmas in long term health care. *Journal of Gerontological Social Work, 5*(1/2), 97–111.

Moody, H. (1992). *Ethics in an aging society.* Baltimore, MD: Johns Hopkins University.

Ryder, R., & Hepworth, J. (1990). AAMFT ethical code: "Dual relationships." *Journal of Marital and Family Therapy, 16*(2), 127–131.

Schick, J., & Schick, T. (1989). In the market for ethics: Marketing begins with values. *Health Progress, 70*(8), 72–76.

Chapter 5

Communication and Information

Communication is the life blood of an organization. The administrator's work is that of communication. The majority of administrative activities, such as speaking with employees, phone calls, meetings, interacting with clients, and writing memoranda and reports, all involve communication skills. Effective administrators are competent communicators (Penley, Alexander, Jernigan, & Henwood, 1991).

Professional communication with clients requires knowledge of later life development and the use of interpersonal skills that are non-judgmental and that demonstrate interest. Communication modifications that overcompensate for perceived barriers, such as speaking very loud or slowly enunciating, may be detrimental to the helping process (Ryan, Hamilton, & See, 1994; Giordano, 2000). Many of the same basic verbal interpersonal skills are appropriate for the gerontologist administrator with clients and staff. The administrator should be an effective communicator who can be a model for staff and who is committed to training in communication skills for staff.

Communication is a complicated process, highly vulnerable to misunderstanding and distortion. Communication within an organization encounters many barriers that must be understood and handled by the gerontologist administrator. Information will be presented on specific aspects of verbal and non-verbal communication, communication in groups, and written communication. This chapter will conclude by highlighting ways in which communication within an organization can be improved.

THE ORGANIZATIONAL ENVIRONMENT AND CONTEXT

The way an organization is structured plus the atmosphere of the organization will impact communication. Traditional bureaucratic structures tend to emphasize top-down communications with very formal feedback loops. Professional organizations, particularly those that incorporate the new leadership principles, use groups and participatory management, which allows for more upward communication. Such structures provide formal ways to transfer information to higher levels, often not following the traditional chain of command: for example, the use of quality teams that cross department lines and report findings and suggestions directly to the organization's executive committee. Formal communication apart from the chain of command becomes more evident if the organization uses task forces and project teams to accomplish goals and objectives.

Communications can also be governed by organizational policies. Certain communications such as those pertaining to personnel matters may need to be written by specific individuals within the organization. Communications that emanate from the organization to the outside environment may be subject to style and vocabulary requirements. In some organizations, informal norms govern who can generate certain kinds of formal communication. Restrictions may be imposed by the organization, such as which employees can communicate with board members and in what fashion, as well as kinds of communications appropriate for employees with clients. As the administrator engages in and seeks to understand communication, these organizational factors must be taken into consideration. Further, communication can be improved not only by developing skills but also by examining and changing the structure and environment of the organization.

Informal Communication Networks

The existence of an informal structure built on a network of personal relationships, quid pro quo relationships, and informal leadership are common to every organization. Informal communication, commonly called "the grapevine," is the life line of the informal organization. Much of this information is gossip and rumor that includes personal information about individual behavior in and outside the organization. Surprisingly, a considerable amount of the informal communication directly relates to the organization's purpose and has come to be considered reasonably accurate. In organizations where the quality of communication is poor, the use of the informal network will be more extensive and rank higher as a source of accurate information (Harcourt, Richerson, & Wattier, 1991).

The informal network of communication, while primarily verbal, also includes written materials, selectively distributed memos or segments of reports that have limited official dissemination, informal notes between individuals, non-verbal communications, and discrete observations, such as reading a memo on the boss's desk while waiting for a phone call to be completed. Further, the informal system may have several networks of communication. This is especially true for the professional bureaucracy—according to Mintzberg (1989), these are complex, stable organizations controlled by professionals producing standardized services—where members of the same profession informally communicate and gossip with one another and systematically exclude others.

The enlightened gerontologist administrator will recognize that attempts to eliminate the informal network of communications are fruitless. It is wiser to accept the existence of this phenomenon and consider it another resource of information. Additionally, the administrator can make use of the informal network to transmit information, usually more rapidly than through the formal process.

A practice of many effective administrators is to informally visit departments or units throughout the organization. This practice, used by administrators for many years, was identified and labeled by Peters and Austin (1985) as management by walking around (MBWA). Routine walking around by the administrator increases visibility to employees and contributes to a sense of stability in the organization (Kouzes & Posner, 1988). MBWA provides an opportunity for informal recognition of accomplishments. The administrator can also identify the informal leaders in the organization and convey information through these individuals.

The administrator should be cautious, however, since misuse of MBWA by engaging in instantaneous problem-solving and decision-making with employees can undermine other's authority and chain of command, thereby weakening the formal structure. The informal communication network is not a substitute for formal communication channels, but rather, it is a supplement which, when used effectively, will reinforce formal communications.

UNDERSTANDING COMMUNICATION

A common expression in organizations when things are operating poorly is, "We have a communications problem around here." While that generality is overused, it usually means that good communication is not occurring; that is, individuals are not receiving or understanding the information sent. Communication is more than simply an exchange of information between a sender and a receiver. The intended meaning of information may or may not be received and interpreted accurately.

Ritual communication in our culture, such as greetings or small talk, is usually brief and has minimal meaning. In the organization, most formal and informal communication is intended to convey meaning for the individual or the organization. Professional communications can be understood by using a conceptual model, such as that presented in Figure 5.1.

A Model of Communication

Communication will always be impacted by the physical environment and the organizational context. An understanding of the complexity of communications can be achieved by exploring the model. Regardless of the method of commu-

Figure 5.1
Communication Model

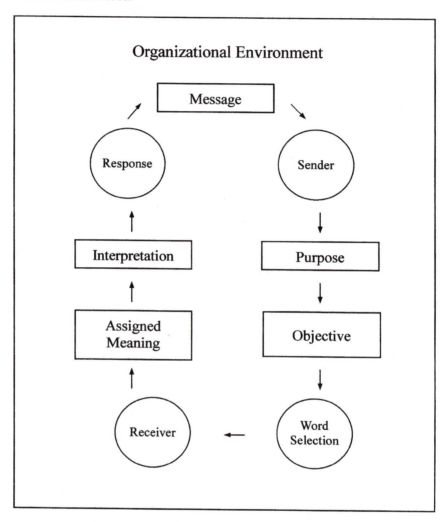

nication, a message is intended by the sender, who has made certain assumptions that the person for whom the message is intended will possess the basic knowledge necessary to understand the message. Thus, the sender has a specific purpose in mind and is attempting to achieve an objective, that is, produce some desired outcome. To ensure this process, the sender selects words consciously or subconsciously.

Next in the sequence, the message undergoes a process whereby the receiver assigns meaning to the words. This is not always the meaning intended. Further, the receiver interprets the message based on the nature of the interpersonal relationship, past experiences, and the context in which it is received. The response of the receiver then may not exactly match the intended objective or purpose of the message. It will reflect the receiver's interpretation of the message. The receiver's response conveys a message, and thus the process begins again.

Thinking through the communication process using this model demonstrates the necessity to pay close attention to communications. To be an effective communicator as a receiver of information, one must give responses that may include asking about information not understood (Dellinger & Deane, 1980). Professional communication requires skill, practice, and diligence.

Distortions and Barriers

One of Murphy's famous laws is, "If something can go wrong, it will." This is clearly the case with communications. The communications model presented in this chapter (Figure 5.1), which is a simplified depiction of the actual process, identifies the steps where something can go awry. A discrepancy between the intended message and the interpretation is all too common. The receiver of a message frequently has a screen through which that communication must pass, and the environment in which the communication is received also plays a role that can enhance or distort the information. Information received that one does not desire can be particularly subject to distortion. For example, the communication by a supervisor to a supervisee that the caseload of older adults is going to be increased by 25 percent could be subject to selective recall. The communicator's credibility and trustworthiness, when questionable, will increase interpretation and speculation as to the meaning of the communication.

Ethnicity, culture, gender, and age all play a role in communication. These differences among individuals require introspection by the communicator on one's own communications style and a demonstration of respect and nonjudgmental behavior to make communication more effective. When people are stereotyped, effective communication is inhibited. For example, talking very slowly and loudly to older adults, simply based on age or status as a client, produces the risk of insulting the older individual (Giordano, 2000). Inappropriate use of terminology characteristic of a particular ethnic group will have the same deleterious effect. The communication skills presented in the next section of this chapter will help the gerontologist administrator overcome these and other barriers to good communication.

The effective communicator will avoid terms and words that may be subject to misinterpretation or may be misunderstood. Acronyms, such as HCFA (Health Care Financing Administration), that are common among professionals, are confusing to clients and volunteers, particularly board members who are not involved with day-to-day direct services. The use of certain slang words or expressions is not likely to be understood where a language other than English is the first language. In talking with a fellow gerontologist of Korean background several years ago, the term (while used positively) "Georgia cracker" was spoken. After using this term, it was evident by the expression on the colleague's face that it had no meaning whatsoever. Similar situations can arise with words, and the associated meaning or lack of meaning among generations or people from different regions. Attending to verbal and non-verbal responses will alert the speaker to these situations.

The use of professional jargon, particularly diagnostic terminology related to health conditions and bureaucratic terminology related to funding sources, can also be subject to lack of understanding and distortion. Memoranda with excessive use of acronyms can be confusing and difficult to read. E-mail that uses "short talk" (abbreviations and cyber symbols) can produce frustration and even avoidance of messages. It is so easy to "delete."

These barriers and communication distortions produce undesirable outcomes, such as behaviors that are inconsistent with the intended goals and objectives of the organization, the withholding of information, and distorted responses. Mastery of these problems comes with the ability of the administrator to form positive, respectful relationships with employees, clients, and volunteers. This is facilitated by guiding communication with a non-judgmental attitude, maintaining one's credibility, and the ability to adapt communications both to the individual and to the group. An administrator also has the responsibility, through supervision and training, to guide staff to improve communication skills.

INTERPERSONAL COMMUNICATION

Face-to-face interpersonal communication with staff, clients, volunteers, and the public is the most common form of communication for the administrator. This communication has the advantage of requiring an immediate response and allowing for observations of non-verbal behavior, and it is the most personal. Communication by telephone, while necessary and convenient, lacks these components and rarely carries the impact of face-to-face communication. In both forms of verbal communication, attending to choice of words, tone, inflections, and pauses will add to the accuracy of the content received.

The amount of information is also an issue, that is, how much detail is essential to convey the message and achieve the purpose? All verbal messages invoke both informational (objective) and emotional (affective) information (Dellinger & Deane, 1980). Individuals begin to make decisions and interpretations and establish a measure of rapport in a very brief period of time (Zunin & Zunin, 1972). Verbal communication, as compared to written communication, is less precise, often unplanned, affected by the surrounding environment, subject to broader interpretation, and often suffers from selective recall. Effective interpersonal communication for the administrator requires a deliberate effort to achieve clarity, accuracy, and focus.

All effective interpersonal communication begins with establishing or reestablishing rapport and a relationship, no matter how brief, with the individual.

Rapport is established by using ritual conversation, showing concern, and finding common interest. For example, a genuine comment to an older adult about an item of jewelry or commenting on a staff member's new auto will often affect the quality of the conversation to follow. With these considerations in mind, four communications skills for the gerontologist administrator are offered: attending to non-verbal communications, listening empathically, confrontation, and giving instructions.

Attending to Non-verbal Communication

Impressions and sometimes conclusions are greatly influenced by non-verbal behaviors. Non-verbal communications convey a major part of emotional messages (Brammer & MacDonald, 1999). These important messages are communicated by volume, tone, facial expressions, choice of words, and body posture. When a department head relates that things are fine, but stares solemnly at the ground, this indicates a contradiction which must be explored. Much non-verbal communication comes from the subconscious, conveys the true state of mind, and can be the most revealing. Also noteworthy is the choice of clothing, including jewelry; and posture, attentiveness to the conversation, and position of limbs such as arms folded across the chest. An attentive communicator would observe all of these phenomena to obtain an accurate picture of the message, and would be conscious of her own non-verbal messages. It is of the utmost importance that the administrator demonstrates consistency between non-verbal and verbal messages and deals with such inconsistencies in others.

Empathic Listening

Empathic listening allows the administrator both to demonstrate concern and to acquire accurate information. While empathic listening addresses feelings with understanding, it is not as probing as therapeutic empathy, such as advanced empathy (Brammer & MacDonald, 1999). This attentive style of listening focuses on spoken words and the emotion communicated by both words and non-verbal communication (Norton, 1983). Feeding back the key words offers the speaker an opportunity to clarify or correct information. When feedback is not offered, the speaker is uncertain that you have received the intended message.

Empathic listening is most effective when the listener maintains a non-judgmental attitude and selectively uses questions. To gain the most accurate information, open-ended questions should be used. Certain questions, such as those that start with "why" or "how come," should be avoided, as they reflect an interrogative posture. This style of listening can be achieved by following three basic principles.

First, allow a person to speak at her own pace, to communicate the essence of the message, while providing feedback about every 10 or 15 sentences. This feedback occasionally should communicate a feeling or emotion that has been conveyed. When a supervisor is explaining to the executive director why the geriatric nurse has "called in" sick again, the executive director might reflect the perceived anger that the supervisor is experiencing. Second, when feedback corrects and clarifies the message, the listener should confirm the clarification or correction by repeating back the information.

Third, a summary of information should be communicated to the speaker prior to changing to another topic or closing the conversation. Further clarification and correction may be required at that time. The summary should include an acknowledgment of the feelings that have been expressed. This kind of communication is especially important for administrators because it encourages others to make decisions for themselves and to take action (Egan, 1975; Norton, 1983).

Giving Instructions

Administrators hold positions that require giving instructions to staff to accomplish various tasks. This is sometimes called directing, giving orders, or requesting with authority. It is essential that the administrator be able to communicate what must be accomplished and what tasks will be undertaken by whom. It is all too common that a discussion occurs and the parties separate without closure as to who is responsible for tasks. Generally, instruction should follow any discussion where a decision has been reached, a problem solved, a task delegated, or when presenting a reprimand.

To give instructions effectively, it is important for the administrator to have a clear purpose in mind, to give consideration to key words, to select a location conducive to the intended exchange, and to have a desired outcome. In giving instructions to a secretary, the administrator might say, "There are three people who need to be contacted before next Friday. Please call them and speak to them directly about their availability for a meeting of the Quality Assurance Committee. Write me a note when you have all of the information and leave it on my desk, next to my phone."

The administrator should also expect the person who has received the instructions to feedback a summary of those instructions to check for clarity and accuracy. For all verbal communications from the administrator, feedback should be expected or requested (Dellinger & Deane, 1980). Indeed, requesting feedback is one way to teach better communication skills to others.

When the administrator decides to give instructions to an individual, contingencies should be considered. Effective instructions should rarely include hedging statements such as, "I know you're busy" or "I realize that this is an extremely difficult task." It is helpful if the administrator also communicates the priority of the instructions that are being given in relationship to other instructions or responsibilities. This method of giving instructions fits well with the empathic listening skills and with the delegation skills discussed in Chapter 3.

Confrontation

Perhaps this communication skill is the most misunderstood. The word "confrontation" conveys for many people a hostile, overly aggressive situation. This is not necessarily the case. Confrontation is used to obtain accurate information and to identify behaviors that are inconsistent with expectations and requirements (Brammer & MacDonald, 1999). Confrontation is used primarily to identify discrepancies. The discrepancy could be between what the individual says and the actual behavior. A confrontation can be offered by simply pointing out the discrepancy; for example, "You stated at staff meetings, and to me, on several occasions that the report would be completed by the last day of this month. It is now the tenth of the next month and the report has not been completed." Confrontation can also be used to point out a discrepancy between what an individual says and the non-verbal behavior that is communicated.

Additionally, confrontation should be used to point out inconsistencies in conversation. The administrator might say to a supervisor, "You mentioned only moments ago that you spent two hours with a problem employee discussing their personal situation, and now you've told me that you believe this is not part of your responsibility as a supervisor."

An effective way to use confrontation is in conjunction with empathic listening. When listening, occasionally insert a confrontive statement to point out a discrepancy or inconsistency. Confrontation placed in the context where one shows concern, listens effectively, and is directed at behavior rather than the person will increase the positive performance of the gerontologist administrator, fellow employees, and volunteers.

MEETINGS AND PRESENTATIONS

Communication in groups is more complex than one-to-one interpersonal communication. Groups, such as staff meetings, committees, task forces, and quality teams, develop a culture with norms, and formal and informal roles for members. The group norms and roles will govern communication. Groups that have cohesion, commitment to tasks, and leadership that demonstrates concern will experience open, meaningful communication that will lead to effective problem-solving and decision-making (Oakley & Krug, 1991). On the other hand, groups that lack trust, seek conformity, and discourage full participation will lack the quality of communication necessary to accomplish objectives and goals efficiently and effectively. Indeed, this latter kind of group typically generates the negative comments associated with meetings.

The gerontologist administrator will experience several communication roles in groups. As a member of a group, the administrator has the responsibility to assist in the facilitation and help create a positive group atmosphere conducive to productivity. Every member of the group has this responsibility. Complaints offered about group meetings outside of the group in casual conversation and

Table 5.1
The Good Facilitator

- Maintain a neutral position, whenever possible, for items under discussion. Offer a position, if necessary, only when bringing discussion to a conclusion.

- Establish guidelines on how to deal with agenda items. This may include determining that an item is for information only, or setting a time limit for discussion.

- Adjust control of the meeting from mild to maximum in accordance with the tasks and the stage of the discussion.

- Elicit information from the low participants and control the overactive, dominant participants to achieve full participation of the group.

- Use empathic listening skills, open-ended questions, and confrontation to keep the meeting moving and to avoid repetition.

- Deal directly with problem participants either within or outside the meeting.

- Strive to be an observer as well as a facilitator.

- Seek to understand dynamics, norms, and group process.

- Share, whenever possible, the facilitator role with group members.

Sources: Adapted from Doyle & Straus (1982); Gatewood, Taylor, & Ferrell (1995).

gossip serve no purpose. Such complaints and criticisms must be addressed within the group and dealt with by the group.

The most common role assumed by the gerontologist administrator is as a facilitator. Those promoted to administrative positions are rarely promoted based on group facilitation skills (Ward & Preziosi, 1994). In this role, the administrator must keep the group on task, encourage participation and feedback from members, and offer leadership. Behaviors associated with good group facilitation are summarized in Table 5.1.

Most administrators will be called upon to present to work groups, staff meetings, or community meetings. In this role, the administrator has the responsibility to prepare adequately, to make an assessment of the audience, and to organize the presentation to fit the subject. In many instances, distribution of material prior to the meeting is useful. Formal presentations will be discussed later in this chapter.

The importance of groups in the modern organization must be stressed. Groups serve many purposes other than the obvious one of transmitting information. Groups are an efficient way of communicating, and there is great benefit in having all participants hear the same communication simultaneously, with the opportunity to clarify and comment on the information presented. Groups also help infuse new ideas and attitudes into the organizational culture, while allowing for a sense of involvement to increase the participants' investment in decisions and plans. Groups can provide the opportunity for employees to learn from observation of others and from the collective knowledge and wisdom of the group. Further, groups are a forum for social interaction that may add to the unity of the organization.

Formal and Informal Meetings

One might ask, "Is every group a meeting and every meeting a group?" Generally, meetings that have only one session for training or information purposes do not have all the components of a group that meets on a regular basis for a specific purpose. The ethics committee discussed in Chapter 4 is an example of an ongoing group with a purpose. Continuity of members is critical since working together allows group norms and skills to emerge. Some meetings are less formal, especially committees or task forces, than regular, scheduled staff meetings or board meetings. The level of formality is guided by the extent of the rules that govern the group. Board of directors' meetings, for example, are more formal and are frequently governed by Robert's Rules of Order, or some modification thereof.

Those planning and conducting a meeting must attend to both the structure and the interpersonal aspects of the meeting. Table 5.2 presents 12 principles for effective meetings. Meetings usually follow a process that begins with identifying the agenda, undertaking decisions, discussing each agenda item, closing discussion, and identifying assignment of responsibility when necessary (Nicole, 1981).

In addition to the principles presented in Table 5.2, any member of the team should be able to question the appropriateness of a particular agenda item, and each agenda item should be scrutinized, in some cases by the group, to determine if there is adequate time for consideration. Certain agenda items can be delegated to a subgroup or task force, or additional information may be required before the item can be discussed. Agendas can also be built or added to in the first part of the meeting. Important content agenda items, those that follow introductions and brief announcements, can be prioritized either by the facilitator or using a group process. Inappropriate and unscheduled agenda items should not distract from the focus of the meeting. Such items may need to be delegated to another group or placed on the agenda of another meeting. Utilizing these ground rules, along with the principles of effective meetings, will save time, reducing misunderstandings that hinder effective communication.

Meeting Presentations

The gerontologist as an administrator will be called upon to make presentations at staff meetings, board meetings, committees, and community groups. This role differs from the role of a trainer where the emphasis is on education. Presentations at meetings are frequently poorly prepared, delivered inadequately, and boring. It has been said that there are no boring subjects, only boring pre-

Table 5.2
Twelve Principles of Effective Meetings

1. The administrator should encourage participation and collaborative norms.

2. Every meeting should have a distributed agenda or should begin with agenda development.

3. Handle easy items in the first part of the meeting and the most difficult items in the middle third of the meeting.

4. Maintain minutes of major activities and distribute and/or post for those who could not attend.

5. Separate informational announcements and problem-solving/decision-making activities.

6. Have pre-announced, routine beginning and ending times that are rigidly adhered to.

7. Avoid information overload by restricting length of meetings and/or provide some information in advance.

8. Interruptions must be avoided or held to a minimum.

9. Seating should allow everyone to be visible to everyone else.

10. The administrator is responsible for recognition and appreciation of individual and team efforts.

11. When tasks must be accomplished, responsibility should be assigned in the meeting and followed by documentation.

12. Conduct periodic informal evaluation of the meeting effectiveness, length, and the scheduled times.

senters. Among complaints offered about meetings are: meetings are too time-consuming, serve little purpose, and speakers are boring.

The capably prepared and delivered presentation can stimulate problem-solving, facilitate decision-making, inject new ideas into the process, and motivate behavior while also being entertaining. While style and approach will vary in relation to the degree of formality and the setting, a systematic approach to developing a successful presentation can be offered (Levy, 1982). This approach has four components: attitude, preparation, innovation, and enthusiasm. These components are used to discuss the details of an effective meeting presentation.

Attitude

A principal attitude that will affect the presentation is one that is directed to the audience about the audience composition. One's attitude, in part, is influenced by knowledge of the audience, past experiences, and an assessment of the material to be presented along with the predicted receptiveness of the audience. Thus, it is important to gain information about the audience. This information helps form an assessment about the group's knowledge in order to plan the presentation. It is constructive, in some instances, to speak with members of the audience or the representative arranging the presentation to pilot a few key concepts.

One's attitude is also impacted by the material to be presented. All administrators will have to present from time to time information that is inconsistent with their interest. Whenever possible, presentation of materials can feature selected areas of interest while other related, necessary material can be handled in another manner, such as through handouts or media. Expression of negative attitudes about the material are sure to bring lack of attention and involvement.

Preparation

Many individuals come to a presentation with minimal preparation, which is perceived by the audience. Such perceptions reflect on the importance of the material and on the importance of the audience. Information overload and information underload will result in a poor presentation. Preparation should follow basic problem-solving and composition tenets to narrow the topic and select key ideas (Doyle & Straus, 1982). One formula for constructing an organized presentation is to use the standard problem-solving model (see Chapter 3). An organized and well-prepared presentation will be placed on cards, or set up in script or outline form.

Innovation

Innovation is designing a presentation that has a new twist, some unusual points of view, or shows creativity in the delivery (Levy, 1982). The most innovative presentations include audience participation. This can be achieved by using open-ended questions, instruments which encourage discussion, or focused interaction with one another. Visual aids, such as cartoons, handouts that summarize key principles, and short media materials, can stimulate interest and learning.

Enthusiasm

Enthusiasm does not require high energy, bubbling, or bouncing around in front of the audience. Yet, a demonstration of interest and involvement with the material will convey enthusiasm. What certainly will not convey enthusiasm is the opening of a presentation or the repeating during the presentation of negative statements that reflect upon the material being presented. For example, "I know this information is boring, but . . ." or "I guess you've heard this before, but I'm going to repeat it because. . . ."

Enthusiasm begins with the selection of the material to be presented orally and in written form. Select material of most interest to yourself and to the audience. Genuine enthusiasm is perceived by members of the audience when there is involvement in the subject matter by the presenter. In a presentation by a geriatric physician on pain control for arthritis patients, enthusiasm was demonstrated by sharing relevant research projects engaged in over the years.

The manner of delivery is often equally as important as content. Doyle and Straus (1982) offer helpful hints on an effective presentation:

• Material that is read or memorized is rarely effective.
• Whenever possible, move around, coming out from behind the lectern to establish better contact with the audience.
• In addition to what is said, one is communicating with body language. Body language can show consistency, enthusiasm, and involvement with the materials.
• Pay attention to the body language of the audience. It may be necessary to modify the presentation based on these observations.
• Explain the conventions of your presentation. If you're going to ask people to participate, take a test, or read materials, tell them early. That is, express your expectations of the audience.

Finally, to assure effective presentations, take control of the presentation environment by reducing interference, interruptions, and potential discomfort for the audience. This may mean closing doors, adjusting the air conditioner, or checking equipment. Thoughtfully prepared and delivered presentations are another indicator of an effective gerontologist administrator.

WRITTEN COMMUNICATION

Written communication tends to be more accurate than verbal communication simply because it requires greater discipline of thinking and precision. When writing, there is an opportunity to focus attention on a single issue and to edit for consistency and accuracy (Brody, 1993). Many times, written communication is necessary because the communication must be documented, as in personnel action, presentation of policy, or communication for negotiations. Written communication is also useful to support and reinforce verbally communicated material. With written communication, content is the most important consideration (Kantz & Mercer, 1991).

The formal or informal style of the written communication is another consideration and will depend on the content of the communications. The administrator may choose to dictate using an electronic device, compose with word processing or e-mail, or write by hand. Most handwritten communication in the modern organization is brief, requiring little effort. An example of a format for a handwritten interoffice memo is provided in Figure 5.2. It is structured to save time and document the communication. The memo is pre-printed with attached duplicate copies.

Other than for brief, handwritten communications, it is useful to set aside time to compose written communications. Many administrators keep notes on the "things to do" list or in a calendar to organize written communication. A similar process is to jot down key words before writing. A slightly more elab-

Figure 5.2
Sample Interoffice Communication Form

```
┌─────────────────────────────────────────────────────────────────┐
│                                                                   │
│              ┌──────────────────────────────────┐                 │
│              │      THE ENRICHMENT CENTER        │                 │
│              │    An Assisted Living Environment  │                 │
│              └──────────────────────────────────┘                 │
│                                                                   │
│  DATE _____          FOR YOUR                          │
│                                   ☐ Information                    │
│  TO _____              ☐ Comments                      │
│                                   ☐ Action                        │
│  FROM _____                                              │
│                                                                   │
│  _____         │
│  _____         │
│  _____         │
│  _____         │
│  _____         │
│  _____         │
│  _____         │
│                                                                   │
│  PLEASE:   ☐ Follow up      ☐ See me      ☐ Other _____         │
│                                                                   │
└─────────────────────────────────────────────────────────────────┘
```

orate process is to develop an outline or a cognitive map (Buzan, 1974). For a cognitive map, the focus of the communication is written in the center of the page; ideas that relate to that communication are jotted down at a rapid pace on lines or branches connected to the concept in the center. Figure 5.3 is an example of the cognitive map used for the summary of this chapter. Another method used in conjunction with these organizing principles is to compose a single statement that encompasses the essence of the written communication as a guide. Regardless of the method—outlines, keywords, or cognitive maps—these guides help organize thoughts and facilitate the writing process.

Many written documents in organizations are memoranda. The most effective memoranda are direct, specific, and limited to one topic. When the topic requires more detail, such as a marketing plan to introduce a new adult day care program, the composed plan is accompanied by a short cover memorandum.

The completed document should meet the following three-point criteria: (1) similar thoughts are grouped together; (2) each group of thoughts is in a logical order; (3) the connected groups provide a coherent document (Kantz & Mercer,

Figure 5.3
Cognitive Map Example

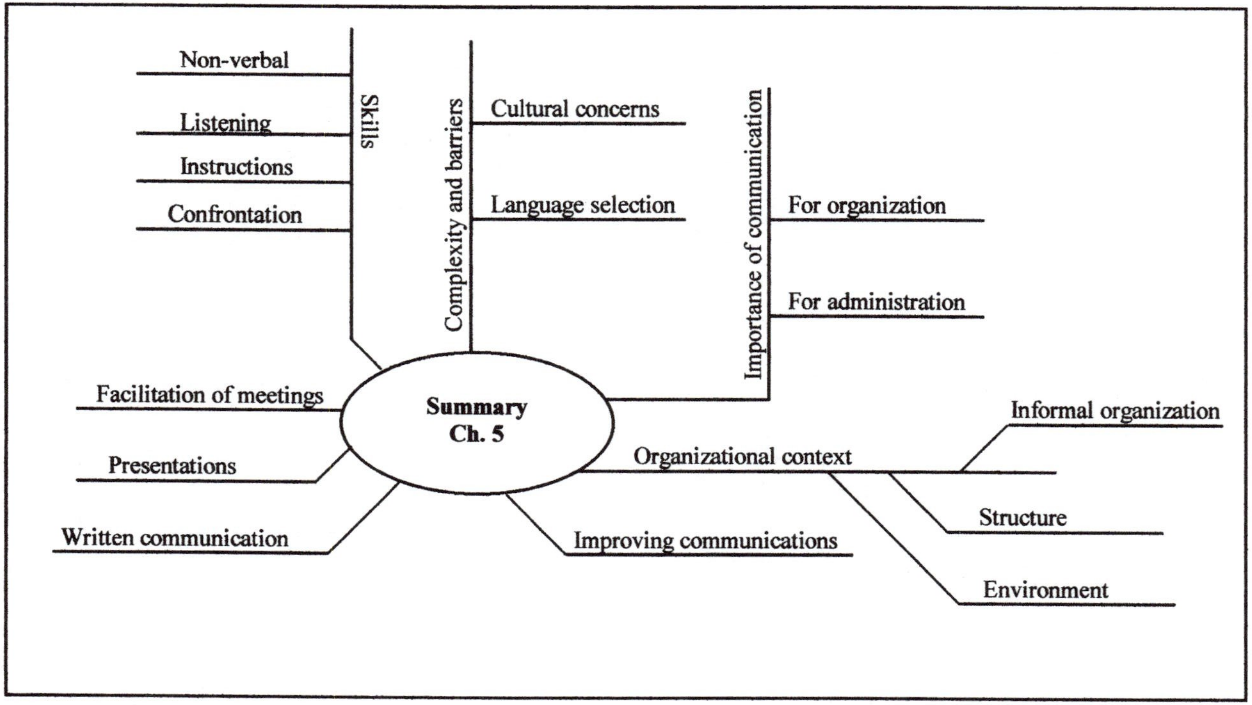

1991). In memos and reports of significance, it is useful to compose the document and set it aside for several days before it is reviewed, revised, and finalized. Equally as helpful is to use the "Napoleon's Corporal" technique. Napoleon, when writing a memo, would frequently have a corporal from the ranks read the memo to receive feedback and check comprehension.

IMPROVING COMMUNICATION IN THE ORGANIZATION

Improvement in communication should be a diligent effort on the part of the gerontologist administrator. Organizations serving older adults must pay special attention to how staff communicate with one another, as well as how multigenerational clients and staff communicate. A common practice is for an administrator to engage in one-on-one, informal meetings with staff to elicit feedback on the kinds and style of communications that affect everyday work performance (Brody, 1993). A more formal method is surveys, systematically distributed, to gather information about the style and accuracy of communication.

Improving communications is one of the primary reasons to engage an organizational consultant. Consultants can be used to identify specific problems and to obtain related recommendations for improvements. Many times, improving communications requires an external, objective review that is free from the traditional practices of the organization. Further, consultants will examine the organizational structure that affects and governs much of the communication.

It is essential that the gerontologist administrator not only pay attention to her own communications but also to the nature of communication throughout the unit, department, team, or organization. More specifically, this means supporting training and education, as well as changes that will improve communication. Overcoming barriers to effective communication for staff will be directly linked to performance (Penley et al., 1991). Centralized organizational structures where there are several layers between top management and staff inhibit the flow of communication (Gatewood, Taylor, & Ferrell, 1995). For these structures, even more intense efforts at enhancing communication and communication systems are necessary. Improving communication in an organization rests with the administration's commitment to use and demonstrate effective communication skills, a commitment to staff development of interpersonal skills, and attention to structure and policy that impact communication.

SUMMARY

The daily operations of an organization are highly dependent on the formal and informal communications system. The manner in which communications are conducted within an organization and on behalf of an organization is related to an array of leadership and management skills and, for the gerontologist administrator, knowledge and understanding of the older adult. The quality of communications is affected by organizational structure, policies, and the extent of the informal network. The informal communications network is linked by personal relationships, informal leadership, and professional allegiances. Its size and complexity vary, depending upon the effectiveness of the formal communications system. The informal network is a useful tool for the gerontologist administrator.

Interpersonal communications are complex. They are influenced by the choice of language, the interpretation of words, and the nature and quality of the interpersonal relationship. Well-developed interpersonal relations skills are necessary to overcome the complexity of and barriers to effective communications. Such skills as empathic listening that provides feedback to the speaker, and the ability to read and understand non-verbal communication are essential. Additionally, judicious use of confrontations to clarify discrepancies and thoughtful, planned instructions to staff will also further effective communications.

Much communication occurs in meetings and groups. The gerontologist administrator plays several roles in groups, the most common of which is as a facilitator. The development of facilitator skills will bring about productive meetings and group sessions. The gerontologist administrator will also be engaged in making presentations at meetings of clients, staff, stakeholders, or citizens. Meaningful presentations include a demonstration of enthusiasm, a positive attitude about the material and the audience, as well as adequate preparation that includes innovative delivery methods.

Written communication must be more accurate than verbal communication, and it requires greater discipline of thinking. A well-written document will have thoughts grouped together in a logical, coherent order. For most written documents, it is important to have someone else review the document prior to distribution.

The gerontologist administrator can improve communications in an organization by modeling effective communication skills and by being committed to training and development for staff. Further, this commitment may require engaging a consultant to look at the communication channels and the structure of the organization. Developing effective communication skills for oneself and the organization, like the lifelong acquisition of knowledge, is a perpetual process.

LEARNING EXPERIENCE

Rate Your Communications Potential as an Administrator

Check the following that apply to you:

_____ 1. Usually plan or give forethought to professional communications

_____ 2. Attend to non-verbal communications

_____ 3. Can identify discrepancies in communications of others

_____ 4. Seek clarification of information presented

_____ 5. Use open-ended questions when appropriate

_____ 6. Able to gain a sense of others' feelings without becoming sympathetic

_____ 7. Place messages in logical sequence

_____ 8. Use notes and other aids to help focus communications

_____ 9. Maintain an awareness of the environment's effect on communications

_____ 10. Retain notes and records for follow-up and documentation

Give yourself 10 points for each check. Total score: _____

Evaluation

100–80	High potential for effective communications
70–50	Need to develop greater awareness of communication behaviors
40–below	Communication problem likely

Now assume you adopt a goal of improving your communications. Write two specific objectives for yourself.

Objective 1 _____

_____

_____

Objective 2 _____

_____

_____

REFERENCES

Brammer, L. M., & MacDonald, G. (1999). *The helping relationship*. Boston: Allyn & Bacon.

Brody, R. (1993). *Effectively managing human service organizations*. Newbury Park, CA: Sage.

Buzan, T. (1974). *Use both sides of your brain*. New York: E. P. Dutton.

Dellinger, S., & Deane, B. (1980). *Communicating effectively: A complete guide for better managing*. Radnor, PA: Chiton.

Doyle, M., & Straus, D. (1982). *How to make meetings work*. New York: Jove.

Egan, G. (1975). *The skilled helper: A model for systematic helping and interpersonal relating*. Monterey, CA: Brooks/Cole.

Gatewood, R. D., Taylor, R. R., & Ferrell, O. C. (1995). *Management: Comprehension, analysis, and application*. Chicago: Austen.

Giordano, J. A. (2000). Communications and counseling with older adults. *International Journal of Aging and Human Development, 51*(4), 71–80.

Harcourt, J., Richerson, V., & Wattier, M. (1991). A national study of middle managers' assessment of organization communication quality. *Journal of Business Communication, 28*(4), 348–365.

Kantz, M., & Mercer, K. (1991). Writing effectively: A key task for managers. In R. L. Edwards & J. A. Yankey (Eds.), *Skills for effective human service management* (pp. 221–257). Washington, DC: National Association of Social Workers.

Kouzes, J. M., & Posner, B. Z. (1988). *The leadership challenge.* San Francisco: Jossey-Bass.

Levy, A. (1982). *The art of effective presentations.* St. Petersburg, FL: Hazlett.

Mintzberg, H. (1989). *Mintzberg on management: Inside our strange world of organizations.* New York: Free Press.

Nicole, D. R. (1981). Meeting management. In J. E. Jones & J. W. Pfeiffer (Eds.), *The 1981 annual handbook for group facilitators* (pp. 183–187). San Diego, CA: University Associates.

Norton, R. (1983). *Communicator style, theory, application and measures.* Beverly Hills, CA: Sage.

Oakley, E., & Krug, D. (1991). *Enlightened leadership: Getting to the heart of change.* New York: Simon & Schuster.

Penley, L., Alexander, E., Jernigan, I., & Henwood, C. (1991). Communication abilities of managers: The relationship to performance. *Journal of Management, 17*(1), 57–76.

Peters, T., & Austin, N. (1985). *A passion for excellence: The leadership difference.* New York: Warner.

Ryan, E., Hamilton, T., & See, S. (1994). Patronizing the old: How do younger and older adults respond to baby talk in the nursing home? *International Journal on Aging and Human Development, 39*(1), 21–32.

Ward, P., & Preziosi, R. (1994). Fostering the effectiveness of groups at work. In J. W. Pfeiffer (Ed.), *The 1994 annual: Developing human resources* (pp. 213–226). San Diego, CA: Pfeiffer & Pfeiffer.

Zunin, L., & Zunin, N. (1972). *Contact: The first four minutes.* New York: Ballantine.

Chapter 6

Organizing Programs and Staff

Every organization starts with a purpose. Given the complexity of an organization's purpose, a structure for cooperation and coordination of individuals within the organization is required. For example, even a relatively small program such as an adult day care center with the purpose of providing respite for caregivers and care for frail older adults requires a structure. In 1996, there were 3,000 adult day care centers nationally, with the prediction that this would grow to 10,000 in the year 2000 (Brunk, 1996). Many adult day care programs will have a board of directors, an administrator, a program director, and staff.

The organizational purpose is embodied in a mission statement, usually with accompanying organizational goals. Table 6.1 provides an example of a mission statement for a not-for-profit senior citizen agency that offers approximately 20 distinct programs. Even organizations that do not have a formal written mission statement operate from established values that serve the same purpose. The more formal mission statement contributes to the focus of the organization and creates boundaries and values to which staff and volunteers can commit. This establishes the functions of an organization, which relates to the formal structure by which goal-related activity is arranged and administered.

There are many reasons why a formal structure is necessary for an organization: First, to reduce duplication of resources by establishing rules and job assignments (Crow & Odewahn, 1987). Second, to establish an administrative structure and work units with lines of authority (Gatewood, Taylor, & Ferrell, 1995). Third, to coordinate work activities by establishing job descriptions and work procedures. Fourth, to limit behavior, thereby enhancing predictability and reducing uncertainty (Scott, 1978).

The understanding of the general principles of organizations using organizational theory is critical for the gerontologist administrator. Several theories will

Table 6.1
Senior Friendship Centers, Inc. Mission Statement

Our Mission

Realizing that in helping others we help ourselves, Senior Friendship Centers' staff, volunteers, and participants form a family of "People Helping People."

As a non-profit charitable organization, we dedicate ourselves to helping older adults live with dignity and respect by providing services which address their needs, including:

- Remaining independent

- Preventing premature institutionalization

- Relieving isolation and loneliness

- Improving quality of life and health for seniors

Source: Used with permission of Senior Friendship Centers, Sarasota, Florida, November 1998.

be presented in this chapter, along with some determinants of organizational structure. Examples of organizational structure in the form of organizational charts will be offered and discussed. Further, organizational structure can be understood by examining components that relate to the administering of the structure. Finally, this chapter will examine the rationale and the manner in which structures are divided into departments, work teams, and special projects.

ORGANIZATIONAL THEORIES

Organizational structure can be viewed from three theoretical perspectives: the professional bureaucracy, open systems, and contingency. The three theories are related, as each provides a perspective on the classic organizational structure of the bureaucracy. Regardless of the perspective, certain basic components of bureaucracy are present to varying degrees in all organizations.

The classic bureaucratic structure described by Max Weber (1986) includes specialization, authority by policies and position, clear hierarchical authority and responsibility, and a rational design of activities (Lewis, Lewis, & Souflée, 1991). Organizational theorists offer strong arguments for sharp variations in organizational structure such as contrasting the classic bureaucracy with the matrix organization. However, for programs that serve older adults, the vast majority of the structures are modified bureaucracies. The most common modification is the professional bureaucracy originally described by Mintzberg (1979) as an organization less centralized than the classic bureaucracy, which shares position authority with those who have professional expertise. Given this common variation of structure, even further modifications occur with open systems and contingency theories. These three theoretical perspectives, as determinants of structure, will be examined further.

Professional Bureaucracy

The professional bureaucracy is the classic structure infused with professional people who retain certain degrees of autonomy, communicate across structural lines, and are significantly involved with decision-making and problem-solving activities. This allows the organization to be more effective at performing highly technical and complex tasks required for delivery of services. In this atmosphere, it is difficult to bring about change. Mintzberg (1979) states, "The professional bureaucracy is an inflexible structure, well suited to producing its standard output, but ill-suited to adapt to the production of new ones" (p. 375).

In the professional bureaucracy, within certain limits, professionals (those who have credentialed competencies) have latitude in interpreting the job, and can negotiate task expectations (Bucher & Stelling, 1969). This frequently results in overlapping job responsibilities, such as attending to social adjustments of older adults in a senior center where the nurse, social worker, and activities person all would identify responsibilities. Different professional values and approaches are merged in these organizations. Consequently, conflict and confusion require strong leadership and management to maximize the contribution of all staff.

The professional in the organization is interested in client outcome, often primarily focused on a specific area of work, and acquires a certain amount of power and influence in relation to the professional group. In the professional bureaucracy, the locus of power shifts in response to different issues (Bucher & Stelling, 1969; Mintzberg, 1989). Frequently, the rational technical orientation of the classic bureaucracy is replaced by a complex political process, with staff interest groups, external stakeholders exerting influence, and a "democratic process" where certain decisions are voted upon.

Indeed, alterations to the classic bureaucracy are often so extensive that some students of organizations have suggested that many organizations cease to be a bureaucracy (Bucher & Stelling, 1969). The extreme of the professional bureaucracy where there is heavy reliance on professional skills and knowledge has been deemed a professional organization (Bucher & Stelling, 1969; Mintzberg, 1989). Many of the modern, older adult service organizations infused with human relations and social science management and new leadership approaches exemplify this departure from the classic bureaucratic structure.

Systems Theory

The systems perspective as applied to organizational structure, and more specifically to professional bureaucracies, expands design possibilities for modern organizations. Systems theory presents a view of an organization in its totality (Scott, 1978). The design and structure of an organization can be understood from an open or closed systems perspective. The classic bureaucracy is essentially a closed system that has well-defined, specific goals and strives for rationality. The professional organization tends to be an open system that considers constant change a given and attends to factors external to the organization.

Modern organizational structures lean toward open systems. In Chapter 3 we discussed and described open systems in relation to manager behavior. Here, open systems is considered as a perspective on understanding and designing organizations. In open systems theory, the organization is composed of inter-related elements, not merely a sum of the parts but a product of the interaction of elements. According to open systems theory, an organization has boundaries that extend into the greater community. For example, most older adult programs network extensively with other services in the community. Great emphasis is placed on subsystems within the organization and the degree to which they impact the overall system. Open systems organizations are seen as adaptable to change and less subject to be modified to meet an individual's characteristics.

Using the open systems perspective is contingent upon three major factors: rationality, steady state maintenance, and feedback (Marion, 1975). Rationality means that the organization has a purpose and identified goals. This purpose guides organizational behavior so there is a striving to integrate the subsystems in relation to the goals. Additionally, the system will make appropriate adjustments in relation to the support and resources in its environment.

Maintenance of steady state is the ability of an organization to use its resources efficiently, although units of the organization may differ from one another. For example, a volunteer physician's program within a large senior citizens' center is the largest department within that center but has only two paid employees, one of whom coordinates that service. This requires a unique supervisory and communications pattern different from the rest of the organization.

Feedback is the ability of the organization to use vital evaluative information. This information is broadly conceived to include formal process and outcome evaluation results, ranging to informal feedback reported by board members or other stakeholders. When the administrator thinks about the organization from an open-systems perspective, all feedback, even from dissident sources, should be considered. This is especially important for the problem-identification phase of problem-solving. When feedback is substantive or can be further validated it will require problem-solving that will lead to change.

The gerontologist administrator who uses this perspective to understand and structure organizations focuses on the resources, the process, and the outcome altering structures. The extent that external factors from the community influence organizations that serve older adults is illustrated by the research on the development of Senior Centers. Senior Centers are developed primarily by older adult leaders in the community, with a local sponsorship and community support (Ralston, 1986).

Further, the systems-oriented administrator would attend to linkages with both the aging network and the network of services throughout the community. The network of services includes those that serve older adults and the broader network of private and profit services that impact older adults. Mechanisms for relating to and communicating with external sources would be as carefully planned, designed, and implemented as those used within the organization. The open systems perspective has generated an even more modern approach to the design of organizations, known as the contingency perspective, discussed in the next section.

Contingency Theory

The contingency perspective is an outgrowth of systems theory, offering a flexible approach to structure. It is perhaps the most characteristic of modern organizations that offer older adult programs. Like systems theory, it offers guides for the manager's behavior. The focus here is on contingency theory's determinants of structure. The best structure, according to this perspective, depends on specific conditions within the organization and the degree of certainty of information and resources in the environment (Lewis èt al., 1991). The contingency organization stresses finding a "fit" with the unique characteristics of the environment, including the characteristics of the client. These characteristics will affect the organization's structure. The administrator's capacity to take into consideration the different organizational characteristics and their interaction relates to the administrator's ability to understand and change the organizational structure.

In summary, contingency theory holds that there is no "one best way" to structure an organization (Lewis et al., 1991). Structures consistent with this theory are highly adaptable, flexible, frequently changing, often different for different parts of the organization, and positioned to take advantage of new developing resources. The gerontologist administrator who administers or creates this kind of structure generally must assume the contingency management style, relying heavily on leadership skills and abilities. A contingency organization's effectiveness is less dependent on structure and more on commitment, collaboration, and meaningful community involvement.

ORGANIZATIONAL STRUCTURE

The structure, also called design, of a formal organization, while influenced by organizational theory, is determined by three critical variables: functions, degree of formalization, and size and complexity. These will result in a formal structure that can be depicted in an organizational chart that identifies staff and line positions. Before examining these determinants of structure, several other considerations need to be discussed to expand understanding of organizational structure. It is well established that most organizations progress through stages. An organizational life cycle model is presented in Table 6.2. While these may vary, depending on the sector (public, profit, not-for-profit), the principles are essentially the same, with one exception. When considering the last stage, re-

Table 6.2
Organizational Life Cycle

Birth
In the first phase, an organization is just beginning. An organization in the birth stage rarely has a formal structure, and the informal structure is characterized by a high degree of centralization but a low degree of formalization and complexity. The identified leader makes most decisions.

Growth
In this phase, the organization is trying to offer more services and garnish financial resources. The emphasis is on becoming larger. The organization shifts its attention away from the wishes of its leader and toward its customers. A formal structure emerges, usually functionally organized departments. This permits delegation of authority. The structure is marked by less centralization, but increasing complexity and an increase in formalization.

Maturity
Once an organization has reached the maturity phase, it becomes less innovative, less interested in expanding, and more interested in maintaining itself in a stable, secure environment. The emphasis is on improving efficiency and income or financial resources. The formal structure is still functionally based departments; the structure remains much as it did in the growth phase. There is more participation in decision-making, but less delegation of authority.

Revival
The maturity phase could lead to decline. At some point, organizations recognize that they are stagnating, usually when financial resources change, the market changes, or customers need change, and they embark on a revival. The organization undergoes significant changes at this time. Strategic planning examines the situation the organization is in and how best to organize the work processes to achieve revised goals. To accommodate the rapid growth, the formal structure abruptly changes from a functional structure to a multidivisional one and may decentralize.

Source: Adapted from Miller & Friesen (1984).

vival, for government organizations, this stage will be more subject to political philosophy, public pressure, or consumer lobbying, often requiring statutory revision.

Structures tend to become more formal over time and, with growth, more complex. In modern organizations, there is a tendency to focus on technology as a major determinant of structure. Two types of technology can be identified. The technologies required for the actual service delivered to older adults, like case management or counseling offered by a senior center, are two examples. This technology influences structure and will be discussed as part of the functions of the organization. The other is support technology such as accounting, word processing, and maintaining statistical data, all of which has become automated. It is a serious mistake to determine organizational structure, lines of authority, or formal relationships based on automated technology or its requirements. Automated computer technology needs to follow and support the desired structure (Gatewood et al., 1995).

Functions

A classic and well-established guideline for organizational structure and design is that "form follows function." Beginning with the organization's purpose, established goals, and objectives, a host of functions with related tasks emerges. Rarely is there the opportunity to begin an organization from scratch. Many of the tasks that must be accomplished initially are directed at establishing the organization as an entity. Most of those tasks, once accomplished, such as incorporating, choosing a name, and, in the case of not-for-profits, developing bylaws will give way to maintaining the permanent structure.

Basically, an organization designed by function results from clustering related tasks. The best way to grasp this notion is to consider a list of all the functions of an organization and then group those functions in relation to one another. These clusters then become departments, work teams, or sections. When the departments are then linked together in an authority and communications hierarchy, this becomes the organizational structure, which can be depicted by an organizational chart.

In organizations that serve older adults, three types of functional clusters can be found. The most common grouping is by activities; for example, all of the financial activities are grouped into an accounting department. Functions can also be grouped into client groups such as an Alzheimer's unit within the large comprehensive community agency. Often, the client groupings identify a set of problems and the professional staff required. Yet a third is clustering by an identified special project. Typically, such projects have specialized funding and a restricted set of activities. An example of a special project, indeed a project that only occurs during certain portions of the year, is home weatherization, where staff are reassigned or specifically hired for this project that has a beginning, middle, and end, each year.

Organizational structures that are common to the agencies that serve older adults often utilize all three forms of clustering in a single organization. The grouping by function is also influenced by the type and range of professionals who must be involved in meeting the organization's goals and objectives. Sometimes this results in overlapping structures that, while not obvious by viewing the official organizational chart, represent an organizational structure that has both formal and informal elements. This is not necessarily a constructive aspect of organizational design, as it tends to mediate against the established lines of authority. Perhaps the best example is the nursing homes which are divided into skilled units and semi-skilled units (also called long-term care). The nurses work for both of these units, each with a separate director, that include other professionals and support staff. Nursing often is also conceived as a separate entity encompassing the entire organization where the director of nursing (DON) and the assistant director of nursing hold direct power and authority over those who work in a functional unit. Nurses may contact the DON directly with concerns.

This is often confusing for employees and creates a duality of supervision that offers opportunity for employee manipulation.

Size and Complexity

An organization with a small number of employees where everyone knows everyone else, operating from a single location, providing a specific set of services has less need for structure and formality. On the other hand, organizations that require standardization and have professional staff specializing in different areas with a broad range of services will be larger. When an organization approaches 50 employees, more formal structure will be necessary to ensure effective functioning (Champion, 1975). These organizations, in short, will be more bureaucratic, often professional bureaucracies.

Organizational growth brings formal work assignments, more delegation, and the necessity for closer supervision. As has been established, many organizations that serve older adults have administrative positions where a person serves a dual role in providing direct service and supervision of other employees. Increased size brings more specialization for administration and a reduction of the dual roles (Zastrow & Kirst-Ashman, 1997). Some organizations increase to the size where those in administration, a level or two beyond the supervisory middle management, do not know the employees who provide the services. In order to maintain productivity and employee satisfaction, mid-level supervisors must give time to communications and building cohesiveness.

The complexity of an organization—that is, the number of different functions that an organization performs, often but not always accompanying growth—is an interrelated determinant of structure (Champion, 1975). Complexity requires greater coordination between departments and increases the need for more specialization of administrators. A home health agency that provides a systematic range of services to individuals in their homes would not require the same extent of administrative staffing as a comprehensive senior center that provides day care, case management, congregate dining, and a specialized Alzheimer's service, where the amount of time committed to administration and the levels of administration are more extensive.

Formalization

While formalization goes hand in hand with increased size and complexity, it may also be necessary for relatively small organizations. In large organizations, it is virtually impossible to operate without a measure of formality. Formalization is the extent and degree to which an organization is governed by policies and procedures, position descriptions, and laws that are documented (Champion, 1975). Regardless of the sector—profit, not-for-profit, or public— even modest formalization means an organization that extends beyond individual influence to the power of written rules. Indeed, the formalized structure often becomes the dominant determinant of behavior.

In the formal organization, norms strongly support "following the rules," and administrators are held accountable to enforce the policies. By the same token, administrators are held accountable for following policy and for encouraging their subordinates' adherence to policy. Policies can be established by boards of directors, executive administrative officials, or a legislative body. Policies and procedures are open to a measure of interpretation, often with debatable boundaries. Formulation of policies and procedures is more participatory in professional organizations that are not directly controlled by a government body. The role of policy and procedure will be explored further, later in this chapter, as an influence on organizational relationships.

Yet another indicator of a degree of formalization is the extent to which an organization socializes staff to the policies and procedures. It, of course, is rare to find an organization that serves older adults without a personal handbook for staff. An even stronger indicator of formalization is the degree of elaboration and detail that comprises new employee orientation and staff in-service addressing established policy and procedure.

Organizational Charts

Most of the time, gerontologist administrators join an organization with an existing structure. Depending on the administrator's level, he will have varying influence on the overall structure. Regardless of the position that the gerontologist administrator holds, understanding the structure is crucial for effective administration and success in one's career (Ehlers, Austin, & Prothero, 1976; Gatewood et al., 1995). To a large extent, the formal structure sets the expectations and determines behaviors as well as impacts relationships within the organization. This structure typically is depicted by an organizational chart.

In the previous section, we discussed the major determinants of structure, functions, size and complexity, and formality. In a subsequent section, the focus will be on departments, teams, and special projects that are subsections of an organization. In this section, the task will be to explore the formal administrative structure of an organization as represented by the organizational chart.

Traditionally, organizational charts are presented as hypothetical designs, such as matrix or bureaucratic charts. However, given the reality that organizations with programs for older adults only approximate the theoretical models, we have opted to present and discuss three organizational charts that represent actual organizations serving the older adult population. These organizational designs, as would be expected, have been influenced by their environment. That is, the marketplace, availability of resources, and public opinion have served to shape these service organizations (Crow & Odewahn, 1987). Thus, both the internal determinants and the environment have shaped and reshaped these organizations.

In short, these organizations, like most, are a product of the reality of the situation (Likert, 1967).

The organizational charts presented are examples of each of the three sectors that provide programs for older adults: not-for-profit, profit, and public. Senior Friendship Centers, a not-for-profit organization (see Figure 6.1), provides a broad range of programs in a three-county area. It has 200-plus employees, and programs that range from adult day care to telephone reassurance. This organizational chart represents only the major administrative units. Some programs are clustered by function, such as health services, while others are organized by region. The governing body (board of governors) has an advisory committee and a staffed fund-raising unit that reports directly to the board. A complete organizational picture of this organization requires eight additional organizational charts that emanate from the chart presented.

The profit organization, Mental Health Programs, Inc., offers mental health diagnostic and treatment services to older adults in nursing homes throughout a 17-county area. The organizational structure is presented in Figure 6.2. This organization has a board of directors made up of three partners, one of whom is a silent partner and does not participate in the operations of the organization. The other two partners hold co-administrator positions where one of the administrators operates primarily as a salesperson and the other oversees the accounting and financial aspects. The operations department head reports directly to both administrators.

The services are primarily presented by therapists who operate outside the office, on-site in the nursing homes. Therapists (clinical social workers and psychologists) are clustered under a field supervisor. The field supervisor could have from three to eight therapists to supervise. This is a relatively flat organization that has the ability to be able to add field supervisor units without restructuring. The disadvantage of this organizational design is the dual roles played by the administrators and the dual reporting relationship for the director of operations.

The example of the public organization that has programs for older adults is the Department of Elder Affairs for the State of Florida, presented in Figure 6.3. This organization perhaps most closely resembles the traditional bureaucracy. One of the most striking features is the clear depiction of staff sections that are available to provide advice and assistance to the organization's head, the secretary. The deputy secretary position directly oversees the operations departments, which represent approximately 200 employees. Under each of the operation's units are clustered similar programs. For example, under the office of long-term care are such programs as Medicaid Waiver, Long-term Policy and Planning, Assisted Living Program, and Hospice. This state agency is engaged in indirect activities that support, regulate, inspect, and fund direct programs throughout the state. In addition, this organization seeks to coordinate those activities that are the responsibility of the not-for-profit Area Agencies on Aging which are dispersed throughout the state by region. That is, the Area Agencies

Figure 6.1
Senior Friendship Centers, Inc. Organizational Chart

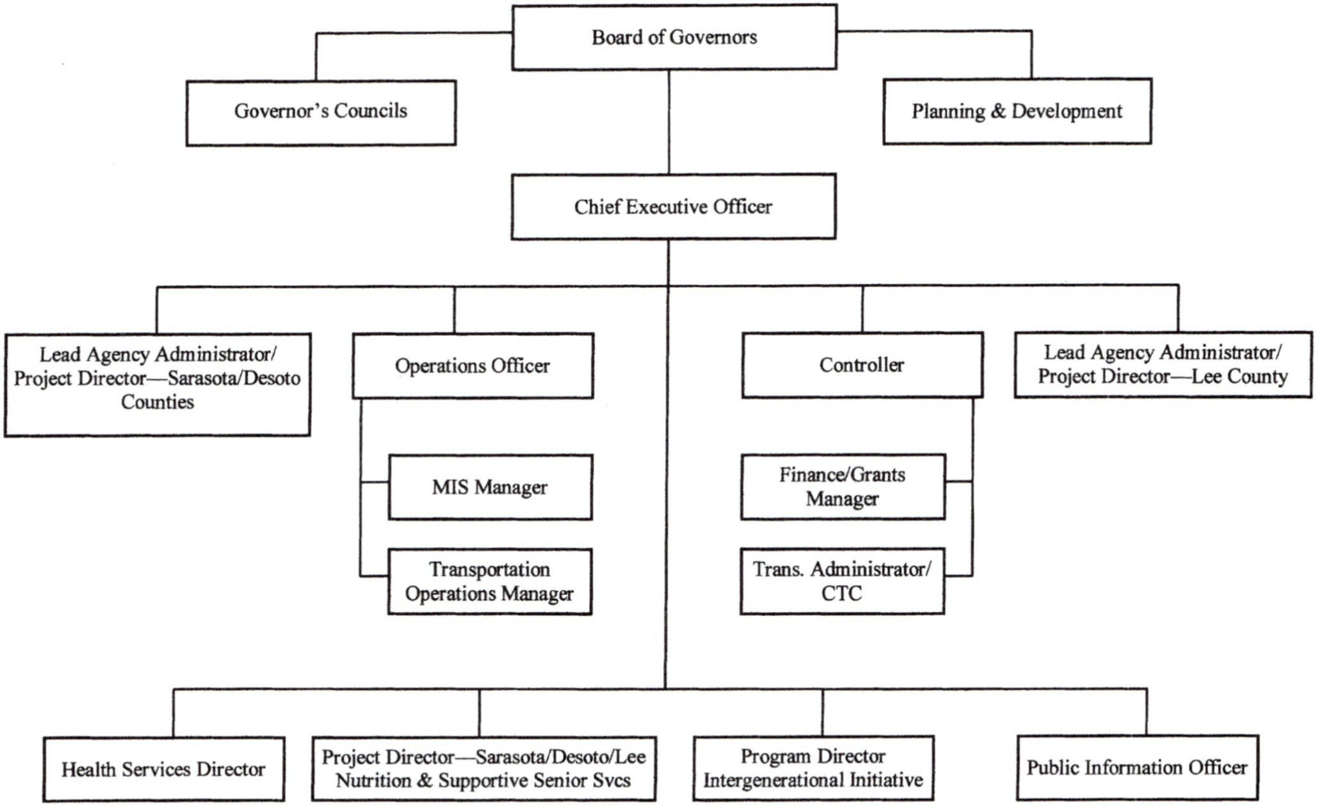

Board of Governors

- Planning & Development
- Governor's Councils

Chief Executive Officer

- Lead Agency Administrator/ Project Director—Lee County
  - Controller
    - Finance/Grants Manager
    - Trans. Administrator/ CTC
- Lead Agency Administrator/ Project Director—Sarasota/Desoto Counties
  - Operations Officer
    - MIS Manager
    - Transportation Operations Manager
- Public Information Officer
- Program Director Intergenerational Initiative
- Project Director—Sarasota/Desoto/Lee Nutrition & Supportive Senior Svcs
- Health Services Director

Source: Used with permission of Senior Friendship Centers, Sarasota, Florida, November 1998.

Figure 6.2
Profit Organization: Mental Health Programs, Inc. Organizational Chart

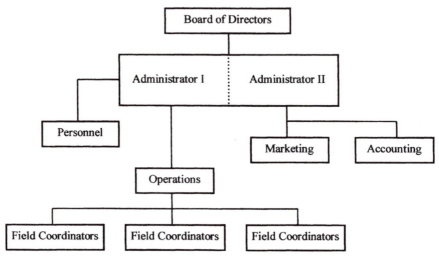

Note: Organization was purchased by a large corporation, after some reorganization became a division, and within a year the division was completely dismantled. It no longer exists. Name is fictitious.

on Aging are part of a network linking the not-for-profit AAA with the government.

These organizations, and most organizations that provide programs for older adults, are not designed based on organizational theory. The organizational theories, however, play a major role as they influence how the designs are operationalized and changed. A portion of this influence will be the organizational orientation of the gerontologist administrators, incorporating such considerations as willingness to delegate, administrative style, adherence to traditional "management" principles, willingness to change, and responsiveness to organizational characteristics. The determinants that will guide the administrator are examined in the next section.

Line and Staff

An organizational structure represented by the organizational chart depicts types and lines of authority for administration at different levels. The structure also shows which individuals and units are entrusted with certain functions and decisions. Two broad categories of employees are line and staff. Staff are those who support and provide auxiliary services to both the administrators and the line units (Schmid, 1990). The staff relationship to administrators in its purest form is advisory with the advice based upon policy, information, and study.

Figure 6.3
Department of Elder Affairs, Florida, Organizational Chart

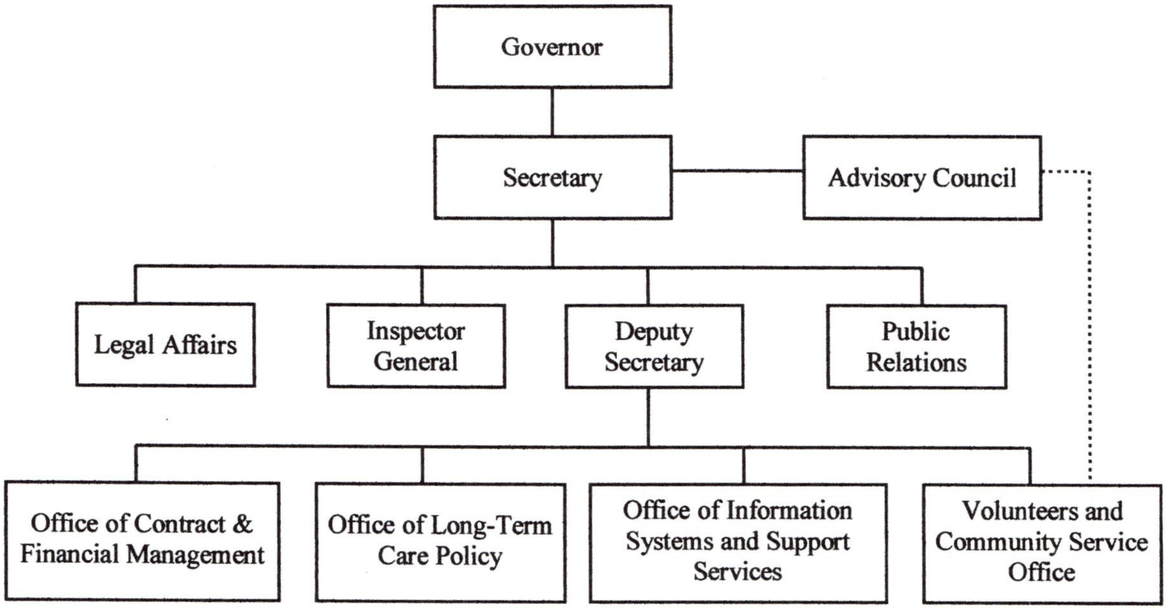

Source: Provided by DOEA, State of Florida, November 1998.

Typically, those in staff positions have only limited final decision-making authority. Staff units in Figure 6.4 are marketing, finance, and human resources. In other organizations, this might include planning and quality control.

Line administrators and units have the responsibility for implementing the programs consistent with the organization's mission (Lewis et al., 1991). Executive-level administrators have final decision-making authority and the prerogative to delegate that authority at varying degrees to administrators at lower levels of the organization. Line positions in Figure 6.4 are the executive director and the associate executive director as well as the administrators of the thrift shop, the assisted living facility (ALF), the nursing home, and the adult day care. Modern service organizations that serve older adults and practice more participatory types of administration blur the distinction between line and staff, particularly in the area of policy and planning.

Where there are clearly designated staff and line units, there frequently exist questionable perceptions of one another. For example, it is not unusual to hear line administrators complain that the support staff lose touch with the actual mission and purpose of the organization and their advice becomes questionable (Weinbach, 1998). At the same time, it is common to hear those in staff positions express concern that line employees do not use their services enough, have a tendency to shirk responsibilities for maintaining proper documentation and records, and when seeking advice do not present a clear problem. The level of authority for those in staff positions frequently fluctuates with the politics of the environment and the availability of resources. As resources shrink or become more difficult to obtain, staff functioning moves away from advice and more toward direct authority.

It is the consensus that the staff-line division within organizations, especially when it is unclear, causes great difficulties, conflict, and loss of time (Dale, 1978; Schmid, 1990; Weinbach, 1998). While it is common practice to attribute conflicts and differences to individuals, in actuality the problems emerge because of the prescribed roles within the organizational structure and, more specifically, because of the transgressions of these roles outside of formally sanctioned relationships. Additionally, the further down the organization the administrator or unit, the greater is the feeling that they are controlled by staff who are in close proximity and perceived as having influence with the top executives (Dale, 1978).

A study of community service agencies that provide recreational, educational, and cultural services was undertaken by Schmid (1990) to examine the nature of staff and line relationships. This study documented support provided by staff units in 11 different areas, such as planning and budgeting, and fund-raising, as well as documenting that line administrators acknowledged this support. Among the findings were that "friction between staff and line units is unavoidable; it can be reduced but not eliminated" (p. 82). Isolation of staff and line units contributes further to conflicts and differences.

Officially sanctioned work teams, task forces, and special projects that com-

Figure 6.4
Line and Staff Organizational Chart

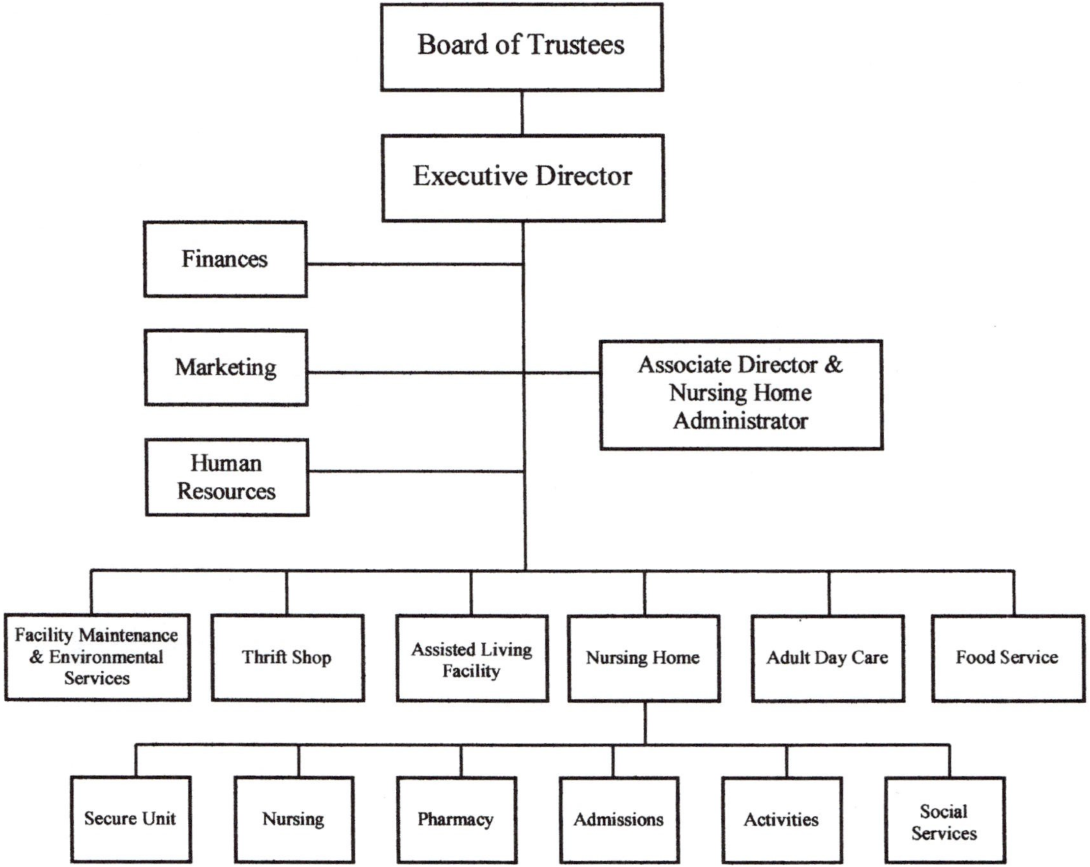

bine line and staff employees increase familiarity and cooperation and maximize the expertise of professionals from both groups. Participatory problem-solving and planning as well as decision-making during staff meetings, retreats, and special initiatives frequently clarify the roles and foster mutual appreciation. The gerontologist administrator with knowledge of the appropriate roles for those individuals holding staff and line positions can reinforce those roles to prevent inappropriate decision-making and maintain a balance of power.

ORGANIZATIONAL RELATIONSHIPS

To understand the nature of organizations, the gerontologist administrator needs to focus attention on the kinds and complexities of relationships in organizations. These relationships are determined, in part, by the established structure that authorizes positions and associated authority and responses to the structure. The formal organization structure will be paralleled by an informal organization. Most formal organizations that provide programs to older adults abide by modernized notions of chain of command and span of control. Further, work relationships are prescribed by policy and procedure, especially in formal organizations. These four influences on organizational relationships—informal organization, chain of command, span of control, and policy—deserve more in-depth discussion.

Informal Organizations

Professional organizations are legendary for their informal networks, because of the existence of professional groups, community involvement, and functional complexities. These networks involve informal alliances, hidden agendas, and activities both in and outside of the organization, and have little relation to the formal organizational chart (Gatewood et al., 1995; Skidmore, 1995). A portion of the organizational culture—the values, beliefs, traditions, and informal leadership—is embedded in the informal organization. The informal organization can be more powerful and influential in shaping behavior than the formal structure.

The informal network is partly composed of subgroups drawn together by professional affiliations, similar tasks, or social activities. These groups develop informal leaders who build cohesion, dispense rewards, and impose sanctions. Sometimes the groups cooperate with one another, depending on the organizational issue. On other occasions, they are in competition and conflict. It is common, for example, to find selected staff groups who socialize, meet together, and have an informal leader. This leader is most frequently the person who plans parties, social events, and other like activities. This informal leader may often have access to information and is a communications link for both gossip and official information.

The subgroups socialize new members and meet needs of members that are not fully met by the formal organization (Longest, 1976). The use and abuse of informal communication channels has been dealt with in Chapter 5. In addition to being a useful communication channel, the informal organization, although not subject to formal administrative control, can be used by leaders to help produce cohesiveness in the organization. This is especially powerful when administrators seek to work with the informal leaders to bring about improvement and change (Skidmore, 1995).

Collaboration with informal leaders may be needed to have successful activities such as company picnics, outings, and other special events like costume dress days. Perhaps the most powerful influence of the informal system, and particularly its leaders, is the ability to provide recognition and acceptance that builds self-esteem of employees. This often takes the form of the "mutual admiration society," verbal praise for someone in the group to members of the group and recognition of behaviors that are consistent with the group's values and beliefs. As one informal group leader said to a case manager, "At the staff meeting today, I especially liked the ways you defended the rights of Mrs. Jones not to participate in certain activities."

Many times, the administrator will need to confront the power of the informal organization, which has a tendency toward stability and thereby makes it resistant to change (Longest, 1976). The informal organization frequently works in opposition to the formal structure. Perhaps the best example of this is the case where the certified nursing assistant (CNA) was taken aside by several colleagues and told that she was completing her task too soon and thereby had time to accomplish other tasks, making the other CNAs look less productive. Informal subgroups often become self-serving, seeking benefits and perks for their group at the expense of the entire organization and the older adult clients.

Often, subgroups are exclusive clubs, rejecting certain members because of lack of compliance to beliefs. Others who do not hold the same credentials may be excluded from decisions and information. These subgroups, particularly those that are affiliated with a given profession, require a certain professional allegiance, thus creating, on occasion, a conflict between loyalty to the organization and loyalty to the professional group. Some authorities suggest that the disadvantages of the informal organization outweigh the advantages (Gatewood et al., 1995; Longest, 1976; Weinbach, 1998).

Chain of Command

The most traditional determinant of organizational relationships is the chain of command, which is depicted by the organizational chart. The chain of command ties all positions together in a hierarchy which represents power, authority, decision-making, and delegation of responsibilities. In professional organizations that provide programs for older adults, there are frequent sanctioned exceptions to the chain of command through the use of task forces, special projects, and committees. Organizations typically enforce employee adherence to the chain of command and usually discipline those who breach the structure. There are two essential components of the chain of command: unity of command and the Scalor Principle.

Unity of Command

This is the principle that each employee should report to and receive directions from only one supervisor, for to do otherwise compromises the supervisor's authority and is confusing and often conflicting for the employee (Fayol, 1949). It is not difficult to perceive how dual supervision can bring about conflicting delegated tasks in terms of priority as well as function. Dual supervisory relationships create enormous problems in organizations. Regardless, many organizations that provide programs for the elderly are structured to produce dual supervising relationships.

The Scalor Principle

This principle holds that authority should emanate from the top of the organizational chart down through the organizational ranks. That is, one person at the top of the organization has final authority and responsibility. Of course, this is not always followed and may create complications. It can be seen in the organizational chart of the for-profit organization presented in this chapter (Figure 6.2) that there are co-administrators. Compromises of the Scalor Principle produce considerable confusion with communication and delegation. Many organizations use the position of chief operating officer or director of operations, who is delegated considerable authority to help maintain the integrity of the hierarchy of authority. This design overcomes the lack of availability of the chief executive, who frequently must spend time in the community relating to the board or working with government or corporate officials.

Span of Control

This is the number of subordinates that is appropriate for an administrator to supervise. Modern thinking suggests that the appropriate number to supervise depends greatly on the level of the organization, the degree to which the work is routine, and, for organizations that serve older adults, the amount of direct service activity engaged in by the administrator. The number of relationships possible between a supervisor and subordinates is extraordinary. If one were to count both formal and informal possible relationships for an administrator supervising five subordinates, the number of relationships is 100 (Longest, 1976). Thus, it must be concluded that some limit, depending on the variables mentioned and the number of supervisees, must be determined or productivity and effectiveness will be seriously compromised.

Gatewood et al. (1995) have suggested that five or six subordinates are appropriate for the higher-level administrators and that where subordinates are doing essentially the same job, lower-level administrators could supervise as many as 30 individuals. Given that service organizations are not known for high levels of routine, the supervision of 30 individuals would seem unwieldy. However, if an administrator were supervising all case managers who had basically the same function, he is more likely to be able to manage that responsibility than if he is supervising a group with different professionals who exercise latitude in interpreting the fulfillment of responsibilities.

Span of control is also less significant for professional organizations that use teams and have appointed team leaders. Often the team leader is of the same professional background and is capable of or spends a percentage of time delivering the same kinds of services as other members of the team. Some of the decision-making and problem-solving is handled by the team, and group supervision is possible. This design works well if teams meet frequently, work to achieve cohesion, and share responsibility for program components. This frequently becomes the desired structure for satellite units that operate semi-independently from the central organization.

Policies and Procedures

Organizational relationships and behavior are also guided by policy and procedures. Policies are statements which emanate from boards, government bodies, or administrators to prescribe both the values and boundaries for decision-making. Procedures are step-by-step actions attached to a particular policy that are expected to be followed by individuals in the organizations. All formal organizations eventually will have extensive policies and procedures. For many organizations that serve older adults, such policies and procedures are required by accrediting agencies, such as the Joint Commission on Accreditation of Health Care Organizations (JCAHO).

Regardless of external requirements, policies and procedure are important for professional service organizations to assist with difficult decisions and to provide consistency and fairness. In order to guide behavior and prescribe areas of responsibility, many organizations adopt a policy on development of policy. Ideally, most policies result from a planning process that involves both the governing body and the administration.

Various staff departments or units within an organization have a primary role of interpreting and enforcing policy throughout the organization. Such is the case with human resources about personnel policy and the finance department as it pertains to purchasing and expenditures. These departments, their administrators, and the staff are there to advise, counsel, and guide those administrators and staff who are operating the programs. Generally, all administrators are expected to follow and enforce adherence to policies. At the same time, a degree of flexibility about policy is desirable as legitimate exceptions will be necessary (Weinbach, 1998). When exceptions are frequent or adherence is poor, it may be time to review and revise the policy.

Not all policies are written (Weinbach, 1998). Policies as ways of behaving are role expectations emerging over time, based on patterns of behavior or an administrator's orientation. Thus, administrative behavior can be precedent-setting. These policies, like written policy, may need to be challenged and reviewed. In some cases, the policies will need to be formalized to remove conflict due to misinterpretation.

ORGANIZATIONAL SUBGROUPS

The tasks and responsibilities within an organizational structure are assigned to a network of subgroups. Three subgroups will be discussed in this section: departments, teams, and special projects. Coordination of subgroups is more manageable than coordination of each position. The most traditional is the department which encompasses a cluster of like activities. Frequently, departments are subgrouped further into units or sections. For example, the case management department of a Senior Center has a crisis unit in addition to the case management program. Both units report to an administrator, who heads the department. In modern organizations, it is common to find "committees" or "teams" without departmental status within a department or crossing departmental lines. These subgroups are usually permanent, have defined tasks, and are formally sanctioned. The ethics committee discussed in Chapter 4 is a good example.

Our survey of administrators shows that for organizations that offer older adult programs, a common subgrouping and an approach to accomplishing tasks is the "special project." These groups cut across department lines and focus on an assignment that can be accomplished in a relatively short duration. Special projects are often called "task forces." A task force is a group of employees representing different aspects of the organization that have an assigned responsibility for accomplishing a project or bringing about some change (Gatewood et al., 1995).

Departmentalization

Organizations may choose a division structure that is subgrouped further into departments. Thus, departmentalization may include three levels of organizational structure: division, department, and units. Sometimes, a program for older adults is a subgroup of a more general division. For example, the outpatient division of a community mental health center may have a geriatric mental health department. For a given department, clustering of activities is usually based upon one of four groupings: functions, clients, professions, or geography.

- *Functions.* Grouping jobs with similar activities, such as in Accounts Receivable.
- *Clients.* Grouping of jobs within a department that serves a specific kind of clients, like an Alzheimer's Day Care and Adult Day Care.
- *Professions.* This is typically used in larger organizations where each profession has a

department. This has been common in hospitals where one can find nursing, social work, psychology, and other such groupings. Representatives of these groupings then may be assigned to areas where services are provided to older adults.

- *Geography.* Generally, when an organization reaches a certain size or has attempted to provide programs in a large geographical area, satellite or regional centers are formed. These entities represent a department where specializations work together and division of labor is less rigidly defined.

Departmentalization has many advantages (such as efficiency) by clustering together like activities or the development of specialized skills through inter- action with those performing the same tasks. It also brings problems. Perhaps the greatest problem occurs when members of a department or the department administrator view and advocate for issues from the perspective of their partic- ular area, lacking a full understanding of the overall organizational goals (Gate- wood et al., 1995). Grouping departments by professions creates conflict among professions and less innovation in the delivery of services.

Greater commonality of purpose occurs when the professions are grouped together to focus on a given population or identified problem area (Lewis et al., 1991). Of course, bringing different professionals together in one department represents a challenge to the administrator of that department to provide the kind of supervision and direction that is relevant for each profession. An in- novative hospital in Tampa, the Moffit Cancer Hospital, solved this problem by breaking with traditional hospital structure and creating a psychosocial unit that clustered together psychologists, social workers, psychiatrists, and other mental health professionals. The multidisciplinary nature of the field of gerontology lends itself to the clustering of work units around functions and clients' needs.

Beyond Departmentalization

Organizing work by subgroups in addition to departments is a common prac- tice of organizations. However, such groups may not always appear in the or- ganizational chart. Work groups exist as independent units within a department or cutting across departments. An example of the latter is the Quality Assurance committee, which is composed of a variety of people from different departments and different levels of the organization, all focused on improving the quality of programs. These groups have many different names: committees, councils, work teams, task forces, and project teams. In the workplace and with the literature, there is little consistency and considerable diversity as to the labeling of groups. Perhaps it is best to consider them all as basically task groups (Toseland & Rivas, 1984). Task groups share the organizational purpose, are composed of a membership that is in frequent communication, and have outcome expectations with a measure of accountability.

Group dynamics, the process that occurs within a group, is addressed in both Chapter 2 and Chapter 5. In this chapter, the focus is on groups as an organizational structural component that represent a division of the labor with assigned tasks. While groups in organizations constitute many forms, two particular models—teams and special projects—are most relevant for the gerontologist administrator.

Teams

Generally, the word "team" is applied broadly to mean any organization, department, unit, or group. These general applications are associated with notions of team building and team work. Often, team is indiscriminately used to apply to all groups (Brill, 1976). The team as an organizational unit is popular with service organizations. The team is distinguished in part because, unlike special projects, it is perpetual in nature. As a work unit, a team has shared leadership roles, works collectively, holds decision-making power, and in addition to individual accountability, has group accountability (Brill, 1976; Gatewood et al., 1995).

Not all groups function as a team. Some departments or sections of an organization may adopt these characteristics to function more like a team than a traditional department. Three specific kinds of teams commonly found in older adult service organizations will be examined further: service teams, quality improvement teams, and self-managed teams.

A specialized service team is designed to address a particular problem area that needs attention. For example, a crisis team in an adult protective services department responds to identified emergencies of elder abuse. After the situation is stabilized, the case is transferred to another section. In some instances, these teams are composed of staff from different segments of an organization coming together as a team to address the service needs or to organize activity.

Quality improvement teams, composed of a variety of professionals, usually from different departments, seek to improve the quality of programs (Townsend, 1986). These teams involve administrators and line staff in an environment that levels position authority. Rather than a formal team leader, there is usually a coordinator who arranges the agenda and facilitates the meetings. The purpose of the team is to engage in systematic review of service products such as records, reports, and customer response information. When working effectively, the team designs corrective action to improve programs and monitors the correction.

A modern variation on the use of teams is the self-managed team. A survey in the early 1990s indicated that 47 percent of the Fortune 1000 companies were using self-managed teams (Lawler, Mohrman, & Ledford, 1992). A self-managed team expands decision-making responsibilities, engages in interrelated tasks, and self-regulates behavior. Some self-managed teams retain the traditional supervisor, who functions as a liaison to other divisions within the administrative structure.

Self-managed teams are consistent with the participatory management approach that characterizes many service organizations. Research findings indicate that self-managed teams are more productive and improve the quality of work life when compared to traditionally managed teams (Cohen & Ledford, 1994). Such teams require a measure of job redesign, task reassignment, and a commitment to the model. Self-managed teams are not appropriate for all work situations.

Generally, the use of teams in service organizations is considered highly beneficial (Brill, 1976; Gatewood et al., 1995; Toseland & Rivas, 1984). The major benefits are:

- Team involvement is regarded as motivating for staff because of the participatory nature and the potential for recognition.
- Teams provide increased options to group problem-solving directed at service delivery and organizational improvement.
- With a team, there is the opportunity for examination and evaluation of activities and processes using a variety of different professionals.
- The likelihood of innovation is increased with teams.
- Teams have the opportunity to utilize pooled knowledge.
- Productivity is enhanced because teams decrease duplication of activities and focus energy.

While the benefits of teams that employ a participatory approach have been lauded, it has also been recognized that many problems and limitations exist. Rees (1991), for example, holds that the actual decision-making should remain with top management. Programs for older adults, like the field of gerontology, are multidisciplinary. This brings additional challenges to effectiveness of teams. Some of the major concerns about teams are:

- Differences among and between professional disciplines that have overlapping areas of expertise and skills produce conflict among members and delays in decision-making (Brill, 1976).
- Team members who lack commitment to the team process are often ill-equipped to participate in the process; for example, there can be a lack of group problem-solving skills (Brill, 1976; Harrington-Mackin, 1996).
- Team meetings can be very time-consuming, often because the team leader and the members lack the skills for conducting an efficient meeting (Brill, 1976).
- The use of teams requires relinquishing of power and authority by middle management staff. Many individuals in these positions are resistant to this requirement (Harshman & Philips, 1994).
- With teams, as in any group that interacts frequently, there is the tendency to focus on the team's task in isolation of the larger organization and to consider non-members of the group threatening.

Teams, as a structural component, are a useful division of labor. Many of the programs for older adults require and benefit from a mix of various professionals. The problems and limitations are not offered to dissuade the use of teams, but to encourage alterations to the traditional authoritative structure that will help maximize the benefits of teams. Achieving the effective use of teams may require employing structured activities such as brainstorming or the nominal group process (Toseland & Rivas, 1984). Training resources available in the literature and the use of administrative consultants can overcome the limitations, leading to successful teams (Brauchle & Wright, 1993; Jessup, 1992).

Special Projects

When researching administration in organizations that serve older adults, one of the distinct features revealed was the frequent use of "special projects" as a structural work unit. These projects, where involvement is voluntary, often have the flavor of a "mission." Motivation and commitment to the goal are usually strong (Odiorne, 1987). The project may extend outside the organizational boundaries, involving other organizations. Special projects may have many other names, such as task force, project team, and committees. The single most distinctive characteristic is that these projects are temporary, having a beginning, middle, and end (Gatewood et al., 1995; Odiorne, 1987).

Special projects either complete the goal or institutionalize the outcome, and then the group disbands. While there is great variation in the structure of special projects, there are some common characteristics, all of which may not be found in a given project. Typically, special projects have a designated leader who has responsibility for completion of the project but does not usually hold the same kind of authority in the formal organizational structure.

Special projects offer opportunities for new leadership to emerge and for regular staff members to learn and practice leadership skills. The leader must be able to tolerate conflict and maintain a commitment to the goal by group members. Members of the project usually come from different departments in the organization. These projects are highly focused endeavors. An example of such a project is an agency's participation in a community health fair. Sometimes projects have no independent funding and must seek resources in order to accomplish the goal.

Since these projects are frequently innovative or different from daily routine tasks, they enjoy heavy involvement and commitment from members. Often it is not necessary to seek a solution or produce a specific outcome, but rather to establish a variety of alternatives or demonstrate an alternative to existing services. Many new service programs are established in this manner. A well-established nursing home complex that already had assisted living, long-term care, and independent living programs sought to add an adult day care center. This was accomplished in part by forming a special project team both to research models of day care and to assess the need in the community. At the end of the project, the team leader reported the findings to the executive director, who conveyed those findings to the Board of Directors.

These projects bring with them a unique set of problems and issues. Project participants may experience role ambiguity because of the multiple reporting relationships (Longest, 1976). The excitement and involvement generated by special projects compete with regular work activity and may result in lower productivity of the participant. Problems will also occur if a special project is managed in the traditional manner instead of with a distinctive leadership approach (Longest, 1976). Projects that lack clear objectives or in which the objectives are changed frequently also are unable to maintain the commitment and involvement of members necessary for success.

Expansion of programs for older adults is frequently tested by a demonstration project. While these projects are occasionally a response to the availability of new funds, it is better if they are in response to an established need based on a systematic inquiry (Wilkerson, 1980). Demonstration projects may be seeking to establish a new approach to an old problem or a response to an area that is underserved. These special projects establish a model of service, a plan, and a budget. Built into these projects are program evaluation procedures. Depending on the findings of the evaluation, the project may be discontinued, altered and piloted further, or may become an established program of the organization.

SUMMARY

Organizations require a formal structure to divide work responsibility and achieve accountability. Theories of organizations assist the gerontologist administrator to understand organizational structure and functioning. Most organizations with programs for older adults embrace the principles of a classical bureaucracy but represent a variation. The variations can best be understood as falling into one of three theoretical categories: professional bureaucracy, systems theory, or the most flexible of the three, contingency theory. Actual organizational structures, which are frequently depicted by an organizational chart, may vary widely, governed by functions, degree of formalization, and size and complexity.

Organizational structure generally becomes more formal as the organization grows in size and complexity. Formal organizations are shadowed by the informal organization that governs many of the relationships and influences staff behavior. Organizational relationships are also affected by the formal chain of command, design of supervision, and policies.

Subgrouping of organizations, traditionally, is by departments, where activities are clustered by function, client needs, professions, or geographical location. Additionally, teams may exist either independently of departments or within a department. Modern organizations are inclined to make extensive use of teams, emphasizing teamwork, commitment, group problem-solving, innovation, and opportunities for leadership. An approach used often by older adult programs is the special project. This is a temporary group, requiring strong commitment focused on a clear objective that will create an opportunity for additional resources or improved programs for older adults.

LEARNING EXPERIENCE

The Community Employment Council

The Community Employment Council was established by members of the human services community and the business community to stimulate employment for youth. The Council met on a monthly basis. As funding became available, the Council established an organization that grew very rapidly to become a significant agency within the community. The original Council became a smaller board of directors, and the purpose of the Council was expanded to include employment for disabled, a special training and placement program for welfare recipients, and the development of employment opportunities for older adults. Staff were hired.

During the 20-year development of this organization, the demography of the surrounding community changed dramatically. The community, a coastal town in Mississippi, became an attractive retirement location. The population of older adults over the age of 65 rose from 9 percent to 24 percent. Adding individuals between 55 and 65 boosted the percentage to 32 percent. Many of these individuals were early retirees searching for employment.

The Community Employment Council had two employees, Jack Black and Sheila White, who focused attention on the employment of older adults. These programs were developed despite the division in the Board of Directors about the direction of the agency. A significant segment felt the agency should stay with its original mission, which was a focus on youth. Jack and Sheila strongly felt that they did not receive the support or resources for the growing demand to assist older adults. After several years of discussion, disagreement, and intense negotiation, the board separated the program offering employment services for older citizens. This became known as the Later Life Career Center, and the two employees, Jack Black and Sheila White, became the staff for this independent program.

As the program emerged, the two employees were also members of a new eight-person board. As in many new organizations, several volunteer board members assisted with the program activities. The two full-time staff members were very creative in obtaining funding beyond that received from the Community Employment Council. They obtained funds from the United Way and from the AAA. They were also creative in their programming, developing innovative media programs emphasizing the benefits of employing older adults, which were to be shown in the community and to employers.

Within a number of years, the organization boasted six employment counselors who were engaged in job development and placement, two professional employees who were involved with public relations, public education, evaluation, and follow-up, and one receptionist-secretary. Jack, much to his disgruntlement, was no longer directly involved in job development and placement. He spent most of his time supervising employees and on personnel issues. Sheila, out of necessity rather than desire, focused on grant writing, fund-raising, and maintaining the budget. The organization had no chief executive. This function was filled in part by Jack and Sheila and the board members, depending on the decision and the situation. The demands for their services continued to exceed the Career Center's ability to meet the need.

Daily activities at the organization were sometimes chaotic and often confusing. Staff turnover, especially in the receptionist-secretary position, was quite frequent. Jack complained of the loss of creativity and ability to be innovative with programs because of the burden of his supervisory responsibilities. Sheila concurred, often asking volunteer board members to assume some of the responsibility she had inherited. Eventually, Jack and Sheila confronted fellow board members, expressing a desire to return to the "front-line" where they felt productive and useful. It took Sheila's threatening to resign from the board and the organization entirely to stimulate the board into several emergency meetings. Out of these meetings came a decision to hire a full-time skilled administrator to reorganize the Later Life Career Center and assume the administrative responsibilities. You are that administrator.

1. What organizational design would you create for the Later Life Career Center?

2. How would you seek to preserve and ensure the creativity and innovation of the two founding staff members, Jack Black and Sheila White?

3. Produce an organizational chart of your proposed design.

4. Given that you have the mandate to add two staff positions, which positions would you add and for what reasons?

5. Even though the board hired you to be the Executive Director, would you recommend bringing in a consultant to assist with the organizational changes?

6. What theoretical approach would be most appropriate for this situation?

REFERENCES

Brauchle, P., & Wright, D. (1993). Training work teams. *Training & Development, 47*(3), 65–68.

Brill, N. J. (1976). *Team work: Working together in the human services.* Philadelphia: Lippincott.

Brunk, D. (1996, October). A rising star: Adult day services find a place in the constellation of services. *Contemporary Long Term Care, 19*(10), pp. 38–46.

Bucher, R., & Stelling, J. (1969). Characteristics of professional organizations. *Journal of Health and Social Behavior, 10*(1), 3–15.

Champion, D. (1975). *The sociology of organizations.* New York: McGraw-Hill.

Cohen, S. G., & Ledford, G. E. (1994). The effectiveness of self-managing teams: A quasi-experiment. *Human Relations, 47*(1), 13–43.

Crow, R. T., & Odewahn, C. A. (1987). *Management for the human services.* Englewood Cliffs, NJ: Prentice-Hall.

Dale, E. (1978). *Management: Theory and practice* (4th ed.). New York: McGraw-Hill.

Ehlers, W. H., Austin, M. J., & Prothero, J. C. (Eds.). (1976). *Administration for the human services*. New York: Harper & Row.

Fayol, H. (1949). *General and industrial management*. London: Sir Isaac Pitman.

Gatewood, R. D., Taylor, R. R., & Ferrell, O. C. (1995). *Management: Comprehension, analysis, and application*. Chicago: Austen.

Harrington-Mackin, D. (1996). *Keeping the team going*. New York: Amacom.

Harshman, C. L., & Philips, S. L. (1994). *Teaming up*. San Diego, CA: Pfeiffer.

Jessup, H. (1992). The road to results for teams. *Training & Development, 46*(9), 65–68.

Lawler, E. E., Mohrman, S. A., & Ledford, G. E. (1992). *Employee involvement and total quality management: Practice and results in Fortune 1000 companies*. San Francisco: Jossey-Bass.

Lewis, J. A., Lewis, M. D., & Soufiée, F. (1991). *Management of human service programs* (2nd ed.). Pacific Grove, CA: Brooks/Cole.

Likert, R. (1967). *The human organization: Its management and value*. New York: McGraw-Hill.

Longest, B. B. (1976). *Management practices for the health professional*. Reston, VA: Reston Publishing.

Marion, D. J. (1975). Open systems. In J. Jones & J. W. Pfeiffer (Eds.), *Annual handbook for group facilitators* (pp. 132–134). La Jolla, CA: University Associates.

Miller, D., & Friesen, P. (1984). A longitudinal study of the corporate life cycle. *Management Science, 30*, 1161–1183.

Mintzberg, H. (1979). *The structure of organizations*. Englewood Cliffs, NJ: Prentice-Hall.

Mintzberg, H. (1989). *Mintzberg on management: Inside our strange world of organizations*. New York: Free Press.

Odiorne, G. S. (1987). *The human side of management: Management by integration and self-control*. Lexington, MA: Lexington Books.

Ralston, P. A. (1986). Senior centers in rural communities: A qualitative study. *The Journal of Applied Gerontology, 5*(1), 76–92.

Rees, F. (1991). *How to lead work teams*. San Diego, CA: Pfeiffer.

Schmid, H. (1990). Staff and line relationships revisited: The case of community service agencies. *Public Personnel Management, 19*(1), 71–83.

Scott, W. (1978). Organization theory: An overview and an appraisal. In J. Shafritz & P. Whitbeck (Eds.), *Classics of organization theory* (pp. 274–290). Oak Park, IL: Moore.

Skidmore, R. A. (1995). *Social work administration: Dynamic management and human relationships* (3rd ed.). Boston: Allyn & Bacon.

Toseland, R. T., & Rivas, R. T. (1984). Structured methods for working with task groups. *Administration in Social Work, 8*(2), 49–58.

Townsend, P. L. (1986). *Commit to quality*. New York: John Wiley.

Weber, M. (1986). The ideal bureaucracy. In M. T. Matteson & J. M. Ivancevich (Eds.), *Management classics* (3rd ed., pp. 220–226). Plano, TX: Business Publications.

Weinbach, R. (1998). *The social worker as manager: A practical guide to success* (3rd ed.). Needham Heights, MA: Allyn & Bacon.

Wilkerson, A. E. (1980). A framework for project development. In F. D. Perlmutter & S. Slavin (Eds.), *Leadership in social administration: Perspectives for the 1980s* (pp. 157–172). Philadelphia: Temple University.

Zastrow, C., & Kirst-Ashman, K. (1997). *Understanding human behavior and the social environment* (4th ed.). Chicago: Nelson-Hall.

Chapter 7

Human Resources Functions

Programs for older adults are staffed by a broad spectrum of paraprofessionals and professionals with different educational levels. Activities related to quality and care of staff comprise what is commonly known as personnel management. Since the 1970s, a more comprehensive approach has emerged: human resources administration and development (Weiner, 1990). Despite the trend to broader activities and the clustering of those activities in a department, many staff question the usefulness and extent of human resources (Ulrich, 1998). The focus of this chapter is on human resources functions regardless of how organized or who has those responsibilities. These functions have the dual, often conflicting, role of protecting and assisting staff and helping the organization meet its goals. A systematic examination of perceived value of human resources departments was conducted. Fitz-enz (1990) asked human resources professionals to provide three main reasons for their existence. The following ranking emerged:

1. Keep out of court
2. Provide standards, consistency, and equity
3. Improve productivity and profits
4. Develop people
5. Provide recruiting services
6. Improve employee relations and communications
7. Support line managers

This ranking emphasizes the need for human resources based on the complexity of laws related to employees and the value placed upon fairness to staff. Given the staff-intensive programs for older adults, an identified human resources department is highly desirable. These activities can be on a continuum of responsibility from being consolidated in a separate human resources department to being extensively shared with administrators throughout the organization.

Human resource functions have expanded from traditional personnel activities such as recruitment and selection of staff and administering benefit plans to reward and recognition programs, organizational safety, and job analysis. Indeed, the list of functions continues to grow with the full complement exceeding the scope of this chapter. Three important areas related to human resources— staff development, performance appraisals, and employee discipline—will be discussed in Chapter 9.

Gerontologist administrators at all levels can expect extensive involvement with human resource functions. In some instances, the administrator will be responsible for assuring that those functions are completed; in others, the administrator will perform those functions. In still other instances, administrators will utilize human resources staff to advise and assist with human resources functions. Where human resources professionals are available, the gerontologist administrator will coach and model for staff cooperation with those professionals. This is accomplished by building a strong relationship with the human resources department.

The administrator will also be required to interpret, enforce, and participate in the development and change of policies that affect staff. Further, the administrator will be expected to foster change, particularly change related to staff and organizational development, and to assist in dealing with resistance to change (Maurer, 1997; Ulrich, 1998). The education of others performing human resources functions, whether an administrative assistant or a human resources professional, will also be required. Hence, it is necessary for the gerontologist administrator to be informed, knowledgeable, and involved with all human resources functions.

EVOLVING DEVELOPMENT OF HUMAN RESOURCES FUNCTIONS

Before elaborating on selected human resources functions, it will be useful to present a brief history on the expansion of human resources activities. Congress, in 1883, passed the Pendleton Act for federal government employees, creating a personnel system. It was not until the 1920s that personnel emerged as a consolidated major function in manufacturing companies with over 250 employees. Forced by the growth in unions, a corresponding growth of personnel departments surged over the next two decades as a necessity to bring fairness to personnel matters (Caudron & Laabs, 1997). By the 1960s, the human relations school of management, which focused more attention on the individual, had become a major influence on administration. At the same time, an increase in government regulations and social legislation added to the complexity of personnel matters (Fitz-enz, 1990).

Personnel activities expanded further to include employee retention programs, recognition and reward to motivate employees, and career development programs. The expanded personnel departments became known as human resources. Human resources functions became viewed as useful for increasing productivity (Caudron & Laabs, 1997; Ulrich, 1998). The growth of human resources functions has moved far beyond the role of finding and securing employees with appropriate skills matched to the organization's purpose. Many of the traditional functions of personnel now fall into the area of human resources administration, and the expanded functions fall into a category known as human resources development. These two clusters of activities of human resources will be discussed in detail throughout the remainder of this chapter. Regulatory compliance constitutes a major challenge for many aspects of human resources (Nobile, 1997). Thus, a review of major social legislation, court rulings, and organizational policy which guide and direct many human resources functions is presented to establish a foundation for this discussion.

The influence of federal legislation and court decisions on employment accounts in part for the phenomenal growth of human resources functions (Goldberg, 1997). Table 7.1 summarizes selected laws and legal decisions that affect employment in most organizations. These influences range from establishing minimum wage (Fair Labor Standards Act) to protecting individuals against discrimination. Laws protecting individuals from discrimination in employment and dismissal have had a dramatic effect on accountability and fairness in organizations. This effect becomes even more powerful when an organization must engage in programs of laying off or dismissing employees, called RIF (Reduction in Force). Serious attention must be given to the possibility of an interpretation of discrimination about decisions. At the same time, the organization's financial situation may require dismissal of some of those in protected categories, making the organization subject to possible legal proceedings.

In 1993, Congress passed a Family and Medical Leave Act challenging administrators to protect the job of a person on leave while assuring that the tasks of the person on leave will continue to be accomplished. Usually, that plan will not allow the hiring of a permanent employee. This legislation applies to organizations of 50 staff or more. Despite the political proclamations as to the simplicity and ease of compliance with this Act, actual practice has produced additional problems (Nobile, 1997). These problems are experienced more by small programs or units that serve older adults. The replacement of appropriate trained professionals and the definition of serious health conditions are difficult tasks for the administrator.

Throughout the 1990s, sexual harassment complaints in the workplace continued to increase. These behaviors are governed by Title VII of the Civil Rights Act of 1964 and enforced by the Equal Opportunities Commission. Considerable misunderstanding and recent redefinition by the courts have altered the definition

Table 7.1

Federal Legislation and Court Decisions Affecting Human Resources Functions

Family and Medical Leave Act	1993	Twelve weeks of unpaid leave for health conditions or care of family member
Americans with Disabilities Act	1990	Prohibits discrimination based upon physical and mental disabilities
Marshall v. Whirlpool	1980	Gives employees the right to refuse job assignments that constitute a physical danger
Pregnancy Discrimination Act	1978	Defines pregnancy as a disability
Albemarle v. Moody	1975	Requires organizations to prove that employment tests are related to the job
Employee Retirement Income Security Act (ERISA)	1974	Protects employees' pension plans from loss due to mismanagement or job change
Spurlock v. United Airlines	1972	Permits college degrees as sole selection criterion for employment
Occupational Safety and Health Act (OSHA)	1970	Safety standards and inspection of workplace
Age Discrimination Employment Act (amended 1978)	1967	Prohibits discrimination against individuals 40-70 years of age
Civil Rights Act (amended 1972 and 1991)	1964	Prohibits discrimination based upon race, color, religion, sex, or national origin. Established the Equal Opportunity Employment Commission (EEOC)
Equal Pay Act	1963	Prohibits discrimination on the basis of sex for pay for jobs of equal requirements
Fair Labor Standards Act (and amendments)	1938	Establishes a minimum wage, requires overtime pay, and provides standards for child labor. Classifies employees as exempt (executives, administrators, professionals, and outside salespersons) or non-exempt (all others) relative to overtime pay regulations
Unemployment Compensation Act	1935	Income for employees who are laid off or fired
Worker's Compensation (dates vary by state)	1935	Provides payments to workers for injury or illness, regardless of fault. Also covers rehabilitation and income for loss due to death.

(Lavelle, 1998). The Act's intention is to prevent discrimination based on gender and unwelcome sexual behavior from persons in positions of authority. Administrations will want to ensure that a highly publicized complaint-resolution policy and procedure is in place (Lavelle, 1998; Nobile, 1997). The procedure should include objective investigation and disciplinary measures.

In addition to the federal influences, most states have laws that also affect human resources decisions. These state and federal laws, along with organizational administrative decisions, become translated into organizational policy. For example, among the greatest influences on employment is the Fair Labor Standards Act, which requires organizations to articulate associated policies for exempt (salaried) and non-exempt (hourly) staff. Non-exempt staff must receive overtime pay for all work over 40 hours per week. Exempt staff are usually those in salaried administrative positions, and payment of overtime is not required by the government.

Most of these policies are accompanied by procedures that appear in the staff personnel handbook. Other administrative and safety policies that are interconnected with personnel policies will also govern behavioral expectations of staff. The safety policy, for example, that requires the systematic removal of toxic substances by certain staff will have compliance and discipline issues. Most organizations' policies extend beyond the legal requirements. These policies seek to provide consistency and fairness in the management of staff and decision-making about staff. Policies also contribute to the total work environment as they affect morale, relationships, and productivity.

HUMAN RESOURCES ADMINISTRATION

Human resources administration is also called human resources management or human resources planning. It involves the traditional personnel functions (French, 1982; Weiner, 1990). These functions are obtaining, maintaining, and retaining staff for the organization. The organization's design, whether it is depicted in a chart or otherwise conceptualized, represents the current and future staffing needs. Human resources administration is responsible for selecting sufficient number of staff with appropriate skills in accordance with the adopted budget and a personnel plan. This process must be accomplished in a way that builds commitment to the organizational purpose and reinforces appropriate work behaviors. A haphazard or systematic organized recruitment and selection process sends a distinct message to the prospective staff member.

These administrative functions require extensive record keeping. Beginning with the employment application through such activities as maintaining a record of annual leave, records of performance evaluation and credentialing, all are part of the personnel process. These routine activities, which can be time-consuming, can partially be handled by the use of human resources computer software programs (Cole-Gomolski, 1998). Quick retrieval of personnel information for supervisors and staff is a major service of human resources.

Responsibility for human resources administration may rest with a designated human resources administrator or a personnel manager within a human resources department. In other instances the activities may be decentralized throughout the organization. The gerontologist administrator will be involved in a number of ways. Where there are designated human resources personnel, there will be the expectation to work cooperatively with human resources and frequently share in the human resources functions. New job applicants for a position may apply to human resources, which conducts a preliminary screening to determine if they meet the prescribed job criteria. Those who successfully emerge from the screening are referred to the gerontologist administrator for interviewing and selection. In other instances, the gerontologist administrator, with the assistance of clerical personnel, especially in smaller programs, will be responsible for all of these human resources functions. A closer examination of the basic personnel functions that constitute human resources administration is useful.

Job Classification and Analysis

The process of assigning a title is the beginning step in job classification. The next step is to group like positions by tasks, duties, and responsibilities (Weiner, 1990); for example, gerontology case managers who are part of a community service agency for the aging would represent a class of positions. The administrative position that supervises the case managers is another class of like administrative positions. This process is a preliminary step to a more formal process, job analysis.

Job Analysis

This is a systematic procedure to obtain information about work-related activities and circumstances of a given job (Gatewood, Taylor, & Ferrell, 1995). This procedure, in its most formal application, examines three distinct areas related to a position: tasks performed; requisite knowledge, skills, and abilities necessary; and equipment and materials for a given job. The process of performing a job analysis can include observations, interviews, and reviews of documents such as job descriptions, and frequently will involve information from supervisors and those performing or likely to perform the job. When a given position has undergone some change deviating from the job description, or when change is predicted, a re-analysis of the position is necessary.

Job Description

A job description is a written document combining narratives and listings that summarizes the job requirements and expectations. Job descriptions are key elements in the personnel system of an organization (Schuler, 1981). Job descriptions are an essential tool for many other personnel activities such as recruitment, supervision, and performance evaluation. The basic components of a job description are as follows:

- Job title and location of the position, such as the department, division, or unit.
- The supervisory position for this job.
- A brief narrative description of the scope of the position.
- A listing of general duties and responsibilities.
- A listing of specific responsibilities.
- Physical and emotional requirements of the job.
- Equipment and machinery used in the position.
- Knowledge, skill, and ability requirements related to the job.
- Education, experience, and credentials required.
- Special requirements for this position such as being bilingual or having a driver's license.

The determination of the essential physical or mental requirements for the job are required to comply with the Americans with Disabilities Act. In some cases, job descriptions take the further step of distinguishing between essential and non-essential tasks associated with the job. For programs that provide services to older adults, it is important for the job description to specify knowledge and skill requirements related to the aging process.

Job descriptions cannot fully reflect all of the job tasks and responsibilities. Jobs within programs that serve older adults frequently change. Job descriptions cannot specify the methods which many people will employ to perform the jobs. While job descriptions are useful and functional for efficient and effective performance, it is important to guard against being overly rigid or too detailed (French, 1982).

The classification of a job, the analysis, and the job description provide a basis for effective recruitment and selection of staff. This is not to suggest that all organizations follow one or all of these steps before they engage in recruitment and selection. It is incumbent upon the gerontologist administrator to ensure the best qualified staff for programs serving older adults by requiring a formal and systematic process. The administrator should either directly participate in, supervise, or expect that job analysis and job descriptions will be part of the organization's policy.

Recruitment and Selection of Staff

Recruitment of qualified staff is a major activity of any organization. The existence of carefully developed job descriptions is essential for an effective recruitment and selection process. Organizations that proceed with recruitment and selection without a job description or even an abbreviated job profile will suffer the consequences. The best recruitment activities produce a sizable pool of job applicants from which to make a selection. Staff selection, guided by external legislation as well as organizational policies, is a serious and elaborate process, involving such activities as interviews, screening mechanisms, and tests. Given the time-consuming nature of these activities, it is advisable that at least some of the activities be centralized into a personnel or human resources section (Laabs, 1998; Schuler, 1981).

We have asserted in this text that diversity in age, gender, ethnic background, and race is an important component of a strong staff. Additionally, the recruitment and selection of staff must comply with Title VII of the Civil Rights Act of 1964 as amended by the Equal Opportunities Act of 1972, in eliminating discrimination on the basis of race, color, religion, sex, or national origin. Where this legislation applies, there may be reasons for rare exceptions in the areas of religion, sex, or national origin where there is a bona fide occupational requirement (French, 1982). For example, in a health center in Miami it was legitimate to advertise for a Creole-speaking geriatric physician, which would give preferential treatment to people of Haitian descent.

Most organizations are required to follow an affirmative action plan, and many other organizations choose to do so. Such plans, of course, are designed to remedy past discriminatory patterns. Organizations that have definitive plans are more likely to reach established affirmative action goals (Lewis, Lewis, & Souflée, 1991). Affirmative action plans apply to disabilities and age as well as to gender and race. Where applicable, compliance with affirmative action plans is enforced by the Department of Labor. The legality of these programs was reaffirmed by the United States Supreme Court in 1979 (French, 1982).

Recruiting

Ideally, recruitment is the process of attracting qualified staff who fit with the organization's goals and who will be compatible with existing staff. With organizations that offer programs to older adults, the gerontologist administrator will strive to find candidates with an interest in older adults and knowledge in gerontology. Aggressive recruiting which extends beyond review of current applicants and maintaining a positive community image for the organization will produce the best pool from which to select staff. A community aging council that offers multiple programs to older adults suffered from turnover in its case management department. After engaging a consultant and spending a year at organizational change which produced positive publicity, the organization's recruitment efforts became more fruitful. Instead of having vacancies in the case management department, this community council now had a battery of applicants from which to choose.

In most instances, recruitment involves both an internal and an external search for applicants. Indeed, many organizations' personnel policies require internal posting of all positions. For some organizations, an internal posting precedes any external advertising for the position, with internal candidates receiving first preference. It promotes morale, provides applicants about whom there is more information, and can serve as a reward for good performance. However, internal recruitment produces a limited pool of candidates.

Selecting applicants from the greater community can introduce new approaches and methods, expanding the collective experience of staff. Placing a lengthy ad that details the job requirements and responsibilities is an important initial step in recruitment. Detailed and lengthy ads are more effective than short ads (Gatewood et al., 1995). These ads provide greater opportunity for individuals to self-select. The position's advertisements can be placed in newspapers, including weekly newspapers, and professional publications and forwarded to university and college career centers.

The use of the Internet has become a common vehicle for recruiting qualified job applicants (Cole-Gomolski, 1998; Hansen, 1998). For example, job banks like American Job Bank, Career Resource Center, and Job Net are among those sites available on the Internet. Professional associations also offer job announcements and search opportunities on the Internet. Organizations are able to have position announcements posted and have access to lists of professionals interested in employment.

Applicants who contact the organization and meet the basic qualifications should be supplied with background on the organization and a job description, and advised of recruitment requirements, such as a police check, prior to the arranging of interviews. Applicants should have the opportunity for self-selection. When recruitment moves to the point of scheduling interviews, then the selection process has begun.

Interviewing Staff Candidates

A multitude of approaches are used for interviews. The process may vary in approach and complexity, based on the level of the staff member. Where human resources staff are available, preliminary interviews are usually conducted before scheduling interviews with administrators. For professional positions, multiple interviews with several staff are common. The interview continues the information exchange begun at recruitment and is essential for successful selection of staff. The interviewer should have at least the candidate's résumé or job application.

The best employment interviews are structured so that the same open-ended, job-related questions are asked of each applicant. For example, the candidate could be asked, "You've seen the job description. Tell me how your qualifications fit the requirements of this position." Structured, job-related questions allow for more accurate comparisons of candidates. Questions that facilitate the candidate's description of work behavior are most beneficial. For example, "Assuming you are visiting an older adult in her home, and her mental state is such that you determine she could be dangerous to herself, what steps would you take?"

To ensure equal opportunity, certain questions are to be avoided (Schuler, 1981). Table 7.2 notes some topics that should *not* be part of an employment interview. It is not simply that these questions are inappropriate and not job

Table 7.2
Topics to Avoid in the Employment Interview

- Marital status, including name of spouse
- Physical characteristics such as height and weight
- Age, even though other information would reveal this
- Children or child care arrangements
- Lifestyle outside of work responsibilities
- Political and religious affiliations and activities

related, but also, if asked, they could lead to an administrative or legal challenge of the selection process.

A useful tool that can be incorporated into the interview or as a supplement is a *training and experience form*. The form lists a series of activities relevant to the position. The applicant then indicates if she has performed or received training in each activity. The more the interview process relates to the actual position's expectations, requirements, and activities, the greater the organizational commitment of the staff person one hires.

Job Applicant Testing

Personnel testing continues to be controversial, but increasingly used to collect information about job applicants. Tests properly administered and appropriate to the position are useful tools for predicting performance (Gatewood et al., 1995; Mali, 1986; Schuler, 1981). The extent and type of testing will vary greatly, depending on the position. At a community center for older adults, which operated a paratransit bus system for older adults and the handicapped, driver applicants were tested. Two tests were used. One test measured attitudes toward people who need assistance, and the other test was a performance test related to driving ability with emphasis on safety. This latter test was an actual performance test. For most professional positions, tests are not used since the applicants have certifications and credentials that verify skills and abilities.

Job applicants should always be informed that testing will be used and should be told the extent to which the results will influence selection. A responsible selection process will use test results to validate criteria for the position in combination with the findings from the employment interview. Wherever possible, standardized tests with established reliability and validity should be used. The human resources literature provides extensive information about available tests: for example, *Handbook of Human Resources Administration* (Famularo, 1986) and *Personnel and Human Resource Management* (Schuler, 1981).

Examination and Background Review

Recruitment and selection will involve investigative activities that may extend beyond the point of employment. Over the years, these procedures have expanded from contact with personal and professional references and verification of credentials, to police and credit background checks and physical examinations, as well as clearance from professional registries. The extent of these personnel procedures has, on occasion, raised considerable question about the employer's right to examine candidates' backgrounds versus the individual right to privacy (Schuler, 1981).

Perhaps because these activities are shrouded in controversy, and background and examination practices have on occasion threatened privacy with resulting legal action, this is frequently the most neglected area of the employment process. The administrator must assure that all organizational policies are followed completely for all potential employees. Reports of such instances as the accounts receivable clerk being found to have deposited checks in a personal account are all too common. Usually, when investigated, it is discovered that references were not called, nor was a police or credit check completed. Information could have been received that would have precluded employment. Investment of time and the thoroughness of the investigative process will prevent many personnel problems, reduce turnover, and protect older adult clients.

Following is a list of activities that are frequently used in examination and background review:

- Contacting references that may include personal friends, professional references, and previous employers.
- Physical examinations to include AIDS, drugs, and tuberculosis testing.
- Police background reports, both local and statewide, and nationally when appropriate.
- College transcripts to verify degrees.
- Credential verification of licenses and certificates.
- Registry clearance, as many states maintain an abuse registry for those who work with older adults.
- Credit bureau information.

Depending on the policies of the organization and the degree to which the activity is related to the job, one or more of these activities can be undertaken. Two areas deserve further elaboration. Physical examinations will generally include tuberculosis, AIDS, and drug testing. For organizations that have a drug-free policy, the identification of drug usage would preclude employment, as would identification of active tuberculosis. Selected physical exam requirements may be completed prior to employment. However, the traditional full physical can only be given after the offer of employment, in compliance with the Americans with Disabilities Act of 1990. Findings of a physical exam will not necessarily preclude employment, unless a specific area in the job description has been designated essential to the position, and a physical exam reveals that this activity cannot be performed. That is, the activity could not be satisfactorily performed even with reasonable job modifications.

Contacting references provided by the applicant and former employers has been criticized because of the limitations imposed by fear of litigation. Nevertheless, this is an extremely important activity that should not be neglected. The probability of success for hiring is increased by checking with at least three references (Lewis et al., 1991). Information received from references is valuable itself and also to cross-validate information obtained from other sources. Contact with the former employer may be limited to verifying factual information such as dates of employment, job title, and whether the organization would re-hire the individual.

Phone conversations or personal interviews with references are equally important. Often, information is revealed without the references intending to sway the prospective employer in one direction or another. A skilled interviewer, taking time to establish rapport and using open-ended questions, can gain valuable information. During one reference check of an applicant's personal friend of 25 years, the friend provided a glowing description. A question was posed about whether this friend thought this person would have any problem in meeting deadlines. The friend, after a chuckle, stated, "Everyone knows she is never on time!" The best practice, especially for administrative and professional positions, is for the future supervisor to contact the references.

Orientation of New Staff

Once the staff person has been recruited and selected, it is essential that she experience a formal orientation to the organization and the job. Unfortunately, many organizations neglect formal orientations, thereby choosing an unstructured and uncontrolled orientation by existing staff. A formal orientation requires thoughtful planning, a systematic presentation, and a substantial time commitment. Orientation is the first training experience offered by the organization. This training experience is of critical importance because, aside from the content, it demonstrates to the new staff member the capabilities and professionalism of the organization. The importance of orientation has become recognized over the years as an essential socialization process (Holland & George, 1986; Webb, Montello, & Norton, 1994).

Orientation is a comprehensive program designed to introduce the new staff person to the complexities of the organization, the mission which includes values and goals, the policies and the scope and expectations of the position. A comprehensive orientation will include at least two components: a general organizational program covering a multitude of topics and a focused position orientation about the requirements of the job. The general orientation is best managed and coordinated by a specialized training professional, usually a member of the human resources department. The position orientation is the responsibility of the department to which the employee will be assigned.

The purpose of orientation, in addition to the sharing of information, is to cultivate attachment and commitment to the organization. According to Schuler

(1981), organizations with orientations have reduced turnover of staff. This is also the opportune time to reinforce the seriousness of the endeavors of an organization providing programs for older adults and link all the support activities of the organization to the program components. An effective orientation will communicate an expectation of accountability and responsibility. Attitudes formed during the early period of employment are most persistent and difficult to change (Holland & George, 1986). Orientations will also increase the learning ability of the new staff member in the first few weeks of employment.

Among the components composing a general orientation for organizations that serve older adults are: (1) welcoming from one or several members of the key administrative staff; (2) history and philosophy of the organization; (3) information about the older population served; (4) overview of personnel policies and staff benefits; (5) safety and emergency requirements; (6) information about cooperative agreements with other organizations, especially those in the aging network; (7) opportunities for growth and development; (8) regulatory and accreditation requirements. These programs tend to be light on organizational politics but heavy on appropriate behaviors of staff, ranging from dress codes to ethical expectations.

Most general orientation programs are presented to a group and involve a variety of delivery methods including films, didactic presentations, and question and answer periods. It is important to leave appropriate time for questions. The best time for the formal, general orientation is before the employee actually begins work. There is a tendency with many service organizations to "throw" the new staff member into the job because of the backlog of work. In service programs for older adults, there is always a backlog. Delaying orientation more than a week creates a situation where competing information provided by other staff (sometimes with a personal agenda) will lessen the impact and value of the organization's orientation (Schuler, 1981).

To be sure, organizations are typically pressed to find enough time to complete an adequate general orientation. Orientations of less than one day are not likely to be comprehensive. Some general orientations may last as long as a week or more for a large, complex organization. This is particularly true of public organizations where there are multiple levels of the organization and strong emphasis on policy and procedure. General orientations also provide an opportunity for administration to obtain feedback from new employees about training needs. This can be accomplished both formally (by administering a training needs assessment) and informally (by observation). Finally, the best orientations include an evaluation process where the new staff member is able to provide feedback as to the effectiveness of the orientation.

The second phase of orientation takes place in the new staff person's department. This is where the specific position duties and responsibilities are described by either the department administrator or members of the department. The interpersonal part of this process is for the new staff member to meet and be greeted by all other staff members in that department. In more sophisticated department orientations, the new staff member is presented at staff meetings, where a brief biographical background is given, facilitating interaction with existing staff. The most effective department orientation occurs when a staff member does not assume responsibilities of the job for several days. A practice that assists with departmental orientation is a checklist of all the contacts and activities that the new staff member will encounter during orientation (Holland & George, 1986). Another mechanism is to pair the new staff member with a mentor who can be a resource, a guide, and in some instances a trainer (Schuler, 1981; Webb et al., 1994).

Staff Compensation and Benefits

Staff compensation is the financial remuneration and the benefit package offered for employment. The extent of the benefit package has increased over the years so that in some organizations that serve older adults it is as high as 35 percent of the financial compensation. Government and not-for-profit organizations tend to offer more extensive benefit plans than profit organizations, while profit financial compensation is usually higher.

The importance of compensation is highlighted by personnel costs. In most service organizations, the compensation portion of the budget ranges from 50 to 80 percent. An organization's compensation plan is directly linked to staff recruitment, retention, satisfaction, and performance (Gatewood et al., 1995; Schuler, 1981). At the same time, the gerontologist administrator should understand that staff often hold strong interests in working with and helping older adults. Many individuals have changed careers, obtained additional education, or directed their professional education in order to contribute to the quality of life of older adults. Administrators must remain cautious to not exploit that motivation, recognizing that it is an intrinsic (as opposed to the extrinsic) form of compensation (Brody, 1993).

Pay Plan

All pay plans are affected by the statutory requirement that employees be classified as either exempt—administrative staff who receive a salary—or as non-exempt—other staff who are paid an hourly wage. The non-exempt staff must be paid for all overtime in excess of 40 hours per week. Exempt staff are rarely paid overtime. In some instances, exempt staff can take compensatory time off for overtime work, governed by organizational personnel policies (Weiner, 1990). This distinction between hourly and salaried staff influences many other aspects of the pay plan. For clarification, the term "pay" instead of salary, which is restricted to one classification of employees, is used throughout this discussion on financial compensation.

To arrive at the appropriate pay for a given position in a systematic manner, a number of resources can be employed. First, the job analysis and job description can be used to characterize the scope and level of sophistication of the position. Second, obtaining information from wage and salary surveys of organizations in the same labor market is a common practice (Gatewood et al., 1995; Schuler, 1981). Third, on a broader scale, many professional organizations publish recommended salaries for levels of education and experience. These usually can be obtained from local affiliates as well as from the national associations.

Two other factors will affect salary. The availability of a particular profession in the community will be subject to the law of supply and demand. Perhaps the most difficult aspect to deal with is the availability of financial resources for positions in the organization. Reduction of standards and qualifications for a given position because the financial resources are not available is a risky practice that will negatively impact the quality of services to older adults. The ethical implications of such a practice should be clear.

Most organizations arrive at a pay classification system that allows for pay ranges for each position (Brody, 1993; Weiner, 1990). Thus, each position has a maximum and a minimum pay. Individuals can be appointed depending on personnel policies that take into consideration experience and education along the pay range continuum. On occasion, exceptions to the pay range can be obtained by special permission from the governing body or other administrative authority.

In professional organizations, it is not uncommon to see great disparity between pay ranges for various professions. This extends to administrators. Thus, it is not uncommon to find a person in a professional position earning considerably more than the administrative supervisor. For example, a psychologist working on the geriatric unit of a large mental health hospital might have a salary twice that of the registered psychiatric nurse who administers the unit. This is both contrary to public view and to the traditional bureaucracy. Such differences are the result of market indicators, availability, and specialized abilities and skill requirements for a given position.

Pay Increases

Many organizations grant a cost-of-living adjustment (COLA) annually. The cost of living is frequently tied to the inflation rate. For some organizations, COLA is guaranteed as a result of contract or union negotiations. COLA is meant to equalize pay with the economy. Across-the-board raises independent of performance are commonly practiced in organizations that serve older adults. A percentage increase is determined based on existing and predicted financial resources. Merit raises are linked to performance and usually influenced by both the formal performance evaluation and job accomplishments. Individual merit raise recommendations are typically made by supervisors to higher levels of administration for final decision. On some occasions, merit raises are awarded to groups within an organization based upon group performance.

Incentive pay increases are commonly used in profit organizations and less frequently used in public and not-for-profit organizations. Two types of incentive programs are bonuses and performance objectives. A bonus is awarded either to an individual or to everyone in a particular job classification for exemplary work. A bonus can be awarded to a team or group in an organization. Bonuses have the advantage of not automatically becoming part of the base pay for the following years. Performance objectives refer to pay increases based on the level of actual achievement of a predetermined goal for productivity while maintaining quality service. For example, if a geriatric physician exceeded the expected number of patient treatments for a given pay period, she would receive a predetermined additional percentage of salary for that pay period.

There are numerous problems with incentive pay (Brody, 1993). Bonuses may become expected after several years, and in a given year, when not awarded, this creates a morale problem. Individuals who are not directly eligible for a bonus or incentive pay may experience jealousy and resentment, especially if their efforts contribute to the extra pay for someone else. Incentives based on productivity by numbers could negatively affect quality of service. Finally, incentive programs are time-consuming and laborious and create a lot of extra paperwork and documentation.

Fringe Benefits

Benefits vary greatly among organizations that provide programs for older adults. Public programs compared to not-for-profit and profit typically have provided a more comprehensive and substantive benefit package. Benefits have become a major factor in recruitment of staff. Certain parts of the benefit program required by the federal government are known as mandatory programs. In addition, organizations offer many optional benefits which, while not mandated by law, contribute to the organization's competitiveness in the labor market. Paramount among benefits is the organization's retirement plan. Retirement plans have become more complex and participatory over the years.

Mandatory benefits include social security, Medicare, and old age survivor's and disability benefits which require contributions from both the employer and the staff member. Unemployment compensation and workmen's compensation are paid for by the employer. The federal government has also enacted legislation (see Table 7.1) that allows for the right to take time off at the birth or adoption of a child, and for family leave that relates to personal illness or care of another member of the family.

The number of optional benefits has grown considerably over the years, along with the growth of service organizations. It would be too lengthy to list all the possible optional benefits, but the primary benefits, those that especially relate to organizations that have programs for older adults, are as follows:

• Paid holidays: These holidays range from six to eleven days per year, often depending on the region of the country.
• Paid vacation: Vacation often depends on the length of employee service and sometimes on the position held. Executives often receive more vacation time.

- Personal leave: This includes leave for illness or death in the family as well as often including leave days known as personal time.
- Group insurance: This can include major medical insurance, dental insurance, income protection, and life insurance coverage.
- Education: This is payment for attendance at workshops and conferences, and reimbursement for college education.
- Day care: Care for children may include the operation of a day care center for staff at a reduced fee, or contributions to assist with payment for day care.
- Employee assistance programs (EAP): These are mental health services to assist employees with emotional and addictive problems that interfere with the job.

Traditionally, employers set aside a percentage of money related to pay for the staff member's retirement plan. This is now rare. Most pension programs are constructed so that employers and staff members share the cost (Schulz, 1995). Under the *defined benefit plans*, payments are made according to a preset formula that involves the length of service and the amount of income. In this plan, the staff member's responsibility is primarily to remain knowledgeable of the benefits related to the plan. More common are the *defined contribution plans*, where the employer and the staff member make contributions to an investment fund. Pension benefits are then related to the value and progress of the investments. In these programs, the staff member has more control and, in many instances, can select the kinds of investments from a list associated with the plan. Further, organizations may offer a private pension plan in which they make no investment but the staff member will choose to participate partly because income taxes will be reduced for contributions.

In recent years, a trend among organizations, recognizing that many staff members may not necessarily want or desire all of the optional benefits, has been to offer a menu of benefits from which to choose. This has become known as a cafeteria plan. Organizations may limit the number of benefits based on cost, and, of course, adjustments in pay may apply. Choice can be made to suit one's family situation. For example, a staff member may choose not to have health insurance, which is frequently copaid by the employer and the staff member, because she is covered by insurance held by her spouse. Instead, she chooses the day care coverage for her two young children. Additionally, because of the Revenue Act of 1998, selection of a cafeteria plan will serve to reduce income taxes.

HUMAN RESOURCES DEVELOPMENT

Much of the growth in human resources functions has occurred in the development area. These are programs and practices focused on existing employees and the work environment that will be mutually beneficial for the individual and the organization. A major area is systematic, fair solutions to staff problems and problem staff. Two primary functions related to problem-solving are staff discipline and grievance. The disciplinary procedures should be detailed in a personnel policy and are usually conducted by the immediate supervisor. Elaboration on disciplinary methods and dismissal will be offered in Chapter 9. Grievance procedures will not be discussed other than to state that every organization needs a formal grievance policy and procedure which can be used if informal mechanisms fail to produce a resolution.

Performance appraisals, when conducted adequately, will contribute to the development of staff. Unfortunately, all too often performance appraisals are seen as simply a tool for determining merit pay increase. Since performance appraisals are most effectively conducted by the immediate supervisor, a full discussion will appear in Chapter 9. The focus of human resources development in this section will be promotion and transfer, career development, selected aspects of training and education, and the quality of work life.

Promotion and Transfer

Many staff in organizations that provide programs for older adults are hoping to be promoted into positions of greater responsibility with increased remuneration. A first step in offering promotion opportunities is the advertising of job openings within the organization. Ideally, a promotion indicates that a staff person will be more valuable to the organization in the new position than she is in the present position (French, 1982). In some instances, staff development is realized by hiring someone at a basic level with the understanding that when she achieves certain credentials she will be promoted. For example, in a large urban community in the northeast, an older adult program hired a Hispanic woman so she could serve as an interpreter for case workers who did not speak Spanish. It was understood at the hiring that this person was already enrolled in a master's program in gerontology and, upon achievement of that degree, she would be promoted to a casework position.

Two positive reasons for transferring a staff member are to place a person in a position more consistent with her skills and knowledge and to institute a new program. Transfers also have a strong retention component as this often offers the opportunity to place a staff member in an area of greater interest. In some instances, a staff member may be dysfunctional in one position and effective in another. It is not good practice to transfer someone who is on probation, as this transfers a problem from one department to another. Should this occur, it is important that ample attention be paid to make certain that the transfer is in the interests of the organization (French, 1982). In general, the administrator should make efforts to solve the problem, following disciplinary and corrective procedures, before considering a transfer. Many organizations require that any transfer be accompanied by another probation period.

Career Development

Career development opportunities are most beneficial to the individual and to the organization. For the individual, there could be professional growth, a greater feeling of personal worth, and eventually promotion. This is likely to produce a greater commitment to the organization and the older adults served, increase productivity, contribute to stability, and foster a positive image in the community. Career opportunities are a major factor in recruitment (Schuler, 1981).

Career development is achieved by career planning, which involves formal and informal activities that help the staff member develop career goals (Weiner, 1990). The career plan can be achieved by supporting formal training and higher education. Many organizations reimburse staff members for college courses relevant to their careers. Further, the organization can promote career development by providing a career ladder: that is, a personnel classification system that offers opportunities for employees to advance from lower positions to higher positions with increased responsibility and authority. It is incumbent upon the gerontologist administrator to identify those individuals with potential talent and assist them in their career development.

Training and Education

Staff development begins with an orientation program, previously described in this chapter. In-service training conducted by or contracted by the organization serves to inform, improve skills and abilities, and socialize staff to the organization's values. Changes in the job tasks and changes in the organization also require training. Informational training usually involves new policies and procedures. Knowledge and skill training may include basic requirements for the position, or enhancement.

Organizations that provide programs for older adults frequently, out of necessity, hire professional staff with limited knowledge and experience in aging. One means of overcoming that deficit is to offer mandatory in-service training on the aging process and aging issues. This is what the Philadelphia Corporation for Aging (AAA) has decided to do for all of its professional employees. All managers and individuals entering a professional position that involves contact with older adults or programs that serve older adults must attend a six-week orientation program that includes training in gerontology and geriatrics. The program topics vary from normal aging to physical and neurological disorders. This program is conducted by the Planning Department in cooperation with a professional with background in gerontology, health, and social work (Brown, personal communication, 1999; Polak, 1999).

Training programs are most effective when addressing staff needs. There are a number of methods for conducting a needs assessment of training. To mention a few, assessment can be done at staff meetings, by listing areas of needs and prioritizing. Also, a needs survey can be conducted at the end of new employees' orientation. Administrators in supervisory roles can frequently identify training needs.

This identification of needs is the first step in a simple but useful model for in-service training. The second step is to develop and present the training program, and the third is to evaluate, to determine the impact of the training experience. Following this model, using all components, will help ensure the success of training programs.

Education external to the organization to increase the skill and ability of staff is an essential component of human resources development. The education can range from technical computer software courses at vocational schools to support of staff working on advanced degrees. The most common method is to reimburse the staff member for tuition and books. Such reimbursement is often dependent upon the criterion of successful completion of course work. These expenditures should be anticipated and budgeted.

Of course, there is often a concern that staff, once educated, will seek other employment. While this is a valid concern, it should not be a reason to curtail such opportunities. The benefits of such programs, such as recruiting talented staff and contributing to the overall professional growth and development of those serving older adults, far exceeds an individual's decision to remain or to seek employment elsewhere. An organization can require a period of continued employment through an agreement with the staff member following completion of educational degrees. Usually, this involves a monetary payback if the employee voluntarily terminates her position prior to the set period.

Quality of Work Life

Policies and procedures that contribute to a positive work environment cover a broad spectrum. The quality of work life is composed of social and professional interactions and policies that relate to the value of staff. Organizational improvement efforts that involve training, restructuring, and consultation will be discussed in the final chapter on organizational change and improvements. Efforts to establish and maintain a positive work environment contribute to staff motivation, and will be discussed in Chapter 8. Three human resources functions have been selected for discussion: flexible work opportunities, recognition and reward, and employee assistance programs.

Flexible Work Opportunities

These practices have become popular because they decrease absenteeism, increase morale, decrease stress, and increase productivity (McNeely, 1988; Schuler, 1981). Flex time is a policy that offers the staff some choice of work hours. The choice is governed by a combination of core time a staff member must work and flex time. Often flex time also serves to further accommodate the needs of older adults and their families.

Table 7.3
Three Forms of Job Sharing

1. **Divided Duties.** Two staff share the duties, hours, and compensation with each receiving related benefits. Each is accountable for her portion of the job.

2. **Job Pairing.** Two equally qualified part-time staff share a single job; each is accountable for the entire job.

3. **Job Splitting.** Two part-time staff with different qualifications perform the functions of a single job. Qualifications and skills are matched to the relevant aspect of the job.

Source: Adapted from Frease & Zawacki (1979).

Part-time work and job sharing offer additional opportunities for staff. Eberhardt and Shani (1984) analyzed information from part-time and full-time employees of a rehabilitation hospital. Part-time employees report higher job satisfaction and hold more favorable attitudes toward the organization. Three types of job sharing are summarized in Table 7.3. Flexible work schedules are especially appropriate for organizations that offer programs for older adults. These programs often have a high percentage of female staff, some of whom seek to balance child-rearing or caretaking responsibilities with a career (McNeely, 1988). These policies also offer opportunities for phase retirement, for older workers.

Recognition and Reward

Many types of recognition and rewards are normative or part of an administrator's style rather than policy. Administrators who praise staff for accomplishments will motivate the individual and contribute positively to the overall environment (Blanchard & Johnson, 1982; Lewis, 1997). Informal social recognition, given verbally, by note, e-mail, or group acknowledgment, contributes to the work environment. More formal programs include staff person of the month, gift certificates for accomplishments, and bonuses. The most desired reward for staff in administrative or professional positions is time off from work (French, 1982). Increased vacation time attached to longevity of service is universally accepted as a form of reward and recognition for those in administrative positions.

Employee Assistance Programs (EAP)

To improve both the quality of the work environment and an individual's satisfaction with her activities, specialized programs that assist with employee problems have become commonplace. Employee assistance programs usually provide 24-hour access to professional counselors who can assist with emotional and behavioral problems (Weiner, 1990). Usually, these programs are the result of a contract with an organization or a number of individuals to provide a variety of mental health services. These services often are available to family members as well. EAP services are generally short term but can be extended through the organization's insurance coverage.

SUMMARY

The day-to-day level of involvement in human resources functions is substantial for the gerontologist administrator, especially for those administrators who head departments or are supervisors. These human resources functions are perhaps the single most important cluster of activities in administering an organization. The importance of the functions cannot be emphasized enough. Consultants can be used to assist with many of the functions, including policy compliance with government regulations and normative personnel practices (Musick, 1997). The legal requirements have become extensive, and dominate human resources practices in terms of amount of time and concerns about legal compliance.

Human resources functions have also expanded over the years from traditional personnel, known as human resources administration, to human resources development. The latter seeks to retain and reward staff. Staff protection from discrimination and security of position are governed by laws that support affirmative action, policies against sexual harassment, and family and medical leave.

Job classification and analysis lead to position descriptions which are tools that will affect recruitment and other human resources activities. Systematic, well-organized recruitment in the selection process is necessary to obtain the best qualified staff by amassing a pool of qualified candidates. Candidates should be interviewed, screened and, if appropriate, tested to narrow the pool. Employee interviews must adhere to certain rules to ensure fairness. The best guide is to pose questions directly related to the position's tasks and requirements. The recruitment and selection process should be an open exchange of information that fosters an informed choice by both parties.

The use of examinations and background checks should be viewed as an essential and serious effort to hire the most qualified staff. The conflict of individual rights to privacy in relation to the organization's responsibility to protect the older adult is guided by legal precedent, organizational policy, and ethical adherence to the principle of gathering job-related information (French, 1982; Schuler, 1981). Additionally, the practice of full disclosure to all job applicants of the extent of the job applicant procedure and background examinations is essential.

Among the most lasting impressions on new staff is how the organization conducts orientation. A two-part orientation that includes a general orientation to the organization as a whole and a job-specific orientation composes a comprehensive program. The use of a checklist and an assigned resource person will enhance the department-level orientation.

Staff compensation for service organizations usually includes a comprehensive benefit package. These benefits may be expanded for those in administrative positions. Personnel costs dominate the budgets of service organizations. Thus, considerable attention is required to ensure a fair and reasonable pay plan that provides a rational process for pay increases. The trend in benefit packages is to offer staff choices in the selection of benefits, including retirement programs.

Human resources development seeks to improve the performance, morale, and job satisfaction of staff. This can be accomplished, in part, by offering educational opportunities along with career development, which could lead to promotion or transfer. Staffs are also affected by the organizational opportunities. Organizations that offer flexible work opportunities will reap the advantages of both effectiveness and efficiency. A work environment that is characterized by recognition, rewards, and available resources to solve personal problems will have the same impact.

Human resources functions have become more sophisticated and complicated and continue to expand, while retaining the basic function of providing qualified staff. While the administrative aspects have become more legally mandated, the expressive developmental aspects have continued to expand. Human resources functions, especially the developmental aspects, require the gerontologist administrator to be versatile and exercise leadership abilities (Laabs, 1998).

LEARNING EXPERIENCE

The Philadelphia Corporation for Aging (PCA) is the AAA for Philadelphia. The PCA operates in relationship with the Philadelphia Department of Aging and is the largest organization of this type in the state of Pennsylvania. This organization has over 400 employees. This organization, like its sister organizations, does not operate any direct service programs. It contracts with community agencies for older adult programs. The staff work to establish, improve, and evaluate these programs. This organization has a Human Resources Department with a professional director and four employees. The Human Resources Department performs many human resources functions independently, and others in cooperation with various administrative staff throughout the organization. The Human Resources Department (HR) has developed a systematic employment process as follows:

Employment Process

1. Approval for hire
   - Job requisition needs to be approved by senior management
   - Need job description/job grading if newly created position
   - See salary administration manual for procedures on job description and job grading
   - For hiring of temporary contract employees, volunteers, etc., see guidelines for using other than probationary/regular employees

2. Internal job bidding
   - New job posted and distributed to all employees:
     —open for five work days
     —exceptions for persons out for legitimate reasons
3. Ads placed in newspapers and other sources:
   - If job not filled internally:
     —ads are requested and reviewed by department heads/managers
     —ads must be received by HR by Wednesday to be placed in next week's local newspapers
4. Affirmative Action mailings of open jobs
   - Once/monthly—to PCA subcontractors and agencies dealing with elderly, minority, and handicapped hiring
5. Résumés received by HR
   - Screened résumé(s) sent to department heads for approval/rejection for interviews
   - Approved applicants called in for interviews by departments
   - Applicants must first report to HR—allow one hour
   - HR will set up interviews upon request
6. HR interview—allow 1 hour
   - Applicant completes PCA Employment Application and EEO data record form
   - Applicant interviewed by HR—allow one hour
   - If applicant is acceptable, sent to department for interview
   - Application and résumé given to department
   - Multiple interview(s) recommended for professional positions
7. Department interview(s)
   - Department interviewer(s) conduct interviews—avoid use of "illegal" questions
   - Department interviewer(s) complete Interview Analysis form—maintained by interviewers unless want to hire
   - If department does not want to hire, department returns application and résumé to HR
   - If department wishes to hire applicant, further interviews may be needed
   - Department will set up interviews—attach Interviewing and Hiring Flow sheet to applicant information
   - If department wants to hire, department will conduct phone/verbal reference checks, as required. HR will do upon request
   - If reference checks are positive, departments need to submit a Personnel Action Request (PAR) form with all documents approved by management: Application, Resume, Interview Analysis, phone references
   - Upon receipt of approved PAR, HR will notify department to formally offer position to applicant

- Offer letter signed by president sent to accepted applicant with any special conditions set by department

8. Rejection letter

- Sent to rejected applicant(s) after position has been filled

9. After hire, HR will require:

- Immigration Work Form I-9
- Physical and drug testing
- Submittal of college degree transcripts/licenses needed, etc.
- Written confirmation of applicant's prior employment
  —title of job
  —length of employment/salary
  —previous employer will rehire or not

Source: Polak (1999).

Questions for Discussion:

1. How does PCA's employment process compare with the discussion of recruitment and selection of staff in the chapter?
2. What specific screening mechanisms are used by PCA with new employees?
3. How are internal applicants for open positions handled?
4. Based on the readings in this chapter, what aspects of the employment procedure would you handle differently from the PCA process?
5. Considering the PCA procedures, how would you characterize the role of the gerontologist administrator who is a department head, in hiring?

REFERENCES

Blanchard, K., & Johnson, S. (1982). *The one minute manager.* New York: William Morrow.

Brody, R. (1993). *Effectively managing human service organizations.* Newbury Park, CA: Sage.

Caudron, S., & Laabs, J. J. (1997). It's taken 75 years to say . . . here's to you! *Workforce, 76,* 70–82.

Cole-Gomolski, B. (1998). HR pros take steps to keep up on issues. *Computerworld, 32*(27), 35.

Eberhardt, B. J., & Shani, A. B. (1984). The effects of full-time versus part-time employment status on attitudes toward specific organizational characteristics and overall job satisfaction. *Academy of Management Journal, 27*(4), 893–900.

Famularo, J. J. (Ed.). (1986). *Handbook of human resources administration* (2nd ed.). New York: McGraw-Hill.

Fitz-enz, J. (1990). *Human value management: The value-adding human resource management strategy for the 1990s.* San Francisco: Jossey-Bass.

Frease, M., & Zawacki, R. (1979). Job-sharing: An answer to productivity problems? *The Personnel Administrator, 24*(10), 35–38, 56.

French, W. L. (1982). *The personnel management process: Human resources administration and development*. Boston: Houghton Mifflin.

Gatewood, R. D., Taylor, R. R., & Ferrell, O. C. (1995). *Management: Comprehension, analysis, and application*. Chicago: Austen.

Goldberg, A. C. (1997). Top 8 legal issues affecting HR. *HR Focus, 74*(12), 1–4.

Hansen, K. A. (1998). Cybercruiting changes HR. *HR Focus, 7*(9), 13–15.

Holland, J. E., & George, B. W. (1986). Orientation of new employees. In J. J. Famularo (Ed.), *Handbook of human resources administration* (2nd ed., pp. 24-1–24-35). New York: McGraw-Hill.

Laabs, J. J. (1998). Targeted rewards jump-start motivation. *Workforce, 77*(2), 88–94.

Lavelle, M. (1998, July). The new rules of sexual harassment: The Supreme Court defines what harassment is and who can be held responsible. *U. S. News & World Report*, pp. 30–31.

Lewis, B. (1997). Praising the right people at the right time and place can be a powerful tool. *InfoWorld, 19*(42), 116–117.

Lewis, J. A., Lewis, M. D., & Souflée, F. (1991). *Management of human service programs* (2nd ed.). Pacific Grove, CA: Brooks/Cole.

Mali, P. (1986). Testing and the employment procedure. In J. J. Famularo (Ed.), *Handbook of human resources administration* (pp. 15-1–15-20). New York: McGraw-Hill.

Maurer, R. (1997). Transforming resistance. *HR Focus, 74*(10), 9–11.

McNeely, R. L. (1988). Five morale enhancing innovations for human services settings. *Social Casework, 69*(4), 204–213.

Musick, J. L. (1997). A helping hand on personnel. *Nation's Business, 85*(8), 38–41.

Nobile, R. J. (1997). HR's top 10 legal issues. *HR Focus, 74*(4), 19–21.

Polak, R. J. (1999, March). *How to hire good employees—how to fire bad ones*. Workshop conducted at the American Society of Aging Annual Meeting, Orlando, FL.

Schuler, R. S. (1981). *Personnel and human resource management*. St. Paul, MN: West.

Schulz, J. H. (1995). *The economics of aging* (6th ed.). Westport, CT: Auburn House.

Ulrich, D. (1998). A new mandate for human resources. *Harvard Business Review, 76*(1), 124–135.

Webb, L. D., Montello, P. A., & Norton, M. S. (1994). *Human resources administration: Personnel issues and needs in education* (2nd ed.). New York: Macmillan.

Weiner, M. E. (1990). *Human services management: Analysis and applications* (2nd ed.). Belmont, CA: Wadsworth.

Chapter 8

Motivation and Productivity

Among the most important challenges for the gerontologist administrator is motivation of oneself and others to maintain and increase productivity. In a study reported by Champagne and McAfee (1989), only one-fourth of the workers indicated that they worked at full capacity. Motivation as an aspect of human behavior has received extensive attention in the literature and popular media. To motivate others, the gerontologist administrator needs to call upon relationship and leadership skills. Motivation requires introspection and self-discipline. This chapter presents concepts and techniques that relate to motivation as it pertains primarily to productivity in an organization.

Productivity means one's effectiveness and efficiency in performing the requisite tasks of a position. Productivity concerns are paramount for administrators and are directly and indirectly related to administrative behavior (Champagne & McAfee, 1989). The supervisor who becomes isolated from staff affects motivation. An all-too-common expression by staff is, "Haven't seen him in two weeks." Conversely, a supervisor could become overly involved and inhibit growth. Administrative characteristics that have been found to contribute to motivation and productivity are empathy, supportiveness, accessibility, fairness, and openness (Gatewood, Taylor, & Ferrell, 1995).

Productivity is a function of staff motivation and abilities. Relevant education, experience requirements of staff, and continuing education contribute to abilities. However, abilities without motivation will not result in good productivity; it requires both; and a highly motivated staff person who lacks the skills and abilities for the position is not likely to be productive.

Motivation, a complex process requiring cognitive decisions and selections of behavior, is affected by many variables. Personal circumstance, such as other interests and obligations, could mean that a person would be motivated by the

Table 8.1
Motivation by Identification and Satisfaction of Needs

Maslow's Hierarchy	Herzberg's Hygiene	McClelland's Achievement
• Self-actualization	• Achievement	• Achievement
• Esteem and status	• Recognition	• Affiliation
• Social (relationship)	• Work itself	• Power
• Security and safety	• Respect	
• Physiological (basic)	• Advancement	
	• Personal growth	

Sources: Based on information from Campbell & Pritchard (1976); Herzberg (1986); Maslow (1986); McClelland (1986).

possibility of extra time off from work. Motivational needs may change over time, depending on where a person is in the life cycle. Personality variations and personal interests, of course, must also be taken into consideration. Another concern is the alignment of the staff member's personal goals with organizational goals. Motivation is also affected by the extent to which one is able to derive meaningfulness from the assigned job (Umiker, 1988). It is unlikely that there is any one particular motivational technique that will be applicable to all staff. The gerontologist administrator must be well versed in time-tested theories of motivation, the impact of the work environment, as well as a variety of motivational methods.

MOTIVATIONAL THEORY

Numerous studies have provided a rich literature on motivational theory. Much of this information pertains to job performance and ways to increase productivity. Motivational theory is divided into two categories: content theory and process theory (Campbell & Pritchard, 1976). Content theory has sought to identify learned and inherited needs that will influence behavior. Process theory focuses on behavior that leads to choice, degree of effort, and persistence. Campbell and Pritchard (1976) suggest that these two categories of theory are complementary rather than contradictory. Process theory identifies what motivates people, and content theory describes how people are motivated.

Process Theories of Motivation

Three major theorists are identified with the human needs that impact motivation. Each of these theorists, Abraham Maslow, Frederick Herzberg, and David McClelland, have formulated a list of needs that are summarized in Table 8.1. Maslow's (1986) well-known hierarchy of needs establishes a particular order in which needs are satisfied. If the most basic needs, those appearing at the bottom of the list, are not met, appeals to higher-level needs will not be motivating. The sequential nature of this list has been seriously questioned. People may experience a number of needs simultaneously (Gatewood et al., 1995).

Herzberg's view of motivation is called the "two factor theory." He identified factors that motivated individuals in the work environment listed in Table 8.1. Herzberg (1986) also described maintenance factors that do not necessarily motivate but, if absent, will be a source of dissatisfaction. The maintenance factors are company policy, supervision, relationship with supervisor, working conditions, relationships with co-workers, salary, status, and security. In Herzberg's (1986) words, "The very nature of motivators, as opposed to hygiene factors, is that they have a much longer-term effect on employees' attitudes. Perhaps the job will have to be enriched again, but this will not occur as frequently as the need for hygiene" (p. 296).

McClelland (1986) identified three basic needs: achievement, affiliation, and power. Closely associated with these needs were certain mechanisms, such as personal goal setting, availability of role models, the seeking of satisfying work relationships, the opportunity to be a mentor, and the opportunity to have control over other individuals. McClelland also placed emphasis on the organizational environment, which will be discussed later in this chapter.

Content Theories of Motivation

Content theories are concerned with how employees are motivated. Perhaps the best known theory is learning theory, which incorporates the principles of behavior modification. The focus of behaviorism is observable behavior rather than feelings or thoughts (Nye, 1992). Behavior can be changed, according to this theory, using rewards and punishments. More specifically, behavior that is rewarded will tend to be repeated, while behavior that results in removal of rewards or is punished will tend to dissipate.

Expectancy theory states that a person is motivated when he perceives efforts will lead to high performance and a valued outcome. This is the activity that occurs when a staff member, perhaps in cooperation with an administrator, selects realistic and achievable goals. Nadler and Lawler's (1977) presentation of expectancy theory states that job satisfaction is the result of expected performance, the value of the task, and the probability of success. Performance leads to two different types of rewards: internal and external. Internal or intrinsic rewards occur while performing job-related tasks that are considered successful. Extrinsic rewards, which are more tangible, relate to recognition for capable job performance. If these rewards are perceived with satisfactory recognition, they will motivate future performance. An administrator making a passing comment about a job well done for a project that involves several months of work including overtime may not be perceived as a significant reward and, therefore, would not motivate the employee.

It should be recognized that there is considerable consistency among these theories. Administrators can draw upon these concepts and incorporate them into behavior directed to the individual and the environment. The remainder of this chapter will focus first on environmental conditions that foster motivation for higher performance, and on a number of approaches to motivating staff members that are derived from the theories discussed.

A MOTIVATING WORK ENVIRONMENT

The work environment powerfully affects motivation and productivity. Stemming from the classic Hawthorne experiments, most motivators relate to social and psychological factors rather than physical factors (Ginsberg & Keys, 1995). Over the years, the factors have expanded, becoming more substantive, to include staff empowerment, participatory management, morale, and job characteristics.

Empowerment is a process by which staff gain mastery and control over the environment (Shera & Page, 1995). Participatory management, discussed throughout this text, relates to shared planning, problem-solving, and selective decision-making by staff and administration. The all-encompassing concept of staff morale is a composite of employee attitudes about their jobs and the organization. High morale is consistently linked to motivation and productivity. Job characteristics that are linked to greater productivity are opportunities for career development, positive professional relationships, and job variety. Generally, the environment is thought to be motivating for staff who feel a sense of involvement, commitment, and importance. The writings and research of a number of students of motivation have identified some specific organizational features that contribute to a motivating work environment (Crosby, 1986; Emmerich, 1998; Shera & Page, 1995; Sonnenberg, 1994; Zimmerman, 1990):

- Opportunities for professional development
- A flexible benefit package
- Availability of job variety and flexibility
- Use of teams
- Sense of hopefulness
- Meaningful recognition and rewards
- Availability of computer technology

Achieving a motivating and productive environment relies heavily on the leadership skills of the administrator. The willingness of the administrator to foster involvement and commitment will impact job satisfaction and motivation (Orpen, 1997; Wiley, 1992). There are many barriers and pitfalls in implementing some of the features discussed. For example, participatory staff involvement and the use of teams for problem-solving can be interpreted as a loss of power by middle managers (Shera & Page, 1995). Greater involvement of staff also requires additional responsibility that some staff are reluctant to accept.

Involvement can also be misinterpreted when there is not a clear distinction between whether the involvement is directed toward influencing or recommending a course of action, or making a decision (Crosby, 1986). In a large, profit home health agency, a staff committee was formed to make recommendations about a merit pay system. After the task force met for several months, it provided three recommendations to administration. The administration selected a method different from any of the three, which negatively impacted staff morale. In some instances where computer technology has been implemented, rather than being motivating, it produced resignations and low productivity. It was found that this occurs particularly when staff have not been involved in the decision-making and have not received the proper training for the technology (Gandy & Tepperman, 1990).

Competition is often encouraged to achieve motivation. Administrators must also guard against excessive competition within the organization. Such competition in the services environment fosters unethical behavior and stereotyping and seriously disrupts effective communication (Weinbach, 1998).

MOTIVATIONAL METHODS

In addition to environmental characteristics, direct methods employed by administrators will motivate staff. Debate exists about whether a person can be motivated by someone else. Those who hold this position maintain that an administrator can merely facilitate motivation. We take the position that gerontologist administrators at all levels can achieve motivation and increase productivity in three ways: first, by practicing behaviors such as goal setting, thus demonstrating the utility of this method and modeling desired behavior; second, by contributing to the features that produce a motivating environment, thereby setting the conditions for motivation and productivity; third, by employing specific methods to motivate staff. This third way, admittedly, is highly dependent on staff personality, stage of the life cycle, and nature of the supervisory relationship. It is difficult, perhaps impossible, for an administrator to motivate a staff member if there is a troubled relationship (Crow & Odewahn, 1987; Gatewood et al., 1995).

Expectancy theory supports the power of satisfying relationships. Relationships with the supervisor and others in the organization improve when the individual perceives performance as enhancing desired relationships (Lewis, Lewis, & Souflée, 1991; Locke, 1975). In a study of six human services programs, two of which served older adults, that were engaged in empowerment activities, the researchers found that the influence of the social service administrator was a key factor (Gutiérrez, Glen Maye, & DeLois, 1995).

The central importance of the work relationship to successful use of motivational method is depicted in Figure 8.1, along with three methods that will

Figure 8.1
Model of Motivation for Productivity of Staff

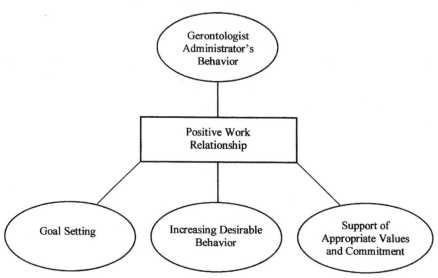

be discussed further. It cannot be denied that motivation may occur when there is a poor interpersonal relationship. Such motivation usually is a result of fear of sanctions or punishment. While this may motivate behavior of staff, it is certainly not recommended, and is considered by some to be irresponsible (Appelbaum, 1975).

Little attention will be given to salary or pay in relation to motivation. It is useful to remember that Herzberg's theory noted that, while pay is related to job satisfaction (considered a hygiene factor), it is not among the top considerations for motivation. Rantz, Scott, and Porter (1996) examine staff motivation in health care, academic, and other private business sectors using Herzberg's theme. Ranking of the group studied, like Herzberg's research, revealed that salary continues to fall in the low end of the scale. Wallsten (1998) reports on a survey conducted by an outplacement firm where money as an incentive was listed as sixteenth. Money, it appears, has varying relevance and, while motivating at times, seems to have no consistent pattern with staff. Indeed, in programs where financial incentives are used with highly skilled workers like physicians, it negatively affects the performance and productivity of the less skilled workers who are not included in the incentive program (Kennedy, 1995).

A vast array of motivational methods are available for self-motivation and to motivate others. From these, we have selected several that take into consideration the nature of the staff that provide programs for older adults and are supported in the literature. The three methods are goal setting, increasing desirable behavior, and enhancing values and commitment.

Table 8.2
Criteria for a Measurable Goal

S Specific—identify the expected outcome

M Measurable—quantify the outcome

A Attainable—likelihood of reaching the goal

R Realistic—assess resources and capabilities

T Time limited—set deadlines

Goal Setting

Goals are so closely associated with motivation that motivation is often defined as goal-directed behavior (Dale, 1978; Latham & Lock, 1991; Longest, 1976). The link between individual and organizational goals and productivity is firmly established. Behavior and resources focused by goals have a positive effect on commitment and attitudes (Lewis et al., 1991). Before continuing a discussion of goals as motivators, two misunderstandings will be addressed.

Goals are often associated with an elaborate process known as management by objectives (MBO). This highly misunderstood process is an elaborate organizational planning model that has proven controversial because of its time-consuming procedures (Albrecht, 1978). Individual goal setting, on the other hand, is a simple, straightforward process that is not excessively time-consuming and relates primarily to personal and professional goals. Also, goals are global notions of a desired outcome but not necessarily action oriented. Most discussions of goals as related to individual motivation speak to "measurable goals," meaning objectives, that is, goals stated in behavioral terms (Blanchard & Lorber, 1985). In our discussion, we will use the term "measurable goals."

Some students of motivation present goal setting as a theory in itself. In actuality, goals represent operationalization of content and process theories of motivation. Measurable goal setting relates directly to gaining satisfaction from the job itself, to personal and professional growth, and to achievement. Measurable, realistically constructed goals that offer a challenge are consistent with expectancy theory. Measurable goals are for solving problems and new opportunities, not for routine work assignments (Albrecht, 1978; Blanchard & Johnson, 1982).

A prescription for successful measurable goal setting is composed of a number of elements: (1) goals must be written, preferably on a single sheet of paper (the same for word processors); (2) for the workplace, goals should be mutually agreed upon, resulting from an interaction with the supervisor; (3) clear, action-oriented goals should meet the SMART criteria (see Table 8.2); (4) a challenging goal will produce high performance as people adjust levels of effort to the difficulty of the task (Latham & Locke, 1991); (5) a goal must be important to the individual, as attachment and commitment are essential to overcoming barriers (Latham & Locke, 1991).

A sense of achievement from measurable goals is facilitated by receiving specific and useful feedback. When a measurable goal is written in behavioral terms, feedback can be automatic, such as when a goal is accomplished by a predetermined date. Likewise, a behaviorally constructed measurable goal allows for feedback from administrators based on observation (Blanchard & Lorber, 1985). Goals, by their nature, are future oriented. Thus, individuals who have been socialized or can learn to hold a future time perspective are more likely to be successful at setting and achieving measurable goals (Seijts, 1998). One can also contribute to the likelihood of achieving goals when the tasks related to these goals are incorporated into the time management practice of a "things to do" list, as discussed in Chapter 3. Lastly, measurable goals for the individual are more likely to be supported, and therefore attained, when the goals are integrated with the organizational goals of the department and the organization.

Increasing Desirable Behavior

Learning theory translated into activity is known as behavior modification. Behavior modification focuses on concrete behavior and states that the consequences of behavior can be motivators. Techniques to increase desired behavior will strengthen the likelihood that the desired behavior will be repeated (Lewis et al., 1991; Nye, 1992) or result in higher levels of effort (Robbins, 1995).

Three dimensions of behavior modification will be discussed. Positive reinforcement occurs when the desired behavior is followed by a reward. Negative reinforcement occurs when the consequences of an undesired behavior will result in weakening or eliminating the undesirable behavior and increasing desired behavior. This is not to be confused with punishment, which is another behavioral technique. Punishment is considered less effective because it results in only a temporary suppression of behavior (Nye, 1992; Skidmore, 1995). Extinction weakens undesirable behavior by not providing positive consequences. These behavioral concepts do not have exactly the same meaning as similar, commonly used terms, and are subject to misunderstanding. This is particularly the case in using behavioral techniques in the workplace, intertwined with other motivators and stimulators of behavior. When motivating employees by using behavioral techniques, it is most effective to follow an established prescription or model.

The list of rewards for and reinforcers of behavior is endless. The most powerful reinforcers are those perceived as valuable by the individual, which are often interpersonal. Among the rewards used by organizations are small gifts; gift certificates; extra educational opportunities; special lunches, perhaps with the boss; exceptions from a restrictive policy; and perhaps the most coveted in today's work environment, time off. These are frequently both rewards and reinforcers. Negative reinforcers include removal of certain rewards or changing one's status, such as placing someone on probation. Extinction is somewhat more complicated, as it requires determining and removing consequences that are inadvertently increasing undesirable behavior. This discussion will concentrate on systematic behavioral methods that use interpersonal interaction, as the effectiveness of interpersonal methods has been well established in the literature (Lewis et al., 1991; Perle, 1997; Robbins, 1995; Wallsten, 1998).

Praise

The use of praise by the gerontologist administrator is the most effective of the three behavioral strategies discussed. Praise is providing a verbal or, in some cases, a written acknowledgment of observed desirable behavior. Praise is most powerful if it follows the event closely and is specific rather than general; that is, simply stating, "That was a good job" is not a particularly effective form of reinforcement. Also, specific aspects of a staff member's work can be praised without praising every aspect of his work (Lewis, 1997). Blanchard and Johnson (1982) offer a prescription for effective praising:

1. Tell people up front that you are going to let them know how they are doing.
2. Praise people immediately.
3. Tell people what they did right—be specific.
4. Tell people how good you feel about what they did right and how it helps the organization and other people who work there.
5. Stop for a moment of silence and let them "feel" how good you feel.
6. Encourage them to do more of the same.
7. Shake hands or touch them in a way that makes it clear that you support their success in the organization.

Praise can also be used in a group situation with peers (Weiner, 1991). Public praising is also useful for team building. Another dimension of praising for the administrator is to reinforce the admission of a mistake made by a staff member. One has to be careful not to reinforce the mistake itself, but to focus specifically on the admission of the mistake (Gatewood et al., 1995). This is a demonstration that admission of mistakes will not necessarily result in punishment, but rather be interpreted as a positive learning experience for the individuals and others in the organization. The most effective praise is accomplished in an exchange that only deals with the praise (Blanchard & Lorber, 1985). Mixing praise with delegations, instructions, or corrections weakens the impact of the reinforcer.

Reprimand

Reprimand is used to inform someone of undesirable behavior and to decrease the likelihood that such behavior will be repeated and desirable behavior will occur. When the gerontologist administrator uses reprimand, it should be in a private session, not in a group, and must specify the exact behavior that was undesirable. Blanchard and Johnson (1982) also provide a prescription for an effective reprimand:

1. Tell people *before-hand* that you are going to let them know how they are doing in no uncertain terms.
2. Reprimand people immediately.
3. Tell people what they did wrong—be specific.
4. Tell people how you feel about what they did wrong, in no uncertain terms.
5. Stop for a few seconds of uncomfortable silence to let them "feel" how you feel.
6. Shake hands or touch them in a way that lets them know you are honestly on their side.
7. Remind them how much you value them.
8. Reaffirm that you think well of them, but not of their performance in this situation.
9. Realize that when reprimand is over, it is over.

Reprimand should be used with all employees, not just problem employees. Concern exists about the use of reprimand because of the feeling that it might disrupt an otherwise positive relationship or be misinterpreted as punishment. This is a valid concern, and that is why this prescription demonstrates an effective way to use reprimand so as not to berate an employee. Reprimand should not be used in anger or in front of colleagues. If a staff person is still in a learning mode, and the mistake occurred because of lack of experience or knowledge, reprimand is not appropriate (Blanchard & Lorber, 1985).

Removal of Reinforcement

This technique is based on the concept of extinction of undesirable behavior. The astute administrator will observe that much of the undesirable behavior engaged in by staff is actually being positively reinforced. The identification of these positive reinforcers and the eventual removal of them will decrease the frequency of the undesirable behavior. For example, a joke made about a staff member who is habitually tardy to meetings is a form of recognition, and thus a positive reinforcer. One might even hear the comment made by the staff person, with an accompanying smile, "That's me!" The combination of removing positive rewards for undesirable behavior and offering rewards for a substitute positive behavior is an effective motivator.

Values and Commitment

One might wonder, amid this discussion of motivation, how it is that organizations who are lacking many of the essentials of motivation accomplish their missions. We all know organizations with poor working conditions, heavy work loads, scarce resources, annual threats of funding losses, and weak administration. In these situations, as well as in more favorable situations where work is accomplished, staff are motivated by values and commitment. Many staff working in organizations that provide programs for older adults are motivated by a strong commitment to the clients. Some staff have chosen education avenues that demonstrate the commitment, like geriatric medicine, gerontology, or gerontological social work. Other staff, even those not members of a profession, have chosen, sometimes for personal reasons, to work with older adults.

Osgood (1992) suggests that staff can develop a committed attitude. Commitment to the mission can override many organizational disadvantages and obstacles (Odiorne, 1987). This is particularly true for staff who choose to work with older adults. The drive and dedication of staff associated with programs for older adults is well-known. This commitment motivates certain staff to work harder and volunteer for extra work, despite certain disadvantages. The wise administrator uses leadership to foster commitment and frequently reminds staff of values associated with the program.

Commitment, which is generally internalized within the individual, is the belief in the mission and goals of an organization (Weiner, 1991). It is related to the sense within the staff person that he can make a difference in the quality of life for older adults. Commitment is associated with the theoretical notions of motivation stemming from the work itself and from achievement where a measure of success can be obtained. Maslow spoke of the need for belongingness, and individuals who work with older adults experience social acceptance. Odiorne (1987) suggests that social acceptance is achieved when there is a commitment to common goals.

The strongest commitment is achieved when an individual's personal growth goals are consistent with organizational goals. This is one means of gaining investment in the activities of a program. As mentioned in this text several times, participation in decision-making and problem-solving achieves ownership. A direct result of ownership is greater commitment (Crow & Odewahn, 1987). Commitment can be to the clients, to the organization and its purpose, or to co-workers. Characteristics of committed staff are identified and summarized in Table 8.3.

Most of the time, the commitment that exists within a staff person is informal, but on some occasions it can be formalized. Written statements of commitment have additional power in motivating individuals. A specific example is the use of a behavioral contract where a well-intentioned staff is seeking to improve their performance (Odiorne, 1987). The behavioral contract specifies particular measurable objectives associated with the shared values inherent in a program. In this way, increased commitment is used to motivate in order to improve productivity.

Values and commitment can be very deeply held and extremely volatile. It is common for staff members to be engaged in the daily routine of work and lose a sense of the values that brought them to their career or employment. Frequent reminders that support and strengthen the values and commitment are essential

Table 8.3
Characteristics of Committed Staff

- Will demonstrate high levels of acceptance for themselves and others

- Are people-centered rather than issue-driven

- Will be more spontaneous than less committed staff

- View problems as deviations from the ideal and accept the challenge to find solutions

- Strive for personal growth, for they are motivated by the possibility of doing a better job

- Will not avoid a calculated risk to improve working conditions or their services

Source: Adapted from Odiorne (1987).

for professionals of all levels providing services to older adults. One way to undermine the motivative power of values and commitments is to suggest that staff members who are motivated by this energy are not appreciated. Equally as negative is for a staff member to feel his commitment is being exploited. Excessive appeals to values and requests for commitment in lieu of concrete or observable relief or reward over time will erode commitment. Exploitation is frequently the reason for the disenchanted, disengaged, previously committed staff member who now lacks motivation and exhibits low productivity and morale.

SUMMARY

Motivation alone will not ensure productivity, as a staff member must also have the capabilities to perform the job. The administrator's behavior is critical to motivation of staff. First, the administrator can model motivated behavior that leads to productivity. Second, an interpersonal style that incorporates empathy, supportiveness, and accessibility contributes to staff motivation. Third, the administrator can employ specific techniques to motivate staff. A close examination of theories of motivation shows there is convergence, especially around such staff needs as recognition (status), achievement, the work itself, and interpersonal relations.

The work environment consistently contributes to behavior of staff and is an important factor in motivation. Work environments that allow for participation, involvement, and commitment, where there is an opportunity for relationships, are found to produce positive motivation. On the other hand, work environments that are characterized by high competition and fear of loss of power or position are not conducive to desired motivation.

Organizational settings that involve high numbers of professional staff providing services are discovering the increasing importance of interpersonal relations to motivation. Among those interpersonal relations are those between staff members and their immediate administrative supervisor. The administrator further contributes to motivation by ensuring an environment that is conducive to motivation. Given a conducive environment, it is incumbent upon the gerontologist administrator to tailor individual approaches to motivate staff.

Mutually agreed-upon and written measurable goals are useful methods of achieving motivation. While goals are important, taken alone without other methods such as reinforcement, they may have limited value (Blanchard & Lorber, 1985). Reinforcement increases desirable behavior or decreases undesirable behavior. This can be accomplished by acknowledging desired behavior, correcting undesired behavior, or removing rewards for undesired behavior.

In programs for older adults, many individuals are attracted to the work because of their commitment. In fact, many staff feel that they have "a calling" to work with older adults. It is incumbent upon the administrator to recognize this commitment, to respect it, and to strengthen it by reminding people of the purpose and values that support the programs.

LEARNING EXPERIENCE

Setting Measurable Goals for a New Program

During a staff retreat, a Jewish family service agency identified the growing number of elderly clients served. This information was presented to the board of directors, and the agency director was given the approval to formulate a new department of aging services. This agency has a variety of services, including individual and family counseling, relocation, employment assistance, temporary housing, and relief. There are five master's level professionals in addition to the executive director providing these services. The executive director converted a vacant position into an aging services coordinator. After interviewing a number of applicants, he hired a master's level gerontologist who had two years' experience as a case manager.

You are the newly hired coordinator of aging services. Your overall goal is to consolidate services to all clients aged 60 and older into a single department. You have no specific budget, as it will depend upon the number of clients and the predicted work load related to those clients. At this point, the executive secretary who works for the director will be your clerical support. The executive director has provided you with background material on the agency that includes a description of all the services, a copy of the organization's budget for the current year, and a copy of the strategic plan. This plan includes a goal statement that reads as follows: "Consolidation of all services for the older population into a single department should be achieved in order to address the unique circumstances of older adults."

You completed orientation last week. Tomorrow you will meet with the executive director. He has asked that you prepare three preliminary measurable goals that will guide your activities in the development of a department of aging services.

Task: Write three measurable goals.

Hint: Measurable goals are phrased in terms of outcome, that is, what is expected. These goals usually begin with a verb and express action. After writing your three measurable goals, check them against the SMART criteria presented in this chapter (see Table 8.2).

REFERENCES

Albrecht, K. (1978). *Successful management by objectives*. Englewood Cliffs, NJ: Prentice-Hall.

Appelbaum, S. (1975). A model of managerial motivation. *Training and Development Journal, 29*(3), 46–49.

Blanchard, K., & Johnson, S. (1982). *The one minute manager*. New York: William Morrow.

Blanchard, K., & Lorber, R. (1985). *Putting the one minute manager to work*. New York: Berkley.

Campbell, J. P., & Pritchard, R. D. (1976). Motivation theory in industrial and organizational psychology. In M. D. Dunnete (Ed.), *Handbook of industrial and organizational psychology* (pp. 63–130). Chicago: Rand McNally College Publishing.

Champagne, P., & McAfee, R. B. (1989). *Motivating strategies for performance and productivity*. New York: Quorum.

Crosby, B. (1986). Employee involvement: Why it fails, what it takes to succeed. *Personnel Administrator, 31*(2), 95–96, 98–106.

Crow, R. T., & Odewahn, C. A. (1987). *Management for the human services*. Englewood Cliffs, NJ: Prentice-Hall.

Dale, E. (1978). *Management: Theory and practice* (4th ed.). New York: McGraw-Hill.

Emmerich, R. (1998). Motivation at work. *Executive Excellence, 15*(6), 20.

Gandy, J., & Tepperman, L. (1990). *False alarm: The computerization of eight social welfare organizations*. Ontario, Canada: Wilfrid Laurier University.

Gatewood, R. D., Taylor, R. R., & Ferrell, O. C. (1995). *Management: Comprehension, analysis, and application*. Chicago: Austen.

Ginsberg, L., & Keys, P. R. (Eds.). (1995). *New management in human services* (2nd ed.). Washington, DC: National Association of Social Workers.

Gutiérrez, L., Glen Maye, L., & DeLois, K. (1995). The organizational context of empowerment practice: Implications for social work administration. *Social Work, 40* (2), 249–258.

Herzberg, F. (1986). One more time: How do you motivate employees? In M. T. Matteson & J. M. Ivancevich (Eds.), *Management classics* (3rd ed., pp. 282–297). Plano, TX: Business Publications.

Kennedy, P. W. (1995). Performance pay, productivity and morale. *Economic Record, 71*(214), 240–248.

Latham, G. P., & Locke, E. A. (1991). Self-regulation through goal setting. *Organizational Behavior and Human Decision Processes, 50*, 212–247.

Lewis, B. (1997). Praising the right people at the right time and place can be a powerful tool. *InfoWorld, 19*(42), 116–117.

Lewis, J. A., Lewis, M. D., & Souflée, F. (1991). *Management of human service programs* (2nd ed.). Pacific Grove, CA: Brooks/Cole.

Locke, E. A. (1975). Personnel attitudes and motivation. In M. R. Rosenzweig & L. W. Porter (Eds.), *Annual Review of Psychology*, Vol. 26 (pp. 457–480). Palo Alto, CA: Annual Reviews.

Longest, B. B. (1976). *Management practices for the health professional*. Reston, VA: Reston Publishing.

Maslow, A. H. (1986). A theory of human motivation. In M. T. Matteson & J. M. Ivancevich (Eds.), *Management classics* (3rd ed., pp. 251–272). Plano, TX: Business Publications.

McClelland, D. (1986). The urge to achieve. In M. T. Matteson & J. M. Ivancevich (Eds.), *Management classics* (3rd ed., pp. 273–281). Plano, TX: Business Publications.

Nadler, D. A., & Lawler, E. E. (1977). Motivation and performance. In D. A. Nadler, M. L. Tushman, & N. G. Hatvany (Eds.), *Managing organizations: Readings and cases* (pp. 101–113). Boston: Little, Brown.

Nye, Robert D. (1992). *Three psychologies: Perspectives from Freud, Skinner, and Rogers* (4th ed.). Pacific Grove, CA: Brooks/Cole.

Odiorne, G. S. (1987). *The human side of management: Management by integration and self-control*. Lexington, MA: Lexington Books.

Orpen, C. (1997). The interactive effects of communication quality and job involvement on managerial job satisfaction and work motivation. *The Journal of Psychology, 131*(5), 519–523.

Osgood, D. (1992). Developing a new kind of motivation. *Supervisory Management, 37*(8), 6–7.

Perle, A. (1997). Have an attitude of gratitude. *Workforce, 76*(11), 77–79.

Rantz, M. J., Scott, J., & Porter, R. (1996). Employee motivation: New perspectives of the age-old challenge of work motivation. *Nursing Forum, 31*(3), 29–37.

Robbins, S. P. (1995). *Supervision today!* Englewood Cliffs, NJ: Prentice-Hall.

Seijts, G. H. (1998). The importance of future time perspective in theories of work motivation. *The Journal of Psychology, 132*, 154–168.

Shera, W., & Page, J. (1995). Creating more effective human service organizations through strategies of empowerment. *Administration in Social Work, 19*(4), 1–15.

Skidmore, R. A. (1995). *Social work administration: Dynamic management and human relationships* (3rd ed.). Boston: Allyn & Bacon.

Sonnenberg, F. (1994). *Managing with a conscience: How to improve performance through integrity, trust, and commitment*. New York: McGraw-Hill.

Umiker, W. (1988). *Management skills for the new health care supervisor*. Gaithersburg, MD: Aspen.

Wallsten, K. (1998). Targeted rewards have greater value—and bigger impact. *Workforce, 77*(11), 66–71.

Weinbach, R. (1998). *The social worker as manager: A practical guide to success* (3rd ed.). Needham Heights, MA: Allyn & Bacon.

Weiner, M. E. (1991). Motivating employees to achieve. In R. L. Edwards & J. A. Yankey (Eds.), *Skills for effective human service management* (pp. 302–316). Washington, DC: National Association of Social Workers.

Wiley, C. (1992). Create an environment for employee motivation. *HR Focus, 69,* 14–15.

Zimmerman, M. A. (1990). Toward a theory of learned hopefulness: A structural model analysis of participation and empowerment. *Journal of Research in Personality, 24,* 71–86.

Chapter 9

Supervision and Staff Development

Administrators, especially those in mid-level positions, spend considerable time and energy supervising staff (Patti, 1983). Generally, supervision is more extensive and elaborate in not-for-profit and government organizations because of the high level of accountability, but this is changing. Profit service organizations are increasingly recognizing the need for and benefits of supervision and expanding the supervisor role. The scope, function, and skills associated with supervision in the human and health services have received extensive attention in the literature (Brody, 1993; Kadushin, 1976; Patti, 1983; Robbins, 1995; Umiker, 1988).

Supervision occurs at all program levels. The extent of supervision will vary with both the level and the professional maturity of the staff person, but the basic functions are expected of all supervisors. For example, most organizations that serve older adults expect the immediate supervisor to conduct the performance appraisal. Supervisors have broad responsibilities for administrative matters relating to compliance and accountability, for providing or facilitating continued professional growth, and for furnishing interpersonal and resource support (Patti, 1983; Umiker, 1988).

Given the commonality of supervisory functions, some distinctions need to be made for supervisors of front-line staff. These supervisors are expected to mediate between line staff and higher administration and are not usually involved in a higher level of decision-making (Robbins, 1995). In programs that provide services for older adults, especially smaller, direct-service programs, supervisors often provide direct services or are expected to substitute for line staff who are absent. While these supervisors perform the same tasks as those whom they supervise, they also hold a position of authority.

Service programs are dominated by professional staff who have high needs for personal and professional development (Lewis, Lewis, & Souflée, 1991). The needs of the organization also dictate continued learning and growth for all staff. A portion of this knowledge and skill relates to those whom the program serves: older adults. Staff development is a major responsibility of all supervisors, extending beyond the direct interpersonal activities of the supervisor. The supervisor is responsible for planning and securing resources for training and growth opportunities. Supporting career development for a staff member is a demonstration of the supervisor's involvement and interest. For many staff, this is perceived as recognition and reward.

Programs for older adults often have a large number of volunteers, especially with community-based services. It is reasonable to believe that volunteers have many of the same needs for supervision as staff (Lewis et al., 1991). We have advocated the inclusion of volunteers in most aspects of the organization's functions, and this is no exception. In certain instances, volunteers themselves may be supervisors of other volunteers.

A model that examines the importance of the supervisory relationship and supervisor roles is offered. The broad scope and intricate nature of the supervisor's responsibilities are elucidated. Additionally, attention is given to the staff development responsibilities of supervisors and the development activities that supplement direct supervision. Information is also presented on styles of supervision and challenges for supervisors.

A MODEL OF SUPERVISION

A number of conceptual models of supervision appear in the literature. Lewis et al. (1991) discuss three corollary roles: the manager, who performs traditional technical functions; the mediator, who links administration with direct services; and the mentor, who accounts for teaching and motivational responsibilities. This is a useful but limiting model that fails to give prominent importance to the supervisory relationship. The relationship is the key to effective and productive supervision. The performance of all the different supervisory roles and responsibilities is dependent on the quality of the relationship.

The Supervisory Relationship

Supervisors are frequently selected based on their technical skills, having achieved higher levels of skill and related knowledge. While in certain instances this may be necessary, it is not the sole nor the best basis for selecting a supervisor. The majority of supervisors have extensive day-to-day contact with their staff. Pincus (1986) conducted a job satisfaction and performance study of hospital nurses. He found that supervisor communication was a major factor related to job satisfaction and performance. For supervisors, communication is frequent and covers a broad range of activities. Effective interpersonal skills and relationship-building skills are the most important criteria for effective supervision (Lewis et al., 1991; Umiker, 1988). For example, the common practice of resolving differences between co-workers to improve the work environment and team productivity is unrelated to the job technology. This activity will require clear communication, conflict resolution, and negotiation skills.

There are many elements to a productive supervisor/staff relationship. Among the key elements are:

- Clarity in communication of expectations.
- Delegation of tasks and detailing of responsibilities that are mutually understood.
- Model interest and commitment to the work. This is achieved by enthusiasm and identification of shared concerns for program goals.
- Regularly scheduled supervisory sessions. A meaningful relationship requires a commitment of time to the staff person and knowledge of that person.
- Use of a collaborative approach. Most, but not all, supervisory responsibilities are collaborative, so that the power relations can be minimized.
- Setting limits on the relationship. The focus must remain on the program and the professional development of the staff person. Extending the relationship to personal problem counseling beyond the initial understanding of the problem will threaten the supervisory relationship.
- Provide frequent feedback about behavior. Expressions about desirable and undesirable behavior, acknowledgment, and recognition are expected from the supervisor by staff. Failure to engage in such activity reduces the value placed on the relationship.

Supervisor Roles

Our conceptualization of supervision has three primary roles. The roles— administrator, consultant, and educator—along with the key position of the relationship constitute the model depicted in Figure 9.1. The administrative role, consistent with the presentation in this text, includes both management and leadership functions. The supervisor as a consultant offers advice and engages in problem-solving with staff. As an educator, the supervisor may be a role model contributing to professional growth, providing situationally oriented instructions and opportunity for learning, both by task assignments and training. The performance of these roles incorporates a large number of overlapping responsibilities.

RESPONSIBILITIES OF THE SUPERVISOR

The supervisor's responsibilities are numerous, sometimes stressful, and often extend across roles. For example, setting mutual goals for productivity may include the selection of opportunities for staff development for a supervisee. Measurable goal setting, discussed in the previous chapter, also provides a form of accountability, always a concern for effective supervisors. The major super-

Figure 9.1
Supervisor Model

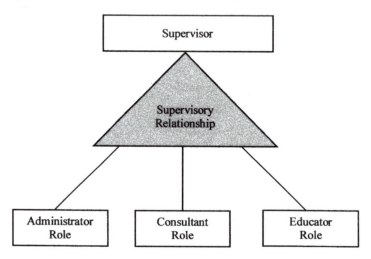

visory responsibilities are clustered into four overlapping areas: management, disciplinary action, performance appraisal, and staff development.

Management

Supervisors hold a position of authority in the organizational structure. Supervisory positions are a link to other departments and to higher levels of administration. Communication, for the most part, flows through the supervisor. Thus, supervisors must mediate between staff and other sources of authority in the organization (Robbins, 1995). These "buffer" activities include interpreting expectations, policy, and changes to staff, often serving to reduce work-related stress (Rauktis & Koeske, 1994).

Supervisors are expected to exert certain controls on supervisees. Basic work behavior, organizational standards, job assignments, approval of absences, and modifications in the job description all fall to the immediate supervisor. In some instances, certain job modifications may require approval from a higher level of administration. The supervisor is also responsible for obtaining the necessary resources for staff members to accomplish tasks. In short, the supervisor facilitates and supports the work of staff members (Umiker, 1988).

Management responsibility is clearly illustrated by the supervisor's responsibility for grievance issues. The supervisor is the first contact for most grievance procedures. A grievance can be sought for any issue that appears to violate the personnel policies, the staff member's contract, or the union agreement. The most common grievances that extend beyond the supervisory level are for discipline and dismissal (Schuler, 1981). In all instances, grievances should begin

Table 9.1

Example of a Progressive Discipline Procedure

1. **Verbal Counseling**—Identify the specific behavior and the correction expected. Document to file with a memorandum.

2. **Disciplinary Session**—Document behavior, corrective activities, and comments from staff member and have signed. Give a copy to the staff person and place a copy in the personnel file.

3. **Disciplinary Session**—Same as above except add statement that next offense will result in more drastic measures (e.g., dismissal, suspension, or demotion).

with informal problem-solving with the immediate supervisor. Most concerns of staff can be resolved at this level. In some instances, the supervisor may advocate for the staff member with higher levels of administration to resolve a grievance.

If concerns cannot be resolved informally, then the more formal grievance procedure, generally outlined in detail by the union agreement or personnel policies, is necessary. This procedure also begins with the immediate supervisor. The most common format involves a step-by-step procedure, written documentation, and time limits for responses as the grievance progresses through the chain of command (Schuler, 1981). Grievances that travel the full course are normally resolved by the top executive, an arbitrator, the board of directors, or a grievance panel composed of staff.

Disciplinary Action

Discipline of the staff member is appropriate for those who choose not to perform duties adequately in accordance with rules or, after training, are unable to perform. Discipline is a consequence of lack of performance, poor compliance, or inability to correct behavior, rather than a punishment. A formal discipline procedure is usually followed if the staff member is beyond the probation period. Less formal and perhaps more frequently used by the supervisor are disciplines such as public criticism and unpleasant job assignments. These practices are not effective, for they are temporary measures (Champagne & McAfee, 1989). Extensive verbal counseling with no record is also an unwise practice. A typical formal, progressive discipline procedure is presented in Table 9.1. Following a systematic discipline procedure often improves the relationship between the supervisor and the staff member (Champagne & McAfee, 1989).

The goal of the discipline procedure is for the staff person to accept responsibility for the behavior and to correct the behavior (Brody, 1993). For the supervisor to achieve an effective disciplinary process, several principles should be followed:

• Start the progressive discipline procedure with a private discussion.

• Consistently follow through with each step of the procedure.

- Focus attention and corrections on specific behaviors.
- Be willing to assist with corrections, but not willing to reduce standards.

There are staff behaviors, usually specified in the personnel policy or the union contract, that circumvent the progressive discipline procedure, leading directly to termination. Such behaviors as physical violence, violating the law, or substance abuse on the job usually fall into this category. Many supervisors in human service organizations are reluctant to take the final dismissal action (Brody, 1993). Generally, a supervisor should consult with her immediate supervisor and human resources staff when termination is indicated. The supervisor must always remember that the first obligation is to the older adult clients, and remain cognizant of the impact of a dysfunctional staff member on the other staff.

In most circumstances, when termination is indicated, staff members should be given the opportunity to resign. Resignation is usually the outcome when progressive discipline is followed precisely. The supervisor should conduct a termination interview (Brody, 1993). If the situation is volatile, the interviewer should have another appropriate staff member present (human resources staff, immediate supervisor, or another administrator). Once dismissal or resignation is complete, all discussion with others should be minimized to maintain confidentiality and to respect the dignity of the dismissed staff member.

Performance Appraisal

A major responsibility of supervisors at all levels is performance appraisal. Robbins (1995) defines performance appraisal as "an evaluation and development tool reviewing past performances to identify accomplishments and deficiencies; and creating detailed plans to improve future performance" (p. 228). The term "performance appraisal" has become more acceptable than "performance evaluations," as the purpose of this procedure has broadened. The purpose of performance appraisals includes (Brody, 1993; Robbins, 1995; Schuler, 1981; Umiker, 1988):

- *Performance Measures.* Establish the relative value of an individual's contribution to the program and evaluate accomplishments.
- *Development Opportunity.* To identify those areas of improvement and procedures that need to be followed to accomplish tasks.
- *Compensation and Promotion.* One of the tools used to help determine compensation in merit pay systems and an established record of performance to be used in making promotion decisions.
- *Adjustment of Job Responsibilities.* This is an opportunity to discuss and agree upon modifications in job responsibilities and to change the job description.

- *Recognition.* Specific acknowledgment of accomplishments and how those accomplishments contribute to the overall mission of the program.
- *Identification of Training Needs.* Cumulative information will provide the supervisor with information to plan for training opportunities.
- *Problem Documentation.* Performance appraisals provide a written statement about problems and corrective actions. This information can play a part in determining transfers, terminations, or job modifications.

Performance appraisals are among the least desirable activities of supervisors and staff. This is especially true for the abbreviated procedure of filling out the form, giving it to the employee, and waiting to see if the employee will schedule a conference. Supervisors often question the need to appraise certain employees. The need for a level of confrontation and the lack of time necessary to complete an effective appraisal raise concerns about disrupting the relationship. Staff who recognize discrepancy in power are often concerned about the supervisor's knowledge of their actual performance and about favoritism, and rarely view the appraisal as helpful (Umiker, 1988).

Despite these concerns, comprehensive, thoughtful performance appraisals actually save time and can improve relationships, enhance performance, and motivate staff. Most performance appraisals are a formal procedure involving an interpersonal exchange and an appraisal form completed by the supervisor. Different performance forms may be used for different classes of staff, and the formats of performance appraisal may be different for those in key administrative or professional positions. For those in these positions, the tendency is to rely more heavily on self-appraisal and measurable goals, dispensing with the traditional appraisal form.

Performance Appraisal Forms

Conventional appraisal forms that include an area for rating and then a scale are the most widely used methods (Schuler, 1981). These forms are highly criticized and maligned. Many forms are too general, use an arbitrary rating scale, and are highly subjective. Many of these forms extend beyond measuring behavior as an indicator of performance to personality characteristics. In contrast, the qualities of a constructive performance evaluation form are as follows:

- Ratings have one or two sentence descriptors.
- Areas of evaluation include performance criteria.
- The form is linked to the job description.
- An area is provided for listing an evaluation of annual goals and objectives.
- The focus is on behavior rather than attitude.
- There is a designated area for goals and objectives for the next year.

The performance appraisal form represents the objective part of the appraisal procedure and is the concrete document that signifies that an appraisal has been accomplished. The most important part of the performance appraisal procedure is the interview.

Performance Appraisal Interview

In conducting performance appraisals, the most useful procedures incorporate an interview prior to the completion of the form. This interview involves an exchange of information and a mutual problem-solving process (Brody, 1993). Of course, the annual performance appraisal interview should not be the first time that performance concerns are discussed. This interview should be the culmination of supervisory sessions and interim informal discussions held throughout the year. Each party should take responsibility for preparing for the performance appraisal. At the minimum, the staff member should bring goals and objectives that have guided behavior for the past year, examples of work, and data that documents accomplishments. In preparation for the interview, the supervisor should review information from interim appraisals throughout the year, review the past performance appraisal, and examine the current job description.

Performance Appraisal Planning

Completion of performance appraisals is often not timely. Thus, a system for ensuring that performance appraisals are conducted is necessary. A system that relies solely on the supervisor for timely evaluations is flawed. Reminders and requirements by administrative staff or human resources professionals are necessary. It is not uncommon to find that the staff member must remind the supervisor that an evaluation is overdue. Untimely evaluations foster suspicion, create unnecessary anxiety, and may give an unintended message to the staff member. A meaningful performance appraisal will include a considerable amount of planning.

In either the performance appraisal interview or a follow-up session, goals and objectives for the coming year that may include changes in duties and expectations should be agreed upon and written (Brody, 1993). Some of these objectives may include corrections of behavior that has been identified as nonproductive, or ways in which a person can be more productive. For example, a case manager who has been found to make inappropriate referrals for some older adults may have an objective of visiting and learning about 10 other programs in the community that offer services to older adults, by a set time during the next year. New objectives that have been tailored to a particular staff member can be incorporated into the performance appraisal for the next year. This is also an appropriate time for the supervisor to share with the staff person her own goals and objectives for the coming year.

Table 9.2
Performance Appraisal Step-by-Step Procedure

STEP 1	Discuss performance with the staff person prior to the interim interview. Establish a time and date for that interview.
STEP 2	The interim performance interview is to be conducted midway (six months) through the evaluation period. At this point, review the performance to date, reinforcing appropriate behaviors, and determine corrective action where necessary. Only complete the performance appraisal form if you feel that the performance has been less than satisfactory.
STEP 3	Prior to the annual interview, review the job description, the employee's material, incident reports, or any other documents relevant to the year's performance.
STEP 4	Before the annual date, conduct a pre-appraisal interview. Hold this interview within five days of notification. It may be useful to require the staff person to prepare materials such as a summary of accomplishments.
STEP 5	Following the interview, complete the standard appraisal form. If further input from your supervisor or other individuals is required, this should be obtained prior to completing the form. The form should not be completed in the presence of the employee.
STEP 6	Provide attachments to the form such as established goals and documentation of unusual circumstances.
STEP 7	Review the completed form with your supervisor. This is best done together.
STEP 8	Deliver the completed evaluation form to the employee for his or her review, comments, and signature.
STEP 9	Conduct a post-evaluation discussion session to clarify the rating and set objectives and/or corrective action for the next period. This should be completed soon after the delivery of the form.
STEP 10	Forward the completed, signed evaluation form and all attachments to your supervisor. Retain a copy for your files and provide the employee with a copy.

Performance Appraisal Problems

Following a systematic performance appraisal procedure that includes inter-personal interactions will avoid many of the common problems. An example of a systematic procedure is provided in Table 9.2. The more a performance appraisal procedure focuses on behaviors that relate to performance and avoids using an evaluation of personality characteristics such as cooperativeness, loyalty, or assertiveness, the fewer problems there will be (Brody, 1993). It is generally understood that the performance appraisal procedure lends itself to many types of errors (Umiker, 1988). Better accuracy and fairness can be achieved by following the fairness hints outlined in Table 9.3.

Actually, most performance appraisal staff satisfaction is related to interper-

Table 9.3
Performance Appraisal Fairness Hints

1. Try to avoid the "halo effect." This is when a person's single accomplishment or failure (mistake) is permitted to overshadow all other areas of concern.

2. Avoid incorrect use of "central" tendency. This would be the excessive use of middle categories or "satisfactory" on the form because of lack of knowledge of the activity or because of length of time in the position.

3. Avoid "recent event" tendency. This is the tendency to use an incident in the last few weeks of activity rather than the entire appraisal period.

4. Avoid focusing on personality or personal likes and dislikes (nice person syndrome). Evaluation is on performance of job-related duties and behaviors.

5. Guard against the "similarity error." Giving ratings in relation to one's own perceived desirable characteristics.

sonal interaction rather than the outcome of the performance appraisal. A study of 217 middle managers who had received and had conducted numerous performance appraisals supported this notion. The study found that when the supervisors solicited input prior to the appraisal and when there was two-way communication during the interview, this accounted for over 90 percent of the positive feelings about the performance appraisal (Greenberg, 1996).

Performance appraisals can be a constructive and meaningful activity that contributes to both high morale and improved performance. While a systematic procedure that includes an effective rating form is important, this is not enough. The supervisor's experience in being appraised is not sufficient. What is required, in addition to a systematic sound procedure, is direct and concrete training in performance appraisal that incorporates the existing policies and forms of the organization.

Staff Development

The supervisor is directly accountable for the performance of staff and the development of staff capabilities to accomplish the goals and objectives of the program (Schuler, 1981). This responsibility involves education and training, sometimes called in-service training, or as a more formal title, continuing education. In addition to providing opportunities for training, the supervisor must assist in transferring the training to performance of duties and responsibilities (Gregoire, Propp, & Poertner, 1998).

Supervisors will require the support of administration as well as the cooperation and collaboration of internal and external resources to accomplish staff development. At the same time, a large measure of responsibility and commitment rests with the individual staff member. Staff participation in development to increase knowledge, skills, and abilities can also serve as a motivator and a recognition of potential. For example, the offering of an opportunity to a geriatric care manager to attend a workshop on supervision anticipates a future possibility.

Determining Need

Many training needs are obvious, as they result from new developments in society (like the advent of HIV) or are linked to future plans of the organization. Needs for development emerge out of supervisory concerns in both informal and formal discussion by administrators. Yet another approach is the use of focus groups where staff members are brought together to discuss topics and kinds of training. A more formal approach to determining training needs is to conduct a written needs survey throughout the organization. Combining survey results with other determinations of training needs allows for proper planning and budgeting.

It is important to recognize that staff development is not simply a means of correcting deficiencies, but is also necessary for professional growth and maintenance of productivity. Experienced staff also require training and development to prevent or deal with stress and burn-out (Moniz-Cook, Millington, & Silver, 1997). Often, training and education are needed to better understand the client population being served. This is particularly true for staff in programs for older adults, as this expanding area of service continues to grow and involve staff who do not have a gerontology background (Wendt & Peterson, 1992). This knowledge base must include biological, sociological, and psychological aspects of aging, as well as knowledge of policies and programs.

Staff Development Opportunities

The opportunities for staff development come in many forms. The core of all staff development is inextricably tied to the attitude of the supervisor and the interactions of the supervisor and the supervisee. The supervisory conference offers a prime opportunity for development. Through these exchanges, other opportunities for development can be determined and agreed upon. Opportunities for staff development range from training at staff meetings to formal college courses, as well as use of consultation to provide guidance and instruction.

Methods and Means

Workshops, seminars, and mini-conferences for those who work with older adults are frequently offered through the aging network, particularly the AAA. These staff development opportunities are open to all who work with older adults, regardless of the sector. Educational opportunities sponsored by the AAA also provide another opportunity to network and learn from colleagues.

On-the-job training (OJT) has many advantages over some of the other venues for staff development (Brody, 1993). OJT is directly related to the task being performed, providing opportunity for consistent reinforcement and correction by the supervisor. Additionally, the vast majority of OJT is experiential. To the extent that the supervisor is viewed as a mentor, this can make OJT even more powerful (Lewis et al., 1991). In a mentoring experience, in addition to the skills and knowledge that can be shared, the supervisor has the opportunity to reinforce the values and the ethics inherent in the program.

An increasingly popular form of OJT emphasizing mentoring is the professional pairing program (Mueller, 1999). This program establishes relationships between a more experienced staff member and a less experienced staff member for a limited period of time. Use of this method has the additional advantages of flexibility and being less formal, along with reducing the power differentiation between the two participants. A more objective approach to OJT is to contract with consultants to work with the staff using process consultation (Weinbach, 1998). This is ongoing consultation that can be related to individual cases, change efforts, program enhancements, or a particular area. These arrangements usually involve written agreements and can extend over a number of years.

Limitations and Concerns

Training that relies on agency employees, whether it is a group session or one-to-one, consumes time that could have been dedicated to clients. Caution should be taken to assure that the designated trainers or mentors have the proper credentials and credibility for undertaking the tasks. There is also the age-old concern, a legitimate one, about the inbreeding of knowledge and skills, placing limits on the development and reinforcing resistance to new methods (Weinbach, 1998).

Staff development experiences external to the agency bring their own problems and concerns. External training may be contrary to practices of the organization and elicit negative reactions from colleagues and supervisors (Brody, 1993). This training, whether workshops, seminars, or college courses, may lack knowledge of the organization's policies, practices, and methods. While a case can be made that in the long run staff development is cost-effective, it is common practice, although not necessarily advisable, for organizations in a financial crisis to eliminate this expenditure first. The gerontologist administrator should keep in mind that if the organization needs to change, develop new markets, and respond to society's needs, staff development is critical.

All staff development activities should incorporate feedback and evaluation. Informal feedback from staff during supervisory sessions, staff meetings, and team meetings can be solicited by administrators. Systematic evaluation of the impact of in-service training and contracted workshops and seminars, using well-designed response forms, is essential. Program evaluation that measures both the impact of the programs and the application of knowledge, skills, and abilities also provides useful data for determining training outcome. Another use for the information obtained from all of these practices is to identify needs for further development and training. Thus, the cycle of staff development begins again, starting with establishing needs, selecting methods, implementation, and finally, with measuring the impact of the experiences.

SUPERVISION STYLES AND TYPES

There is considerable evidence that the style of supervision used by the gerontologist administrator will influence the motivation and productivity of the supervisee (Lewis et al., 1991; Richer & Vallerand, 1995; Rosengren, 1974). Many variables influence style such as personality, personal history of supervision, and professional education. These variables have received less attention than environmental influences. Clearly, the size of an organization, its communication patterns, and its organizational policy will influence supervision style. Government programs, many of which provide indirect services and are of considerable size, tend to encourage compliance-oriented supervision (Rosengren, 1974; Russell, Lankford, & Grinnell, 1985). Private profit programs often lean toward production (task)-oriented supervision (Rosengren, 1974). In not-for-profit programs, supervision is more likely to be people oriented (Patti, 1983). This is not to suggest that supervision style will always fall into the respective organizational category or that these are the most desirable approaches. These three styles will be explained more fully in this section.

There are many other variables that affect supervisory style. The less experienced or uncertain supervisee will require more direct and detailed supervision (Lewis et al., 1991). De Vries, Roe, and Taillieu (1998) studied supervisors in a large private organization and found that the need for supervision, not surprisingly, was greater for those with fewer years of service and less knowledge. The style of supervision can change over time for a given supervisee. The expectations and demands for supervision may also vary with the career interests of the supervisee (Lewis et al., 1991). For example, a gerontologist working as a case manager with aspirations to be an administrator might ask for task-oriented supervision and challenging assignments.

The level of employee satisfaction with the job, the kind of organization, and the style of supervision will vary the demands placed on the supervisor. A dissatisfied staff member may require more supportive supervision to bring about motivation and productivity. To be sure, a single style or approach to supervision will not be effective with all staff. The proficient gerontologist administrator must have the ability to adapt and adjust her supervisory style to the needs of the supervisee, while maintaining standards of accountability and remaining focused on the program's goals.

Compliance-Oriented Supervision

This style of supervision exerts a large measure of control over the supervisee. It emphasizes the management aspects of the administrative role and discourages autonomy. Some characteristics of compliance-oriented supervision are (Richer & Vallerand, 1995; Rosengren, 1974; Russell et al., 1985):

• Communication is mostly lateral.
• Tasks and assignments are typically limited to the job description.
• Emphasis is placed on work behavior, like office tidiness and attitude.
• Heavy reliance on tradition and policy.
• Difficult decisions and information are attributed to superiors.

This approach to supervision takes low risks and seeks to protect both the supervisor's and the supervisee's position in the organization. This approach is taken often when the supervisor sees a conflict between a person-centered style and production requirements. While compliance is a general concern, non-compliance does not necessarily result in punishment. However, there is a sub-category of this, known as punitive-controlling–oriented supervision (Richer & Vallerand, 1995). This style employs punishment or threats of punishment to gain compliance. This highly directive style has been found to result in low levels of self-determination and intrinsic motivation (Patti, 1983; Richer & Vallerand, 1995).

Production-Oriented Supervision

This style of supervision is also called task- or performance-oriented supervision. Its thrust is on outcome of work activities. The supervisor's efforts are directed toward decreasing interference with productivity. The administrative role, with emphasis on the management aspects, is evident, since there is a reliance on authority. Elements of the consultant role, particularly as it pertains to technical assistance, are also evident in this style (Robbins, 1995). The characteristics of this particular style are as follows (Patti, 1983; Russell et al., 1985):

• Task accomplishment is seen as totally related to the supervision provided.
• Focuses on both quantity and quality.
• Tendency is to work with preset objectives.
• Objective measurement of work activities is used.
• Staff job satisfaction is desirable but not necessary.
• The supervisor is concerned with who is blamed for mistakes.

The extreme of this style is a tunnel perspective on the bottom line, that is, a focus on outcome to the extent that the value of the process is lost. Tangible and expressive rewards are offered for high productivity. Overemphasis on productivity can produce value conflicts and unethical behaviors.

People-Oriented Supervision

This style also has many names, such as human-oriented, supportive, or person-centered supervision. In essence, person-oriented supervision is a partnership with the supervisor being the senior partner. It emphasizes the leadership aspects of administration and fully utilizes the consulting role. The major principles of this style are (Lewis et al., 1991; Richer & Vallerand, 1995; Russell et al., 1985):

- Shared problem-solving and decision-making.
- Concern with production is achieved by development of people and gaining a commitment.
- Concern for staff satisfaction.
- Emphasis is placed on successes.
- Assistance with personal and professional growth.
- Infusion and reinforcement of values related to organizational goals.

Research indicates that this supportive, collaborative approach increases extrinsic motivation (Richer & Vallerand, 1995). However, the extreme of this style may prove to be counterproductive. When the supervisor becomes a confidante, who feels she must shelter and protect the supervisee, there is a tendency to avoid failures and problems with productivity. That is, conflicts between productivity and personal growth are resolved in favor of the latter. This extreme style is particularly true when the supervisor has high needs for acceptance by the supervisee (Russell et al., 1985).

Combined Styles

Supervision roles and responsibilities are heavily affected by the organization and the type of program. A supervisor's style is also subject to the individual choices and attitudes of the supervisor. Most supervisors will adopt a combination of these styles, adjusting the style to meet the needs of the person and the program.

Blake and Mouton (1978) offer two combined styles, one of which has a moderate concern for both people and production. The other suggests that a maximum concern for production and people is possible. This classic conceptualization of managerial styles, known as the "managerial grid," fails to account for decisional conflicts that surely arise in the combining of styles, especially the maximum concern approach (Russell et al., 1985). For example, a supervisor in an adult protective services unit has a backlog of investigations needing to be assigned to a new staff member. The new staff member is currently involved in intensive and frequent supervision, experiencing dramatic professional growth. Assigning the additional investigative cases will reduce the time avail-

Table 9.4
Conditions Conducive to the Coaching Style

- A general climate of openness and mutuality
- A helpful and empathic attitude
- An effective dialogue that is not overly prescriptive
- A focus on work-related, measurable goals
- Recognition of the uniqueness of each staff person supervised

Sources: Adapted from Evered & Selman (1989); Pareek & Rao (1990).

able for supervisory sessions. Furthermore, the Blake and Mouton conceptualization does not directly address the importance of compliance.

Any combined style will typically reveal a slight dominance of one of the three supervisor orientations: compliance, production, or people. An "equally balanced style" is difficult and perhaps not desirable. An emerging supervisory style called "coaching" is appropriate for the gerontologist administrator. This style leads with the productivity orientation, yet incorporates the useful aspects of compliance and concern for people.

The term "coaching" brings the familiar association with sports. However, supervisor coaching, while accepting the performance focus, is not entirely synonymous with sports coaching (Evered & Selman, 1989). Coaching is essentially job skill development that involves analysis of behavior and collaborative problem-solving for the purpose of increasing effectiveness. This style is consistent with the supervisory model presented in this chapter, since at the core of its effectiveness is the relationship.

Conditions that are necessary for effective supervision using this style are presented in Table 9.4. According to one conceptualization, coaching involves three processes: communication, influencing, and helping (Pareek & Rao, 1990). Frequent communications incorporate active listening, open-ended questions, and feedback. Influencing means encouraging autonomy, using positive reinforcement, and fostering identification with the coach. Lastly, the helping process is to identify needs, establish mutuality, engage in planning, and express genuine interest and concern.

With coaching, the supervisor is clearly responsible for the behavior of the supervised staff member (Evered & Selman, 1989). Consistent with sports coaching, efforts are often directed at staff stretching beyond one's self-perceived capabilities. Also consistent with sports is the emphasis placed on following the rules (compliance with policy).

Because of the nature of the coaching style, which is collaborative, cooperative, and mutual, both the supervisor and the supervisee can experience growth and development. It can be facilitated by actually discussing the approach to supervision with staff members. This style is effective with both individuals and groups. Group supervision is especially useful in programs that provide services to older adults because the multiprofessional staff compositions offer an opportunity to benefit from the various backgrounds.

Group Supervision

Group supervision has the same goals as individual supervision: service effectiveness, professional growth and development, motivation, and job satisfaction. Bringing a group together to supervise is no simple matter, because of multiple relationships, complexity of communications, and possible increased competition. Group supervision is perhaps most appropriate for professionals, paraprofessionals, and volunteers who have complementary skills and a common purpose (Robbins, 1995). Russell et al. (1985) conducted a study of supervisory styles at a department of human resources in Texas. The researcher used Blake and Mouton's managerial grid to identify different styles of supervision. They were surprised to find that the predominant style of supervision showed minimum concern for both people and production. Their recommendation was to move toward team management and group supervision.

When to use group supervision is usually the individual supervisor's decision. Thus, it is useful to identify the advantages and disadvantages of this method.

Advantages of Group Supervision	Disadvantages of Group Supervision
1. Time efficiency	1. Places heavy demands on the supervisor for group facilitation skills
2. Mutual support from one another	2. The possibility of straying from the purpose
3. Pooled knowledge and insight	3. The potential of competition and rivalry
4. Learning from one another	4. Adjustment of the supervisor to the sharing of the supervisory responsibility
5. Group problem-solving	5. Group turning into therapy sessions
6. Lessens dependency on a single supervisor	6. Less assertive individuals do not reap as much benefit
7. Makes use of existing interpersonal skills of members	7. More experienced members become bored with beginning staff issues
8. Cost-effectiveness	

To conduct effective group supervision, the number of staff needs to be small. The members should not exceed 10, and the ideal is between five and six. The supervisor must possess both supervisory skills and skills in group facilitation. As the group leader, the supervisor will need to encourage participation, be responsive to group cues, and maintain a focus on increasing effectiveness and efficiency (Kaslow, 1972). For successful group supervision, it is important to separate administrative aspects of supervision from other discussions. Combining group supervision with individual supervision can reduce the frequency of individual supervision while realizing the benefits of both methods.

CHALLENGES FOR SUPERVISORS

The importance of the relationship between the administrator and the staff for motivation and supervision has been stressed. The transition to a supervisory position demands necessary changes in prior relationships with most members of the organization. Many of the challenges for supervisors stem from inappropriate relationships. Simply stated, supervisors who cross the line of the professional relationship are not able to establish the appropriate professional relationship with the supervisee. The supervisory relationship represents an area where there are many ethical considerations.

In addition to the appropriate supervisory relationship, the supervisor as a representative of the organization, a profession, and the commitment to clients is subject to numerous challenges. The effective supervisor is expected to make adaptions related to certain characteristics of supervisees, but not to violate norms or rules. This often requires a transition to an administrative role that will be quite different from her previous career experience. Further, with service programs, supervisors are expected to deal with supervisees' personal problems, but there are limits.

Necessary Adaptions to Supervision

It has been established that supervisory approaches and perhaps effectiveness are dependent, in part, on the type of organization, the quality of the relationship, and the supervisor's style. Within that context, supervisors must also be able to adapt to the experience, level of education, and circumstances of the supervisee. More specifically, the supervisor in organizations that serve older adults will encounter volunteers, students, older workers, and individuals with different cultural backgrounds from her own. The absolute first task for the supervisor is to make an assessment of the supervisee's skills and knowledge, independent of the circumstances.

Certain circumstances could result in a low level of supervision. While the nature of service programs necessitates regular, routine supervision, the type and intensity may vary. Continued development of knowledge and skills is a lifelong process. This phenomenon is emphasized because different professional backgrounds bring a diversity of views about the need for supervision (Royster, 1972).

In making adaptions, the supervisor must guard against changes that occur because of identification or unprofessional expectation. For example, likeness of age, gender, race, and professional background, taken alone, are not appropriate for altering standards, goals, or the need for supervision. The supervisor is an administrative officer in the organization expected to function consistently with the purpose, focus, and goals of the organization (Royster, 1972). Identifications with or conflicts that the supervisor may have with the supervisee are not a basis for making inappropriate adaptions. However, tailoring supervision of supervisees who are volunteers, older workers, students, professionals, or paraprofessionals is necessary.

A supervisor may be supervising a volunteer coordinator or a group of volunteers. Most volunteers have many of the same needs and interests as regular staff for development, problem-solving, and support. In fact, the absence of remuneration provides an opportunity for focus on other aspects of supervision and evaluation that pertain primarily to the programs. Supervising students who have time-limited exposure to the supervisor and whose experiences are integrated with course work is usually structured. The best supervisory situation is where the student has a learning contract which has been mutually agreed upon by the institution of higher education, the student, and the supervisor.

In supervising both staff and volunteers, it is common with services to older adults to find young supervisors and older workers. Supervision is a two-way process and never more so than when one has the opportunity to supervise a more experienced or older supervisee. The mutuality of the learning experience relates to the staff development role of the supervisor. While the administrative role remains essentially the same, where appropriate, the supervisor can make use of the experience of the older worker by asking for assistance with other members of the staff or in special projects.

Supervising highly trained professionals, depending somewhat on experience, means recognizing that a level of motivation and commitment to the program already exists. Depending on the assessment of knowledge and skills, a greater level of autonomy can usually be offered to professionals (Lewis et al., 1991). Paraprofessionals working in organizations that serve older adults may have had some college training. Those with college training will be career-focused like professionals (Lewis et al., 1991). The supervisor needs to refrain from expecting paraprofessionals to perform work of people who are professionally trained. At the same time, the supervisor must recognize that paraprofessionals occupy a certain status that may be undervalued and that support and encouragement, along with continued development, will produce a more effective staff member.

Transition to Supervisor

Becoming a supervisor brings a change in status and authority, new relationships, and the expectation of greater compliance. The transition is often difficult as one joins the administration. Initially, a deceptive "honeymoon" exists where cooperation and observation eventually give way to cautious acceptance and resentment (Umiker, 1988). Reports of first-time supervisors in workshops and in the literature document the numerous difficulties experienced during this transition (Lewis et al., 1991).

The transition is less disruptive and more accepted when the promotion or appointment is perceived as fair and the new supervisor has been previously recognized as an informal leader. A gradual change, with progressive performance of administrative tasks and formal preparatory training, also contributes to a smooth transition (Umiker, 1988). The transition is less dramatic if the appointment to supervisor is in another organization where former co-workers are not present.

Some supervisors resist, never breaking from the former status and role, often maintaining that "nothing has really changed." This is a sure sign of ineffective supervision, which will manifest itself in the reluctance to evaluate staff, difficulty with decisions, inappropriate relationships with staff, and inevitable problems with acceptance from other administrators. Some supervisors who insist on retaining many of their former activities do so not out of necessity but because of reluctance to assume the supervisory role. To make this transition, old friendships may suffer, as one must guard against the appearance of favoritism, and the character of social activities with former peers will change (Umiker, 1988).

The new supervisor will have a new reference group: other supervisors and administrators within the organization. There are conversations and information that can be shared with this reference group that would not be appropriate for other members of the staff. Support of the supervisor comes from her direct supervisor and from this reference group. Typically, this reference group will have a perspective on the organization that is broader in scope than the new supervisor previously experienced.

Moreover, there is a shift in the informal system of rewards. A supervisor may previously have received rewards and recognition for her direct work. As one moves up the ladder of administration, becoming more distant from the direct activities, rewards and accolades increasingly must come from the successes of one's supervisees and from the administrative peer group. By the same token, the supervisor will need to accept responsibility for the mistakes of supervisees (Umiker, 1988).

Personal Problem Counseling

To what extent should a supervisor be involved in personal counseling? Personal counseling, although intertwined, is distinguished from performance and compliance counseling, as it concentrates on the person's private circumstances which may or may not directly interfere with the work. Frequently, the relation to the work problem is difficult to establish, such as absenteeism as possibly related to excessive drinking of alcohol. Many supervisors are opposed to personal counseling in any form and avoid all personal discussions (Hopkins, 1997;

Sonnenstuhl & Trice, 1990). Indeed, many supervisors delay confronting performance problems so as not to enter the personal arena.

For the gerontologist administrator in the modern supervisory role, limited personal counseling is not only appropriate, but necessary (Hopkins, 1997; Loen, 1994; Umiker, 1988). The limits involve both time and depth of counseling and should not be dependent upon the supervisor's training in counseling or psychotherapy. Possessing the techniques, knowledge, and skills is not a license to extend the supervisory role to becoming a personal therapist. Supervisors, both with therapy skills and without, found in-depth counseling to be counterproductive, as it changes the relationship and breeds manipulation (Lewis et al., 1991). Given the necessity to enter into limited counseling, all supervisors need basic interpersonal skills and a systematic approach (Umiker, 1988).

It must always be kept in mind that a personal problem can reach the extent where it will affect the behavior of the staff member with customers, clients, stakeholders, and the supervisory relationship itself. It is neither constructive nor cost-effective to lose an employee without first making attempts to deal with personal problems. Often, confronting these problems in the early stages will prevent them from becoming more complicated and serious, not only for the individual but also for the organization. Part of the rationale for engaging in limited personal counseling is to prevent a major personal or job-related crisis.

On occasion, the supervisor engaged in limited personal counseling will encounter resistance, minimizing of the identified problem, and divergence of discussion (Umiker, 1988). Discussion of personal problems is frequently emotionally charged, with expressions of fear, anger, and sorrow. Even in limited counseling, the supervisor must guard against sympathetic responses that result in a change in standards or requirements of the job. While some adjustments may be appropriate, any adjustments that impact the quality of the program and place additional burdens on other staff are inappropriate and ethically questionable. The most useful control when entering into personal counseling with a staff member is to discuss the situation with one's own supervisor. This is not a breach of confidentiality. The supervisor cannot promise confidentiality to the staff member that would preclude discussion with her own supervisor.

The limited counseling role suggested is listening to staff expression of problems, helping to clarify those problems, facilitating problem-solving by the staff member, and when appropriate, referring the staff member to a professional helping source (Hopkins, 1997). The supervisor should avoid giving advice, making interpretations, or displaying sympathy, yet, at the same time, communicate concern, interest, and encouragement.

Referrals can be made to an employee assistance program (EAP), and if not available, the employee can be encouraged to seek assistance through private practitioners or community mental health programs. This is a prime opportunity to seek the assistance of human resources in helping the staff member find professional help. Once a staff member has engaged professional services, personal counseling should be limited even further to simply encouraging the continuation of professional help.

Supervisor Training

Promotion to supervisor for some is the enactment of "the Peter Principle," that is, being promoted to a level of incompetence. Generally, this is because additional skills, knowledge, and experience place demands upon the supervisor, for which most supervisors are initially unprepared. Unfortunately, supervisory training is often left to on-the-job-training, with a large dose of trial and error. Considering the roles, relationships, and challenges to supervisors, special training and instruction are essential. Most supervisors in programs serving older adults have a supervisor with experience who can contribute to the new supervisor's development. However, the best method is expressed by Walsh (1990): "Continuing education and inservice training for supervisors, as they begin to immerse themselves in that role, are the most effective methods for helping to inculcate supervisory skills, attitudes and behaviors" (p. 82).

Supervisor training that restricts the group to a single organization is preferable since the mission, policies, and management expectations can be incorporated. This is not always possible, especially for training directed at the transition to supervisor. One of the authors of this text has developed and conducted supervisor transition training for many years. This training is focused upon supervising friends, use of authority, conducting an effective performance appraisal, supervising the older worker, and delegation. A more broadly based, 15-hour training design for new supervisors has been prepared by Walsh (1990). It includes such topics as the role of authority, values and ethics, and dealing with different levels of staff.

Supervisors in programs that serve older adults will need to assess their own knowledge of aging to determine if a broader base of knowledge is now required. Frequently, moving to a supervisory position requires increased knowledge of policies, programs, and funding sources related to older adults. For example, reimbursement from Medicare Part B guidelines as they pertain to home health programs will determine to some extent the directions that the supervisor will provide to the direct service staff member.

SUMMARY

Supervision of staff is a primary responsibility for gerontologist administrators. Many supervisors share this responsibility with other program-related activities. In organizations that offer programs for older adults, gerontologist administrators may find themselves supervising volunteers, student interns, professional and paraprofessional staff. In some instances, professional staff will have expertise and technical skill not possessed by the supervisor. It is not necessary or even possible to know all of the technical skills of those supervised.

However, it will require a broader base of knowledge about older adults and related policies and programs, as well as acquisition of supervisory skills.

An integrated model of supervision that emphasizes the professional relationship was offered. This model divides the roles into administrator, consultant, and educator, accounting for the interconnectedness of these roles. The relationship between the roles is demonstrated by examining four critical areas of responsibility: management activities, disciplinary action, performance appraisal, and staff development. The supervisor as a manager is a buffer for information and communication, as well as for administration and employee problems. Discipline responsibility requires counseling and systematic, progressive approaches to correct behavior. Conducting performance appraisals also requires a systematic approach, fairness, and maintaining the appropriate relationship. Effective performance appraisals will increase performance and contribute to high morale. The supervisor has both direct responsibility for developing staff and indirect responsibility for identifying and supporting educational opportunities.

The supervisory style will be affected by the organizational setting, professional background of staff, expertise of staff members, and the personality of the supervisor. Three distinct styles—compliance-oriented, production-oriented, and people-oriented—were discussed. Each possesses necessary aspects of effective supervision, but extremes of these styles are non-productive. A fourth combined style that features a production orientation, called "coaching," is thought to be appropriate for the gerontologist administrator in most supervisory positions. Additionally, group supervision can add another dimension to the accomplishment of these responsibilities.

The supervisor will be challenged to adapt supervision while maintaining standards. Decreases or increases in supervision or adjustments in style are related to assessment of the staff member and the tasks at hand (Kaslow, 1972). New supervisors must make a transition to the ranks of administration. This requires changes in relationships and acquiring or use of new skills and abilities.

In organizations that serve older adults, the supervisor may be expected to engage in limited counseling of employees. It is important to keep in mind that emotional learning related to staff growth and development often comes from such counseling (Gitterman, 1972). The tendency to take this activity too far, becoming a staff member's therapist, must be guarded against. When therapy or lengthy counseling are required, the staff member should be referred to the appropriate resource.

Supervisory skills and abilities can be taught and learned. Few people enter supervision with the knowledge and experience required to be effective. Relationship-building skills that include interpersonal abilities are the key to effective supervision. Many first-time supervisors who are joining the ranks of administration must develop management and leadership skills and abilities. It should always be kept in mind that the nature and quality of supervision will impact the programs and services offered.

LEARNING EXPERIENCE

Selection of a first-time supervisor represents a critical decision for administrators. We have emphasized the need for supervisors to have multiple skills and abilities, with strong emphasis on relationship skills. Recognition has also been given to a need for compliance and commitment to self-development and development of staff. The following instrument, using slightly different terminology—technical competency, interpersonal competency, and conceptual competency—seeks to assess a range of abilities needed to become a supervisor. As a learning experience, this scale can be used to conduct a self-assessment or to assess a present or past co-worker's readiness to be a supervisor. Indicate the approach selected in the box below and follow the instructions:

☐　Self-assessment　　　　☐　Assessment of past or present co-worker

The Supervisory Assessment Instrument

Abstract

In too many cases, senior managers look back at their decisions to promote others to management with regret. Many managers are not competent and contaminate their organizations with uninspired leadership and inefficient administration. This instrument addresses a major cause of poor performance by managers: the criteria used to promote people into managerial positions in the first place.

The Supervisory Assessment Instrument (SAI) assesses three competencies essential to managerial performance: technical skills, interpersonal skills, and conceptual skills. Assessors rate prospects for supervisory positions on 20 items, measuring observed proficiency in each skill area. The results indicate a prospect's readiness to assume a supervisory position.

In addition to assessing a prospect's readiness, the instrument can be used to determine training and development needs for prospective managers. It can also be used in orientation programs to explain performance expectations of supervisors. Finally, the instrument can be used to design a performance appraisal system appropriate to managerial work.

Assessment of Prospect

Directions

Using the rating scale below, place an X in the appropriate column by each numbered item to indicate the consistency with which the person you are rating exhibits the behavior.

Rating Scale **SA** = Strongly Agree **A** = Agree **D** = Disagree **SD** = Strongly Disagree	SA	A	D	SD
Technical Competence				
1. Interprets instructions accurately.				
2. Follows task procedures correctly.				
3. Verifies the accuracy and completeness of assigned tasks; rarely has work returned because of errors/ mistakes.				
4. Uses required tools and/or equipment correctly; i.e., follows proper start-up, shut-down, and/or operating procedures.				
5. Follows administrative procedures correctly; i.e., follows proper safety, security, routing, and/or documentation procedures.				
6. Writes clearly and accurately; rarely has to explain the content of written work orally.				
7. Learns new technology applications correctly.				
Interpersonal Competence				
8. Maintains composure with difficult people and in difficult circumstances.				
9. Gives credit to others for their accomplishments and efforts.				
10. Seeks the opinions of others and incorporates their concerns into plans and actions.				
11. Speaks clearly and confidently to others.				
12. Obtains the willing support of others for tasks requiring cooperation and teamwork.				
13. Listens respectfully to others in order to understand their positions or concerns.				
14. Disagrees with others without being rude or offensive.				

Rating Scale **SA** = Strongly Agree **A** = Agree **D** = Disagree **SD** = Strongly Disagree				
	SA	**A**	**D**	**SD**
Conceptual Competence				
15. Sets appropriate priorities for work assignments.				
16. Understands the job's contribution to organizational goals.				
17. Shows the importance of continuous learning by taking the initiative to improve current skills and to learn new skills.				
18. Takes the initiative to determine a course of action when assignments are unclear or ill-defined.				
19. In handling job-related problems, demonstrates an awareness of long-term implications of a course of action; i.e., avoids quick fixes or expedient solutions that may later prove to be inadequate.				
20. Shows the importance of networking as a means of learning about issues and trends outside the company by becoming involved in professional and community organizations.				
Determining Total Score				
Step 1: Total the Xs marked in each column	—	—	—	—
Step 2: Multiply numbers in Step 1 by:	×4	×3	×2	×1
Step 3: Add column totals:	+	+	+	+
Step 4: Add four column totals for aggregate score:	= _____			

Now use the same scoring system to determine the total score under each scale: Technical Competence, Interpersonal Competence, and Conceptual Competence.

Do Not Recommend if:

☐ Candidate excludes self from consideration.

☐ Candidate scores below:

    21 on Technical Competency Scale

    18 on Interpersonal Competency Scale

    14 on Conceptual Competency Scale

Recommend if:

☐ Candidate's aggregate score is between 53 and 60 points (Long-Term Prospect)
☐ Candidate's aggregate score is between 61 and 70 points (Intermediate-Term Prospect)
☐ Candidate's aggregate score is between 71 and 80 points (Near-Term Prospect)

Developmental Needs:

☐ Long-Term Prospect: Needs Skills Training in:

_____

_____

_____

_____

☐ Intermediate-Term Prospect: Needs Skills Training in:

_____

_____

_____

_____

☐ Near-Term Prospect: Needs Skills Training in:

_____

_____

_____

_____

Source: Benham (1999). Reproduced with permission of Jossey-Bass/Pfeiffer.

Guidelines for Interpreting the SAI

Prospect Not Recommended

1. *Prospect Excludes Self.* Identify the reason and note whether it is circumstantial or attitudinal in nature. Circumstantial refers to temporary situations of a personal nature that make the timing inconvenient for the prospect. Prospects who exclude themselves for circumstantial reasons should be reconsidered for supervisory opportunities at a later time. Attitudinal refers to a prospect's unwillingness to become a supervisor. Some people object to the increased complexity and ambiguity of supervisory work. The discomfort caused by the complexity and ambiguity is so unsettling that it preempts any attraction that increased pay and status accompanying a promotion may have. Prospects who exclude themselves for attitudinal reasons should probably be removed from the

prospect list. Unless the attitude is caused by misinformation about what is expected in a supervisory role, the person probably will not succeed as a supervisor.

2. *Prospect's Ratings Are Too Low.* If the prospect fails to obtain the minimum score in one or more competencies, note the nature and severity of the difficulty. For example, did the prospect fail in one competency or in all three? Did the prospect miss the minimum score by only one or two points? Assess the likelihood that the prospect will receive a passing score after completing remedial training and some on-the-job coaching. If the likelihood is low, the prospect should be removed from the list. If the likelihood is high, however, use the data profile from the SAI to develop a plan for remedial work. As the employee responds to the training and coaching, showing improvement in the competencies targeted for development, consider reclassifying the person as a prospect.

Prospect Recommended

1. *Long-Term Prospect.* Generally, long-term prospects (those scoring between 53 and 60 points on the SAI) need additional training and exposure to certain performance situations before they will be strong candidates for promotion to supervisor. Normally, the time required to make the improvements will be 12 to 18 months. Long-term prospects usually need improvement in interpersonal and conceptual skills.

2. *Intermediate-Term Prospect.* Generally, intermediate-term prospects (those scoring between 61 and 70 points on the SAI) need training in just a few skills before they will be strong candidates for promotion to supervisor. Normally, the time required to make the improvements will be 6 to 12 months. Intermediate-term prospects usually need improvement in their interpersonal skills.

3. *Near-Term Prospect.* Generally, near-term prospects (those scoring between 71 and 80 points on the SAI) require coaching on a limited range of techniques before being nominated for promotion to supervisor. Normally, the time required to make the improvements will be one to six months. Near-term prospects usually need improvement in coaching and counseling techniques, especially those needed to implement the organization's performance appraisal system.

Developmental Needs

Although training that is experiential in nature, such as role playing, is very helpful in developing skills targeted by the SAI, selected job assignments are powerful learning opportunities that often go unrecognized by managers. For confirmed supervisory prospects, a task force assignment can be quite helpful in developing interpersonal and conceptual skills.

REFERENCES

Benham, P. (1999). Supervisory selection: The Supervisory Assessment Instrument. In Jossey-Bass/Pfeiffer (Ed.), *The 1999 annual: Vol. 1. Training* (pp. 93–105). San Francisco: Jossey-Bass/Pfeiffer.

Blake, R. R., & Mouton, J. S. (1978). *The new managerial grid.* Houston, TX: Gulf.

Brody, R. (1993). *Effectively managing human service organizations.* Newbury Park, CA: Sage.

Champagne, P., & McAfee, R. B. (1989). *Motivating strategies for performance and productivity.* New York: Quorum.

De Vries, R. E., Roe, R. A., & Taillieu, T.C.B. (1998). Need for supervision: Its impact on leadership effectiveness. *Journal of Applied Behavioral Science, 34*(4), 486–501.

Evered, R. D., & Selman, J. C. (1989). Coaching and the art of management. *Organizational Dynamics, 18*(2), 16–27.

Gitterman, A. (1972). Comparison of educational models and their influences on supervision. In F. W. Kaslow and Associates (Eds.), *Issues in human services* (pp. 18–38). San Francisco: Jossey-Bass/Pfeiffer.

Greenberg, J. (1996). *The quest for justice on the job: Essays and experiments.* Thousand Oaks, CA: Sage.

Gregoire, T. K., Propp, J., & Poertner, J. (1998). The supervisor's role in the transfer of training. *Administration in Social Work, 22*(1), 1–18.

Hopkins, K. M. (1997). Supervisor intervention with troubled workers: A social identity perspective. *Human Relations, 50*(10), 1215–1231.

Kadushin, A. (1976). *Supervision in social work.* New York: Columbia University.

Kaslow, F. W. (1972). Group supervision. In F. W. Kaslow and Associates (Eds.), *Issues in Human Services* (pp. 115–141). San Francisco: Jossey-Bass.

Lewis, J. A., Lewis, M. D., & Souflée, F. (1991). *Management of human service programs* (2nd ed.). Pacific Grove, CA: Brooks/Cole.

Loen, R. O. (1994). *Superior supervision: The 10% solution.* New York: Lexington Books.

Moniz-Cook, E., Millington, D., & Silver, M. (1997). Residential care for older people: Job satisfaction and psychological health in care staff. *Health and Social Care in the Community, 5*(2), 124–133.

Mueller, N. V. (1999). The professional pairing program: A new way to mentor. In Jossey-Bass/Pfeiffer (Ed.), *The 1999 annual: Vol. 2. Consulting* (pp. 187–198). San Francisco: Jossey-Bass/Pfeiffer.

Pareek, U., & Rao, T. V. (1990). Performance coaching. In J. W. Pfeiffer (Ed.), *The 1990 annual: Developing human resources* (pp. 249–263). San Diego, CA: University Associates.

Patti, R. J. (1983). *Social welfare administration: Managing social programs in a developmental context.* Englewood Cliffs, NJ: Prentice-Hall.

Pincus, J. D. (1986). Communication satisfaction and job performance. *Human Communication Research, 12*(3), 395–419.

Rauktis, M. E., & Koeske, G. F. (1994). Maintaining social worker morale: When supportive supervision is not enough. *Administration in Social Work, 18*(1), 39–60.

Richer, S. F., & Vallerand, R. J. (1995). Supervisor's interactional style on subordinates' intrinsic and extrinsic motivation. *The Journal of Social Psychology, 135*(6), 707–723.

Robbins, S. P. (1995). *Supervision today!* Englewood Cliffs, NJ: Prentice-Hall.

Rosengren, W. R. (1974). Structure, policy, and style: Strategies of organizational control. In Y. Hasenfeld and R. A. English (Eds.), *Human service organizations: A book of readings* (pp. 391–412). Ann Arbor, MI: University of Michigan.

Royster, E. C. (1972). Black supervisors: Problems of race and role. In F. W. Kaslow and Associates (Eds.), *Issues in human services* (pp. 72–84). San Francisco: Jossey-Bass.

Russell, P. A., Lankford, M. W., & Grinnell, R. M. (1985). Administrative styles of social work supervisors in a human service agency. In S. Slavin (Ed.), *Social administration: The management of the social services: Vol. 1 of An introduction to human services management* (2nd ed., pp. 150–167). Binghamton, NY: Haworth.

Schuler, R. S. (1981). *Personnel and human resource management.* St. Paul, MN: West.

Sonnenstuhl, W., & Trice, H. (1990). *Strategies for employee assistance programs: The crucial balance.* Ithaca, NY: ILR Press.

Umiker, W. (1988). *Management skills for the new health care supervisor.* Gaithersburg, MD: Aspen.

Walsh, J. A. (1990). From clinician to supervisor: Essential ingredients for training. *Families in Society, 71*(2), 82–87.

Weinbach, R. (1998). *The social worker as manager: A practical guide to success* (3rd ed.). Needham Heights, MA: Allyn & Bacon.

Wendt, P. F., & Peterson, D. A. (1992). National survey of professionals in aging network supports need for formal training in gerontology. *AGHE Exchange, 15*, 1–4.

Chapter 10

Funding Programs and Financial Management

Involvement in financial matters has increased for administrators of service programs because of the emphasis on accountability and the multiplicity of funding sources (Gross, 1985; Lohmann, 1980; Slavin, 1985). Financial management knowledge and skills are essential, and these areas frequently need development. Many administrators emerge from conceptual, program-oriented staff positions lacking the leadership skills necessary for effective acquisition of funding. Creative decision-making, influence, and vision are all important skills for fundraising. A combination of management and leadership skills is required of the administrator. For example, the systematic and competent development of a grant proposal for a new project submitted to a funding source may also require an executive presentation to a decision-making group.

The gerontologist administrator will be involved in obtaining, managing, and monitoring financial resources. The extent and kinds of activities will depend on the level of the administrator and the organizational setting. Many administrators will be deeply involved in all three areas. Generally, the higher the level of administration, the more time dedicated to obtaining funds. The size and sector—public, not-for-profit, or private—will also determine the extent of involvement with financial management. In most public programs, much of the financial management is accomplished by other departments, like accounting, budgeting, systems, or capital expenditures (Weiner, 1990). Regardless of the setting or size, the gerontologist administrator must give attention to and be thoroughly informed of the financial aspects of the organization or his unit. The perception that an organization has effective financial management and funding directly relates to the conclusion, although not always accurate, that the programs are effective.

SECTOR DIFFERENCES IN FUNDING AND FINANCIAL MANAGEMENT

Funding sources differ considerably for the three sectors that provide programs and services for older adults. The major difference is in the funding motives. Profit organizations are driven by efficiency and the bottom line (Elkin, 1985; Gatewood, Taylor, & Ferrell, 1995). It may be that a given profit organization adopts a mode of operation that claims service first and profits will follow; however, without profit there is no reason for service. Profit is understandably the primary measure of success. Not-for-profit organizations, whose funding is typically more diverse, strive primarily for effectiveness of programs with efficiency as a dual goal. Not-for-profit organizations are often expected to show revenues above expenditures, sometimes called "earned income," and demonstrate impact of programs to funding sources. Public organizations derive most funds from taxes and are driven by maintaining stability, control, and accountability to government bodies and the public (Weiner, 1990). Thus, all three sectors have different kinds of dependencies on funding sources.

Many government organizations provide programs and are also a source of funding by contract or purchase of service for profit and not-for-profit organizations (Elkin, 1985). Funding efforts are frequently political. For example, the chief executive may become involved with the state legislature or Congress to maintain or increase appropriations. Not-for-profit funding sources are by far the most complex, utilizing local, state, and federal funding, government and foundation grants, reimbursement for service, fees for service, community resources, fund-raising events, membership fees, and philanthropic contributions. Profit organizations that offer services are not typically eligible for most grants from government or foundations, but may receive government funding by reimbursement for services such as with social insurance (Medicare) and service purchase contracts.

It is desirable for most gerontologist administrators to have a large measure of control over financial planning and financial management. However, such controls are often limited in large profit corporations and public organizations. For many large corporations, where the majority of gerontologist administrators are in community-based services such as in nursing homes, much of the financial decision-making about budgets as well as control of accounts payable and purchasing is performed by a central office, either within a region or a central location. On the other hand, for small businesses which have employees of fewer than 25 and do not dominate the marketplace, business owners who are frequently owners-managers have extensive control over finances. A very high percentage of profit organizations that serve older adults are small businesses, like case management, home health, or professional offices. Many of these small businesses operate without a formal budget and use basic financial management techniques.

Gerontologist administrators in public organizations may have a limited role in financial management because other units within the government bureaucracy handle the financial aspects (Weiner, 1990). The gerontologist administrator's responsibility is to gain an understanding of the regulations and requirements that pertain to the financial aspects. For state and local governments, the Government Accounting Standard Board (GASB) has established standards for accounting and financial reporting (Martin & Kettner, 1997). In 2000, GASB extended its authority beyond generally accepted accounting principles and standards to require performance data annually. This will affect many not-for-profit organizations as well. Generally, it is advisable for the administrator to maintain a parallel financial management system in order to maintain some measure of control (Weiner, 1990). This practice becomes part of an elaborate checks-and-balances system that characterizes government finances, which are highly subject to public scrutiny.

Not-for-profit organizations that serve older adults with the infusion of federal funds through a variety of sources operate most programs. These organizations with multiple funding sources have multiple reporting requirements and frequently different budgets that respond to different fiscal years. Indeed, one community program that served older adults received funds from the federal government, the local government, and the United Way, all of which had different fiscal years requiring budget proposals and reports.

Standards for audits and accounting are offered by several national organizations, such as the United Way and the National Health Care Council, to provide these not-for-profit organizations acceptable standards for financial management (Elkin, 1985). Accounting practices in not-for-profit corporations differ in many ways from those of government and private business. Some not-for-profit organizations' budgets include an expected deficit, and many not-for-profit organizations' revenue flows do not parallel operating cash requirements. These differences are extensive enough that many business schools at universities have set up separate departments and degrees for not-for-profit accounting.

The differences in funding sources and financial management have been offered because they are frequently ignored in the literature and because the gerontologist administrator who moves between different sectors must have a basic understanding of these differences. It would be difficult, if not impossible, to refer constantly to these differences throughout the remainder of this chapter. Thus, some emphasis will be placed on certain funding and financial practices that are common to all three sectors. Because of the complexity and dominance of not-for-profit organizations, much of the elaboration of information will be in relation to this third sector. The remainder of the chapter will provide information on funding sources and fund-raising, financial management and accountability, and use of financial technology.

FUNDING SOURCES AND FUND-RAISING

Funds are obtained from multiple sources for organizations providing older adult programs. The sources available are often determined by the sector of the organization. Profit organizations are less likely to receive donations because there is no tax advantage for the donor and because of the profit orientation of the organization. Government policies will determine who is eligible and the conditions for receiving government funds (Jansson, 1990). Government organizations are more dependent than not-for-profit and profit organizations on direct government appropriations. Not-for-profit organizations are dependent upon philanthropy, grants, fees, and contracts. Profit organizations usually obtain most funds from fees generated by programs. Organizations in all three sectors may be in competition for certain funds.

Gerontologist administrators are in positions that will require tough decisions about funding priorities and justification of the purpose of programs to funding sources. This means becoming and remaining informed, maintaining contact with potential and existing funding sources, and cooperating with a number of organizations. The demonstration of sound financial management and accountability for funds is crucial to continued funding and the development of new resources. As a beginning step, a general overview of funding sources is offered.

Major Sources of Funding for Older Adult Programs

- *General Revenue.* Funds from taxes, fees, fines, and investments of state, local, and federal government are allocated by governing bodies to departments or programs annually. The federal government dominates this source, and while several departments provide funds, the major funding over the years has been authorized by the Older Americans Act.

- *Insurance.* Both private insurance and social insurance reimburse or make direct payment for health, mental health, and human services. Private insurance is frequently paired with social insurance, providing co-payment for a percentage of the fee. The major sources of social insurance programs are Medicare and Medicaid.

- *Consumer Payments.* Fees for service, sometimes on sliding scales, other times as co-payments with insurance, represent a significant share of funding. Increasing numbers of older Americans can pay fees, as many have considerable savings and investments, as well as multiple pensions in addition to social security (Schulz, 1995).

- *Foundations and Federated Agencies.* Private, national, and local foundations set funding priorities and accept grant applications for specific projects or programs. Many communities have federated foundations called community foundations. Other federated funding sources exist, the best known of which is the United Way. Some enterprising organizations that serve older adults have established their own foundation in which they are the sole recipient of that foundation's awards.

- *Private Philanthropy.* Direct charitable contributions from individuals, clubs, churches, and corporations are a cornerstone of funding for community not-for-profit organizations. The contributions include endowments and bequests that can provide great funding stability. Many organizations also have membership fees and hold fund-raising events.

- *In-kind.* This is the provision of goods, services, or properties at no cost to the organization. Volunteers are an example of in-kind services. Another example is a congregate meal program which had free desserts provided several days a week by different restaurants in the community. The possibilities are endless.

The Older Americans Act

The Older Americans Act (OAA) is a unique and extensive resource for funds for programs that serve older adults. First enacted in 1965, the OAA has features unlike other social legislation. The Act created the Administration on Aging (AOA) as an independent agency that reports directly to the Secretary of the Department of Health and Human Services. In 1973 the Comprehensive Service Amendment required each state to establish regional Area Agencies on Aging (AAA) and authorized additional funding for programs. The funding stream goes directly to a network of AAAs. There are approximately 700 AAAs which in turn fund not-for-profit and profit organizations to deliver programs for older adults. The AAA concept allows for considerable flexibility in the use of local service organizations (Atchley, 2000). Funds are allocated for all those over the age of 60, rather than requiring eligibility for services based on income testing. Programs and services are free, but the government allows voluntary contributions by older adults.

Title III of the OAA establishes authority for grants to states for community planning and social services, research and development projects, and personnel training in the field of aging (Holt, 1994). The AAAs are expected to stretch the limits of Title III funds by brokering and pooling public and private resources (Liebig, 1996). Historically, specific guidelines for the definition of need have been flexible, allowing the states to be responsible for defining the target population. No state uses the same formula for applying for allocations. The appropriations are provided to each state in accordance with the proportion of population aged 60 and over.

The OAA has been reauthorized and revised numerous times over the years. During the fall of the 106th Congress, re-authorization of the Older Americans Act (OAA) was under consideration. The re-authorization is for the years 2000–2004 and, assuming that adjustments are made for inflation, the amount is estimated at $7.6 billion for this period. More specifically (as this text is prepared for press), $1.6 billion has been proposed by Congress for the year 2000, representing a modest increase. A portion of the increase is for a new program to provide information and support for family caregivers. It would require a 25 percent match from states. In his year 2000 budget, President Clinton proposed expansion of programs under the OAA to increase home-delivered meals and funding for family caregivers (Blancato, 1999). Since 1984, the language of the legislation has attempted to target the funds more to those who are poor. However, with the expansion of funding for programs, numerous contradictions and policies on the targets of funds have emerged (Ellis & Roe, 1993).

In recent years, the debate has centered around enhanced funding formulas for older adults in rural areas. One study that explored funding by taking a random sample in five states found that enhanced funding that favors a rural population is an inappropriate strategy (Harlow, 1993). Although many arguments have been made and research has been conducted about the targeting of funds, it has not significantly impacted funding formulas over the years. However, the ambiguity has negatively affected delivery of services (Ellis & Roe, 1993).

Each reauthorization of the OAA brings changes. In 1992, support services for family caregivers of frail elderly were added (Cannon, 1993). Although OAA authorizes a large number of services, the level of funding is low ($900 million in 1992) which forces a focus on low-income, minority, or frail elderly (Hooyman & Kiyak, 1993).

Medicaid and Medicare

Major funding comes from the reimbursement system established by the social insurance programs of Medicaid and Medicare. Eligibility for Medicaid is based on income, and all older adults upon reaching age 65 are eligible for Medicare. The reimbursement is such that individuals may be eligible for either or both, depending on the circumstances. Funding through these sources supports such programs as nursing homes, day care, home health, hospice, hospitals, and health clinics. Many of these programs would not exist without payments from Medicaid and Medicare.

Medicaid, a comprehensive health care program for the poor, was an amendment to the Social Security Act in 1950. However, it was not until 1965, when it was expanded by Title XIX of the Social Security Act to increase eligibility to cover basic health services, that the true impact of this funding was experienced (Schulz, 1995). While it is a federal program with accompanying guidelines, eligibility requirements are determined by each state. In addition to eligibility, states determine the duration and amount of service offered, as well as the reimbursement procedures and rates. Medicaid covers the same medical service paid for by Medicare, plus drugs, eyeglasses, medically related transportation, and extended residence in long-term care (nursing home) facilities (Atchley, 2000). A substantial percentage of the Medicaid expenditure for long-term care is for older adults in facilities. Medicaid, through its optional waiver home care, offers an alternative to institutional long-term care (Rosenzweig, 1995). Most states contract with a private profit contractor to administer the payments.

Medicare, which provides universal medical coverage for older adults, was added to the Social Security Act in 1965. This totally federal program, which receives financing from compulsory payroll taxes, is administered by the Health Care Financing Administration (HCFA) of the federal government. All older adults eligible for social security or the railroad retirement system and most social security disability beneficiaries under the age of 65 are eligible for Medicare. The Medicare program has two parts: hospital insurance (Part A) and supplementary medical insurance (Part B). Part B of Medicare covers outpatient services including physical therapy, psychotherapy, and others.

Program reimbursements range from 50 to 100 percent of reasonable charges. Medicare establishes fees for health care institutions and providers. Many medical needs are not covered by Medicare, the most significant of which is reimbursement for medication. The addition of medication is under consideration by Congress at the present time. A significant portion of these funds pay for services at hospitals and nursing homes, as well as for services by private practice health care professionals.

Complexity of Funding

Programs for older adults, especially community direct service programs, are characterized by complex funding which may change from year to year. While not a desirable phenomenon, it is the reality, and it presents many challenges for the gerontologist administrator. Two examples, one demonstrating multiple funding, the other transition of funding sources, will serve as cogent illustrations.

A study of geriatric health services at 10 community health centers provides an illustration of a not-for-profit, quasi-government organization's use of multiple funding sources (Yeatts, Ray, List, & Duggar, 1991). Community health centers offer preventative and primary health care principally for the underserved rural and urban areas across the United States. Typically, these programs have concentrated on care to children and middle-aged family members. To develop the geriatric services, as an addition to existing health programs, information was obtained from community surveys, public hearings, AAAs, and older adult focus groups. Once established, these programs, in addition to traditional primary medical care, offered mental health services, case management services, weekly check-ups for those in day care, health counseling, medication review, homemaker services, respite care, and transportation. The primary funding sources were Sections 329 and 330 of the Public Health Act, which is supported by general revenue, Medicare, Medicaid, state and local government, private foundation grants, and corporate donations. Other sources of funding were sliding scale patient fees and Medi-gap private insurance, which provides reimbursement for that portion not covered by Medicare. Income from the primary sources was used to offset lack of income for the non-refundable services.

Grant funding, whether from government or foundation, is often used to demonstrate the efficacy of a program. Therefore, alternative funding must be part of the planning process. Unfortunately, some innovative programs for older adults are shrunk or ended when the grant period is over. The Rural Elderly Outreach Project of the Abbe Center for Community Mental Health, "survived and even flourished well beyond the initial three year grant period" (Smith,

Buckwalter, Zevenbergen, & Kudart, 1993, p. 212). The program was to assess and treat mentally ill older adult clients in their own homes, integrating health, mental health, and human services. A multidisciplinary team consisting of a social worker, a nurse, and a psychiatrist formed the core for the mental health team that operated and coordinated the services.

Over the three-year grant period, the services and the personnel were expanded. Approximately three months before the end of the grant, the planning efforts culminated in a retreat conducted by the organization's executive director that formulated a plan for continuing the program. It was necessary to put several small aspects of the program on hold. Mental health in-home services, previously offered for free, would now charge fees using Medicare, Medicaid, and private insurance along with private co-payment. Initial assessments would continue as a free service. These changes required the staff to become involved in discussing financial matters and handling insurance forms. The project, which had been semi-autonomous, was renamed Elderly Services and integrated into the permanent structure of the community mental health center. After the transition period, Elderly Services continued to expand.

The gerontologist administrator must be aware not only of the variety of funding sources but also of the mechanisms for funding. This requires knowledge of the policies and procedures. It also may mean becoming involved in efforts to influence the policies and laws.

Fund-Raising Efforts

Gerontologist administrators of all levels will be involved in requesting and raising funds. The skills of both management and leadership are necessary for successful fund-raising. Acquiring funds is a basic survival function that for many administrators is a substantive part of the work requirements. This involves translating the programs to stakeholders and the broader community. No matter what the fund-raising method, the public image that includes the perceived accomplishments and failures of the organization will affect the funding. The most straightforward method is requesting government funds by submitting an annual budget. In addition to the mechanics of budget development, which will be elaborated upon later in this chapter, this can require presentations, supplementary explanations, and lobbying efforts with governance bodies or within the larger organizational structure. Most of the time, these efforts are for operating and capital funds to support programs. In some instances, organizations acquire funds to be the source of funding for other programs.

When the organization is the grantor or contract manager, such as with AAAs, they typically issue requests for proposals (RFP). Weiner (1990) offers a useful RFP format for potential grantees:

1. Specifications include selection criteria and procedure, program design, funding limits, time frame, and monitoring procedures.

2. The written RFP document is issued to prospective grantees with deadlines.

3. Proposals received by deadline are given an initial evaluation to determine finalists.

4. Finalists are interviewed and selected.

Not-for-profit and profit programs, depending on the criteria, may compete for these funds. Programs in these two sectors also obtain funds from third-party reimbursements, fees, purchase of service agreements, and contracts. Private, not-for-profit programs historically have developed a broad base of additional fund-raising activities. These efforts, some of which in the changing service environment are available to profit organizations, are contracts, philanthropic activities, grants, and exchanges that produce revenue.

Contracts

These are legal agreements for specific services that usually require competitive bidding (Jansson, 1990). The bid is in response to an RFP that sets forth organizational qualifications, project criteria, and the details of the desired service. In some instances, a "sole source" contract is used, when it can be demonstrated that only one organization in the geographical area can provide the service. Contracts for service are highly enforceable, are usually monitored closely by the contractor, and are occasionally subject to third-party evaluations. Under certain circumstances, contracts can be issued to profit organizations. For example, HCFA of the federal government, which is responsible for Medicare, contracts with private profit insurance companies called "intermediaries" in each state to administer Medicare funds in response to claims related to health and mental health services.

Philanthropy

Voluntary contributions by individuals, families, service clubs, corporations, and foundations are the heart of funding for not-for-profit programs that serve older adults. These contributions range from a few dollars to millions. Many programs rely heavily on direct philanthropic financial contributions. Contributions of this nature are solicited both by members of the board of directors and by staff. Many boards of directors have a fund-raising committee. Larger organizations employ staff, such as a development director or a public relations person, who has responsibility for soliciting funds.

Most of the funds donated come from a small percentage of people (Weiner, 1990). People donate primarily to causes and identified needs. The reasons are varied and multiple: consistency with family history, to repay the community, enhance business opportunities, or experience positive feelings. A small percentage of people are motivated by the tax deduction.

Donations take many forms, such as direct cash contributions, pledges, items such as a car or house, stocks, bequests, or insurance policies. Most of the time, funds are sought to support the service aspect of programs for older adults, but

Table 10.1
Formula for Successful Fund-Raising

- Acknowledge all contributions immediately in writing
- Maintain detailed records of donors
- Personal contact, often several, is best
- Have a project or specific item to identify
- Contact people who have a history of philanthropy
- Boldly present the successes and accomplishments of your organization
- Be able to explain how a person's contribution will meet a need
- Whenever possible, offer methods of public recognition

it is also common to engage in fund-raising for construction or equipment. For example, one large residential complex chose to convert a portion of its long-term care facility into an Alzheimer's unit. This organization then solicited funds for both the renovations of the unit as well as the program for the patients. There are time-tested principles that will maximize the likelihood of success in obtaining contributions. These are summarized in Table 10.1.

In addition to direct personal contact, funds can also be solicited by mail. It is generally a goal of direct fund-raising to have people increase their donations over the previous year (Weiner, 1990). The combination of a mail solicitation with a personal follow-up will prove to be fruitful. Fortunately, some parties will choose to give annual contributions and place the organization on an annual donor list. It is essential to maintain accurate records of contributions. This is best accomplished by using a computer database program that provides basic information on contributors and a history of contributions.

Grants and Grantsmanship

Grants are funds provided to organizations that demonstrate the expertise and the ability to meet the objectives published by the granting source. Grants are available for capital expenditures, service programs, staff training, and research. Some grants incorporate two or three areas. Applications for grant funds are made in accordance with grantor published guidelines, must follow a required format, and usually require an evaluation (Skidmore, 1995). Adherence to the detailed expectations of the funding source is essential for success.

All grants will require an initial investment of time and resources as well as the involvement of a number of staff. Most grants will require matching funds or in-kind resources. Some of the administrative requirements will increase the work load for staff beyond the grant-funded activities. Consequently, the gerontologist administrator must, with the assistance of other staff, carefully assess and analyze the grant announcement to determine that the resources exist to make application and complete the project. This assessment should include the determination and support from higher levels of administration (Patti, 1983).

During the initial phase, it is also important to contact the funding source to establish rapport, clarify objectives, gain additional information, and determine the nature of the competition or chance of success.

When it comes to the availability of grants, a play on an old adage comes to mind, "So many grants, so little time." Grants are available in abundance from all levels of government, foundations, and corporations. Foundation funding of programs has lagged behind government and corporations with a definite trend toward increased funding (Sontz, 1989). It depends greatly on the nature of the organization as to the availability. There must be a match with the organization's purpose and the funding priorities of the source.

Certain grants are available only to not-for-profit organizations. Information on funding sources can be obtained by computer searches by subject, using key words or accessing such sources as the Foundation Center or the *Foundation Grant Index Annual* (Rubin & Rubin, 1992). Even the local phone directory provides information on foundations. Government organizations issue numerous bulletins and announcements, far too many to mention. One generic publication is *The Catalog of Federal Domestic Assistance*. A rule of thumb is that private foundations allow more freedom than government with project creativity, while government will have more stringent guidelines and elaborate reporting procedures (Brody, 1991).

Once a decision is made to pursue a grant based on the announcement, the best procedure is to submit a brief prospectus to the funding organization and follow with a phone conversation. This "testing the waters" will provide valuable information and also contribute to maintaining contact with an individual in the granting organization. The most successful applications are written in clear, concise, and forceful language incorporating a unique approach to the problem (Skidmore, 1995). Above all, follow the directions of the granting organization.

Grant proposal guidelines and instructions vary considerably, but the federal government has a standard format. A sample format is presented in Table 10.2. The ordering of the items will differ from agency to agency. Sometimes following the submission of a written proposal, an oral presentation or a site visit will be required. Never assume that the reviewers have read the entire application (Rubin & Rubin, 1992). The administrator in these situations must be capable of enthusiastically summarizing the proposal information, with emphasis on the capacity of the organization to succeed.

Funds from Exchanges

Fund-raising by exchange of a product or services is common in not-for-profit organizations. For these fund-raising efforts, all or a portion of the funds may be a donation, depending on the type of exchange. Perhaps unique to these particular methods is that many individuals may participate who do not have a particular interest in the purpose of the organization. For example, a widely recognized older adult program was conducting a capital campaign for a new administrative center. On the donated land was an old brick structure. The bricks

Table 10.2
Sample Format for a Grant Proposal

1. **Cover Letter.** The letter should be on letterhead, signed by the chief executive. Content should include a brief restatement of the purpose, the goals, and the amount requested.

2. **Table of Contents.** A detailed outline of the grant proposal.

3. **Summary Statement.** A concise overview of the goals, objectives, methods, and budget.

4. **Statement of Need.** Documentation with evidence of problems and needs. Extensive data should be placed in the appendix.

5. **Goals and Objectives.** The ultimate intentions of the project and the specific, measurable objectives.

6. **Methods.** The components of the program detailing the tasks related to the objectives.

7. **Evaluation.** The plan to measure and document accomplishment of objectives.

8. **Qualifications.** The capabilities and characteristics of the organization that will contribute to the success of the project, including staff credentials and resources.

9. **Future of the Project.** A plan to continue the project.

10. **Budget.** A line item presentation of the funds requested, with delineation of other sources if appropriate. This must be accompanied by a narrative explaining expected costs within each line item. Include the organization's total budget and audit.

11. **Appendices.** Support data, letters of support from relevant organizations and people, résumé of key project personnel, and major equipment or construction quotes.

were dismantled, and each was painted with a picture by an artist. Individuals who made a contribution of a thousand dollars or more to the capital campaign received a painted brick. It became a status symbol in the community to have a painted brick displayed.

Establishing a supportive membership to an organization where different categories of members may join for a fee—typically individual, family, and corporate—is a common practice. Members then receive certain benefits, such as a newsletter or invitations to events. In some instances, the members are an extension of the not-for-profit organization, and they can attend the annual meeting and vote on changes in the board.

Members also provide a distinct audience for fund-raising events. Such events can have the dual purpose of raising funds and highlighting an organization's program and successes. The list of possible events that an organization, usually with the help of a board of directors, can offer the community is endless. Events such as award dinners, special luncheons, black tie balls, golf tournaments, and auctions all have the capacity to raise funds. For most of these events, some of the products are donated, and the work activities are conducted by volunteers. Therefore, the ticket sales represent a donation to the organization. Such community events, if successful, are morale builders for both volunteers and staff.

Sales of products in which the proceeds or a portion of the proceeds are donated to the organization is yet another method of fund-raising. Two illustrations of this method are offered. First, local businesses in town can establish a day or a period of a day in which a percentage of the sales are contributed to the organization. Second, some organizations, through a volunteer committee, operate a thrift shop where donations of goods are then sold with the proceeds going to the organization's programs.

Money is a product. It can be invested in an assortment of income opportunities like CDs, money market funds, stocks, mutual funds, and index funds. While sometimes controversial, this is usually a decision of the board of directors. When the decision is made to make such investments, it is wise to adopt by vote of the board an investment policy and to work through a reputable broker to manage the account. The opportunity to raise funds in this manner is more available than most organizations realize. For example, instead of keeping operating funds in a regular checking account, why not place them in a money market checking account?

FINANCIAL MANAGEMENT

The discussion thus far has focused upon funding sources and fund-raising. This represents the revenue side of the financial picture, which is completed by detailing the expenditures. The gerontologist administrator, to varying degrees, will have responsibility for developing and monitoring the organization's budget. The efficiency and effectiveness of the use of funds vary greatly among organizations. The successful gerontologist administrator will clearly understand the importance of budgetary processes and decisions. The budget serves as a major means of control, is a reflection of the program priorities, and in part results from a political process (Gatewood et al., 1995; Meenaghan, Washington, & Ryan, 1982; Weiner, 1990). Detailed accounting, a highly important and technical area, should not be confused with budgeting and will not be elaborated upon in this text. The responsibility of the administrator to understand the different formats and types of budgets, budget planning and development, monitoring of the budget, and financial accountability are critical areas of expertise that will be discussed.

Budget Types and Formats

Among the beginning steps to gain competency in financial management is learning about budget techniques. A budget is a formal, written plan that predicts revenue (income) and expenditures (costs). There are basically two types of budgets. The operating budget details the day-to-day activities of the organization, such as payroll and supplies. In the section of this chapter on budgetary monitoring, a monthly statement will be presented in Table 10.3. This also provides an example of a line-item operating budget. Generally, these are annual budgets, but recently, emphasis on planning has encouraged two-year budgeting.

Table 10.3
Day Care for Older Adults Monthly Statement

	CURRENT PERIOD		
REVENUES:	**Actual**	**Budget**	**Variance**
Grants and Contributions	4,500	5,000	-500
Daily Fees	12,559	16,146	-3,587
TOTAL REVENUES—NET	17,059	21,146	-4,087
EXPENSES:			
Salaries	12,356	9,544	-2,812
Payroll Taxes	990	730	-260
Pension Benefits	239	239	0
Health Insurance	391	391	0
Workers Compensation	370	294	-76
Employee Education	42	53	11
Other Employee Benefits	0	0	0
Licenses and Fees	0	25	25
Advertising—Help Wanted	961	0	-961
Advertising—Promotion	502	210	-292
Activities Expenses	12	63	51
Utilities	616	622	6
Supplies and Postage	154	414	260
Supplies—Food	1,710	1,656	-54
Other Expenses	5	50	45
Dues and Subscriptions	25	10	-15
Repairs to Building	0	50	50
Repairs to Equipment	0	50	50
Insurance	135	260	125
TOTAL EXPENSES	18,508	14,661	-3,847
NET INCOME (LOSS)	-1,449	6,485	-7,934

YEAR-TO-DATE

Actual	Budget	Variance
15,000	20,000	-5,000
99,958	107,991	-8,033
114,958	127,991	-13,033
75,780	65,192	-10,588
5,424	4,987	-437
1,629	1,629	0
3,408	3,128	-280
2,151	1,995	-156
134	318	184
193	279	86
0	150	150
2,867	0	-2,867
888	1,680	792
215	450	235
6,069	6,023	-46
1,869	2,769	900
12,861	11,076	-1,785
429	400	-29
145	110	-35
422	400	-22
1,036	400	-636
1,236	2,080	844
116,756	103,066	-13,690
-1,798	24,925	-26,723

Note: Monthly statement for the period ending March 31, 1999.

227

The second major type is a capital budget that presents revenue needs and expected expenditures for high-cost equipment, renovations, purchase of property, construction, and related planning activities, such as construction feasibility studies and engineering reports. These budgets can relate to annual expenditures or to expenditures for many years in the future. Frequently, more stringent requirements on the expenditures of these funds are placed on administrators.

Three formats are used by service organizations for constructing budgets: line-item, program, and performance. A particular approach to budgeting, which is not a separate format, is zero-based budgeting. These formats and the zero-based approach are not mutually exclusive and can be used in combinations that best serve the organization's purpose (Skidmore, 1995):

- *Line-item Budget.* This is the most common format. It systematically lists the expected revenues from different sources and group expenditures, such as salaries, benefits, travel, and supplies. Typically, it presents the previous year's information for historical comparisons. The line-item budget lends itself to tight financial control but lacks program orientation.

- *Program Budget.* The program budget is organized by functions and relates directly to goals and objectives. This format utilizes milestones and performance criteria and identifies cost centers, but has somewhat less control than the line-item budget. It also offers greater flexibility for the administrator, as all costs for a given program within an organization are lumped together. For example, a senior center with three programs would have a lump sum for day care, meals and activities, and case management.

- *Performance Budget.* This is the least used format, but the most useful for reporting the actual service expenditures. That is, it relates unit of work performance to financial costs. These units can be compared to production standards or benchmarks.

Zero-based budgeting is an approach to the budget process. The zero-based budget has wide popular appeal partly because of the name and the association with budget restraints. It is actually not a separate format and typically is not used independently. When completely implemented, it is actually a form of program budgeting (Crow & Odewahn, 1987; Meenaghan et al., 1982). One element of this approach is budgeting by starting with no allocations at the beginning of each budget preparation cycle, requiring justification of all requested funds. This can be a comprehensive and elaborate process, depending on the criteria for justification of funds. The intent is to force administrators to re-examine each budget area to achieve more efficiency (Gatewood et al., 1995). This practice differs from the common procedure of simply adjusting the budget of the previous year.

Budget Planning and Development

For organizations that provide programs for older adults, several budgets or variations of the main budget are frequently required because of the multiple funding sources that may have different fiscal years. This is especially the case for community-based not-for-profit agencies. Also, for older adult programs, most of the budget is personnel costs. The budget establishes parameters for all elements of the organization's operation. It is advisable to involve administrators from throughout the organization and other staff in the development process. Executive administrators, with assistance from technical staff, will ultimately need to complete the final document following discussions and negotiations. Steps for the budget planning process are offered by Crow and Odewahn (1987):

1. Establish measurable goals and specific objectives to determine the financial plan.
2. Examine alternative methods and resources to meet the objectives.
3. Estimate the cost involved.
4. Predict the expected revenues.
5. Formulate into a budget format.

It is important to notice that the process begins with needs rather than resources. Beginning with predicted funding will limit the creativity of the budget process and stagnate programs.

Two additional, important considerations are budget padding and contingency funds. If the gerontologist administrator chooses to enhance the budget in anticipation of cuts, this common practice would likely be detected and could result in less, not more, funds. The nature of service organizations assures that unpredictable expenditures will emerge. Consequently, a contingency fund for the gerontologist administrator to use at his discretion is essential.

Once the budget document is composed, often in draft form, it is necessary to seek approval from higher levels of administration or governance bodies. This will require a verbal presentation of the budget. It is advisable for the top administrative executive to make this presentation himself. One can anticipate that negotiations will continue with administrators in higher positions in the organization or with board committees ultimately to gain approval. These negotiations and approval processes are critical to the operations of an organization. These processes render the budget a mutually agreed-upon plan and further the understanding that the plan can be altered by mutual agreement.

Budget Monitoring

The gerontologist administrator must keep abreast of the revenues and expenditures to ascertain potential surpluses and deficits, as well as to identify important indicators of operation. This can be accomplished by close review of the monthly balance sheet and financial statement (also called income statement or profit and loss statement). The balance sheet summarizes the organization's financial position, including the value of assets, debts, holdings, and accumulated depreciation (Gatewood et al., 1995). The monthly financial sheet typically includes revenues and expenses for the month and year to date, allowing the actual figures to be compared with the budgeted amounts. In some instances, this statement will include the total budget and the percentages of the revenues and expenses (Skidmore, 1995). These statements are especially useful if budget variances are included, as in the not-for-profit example in Table 10.3. This example illustrates both the format for a line-item budget, as well as a monthly statement. In profit organizations, documented profitability will directly affect annual compensation and bonuses. In most organizations, this data can be accessed at any time by computer. Prompt and timely reporting of these financial tools by responsible staff should be required by the gerontologist administrator.

Another method for monitoring financial matters is *ratio analysis.* As mentioned before, a line-item budget does not provide information for detailed analysis of programs. Thus, the administrator may want to obtain additional information to monitor the expenditures of programs. Such information will allow a ratio analysis which establishes the proportional relationship between two variables. Crow and Odewahn (1987) provide an example: "Administrative costs divided by total service dollars yields the proportion of administrative costs to total service costs, allowing the manager to identify critical program dimensions" (p. 158). These ratios can be compared to established standards and goals or national benchmarks.

Budget Adjustments

The gerontologist administrator in the chief executive position will find it necessary, and often required, to conduct these analyses and review these reports with a committee of the board of directors, a district administrator, or another party higher in the organizational structure. Mutual analyses are constructive and lead to early problem identification and corrective action. The budget represents an estimate of anticipated revenues and expenses. It is not a fixed document that cannot be altered. Although there is considerable misunderstanding about the fixed nature of budgets, budget adjustments are usually necessary. Some organizations allow the chief administrator to make adjustments within a certain percentage so that funds can be transferred from one area to another.

Anticipated surpluses can often be identified and reallocated. For example, personnel changes and time lapses in filling positions may provide surplus funds. Mid-year budget adjustments of significant proportion may be necessary. Organizations may experience cutbacks in funds or the failure of an anticipated grant. Some organizations that experience cutbacks use the flawed procedure of cutting a percentage from all areas, rather than analyzing programs and selectively reducing expenditures. When budget reductions are necessary as a result of reduced funding or loss of profit, specific programs must be evaluated with consideration given to discontinuing or consolidating them.

Depending on the sector, different values are associated with expenditure of budget funds. In government organizations, failure to expend all funds is often thought to result in a negative reaction toward increased expenditures in years to come, but at the same time can be viewed as evidence of a frugal administrator. In profit organizations, accomplishing goals and objectives without expending the full budget is highly valued. In not-for-profit organizations, administrators who do not expend the budget allocations, which are often less than is needed to provide the programs, raise questions about the commitment to the programs and the level of monitoring.

Financial Audits

Financial audits are essential and usually required for organizations. This is an annual examination of the financial records, the legal and policy compliance, and the management of the financial system. Generally, the annual audit is conducted by an external organization that has no potential conflicts of interest with the organization's activities. External audits have the advantage of utilizing consultants who have the most current information on innovative accounting methods and can offer improved accounting procedures (Gatewood et al., 1995). Internal audits can be conducted for any specific area of the organization or the entire organization at any time. The gerontologist administrator may request internal audits when a particular program or segment of the organization is of great concern. It is a prudent practice to request a financial audit of the organization when assuming the chief executive position.

Financial Accountability

Organizations that provide programs for older adults from all sectors have stakeholders and funding resources to whom they are accountable. Often accountability is viewed as an effort to satisfy political pressures (Meenaghan et al., 1982). Even though accountability procedures are often viewed with a jaundiced eye, or at the extreme as an inquisition, they are essential for modern organizations. Indeed, continued or enhanced funding and even survival of a program may rest on a demonstration that the funds are used for the intended purpose and are used efficiently. When resources for programs tend to be scarce, it leads to greater emphasis, often overemphasis, on financial accountability (Meenaghan et al., 1982).

Cost Reporting

Cost reporting (cost accounting), originally associated with the manufacturing of products, has been adapted and improved to measure services. A number of cost reporting areas may be used: reimbursable cost reporting, average per-person cost reporting, functional cost reporting, unit cost reporting, and needs cost reporting (Skidmore, 1995). To illustrate this procedure, unit cost reporting was chosen. Program information and financial costs must be used. First, fixed costs must be allocated to a given program. Then variable costs, such as salaries, are determined. The sum is divided by the number of clients to establish a unit cost. This can be compared against established standards or national benchmarks.

Accountability Problems

The gerontologist administrator will understandably strive for effective financial management and accountability. Some accountability measures become extremely intrusive and cumbersome, measuring actual time spent by using detailed logs, or using videotapes of the activities. Equally as dubious is leaving accountability procedures entirely to those in charge of accounting; that is, individuals who may have no clear understanding of the programs offered. In the same vein, if the gerontologist administrator remains solely focused on the "bottom line," this will have an impact on morale and be morally questionable. Administrators must carefully consider the ethical aspects when instituting and using accountability procedures.

FINANCE AND FUNDING ELECTRONIC TECHNOLOGY

Financial operations and management are among the first aspects of an organization to be automated, and often the only aspects. This usually involves software that includes the general ledger, payroll, and purchasing (Miranda & Keefe, 1998). While some software resources include funding sources, fund-raising database modules frequently lag behind. Management information has always been maintained and used by organizations. Automation permits a better organized rapid retrieval system (Gatewood et al., 1995).

A modern automated management information system (MIS) has many advantages, although doubts are frequent, especially when the system is "down." An MIS can assist by providing a rapid reaction to changes and opportunities. In fund-raising, for example, demographical data on clients can be stored and retrieved instantly to incorporate into a last-minute grant. When key executives are tied into the MIS, coordination of activities becomes less time-consuming and more convenient. With an MIS, it is easier to outsource aspects of financial activity (Cormier, 1996). For example, one housing authority for older adults electronically transmitted employee data each month to a contract organization that then handled the payroll. In some advanced systems using current and historical data, budget development modules assist in coordinating the operating and capital budget preparation process (Miranda & Keefe, 1998).

The most effective MISs are "user friendly" and are constructed to minimize frustration. There are executive information systems which require only limited technical experience and knowledge to access the data. This requires careful selection of software. For the selection of software it is best not to rely totally on the word or demonstrations of vendors. The administrator should also engage in research of references, on-site visits, and read professional reviews. The pace of change in the technology industry offers a significant challenge for the gerontologist administrator.

The gerontologist administrator should keep in mind that the computer-stored data is meaning-free (Weiner, 1990). The use and interpretation of the data by a human being supplies the meaning. Further, the technology should support the organization; that is, support operations and the programs should not be adjusted to satisfy the limitations of computer technology. Finally, the administrator can find staff or consultants to apply the technology, but must be sufficiently knowledgeable and skilled to manage and monitor these individuals.

SUMMARY

The gerontologist administrator will be involved in all aspects of acquiring, developing, and monitoring financial resources. The kind and level of involvement will vary with the sector. There are differences among sectors in obtaining financial resources, accounting practices, and extent of decision-making in relationship to the budget. Major sources of funding for programs across sectors involve general revenues, insurance, consumer fees, grants from the government and foundations, private philanthropy, and in-kind services and equipment. A major source of funding for programs in the community comes through the OAA and the aging network that was established by Congress. Funds based on the annual state plan are filtered down through the AAAs. Another major funding source is reimbursement through social insurance, particularly Medicare and Medicaid.

For community-based programs that serve older adults, both private and not-for-profit, funding is derived from multiple sources. The complex nature of these funding patterns will require the gerontologist administrator to be knowledgeable and involved in many different kinds of financial resources. The nature of these funding patterns also requires attention to alternative funding sources. Among the funding efforts that the gerontologist administrator is involved with are lobbying, detailed presentations of proposed budgets, grant writing, solicitation of funds from organizations and individuals, and fund-raising through exchange of donated products and services.

Financial management requires an in-depth understanding of the total financial situation for the organization or program and the development and monitoring of budgets. Working with technical staff in accounting and in MIS, the annual or bi-annual development of the budget is a major task. There are two types of budgets: the operational budget, which funds the daily activities; and the capital budget, which funds larger expenditures for equipment, property, and structures. There are three formats for budgets: line-item, program, and performance, of which the line-item budget is the most common. An approach to budgeting used frequently that has great public appeal is zero-based budgeting. The most common aspect of this approach is to start with no allocations at the beginning of the fiscal year for each area that requires funding.

Budget planning and development involves the participation of many staff and the interaction of the administrator with superiors. Negotiations are continual throughout the development of the budget and the approval process. Frequent monitoring of budget expenditures and negotiating and accomplishing adjustments in the budget are necessary to exert proper controls. Programs are expected to justify expenditures for the intended purpose and ensure that the program is effective. Cost reporting can be utilized to make sure that expenses for the program are within established parameters.

Most organizations have automated all or a large percentage of the financial aspects. These are computer software programs, management information systems (MISs) that store and retrieve financial data. This information is available to gerontologist administrators for monitoring the financial aspects and in developing budgets. MISs have become increasingly "user friendly." Administrators will be involved in the selection of new or updated hardware and software as well as the supervision of technical staff.

LEARNING EXPERIENCE

Funding and Financing Adult Day Care

Adult day care is a familiar program in the network of community-based services for older adults. Programs continue to open and expand. Program administrators are faced with the necessity to draw upon multiple resources for funding. Medicare does not reimburse for adult day care services, although Medicare Part B will reimburse individual providers for certain contracted services, like physical therapy and psychotherapy. However, these funds do not contribute to the basic operations of the program and are not budgeted services. Consistent with adult day care funding throughout the country, the highest proportion of the revenue is from client fees (Bradsher, Estes, & Stuart, 1995). In the monthly statement example provided in Table 10.3, the daily fees consist of private pay, insurance co-payment, and a small percentage of Medicaid. Not all states permit the use of Medicaid funds for adult day care.

Review, study, and closely analyze the monthly statement provided in Table 10.3. Considering the content of this chapter, complete the following tasks and questions:

1. Calculate the total amount of revenue and expenses budgeted for this program.
2. What is the general state of the financial picture at this point in time?
3. Examining the expenses, what major expense items are missing from the list, and what are the possible explanations?
4. How would you change this statement to reflect more details about the revenues?
5. What other funding sources could be available to assist with this program?
6. You have just been notified that an anticipated grant for $5,000 used as part of your revenue prediction will not be funded. What actions are necessary, as this is a program operating at a deficit?

REFERENCES

Atchley, R. C. (2000). *Social forces and aging: An introduction to social gerontology* (9th ed.). Belmont, CA: Wadsworth Thomson Learning.

Blancato, B. (1999). Prospects brighten for action on Older Americans Act. *Southern Gerontologist, 7*(5), 1.

Bradsher, J. E., Estes, C. L., & Stuart, M. H. (1995). Adult day care: A fragmented system of policy and funding streams. *Journal of Aging and Social Policy, 7*(1), 17–38.

Brody, R. (1991). Preparing effective proposals. In R. L. Edwards & J. A. Yankey (Eds.), *Skills for effective human services management* (pp. 44–61). Washington, DC: National Association of Social Workers.

Cannon, N. (1993). Older Americans Act reauthorization targets more services to minorities; funding for low-income aged. *Aging, 365,* 58.

Cormier, K. A. (1996). Outsourcing accounts receivable and other, serendipitous, benefits. *Management Accounting, 78,* 16–17.

Crow, R. T., & Odewahn, C. A. (1987). *Management for the human services.* Englewood Cliffs, NJ: Prentice-Hall.

Elkin, R. (1985). Paying the piper and calling the tune: Accountability and the human services. In S. Slavin (Ed.), *Managing finances, personnel, and information in human services. Vol. II of Social administration: The management of the social services* (2nd ed., pp. 138–153). New York: Haworth.

Ellis, L., & Roe, D. A. (1993). Home-delivered meals programs for the elderly: Distribution of services in New York State. *The American Journal of Public Health, 83*(7), 1034–1037.

Gatewood, R. D., Taylor, R. R., & Ferrell, O. C. (1995). *Management: Comprehension, analysis, and application.* Chicago: Austen.

Gross, M. J. (1985). The importance of budgeting. In S. Slavin (Ed.), *Managing finances, personnel, and information in human services. Vol. II of Social administration: The management of the social services* (pp. 11–25). New York: Haworth.

Harlow, K. S. (1993). Proxy measures, formula funding, and location: Implications for delivery of services for the aging. *Journal of Urban Affairs, 15*(5), 427–444.

Holt, B. J. (1994). Targeting in federal grant programs: The case of the Older Americans Act. *Public Administration Review, 54*(5), 444–449.

Hooyman, N. R., & Kiyak, H. A. (1993). *Social gerontology: A multidisciplinary perspective* (3rd ed.). Boston: Allyn & Bacon.

Jansson, B. S. (1990). *Social welfare policy: From theory to practice.* Belmont, CA: Wadsworth.

Liebig, P. S. (1996). Area Agencies on Aging and the National Affordable Housing Act: Opportunities and challenges. *The Journal of Applied Gerontology, 15*(4), 471–485.

Lohmann, R. A. (1980). Financial management and social administration. In F. D. Perlmutter & S. Slavin (Eds.), *Leadership in social administration: Perspectives for the 1980s* (pp. 123–141). Philadelphia: Temple University.

Martin, L. L., & Kettner, P. M. (1997). Performance measurement: The new accountability. *Administration in Social Work, 21*(1), 17–29.

Meenaghan, T. M., Washington, R. O., & Ryan, R. M. (1982). The planning model:

Content and phases. In T. M. Meenaghan, R. O. Washington, and R. M. Ryan, *Macro practice in the human services: An introduction to planning, administration, evaluation, and community organizing components of practice* (pp. 19–34). New York: Free Press.

Miranda, R., & Keefe, T. (1998). Integrated financial management systems: Assessing the state of the art. *Government Finance Review, 14*(2), 9–15.

Patti, R. J. (1983). *Social welfare administration: Managing social programs in a developmental context*. Englewood Cliffs, NJ: Prentice-Hall.

Rosenzweig, E. P. (1995). Trends in home care entitlements and benefits. *Journal of Gerontological Social Work, 24*(3/4), 9–30.

Rubin, H. J., & Rubin, I. S. (1992). *Community organizing and development* (2nd ed.). Boston: Allyn & Bacon.

Schulz, J. H. (1995). *The economics of aging* (6th ed.). Westport, CT: Auburn House.

Skidmore, R. A. (1995). *Social work administration: Dynamic management and human relationships* (3rd ed.). Boston: Allyn & Bacon.

Slavin, S. (Ed.). (1985). *Managing finances, personnel, and information in human services. Vol. II of Social administration: The management of the social services* (2nd ed.). New York: Haworth.

Smith, M., Buckwalter, K. C., Zevenbergen, P. W., & Kudart, P. (1993). An administrator's dilemma: Keeping the innovative mental health and aging programs alive after the grant funds end. *Journal of Mental Health Administration, 20*(3), 212–222.

Sontz, A.H.L. (1989). *Philanthropy and gerontology*. Westport, CT: Greenwood.

Weiner, M. E. (1990). *Human services management: Analysis and applications* (2nd ed.). Belmont, CA: Wadsworth.

Yeatts, D. E., Ray, S., List, N., and Duggar, B. (1991). Financing geriatric programs in community health centers. *Public Health Reports, 106*(4), 375–384.

Chapter 11

Planning and Evaluation

Planning and evaluation are inevitably bonded to one another in the practice of administration. Indeed, evaluation is the first and last step in planning (Meenaghan, Washington, & Ryan, 1982). Furthermore, collection of data for evaluations is part of planning, and planning itself can be subject to evaluation. The successful gerontologist administrator must be knowledgeable about, committed to, and involved in the planning and evaluation process.

Planning can be defined as a systematic, thoughtful process to determine priorities for what needs to be accomplished, how to accomplish selected goals, and what methods to use (Albanese, 1975; Gatewood, Taylor, & Ferrell, 1995). Development of a budget, described in Chapter 10, is a classic example of planning. Planning has been described as a highly rational management process that lends itself to sequential linear thinking (Mintzberg, 1989). In actuality, planning requires both management activities and leadership. Planning, like most administrative activities, is more effective with commitment, participation, and enthusiastic implementation. A plan brings order to an organization and serves as a means of control.

Evaluation is the examination of an organization, programs, or functions to assist with decision-making, establishing policy, and documenting accountability (Lewis, Lewis, & Souflée, 1991; Meenaghan et al., 1982). In short, it is a systematic process for making informed judgments. For administrators, evaluation must be broadly conceived, ranging from informal feedback to assessment of needs and objective measurements of outcome. It is important to recognize that evaluation is not subject to all the rules of scientific research or limited to classic research designs.

Goals and objectives, whether formal or informal, are intimately related to planning and evaluation. Previously, we discussed measurable goals in relation to individual performance. For planning and evaluation methods, goals emanate from the mission and the organization's purpose. Goals are typically a reflection of values and an expression of intentions for an organization or program. They are difficult to measure. A goal set by a hospital-based gerontology educational program for the community was "to extend gerontological education to adult children." Objectives are typically specific, stated in behavioral terms, and are measurable with associated tasks. Objectives often include deadlines, percentages, and target numbers. Thus, goals, objectives, and tasks and similar terminology have become an integral part of planning and evaluation. The discussion of planning and evaluation in this chapter is oriented to the establishment of goals and objectives.

All three sectors—public, profit, and not-for-profit—which offer programs and services for older adults will be involved in several types of planning and many kinds of evaluation. Some organizations have specialized staff for these areas. The gerontologist administrator must be diligent in ensuring involvement of administrative staff in both of these processes and in sustaining the relationship between planning and evaluation. A basic, widely applicable planning process with three different levels of planning will be examined: strategic, development, and operations. Evaluation, broadly conceived, will be discussed under four general categories: needs assessment, process, outcome, and efficiency.

PLANNING

Planning is highly valued, discussed often, and has a vast literature of models and methods. Yet, formal, systematic planning, with the notable exception of budgeting, is often avoided or delayed indefinitely. In the field of services to older adults, such remarks can be heard as, "We do not have time to plan"; "We are under too much pressure to provide services"; "Things are always changing, so why bother?" Perhaps some of these remarks have merit for some organizations, but it is common also to hear, "If you don't know where you're going, you don't need to plan." Increasingly, planning is mandated, such as in the federal government requirement that each state submit an annual plan for funds administered by the AAAs. AAAs place requirements for planning and evaluation on community service organizations that offer services to older adults. Feasibility studies and plans are frequently required by profit organizations that are seeking to expand their services to the older adult population.

Benefits of Planning

While the phrase "plan or perish" is overly dramatic, there are important benefits to routine, systematic planning:

- *Efficiency and Effectiveness.* The process typically reveals a modified focus of inter-related problems that differ from perceptions and original concerns. Additionally, every good plan sets priorities, thus focusing attention and resources.

- *Coordination.* Planning requires thinking through the order of activities and assigning responsibilities.

- *Accountability.* Planning involves the establishment of objectives and evaluation to document activities, correct mistakes, and adapt to change. It provides important information for funding sources, stakeholders, and the public.

- *Generating Alternatives.* Planning brings together people and resources to generate different ways and means to accomplish goals. Alternatives can be compared for impact, cost, and value.

The planning process is motivating and good for morale (Gatewood et al., 1995; Skidmore, 1995). This identified benefit of planning is highly dependent on many factors. Planning can be motivating if it involves a large number of people, if the plan is implemented as intended, and if the results are relatively positive. However, planning can have the opposite effect if the planning process was a façade or if the planning process was so extensive that it exhausted the resources of the organization. Having a plan does not ensure success.

The Planning Process

We have characterized planning as a formal, systematic process that begins and ends with evaluation. This process is the best way to avoid the inevitable errors of dedicating resources to a poorly defined concern, unnecessarily consuming time, or compromising effectiveness. Consequently, systematic planning models offer a step-by-step procedure. Longest (1976) presents basic steps for planning. Using the core of his presentation, an enhanced planning process is offered:

1. *Statement of purpose.* Depending on the type and level of planning, the statement of purpose can take many forms. Whatever the form, the statement of purpose should incorporate the goals of the plan. In strategic planning, or planned organizational change, the mission would constitute the statement of purpose. If a mission statement exists, it may be necessary to reconsider and redefine the mission in this first step of the planning procedure. Information from previous planning sessions, evaluations, and opportunities for new resources can also be used to formulate a statement of purpose. On occasion, the statement of purpose is cast as a problem statement. In this situation, the preliminary extent and the causes of the problem will lead to a statement of goals which will constitute the purpose. Whatever the form, the statement of purpose will serve to reduce ambiguity, forming the basis for the remainder of the plan.

2. *Establishing objectives.* Objectives provide further focus to the planning and the expected outcome. Task assignments and activities are organized around the objectives. To state the objectives, it is useful to engage in analysis that

examines past efforts, the current situation, and, in some instances, the activities of other organizations, all in relationship to the stated purpose. Information from needs assessments and evaluations can be useful in both the first step and this step.

3. *Forecasting.* Systematic planning involves assumptions about the future. These assumptions should be based on further analysis of the situation. The expanded analysis should include limitations and estimations of existing resources. Predictions as to the changes, both within the organization and externally, that affect the purpose need to be factored into the planning process. For example, the consideration by Congress of including reimbursement for medication in Medicare may need to be considered when planning to establish a pharmacy in a multilevel residential complex for older adults.

4. *Determining alternatives.* The very essence of planning is establishing alternatives. If alternatives do not exist, it may not be necessary to engage in all steps of the planning process. This is the point where extensive information is solicited from staff and, on occasion, certain stakeholders. Generating alternatives is a creative process. Initially, one should withhold judgment of the possible alternatives. Indeed, the most useful alternative for a given objective may first appear outrageous or unavailable.

5. *Choosing alternatives.* This is the time to evaluate the various alternatives by making judgments about feasibility and by anticipating the outcome. It will require further examination of constraints and compromise. Prioritization of alternatives in relation to objectives is essential. Conditions such as time restraints, available resources, and receptivity to the alternative all need to be considered. The result of this step is the formulation of a plan.

6. *Implementing the plan.* The success of the planning process thus far, particularly as it pertains to involving relevant staff, will determine to a great extent the success of implementation of the plan. This is the stage where the leadership qualities of the gerontologist administrator will be necessary to maintain commitment to the alternatives selected. At this point, she will require staff to carry out assignments in relationship to the objectives and the design agreed upon. The plan is useless unless it is carried out as intended. This is not to suggest that there could not be some flexibility, but such flexibility requires agreement among the parties involved and usually pertains to tasks, rather than goals and objectives.

To implement a plan, a time schedule is required. Among the most common systems used is the Program Evaluation and Review Technique (PERT). PERT allows for three time estimates for each activity to be accomplished: an optimistic time, a pessimistic time, and the most likely time. All the identified events necessary to complete the plan are arranged on a time line. Some events are arranged so that they can be completed simultaneously, while others are in a lock-step sequence. The amount of time to complete each event is indicated. This scheduling scheme offers a time line for the implementation of the plan and a way of evaluating progress.

7. *Evaluation and alterations.* Evaluation is the final step in the planning process. It involves two facets: evaluating (monitoring) the implementation process (using PERT, for example) and determining the impact of the project objectives. Evaluating objectives means measuring outcome in terms of quality and quantity. Implementation will inevitably undergo change, for even the best of plans requires flexibility and alteration. The actual program objectives based on data may also require alterations. The challenge is to make the necessary alterations without compromising the goals.

This planning process is not problem oriented, as it is not necessary to have a problem to plan. Planning is conceived as more broadly applied and relevant for established organizations and programs to make improvements, prepare for the future, and, when appropriate, solve problems. The planning process steps are universal and can be used for programs, organizations, departments within organizations, special projects, and cooperative community programs. In the next section of this chapter, there will be discussion of levels of planning. The planning process applies to all levels. Some aspects will be more elaborate, depending on the level of planning. For example, strategic planning will require formulation or reformulation of a mission statement, while operation planning will begin with modifying or formulating new objectives.

Planning steps do not always occur in a linear sequence (Skidmore, 1995). Since planning is a dynamic operation, the starting point may not be at step one. A mental health center subject to political and economic pressures adopted several program alternatives for expanding mental health services to older adults during a crisis. Several months later, planning can now retrack to complete the other steps as appropriate, perhaps considering other program alternatives.

Levels and Types of Planning

The planning process, not the written document, brings clarity and focus to the organization. The resulting planning document establishes boundaries that hopefully achieve the best use of resources, curtail attempts to accomplish more than is effectively possible, and reduce confusion as well as conflict. The plan, with a measure of flexibility, becomes a reference point for decisions and actions.

There are different levels of planning, and within levels there are different types. The levels are strategic planning, development planning, and operational planning, which are shown with brief descriptors in Figure 11.1. When planning moves from strategic planning to implementation, the planning process moves from the envisioned to the reality and from the long range to the short range. As will be discussed, the purpose, approach, and participants help distinguish the levels. Although the best scenario occurs when the levels are sequential, beginning with the strategic plan, this is rarely the case, nor is it necessary. However, all levels are important to gain the maximum benefit of planning.

Figure 11.1
Levels of Planning

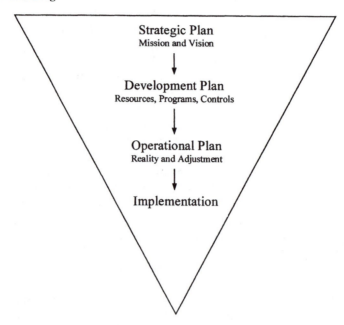

Another form of planning, contingency planning, which can be combined with the levels or accomplished independently, will also be defined and discussed.

Strategic planning was originally designed for organizations (Bryson, 1988). Developmental planning, sometimes called program planning, has usually been applied to specific, discreet programs. Operations planning, formal and informal, which is tied to available resources and is the most common, can be found in a wide variety of circumstances. Currently, all three levels of planning are used with organizations, departments, programs, and projects. To maintain a clear view of the characteristics of each planning level, the discussion will center on planning for organizations.

Strategic Planning

This is a structured planning effort to produce fundamental decisions and actions about the future of an organization (Bryson, 1988). It is a long-range plan usually for three to five years, but can be as much as 15 or 20 years. In planning for expansion of paratransit for older adults and persons with handicaps, the Hillsborough Transit System in Tampa, Florida produced a 15-year strategic plan. This was necessary so that land acquisition for eventual terminals and stops could be secured and, in some instances, purchased in advance.

Strategic planning differs from other planning primarily because it is highly vision-directed, speculative, and not restricted by the available resources. The

Figure 11.2
Goal-Oriented Strategic Planning Model

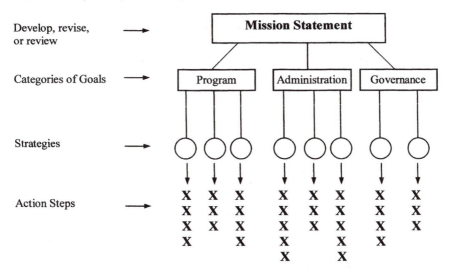

last point is the most difficult for planning participants to comprehend, since the norm that guides many planners is "can we afford it?" Furthermore, the effective strategic planning process requires creativity, intuition, opinions, and outrageous suggestions (Agor, 1989).

There are three types of strategic planning: direct, scenario, and goals (Bryson, 1988). In the direct model, the planning effort goes from the mission statement to a listing of issues. This is used more often when there is anticipated difficulty in getting agreement on goals. In the scenario approach, the organization develops a profile of an ideal organization of the future, then examines means for moving from the present state of the organization to that ideal profile. The third approach, the most commonly used and the most consistent with current planning literature, is goal-oriented strategic planning. This approach to strategic planning will be elaborated.

The goal-oriented strategic planning model is presented in Figure 11.2. The model starts with the mission and leads to categories of goals. The figure gives examples of categories, but they can vary as determined by the planning participants. Each goal, then, has a list of strategies (sometimes called objectives) which in this model are more comprehensive than objectives since they provide several alternatives. Following from each strategy is a list of action steps. The best strategic plan will have people who are assigned to overseeing each of the strategies and individuals who will be responsible for completing the action steps. Action steps are to be accomplished within a certain time frame.

An effective strategic planning process will involve many hours of activities for staff, volunteers, and, in many instances, consultants (Brody, 1993). Prior to the beginning of a strategic planning process, it is useful for administrators throughout an organization to solicit from staff observations, opinions, and suggestions. Strategic planning is not a process left to planning personnel or a few select administrators. The actual planning sessions should be composed of key executive and administrative staff, board members, and volunteers. It is constructive to set aside blocks of time for group interaction to accomplish the various phases of goal-oriented strategic planning. The sessions should be free from interruptions, interference, and attempts to solve current daily operational problems.

When the planning group develops, revises, or reviews the mission statement, this is intertwined with several analyses of the organization and the environment. At a minimum, a facilitative session should be held to examine and list organizational strengths and weaknesses. Similarly, a session should be held that identifies opportunities and threats, both within the organization and in the community at large.

These activities, or similar activities, will lead to the mission statement. As a rule, this is the most time-consuming part of the strategic plan, since the mission statement, as previously described in Chapter 6, is a reflection of the values and the purpose of the organization. From the mission statement flow categorized goals, strategies, and action steps.

A multiprogram senior center planning group that establishes a goal of expanding services into an adjacent rural county provides an example of the strategic planning process. One of the strategies listed in relation to this goal is to contact government officials, both elected and appointed, to explore the receptivity and support for the expansion. Flowing from that strategy are specific action steps. Contact is to be made by the executive director with the two city managers and the one county manager. Three volunteer board members will contact key elected officials in each one of these political entities. Brief reports will be accumulated by the person who is designated to oversee the goal, who will then integrate the material into a brief summary.

The strategic planning process results in a written document. The document specifies those elements of the goal-oriented strategic plan previously described. It is primarily a listing rather than a narrative. Developing an initial strategic plan or revising an old plan can be laborious and require a substantial commitment of time. Thus, once a plan is devised, it is useful to revise it on an annual basis. Such annual reviews result in an efficient use of time and the infusion of new information to update the plan. In some instances, the mission does not need to be revised, but rather reaffirmed. It is not unusual for planning sessions to extend over two or three months to produce a strategic plan (Brody, 1993).

Developmental Planning

The strategic plan, if available, should guide the developmental plan. It is incumbent upon the gerontologist administrator to assure linkage between the levels of planning and to see that the plans are used to guide work behavior.

This, in part, can be accomplished by linking specific program administrators and staff, goals, and objectives with the strategic plan. Developmental plans generally focus more on functions of an organization (Gatewood et al., 1995). These include programs of service, finance, or marketing. Goals, as compared to strategic plans, become more specific, leading to measurable objectives and a listing of associated discreet tasks for each objective.

Continuing the example presented on strategic planning about expansion of services into an adjacent county, a developmental plan would now establish program goals. More specifically, one of the goals could be "to establish case management-outreach services in Boxmore County, beginning with the next fiscal year." One of the related objectives could be to "secure a letter of funding assistance from the county commission for twenty percent of the project cost by August, 2000." To illustrate further, consider two likely tasks: (1) "write a formal letter requesting funds from the county commission" and (2) "secure a place on the county commission agenda."

Developmental planning generally occurs about one or two years in advance. It precedes budget development and will drive the budget process. This planning level is directly associated with estimating both the source and the use of financial and human resources. Information from needs assessments and evaluations contribute to the expansion, reduction, or establishment of new programs or functions. The participants in developmental planning include executive administrators and middle managers. In not-for-profit organizations, there will be board involvement, particularly through the program and finance committees. In the government sector, involvement should include higher levels in the structure to ensure acceptance and commitment to the programs. For profit organizations, this could include board members, owners, or, in the case of large corporations, district-level administrators who would participate in and contribute to the plan. Of course, for some large organizations, regardless of the sector, there may be professional planners who manage or facilitate the developmental planning process.

Operations Planning

The operational plan is driven primarily by the known, available resources. Once the budget has been established and limits set, modifications of the development plans will be required. Sometimes it is a matter of "picking up the pieces" as the visions turn to the reality of available resources. The primary principle of short-range operational planning is to remain committed to the goals whenever possible, focusing upon changing the objectives and the tasks. This will involve reallocation of existing resources, transfers of personnel, or selection of alternatives.

Once again, it will be useful to pursue the example of service expansion by the senior center to an adjacent county. Unfortunately, the budget process and the resource pursuit did not produce the funding at the level necessary to establish a full outreach program in Boxmore County. However, some resources were secured. Thus, the objective now is to "establish a pilot project of outreach in a segment of the county with a heavy concentration of older adults by mid-year." Among the tasks to be accomplished to achieve this objective is the reassignment of one staff member. Thus, a small-scale version of the original goal will be implemented. Perhaps there is some advantage to an incremental approach that can demonstrate the program while avoiding a large-scale failure (Brody, 1993). At a later date, given a positive evaluation, adjustments can be made if expansion is indicated.

An operational plan differs from a strategic plan or a development plan in that some aspects will be applicable for only a year, to be replaced in the future. Other aspects will be recurring, and may result in permanent policies. These plans are usually annual, include implementation steps, and involve monitoring and evaluation. The participants' planning group is generally small, composed of mid-level program administrators, executive administrators, and individuals in support (staff) positions, such as a chief financial officer or a human resources director. Unfortunately, some organizations skip this critical planning level, and jump to implementation and adjustments without giving time to a systematic, thoughtful process (Brody, 1993).

Contingency Planning

Even with a productive planning process and a good plan, the administrator can count on one certainty: something will go wrong. Assumptions used with a plan can change; a resource is lost; or the clients' response is different than anticipated (Gatewood et al., 1995). It is constructive to contemplate in advance the possible undesirable events. Indeed, a plan's likelihood of success often depends upon the ability of the administrator to predict problems (Brody, 1993). Thus, once a plan is almost complete, it is constructive to conduct a "fail-safe" analysis. This is a group session focused wholly on what can go wrong. The session should include a talented "flaw finder," perhaps a consultant or a colleague from another organization, preferably someone not yet vested in the plan.

More specifically, contingency planning can be fostered by the gerontologist administrator who is willing to engage in "what if" possibilities. Of course, preliminary decisions can be made about alternatives and resources available to respond to possible problems: that is, the well-known and useful "plan B," and it may be useful to have "plan C" and "plan D" as well.

Unfortunately, even with thoughtful predictions, there will be unanticipated events. According to Mintzberg (1989), some could be opportunities. For these circumstances, the administrator will want an established procedure for responding, that is, a real-time decision process that can be rapidly arranged. This can be a group session that begins with a brief analysis of the event and then generates alternatives. In these situations it is incumbent upon the gerontologist administrator to act quickly and decisively.

Prescription for Successful Planning

Planning activities are systematic, sequential, and detailed, requiring management skills. Having a complete and successful plan requires collaboration, commitment, vision, and legitimization of the process and influence (Bryson, 1988; Goldberg, 1995). All of these conditions are fostered by leadership. The complete planning process disciplines the organization to make important, thoughtful decisions about itself, the programs, and the future. Considering the complexity and the multiple requirements for successful planning, the following prescription can serve as a guide (Brody, 1993; Bryson, 1988; Goldberg, 1995; Mintzberg, 1989):

- Knowledge of the client group and subgroups that includes needs, characteristics, behaviors, and attitudes. For example, in planning a program for older adults, these considerations, as well as demographic data, may need to be analyzed based on Neugarden's age categories of the young-old (65–74), the old-old (75–84), and the oldest-old (85 years and older).
- Involve the appropriate people, depending on the level and type of planning. Planning is best accomplished as a group effort.
- Every plan must have mutually agreed-upon priorities. A plan without priorities is an overwhelming enterprise.
- Concentrated, uninterrupted time must be set aside to plan. Serious planning will require blocks of dedicated time.
- Follow a rational planning model using logical analysis and, whenever possible, empirical data.
- Hold to the goals of the plan, but remain flexible about the objectives (strategies).
- Use external professional consultants to facilitate the planning process and to supply knowledge, but not to decide on the elements of the plan.
- Never be reluctant to reformulate the plan based on new, reliable information and evaluation.

Planning and evaluation are clearly connected, and evaluative findings are useful to start the planning process as well as throughout the planning process. Evaluation is necessary to monitor the planning process and to measure the results of the implementation. Consequently, a more comprehensive and detailed discussion of evaluation is indicated.

PROGRAM EVALUATION

Programs for older adults will require the involvement of the gerontologist administrator in a multitude of tasks, but not necessarily as an evaluator. At a minimum, it is the responsibility of the administrator to value, support, and integrate evaluation into all aspects of the organization (Hirschhorn, 1980). All activities that affect clients (individuals, groups, programs, and communities) and the broader group of consumers (employees, volunteers, and stakeholders) can be part of formal or informal evaluation.

Evaluation includes needs assessment, the manner in which programs are conducted (process evaluation), the impact of programs (outcome evaluation), and a determination of efficiency. Evaluation most commonly pertains to the effectiveness of a particular intervention or a support function. An entire organization can also be evaluated, and this facet will be discussed in Chapter 13. Some types of evaluation are more rigorous in design than others. While design for evaluations will be noted, detailed information on all design models is beyond the scope of this textbook.

To understand evaluation, it must be distinguished from research; both research and evaluation are systematic inquiry. The mere mention of the word "research" often sparks anxiety in administrators and service practitioners. Nevertheless, evaluation is an integral part of almost all programs for older adults. Scientific research, as contrasted with evaluation, is more theoretically based, is value free, uses more complex designs, requires more controls, and seeks to produce new knowledge (Lewis et al., 1991; Morgan & Hiltner, 1992). Evaluation involves collection of data to provide information to decision makers about the delivery of the program and the level of impact on the clients. Information is generally compared to goals and objectives or preselected criteria. Lohmann (1991), writing about evaluation of programs for older adults, offers four requirements:

- It requires the measurement of the effect of programs, which means the evaluator must know what effects are anticipated and have a means of measuring them.
- It requires that effects be measured in comparison with the goals that were set in advance for the program.
- It requires that results of the evaluation have an impact on the decision-making, which means that those making decisions about the programs must be informed of the results.
- It requires that results contribute to future programming, which means that outcomes must be disseminated to those involved in this program, as well as more broadly, so they can impact on program design and development.

The literature on evaluation is often confusing, mixing evaluation methods (techniques and tools) with types. We have organized evaluation into four general categories: assessment of need, process evaluation, outcome evaluation, and evaluation of efficiency. These categories are briefly described in Table 11.1 and elaborated upon in this chapter. Categories are distinguished from evaluation tools, presented in Table 11.2, which may be applied across categories. The use of several categories and multiple tools for a given evaluative effort is encouraged (Rog & Fournier, 1997; Hirschhorn, 1980).

Table 11.1
Categories of Evaluation

- **Needs Assessment.** Systematic survey of perceived wants, desires, or expectations to use for planning and designing training, programs, and projects.

- **Process Evaluation.** Measures of activities to assess the extent of activity and if it is being conducted as intended.

- **Outcome Evaluation.** Structured assessment, usually using research designs to determine if the activity has resulted in a change as intended.

- **Evaluation of Efficiency.** Mechanism to determine costs of an activity and the relation to benefits.

Table 11.2
Tools Used in Evaluation

- Surveys; for example, consumer satisfaction and needs assessments
- Case studies
- Cost analysis
- Focus groups or public hearings
- Experimental and quasi-experimental research designs
- Appraisal forms
- Standardized instruments
- Group information; for example, environmental scan
- Financial and administrative audits
- Quality assurance programs
- Established norms, benchmarks, indicators
- Adopted criteria or objectives
- Key informants

Note: The "tools" listed are only a sample of those available for assessment and evaluation.

Purpose and Categories of Evaluation

The value and use of evaluation has increased so that some administrative practices, like TQM, have incorporated it into the management approach. Government funding sources have increasingly required evaluation to justify the allocation of financial resources. The growth of programs for older adults coincided with the increased emphasis on evaluation; thus, programs in all sectors have made extensive use of evaluation. Program evaluation costs money, takes time, and may provide findings not desirable to administration or staff. For these reasons, evaluation may be avoided, ignored, or worse, provided by a "friendly" evaluator who avoids the issue. Therefore, the purpose and importance of evaluation must be stressed. We wish to emphasize the positive value and use of evaluation to assist with rational decision-making about programs, policies, and services. Evaluation provides:

- information and data for planning to assist with decisions about resources
- knowledge about programs for older adults as it relates to age groups and other characteristics (Lohmann, 1991)
- a measure of effectiveness of a program or intervention, and can establish credibility (Lewis et al., 1991; Lohmann, 1991)

- information on the continued relevance of goals and objectives (Rubin & Rubin, 1992)
- assistance with administrative control over programs and services (Crow & Odewahn, 1987)
- data for corrections, improvements, and refinements in programs to achieve quality (Crow & Odewahn, 1987; Lewis et al., 1991)
- a basis for support for, involvement with, or justifying a valued program (Lewis et al., 1991)

Both the value and the utility of evaluation become even more relevant for the gerontologist administrator when considering the scope of evaluative categories. The discussion of the categories—needs assessment, process evaluation, outcome evaluation, and evaluating efficiency—and selected, associated tools will show that evaluation is more than a paper compliance requirement and that it is common to the daily work activities.

Programs for older adults have not always continued to exist because of evaluative information, nor do they necessarily emerge from an orderly, logical planning process. Programs may exist because:

- A source of funding for the program became available and was accepted.
- The staff favor the activities of the program.
- An evaluation of the program does not exist or is superficial.
- It is popular, despite any lack of documentation of effectiveness.
- It is politically expedient.

These conditions, with the exception of the last one, are being replaced by the trend to establish programs based on feasibility information. Programs are subject to modification, alterations, or reduction based on prior evaluations. Of course, a mixture of evaluative information and other reasons will continue to influence programs, sometimes producing unfortunate compromises. The gerontologist administrator who supports and is committed to systematic assessment and evaluation will direct programs with demonstrated benefit for older adults.

Needs Assessment

The needs assessment is the first stage of most systematic planning, problem-solving, and decision-making (Lohmann, 1991). A useful definition is offered by Rossi, Freeman, and Wright (1979): "Systematic appraisal of type, depth, and scope of problems as perceived by study targets or their advocates" (p. 82). To expand this definition, it is not necessary to have a problem to assess interests or to determine what needs are or are not being met. Perhaps needs assessment can best be explained by a simple but useful formula: discover what is needed; determine what exists; subtract, and the difference is what needs to be accomplished.

There are many ways to conduct a needs assessment. Not all are expensive and time-consuming. Needs assessments can be as simple as a focused discussion with staff on training issues or as complex as a community random sample survey with an assessment instrument like the Older Adults Resources and Services model (OARS). The OARS is a structured, unidimensional scale for determining need and ranking problems (Lohmann, 1991). The approach will vary, depending on the issues, availability of staff, and financial resources. A good needs assessment, regardless of its complexity, extends beyond the degree of severity of the issue to gain understanding of the characteristics of the target group. For example, a needs assessment of issues with an older adult population could primarily be related to a segment of that population who are the old-old (between 75–84) and living alone.

To demonstrate the extent and nature of needs assessment, two tools, among the many available, have been selected for discussion: environmental scan and key informants. Additionally, an example of a needs assessment using multiple tools will be presented in detail.

Environmental Scan

Used often with strategic planning, the environmental scan is also appropriate for program planning (Lohmann, 1991). It can be accomplished in several hours with no preparation using participants' knowledge, or with extensive preparation in a retreat for a number of days. Techniques range from tapping the knowledge of the participants to obtaining data from a systematic inquiry. Generally, the first step is to conduct a "self-audit," examining strengths and weaknesses (Crow & Odewahn, 1987; Edwards & Eadie, 1994).

The second step is to focus on the environment. These are conditions over which the program usually has no direct control, such as population growth and characteristics, economic conditions, identification of stakeholders, government regulations, and competition. With older adult programs, it is essential also to examine public attitudes and myths about aging. The final step is the formulation of a problem statement or statement of purpose with associated goals. Group involvement and objective facilitation will instill greater commitment to the goals (Crow & Odewahn, 1987).

Key Informants

One of the simplest and least complicated approaches to needs assessment is key informants. It is a relatively informal tool that uses the knowledge of leaders, experts, staff, or volunteers to learn about the target population's needs (Rossi et al., 1979). This approach can be used to establish goals or to narrow the focus for more rigorous and elaborate needs assessment. Typically, information is gathered in group meetings, by surveys, or by individual interviews (Lewis et al., 1991). Interviews are the most common, using a structured interview format or a data guide that is completed after the interview.

Rossi et al. (1979) hold that this approach works best when specific and concrete information is asked of the respondents. Information-gathering techniques can be used with groups. For example, a nominal group process, that allows for broad participation with interposed discussion, was used with seven groups of older adults and two groups of professionals who work with older adults to determine communication difficulties (Hickson, Worrall, Yiu, & Barnett, 1996). This information was then used to determine the content of an educational program.

Perhaps the main advantage of this technique, besides being relatively simple and easy, is that it builds support and involvement for the eventual program. This is especially the case when the tabulated information is fed back to the informants for review. The obvious limitation is that this may include the biases and possibly the narrow perspective of the informants. Thus, it is best to use this tool in combination with other needs assessment techniques or as a precursor to a more elaborate and rigorous needs assessment.

Multiple-Input Model of Needs Assessment

The best needs assessments combine several tools and collect data from multiple sources (Parsons, Higley, & Okerlund, 1995). Wherever appropriate, community or agency policies relative to human subject research should be followed. A four-step model that combines various assessment tools is presented by Parsons et al. (1995):

1. Information is gathered from focus groups, the older adult population, caregivers, and family members.
2. Based on the focus group information, a survey instrument is designed to be used with a broader range of citizens in the community.
3. Using information from both of these tools, a revised questionnaire is then developed to survey the community's older adult population. This data, along with previously collected information, is coded and statistically analyzed.
4. Twelve older adults from the community, six frail and six healthy, were identified as case studies to validate the findings.

With needs identified and prioritized, a plan to meet the needs can be formulated. Confidence in the findings is secured by using a multiple method that cross-validates findings.

Process Evaluation

Process evaluation is used to determine whether a program was implemented as intended. The focus is on how services are rendered, who receives the services, and whether the methods are being used as prescribed. Typically, these evaluations are frequent, weekly or monthly, with data continuously collected. Process evaluation is a precursor to outcome evaluation. Often the two categories are combined (Lewis et al., 1991). Actually, meaningful outcome evaluation requires that process evaluation take place (Rossi et al., 1979). Differences in actual and implemented program components will dramatically affect outcome, thus sometimes producing a dilemma, as process evaluation is, in part, for the purpose of changing or adjusting program elements. Such improvements or changes must be justified and documented. More specifically, Meenaghan et al. (1982) state that the purpose of process evaluation is to:

- detect malfunctioning in procedures or implementation
- identify sources of difficulty
- provide information for program revision
- check for adequacy of resources
- identify unintended developments

The design of process evaluation is rarely an experimental design (Lewis et al., 1991). The approach is usually a logical, qualitative, and analytical design using criteria, standards, and principles against which to compare program components. Compared to outcome evaluation, the information obtained is less stable, not germane to cause and effect, and never generalizable (Rutman, 1977). Two types of process evaluation have been selected for discussion: monitoring and quality assurance.

Monitoring

A senior center provides congregate dining for older adults. The contract with the AAA states that there will be an average of 37 meals a day for five days a week; they are to be consistent with the nutritional plan and within a certain temperature range when served. A gerontologist professional from the AAA reviews and validates data monthly. If the gerontologist finds deviance from the contract, she will expect changes to correct the situation.

Monitoring generally focuses on the process, but can also include outcome measures. Outcome measures are more difficult because of the design requirements to obtain qualitative and objective data. Monitoring of process faces other issues. First, measuring objectives requires using performance indicators to judge activity (Brody, 1993). Second, many professionals resent monitoring and the requirements to collect data (Simyar & Lloyd-Jones, 1988). Third, monitoring will require corrective measures, meaning changes that may be responded to by resistance, poor follow-through, or minimal compliance. Monitoring will reveal both strengths and weaknesses in programs. It is certainly more difficult to respond to unfavorable findings.

As with all evaluation, the gerontologist administrator will be expected to make decisions and be willing to make changes. Understandably, decision-making will be influenced by certain political considerations, level of independence of the program, and the age-old dilemma that solving one problem may create another. In addition to making tough decisions, it will require leadership

Table 11.3
Quality Assurance (QA) Basic Formula

1. Identify and monitor a specific activity.
2. If necessary, adopt corrective action.
3. Implement corrective action for a set period of time.
4. Evaluate the results of the corrective action.
5. Monitor for stability and consistency.

skills on the part of the gerontologist administrator to obtain commitment and compliance with those decisions.

Quality Assurance

This is the first cousin of monitoring, but generally is internally controlled, highly specific, and concentrated on pre-selected areas at different periods. This highly focused procedure, which first flourished in the area of medical services, has become more broadly used for all services for older adults. Government regulations and accreditation organizations often require a functioning quality assurance program (QA). These programs have many names, such as quality improvement or quality control. Formal programs will have highly systematic procedures to measure quality of service and will require specific documentation (Patchner & Balgopal, 1993).

QA programs use checklists, protocols, and established criteria. For example, in a geriatric clinic, the protocol for diabetes calls for 80 percent follow-up visits. A QA committee composed of service professionals, administrators, and, in some cases, board members and a community member, meet routinely to discuss data collected on specific, pre-identified areas. It is not necessary to have a problem for this system to be employed. In fact, one of the benefits of this system is that it monitors areas that may not have a readily identified problem. The committee also reviews previously identified areas of correction and evaluates those corrective measures.

The committees are facilitated by an appointed QA coordinator, which is usually a part of an assignment for a staff member with a broader job scope. The programs require a large amount of paperwork and documentation, much of which can be automated. The committee can direct other committees to take action or can refer action through administrative channels. The committee's authority crosses over unit or department lines. A basic formula for the process of QA programs is presented in Table 11.3. These are sequential steps, except if the evaluation results indicate that the corrective action is not making the desired change; then the committee, or a designee, will formulate different corrective action.

QA programs are perpetual. The number of areas to be monitored is endless. QA committees need to make an annual plan about areas that will be investigated and be ready to examine other areas brought to their attention as a result of staff observations. The gerontologist administrator has a responsibility to see that effective QA programs are operating as intended.

Outcome Evaluation

Process evaluation asks if the program was implemented and conducted as intended, while outcome evaluations determine the change or impact of the program. Thus, outcome evaluation requires systematic measurement sensitive to the program goals. For example, a psychotherapy program to reduce depression in older adults would use a valid and reliable scale that has been designed for measuring levels of depression in older adults.

Commonly, outcome evaluations seek to determine if programs are approaching, meeting, or exceeding predetermined goals. The evaluation questions and the evaluation design determine the range of measurement tools used. Evaluations, unlike many research projects, take place in the real world and are affected by philosophical beliefs, ethical standards, and political realities.

The gerontologist administrator will find the results of outcome evaluations useful to document the value of programs to funding groups, to make decisions about program approaches, and to adjust and change methods to create a greater impact (Lohmann, 1991; Rossi et al., 1979). Additionally, information from outcome evaluations can assist administrators in policy formation and organizational change and improvement. Information from these evaluations along with process evaluations and efficiency evaluations all contribute to a broad concept of accountability.

A basic decision about outcome evaluation is whether it will be formative, summative, or both. A formative evaluation collects data and makes measurements while the program is in progress and may be used to alter the program over time. A summative evaluation waits until the end of a program to determine the impact. This information can be used to alter the future of the program being measured or for the establishment of other programs. The information can also be disseminated to contribute to the overall knowledge base for the development, design, and implementation of programs for older adults.

Outcome evaluation means measuring the dependent (experimental) variable. The classic experimental design examines alternative hypotheses to determine the cause of an outcome. This design involves random selection and assignment to a treatment group or a control group. A statistical comparison of the findings will show if the difference between the groups is by chance or a result of the treatment. Thus, cause and effect can be established.

For most service program evaluations, it is difficult, sometimes impossible, and often ethically questionable, to randomize and use a control group (Hirschhorn, 1980; Lohmann, 1991; Miringoff, 1980). Thus, alternative designs and approaches to outcome evaluations must be used. Unfortunately, without random assignment to groups, it is difficult to obtain validity or ascertain the influence of rival variables on outcome.

Consequently, evaluation approaches have evolved over the years so that less attention is given to adherence to classic research design and more toward using designs that consider the complexity and limitations of the service programs (Kuechler, Velasquez, & White, 1988; Light, 1994). Despite arguments to the contrary, program outcome related to the quality of the service can be evaluated. A full range of basic quasi-experimental and non-experimental designs is provided by Campbell and Stanley (1963). It is also important to recall that effective program evaluation employs several categories and multiple methods of evaluation.

Meaningful program outcome evaluations have at least four basic requirements:

- A question or hypothesis
- A systematic, established evaluation design
- Data that has been accurately and carefully collected
- A qualified external evaluator who has no association with the design or delivery of the program

To demonstrate and distinguish between commonly used outcome evaluations, a non-experimental design and a quasi-experimental design will be discussed. Additionally, the use of multiple methods with an adult day care program will be presented.

Before and After Evaluation

This non-experimental design, also known as a pre-test post-test, uses a single group. As suggested by the design name, observations or measurements are made before participation in a program; then, the same measurements are taken at points throughout the program. With older adults, it is advisable to have several postmeasurement points to reduce the influence of other causes for the findings. For example, a single measure of memory could follow the recent loss of a friend, influencing the impact of a memory improvement program only temporarily. It is relatively easy to build before and after evaluations into service programs (Lohmann, 1991).

Control Group, Non-randomized

When the pre-test post-test can be used with non-equivalent control groups, this becomes a quasi-experimental design. The pre-test provides baseline comparative measures, while the post-test offers comparisons to determine the extent of the differences, if any, as a result of the program. Non-equivalent control groups can be found on waiting lists, from community volunteers, or clients of a related program that had no exposure to the program being evaluated. This is a frequently used evaluation design with programs for older adults (Lohmann, 1991).

Evaluating Adult Day Care

The adult day care program was initiated by a not-for-profit, community-based nursing association to help frail or disabled older adults maintain independence while living in their homes (Strang & Pearson, 1995). The authors report an evaluation design that focused on two questions consistent with the goals: Does the adult day care provide respite to caregivers? Does it delay institutionalization?

Interviews were conducted with adults receiving the service, caregivers, and professionals and volunteers providing the service. In addition, the older adults received a mental and physical functioning assessment at admissions and three months later. The caregivers were assessed for caregiving burden at admissions and three months later. Content analysis was used to analyze the interview data, and t-tests for the analysis of variants on client functioning and caregivers' burden.

The findings indicated that the adult day care program did not provide the intended relief to caregivers as expected, and it did not delay long-term care placement. Indeed, Strang and Pearson (1995) state, "The major impact of the program seemed to lie in helping clients and their caregivers to realize the benefits of placement and then the ease of pain of adjustment to inevitable placement" (p. 79). No significant difference in physical and psychological functioning was found when comparing measures from the time of the first assessment to the assessment three months later. Thus, this evaluation revealed an unintended outcome—the program amounted to an incremental step toward institutionalization.

Efficiency Evaluation

A process evaluation is conducted to determine if programs are implemented as intended, while outcome evaluation is designed to measure the impact of the program. Efficiency evaluation is concerned with the cost as it is related to outcome; that is, can the same impact be achieved more economically? Human and health services are legendary for establishing successful delivery models that later undergo certain efficiency decisions that negate the impact. As Lewis et al. (1991) state, "Efficiency does not involve simply cost cutting; it involves recognizing that alternative methods might differ in the amount of resources used to arrive at the same ends" (p. 243). Cutting costs often means reducing the quality and compromising the desired change. On the other hand, appropriately applied, this category of evaluation can contribute to expanded service, greater profits, and better resource allocation.

Improvements in data collection, storage, and budget developments using computers have made efficiency evaluations common practice. The actual time and cost required for these analyses have been reduced over the years (Rog & Fournier, 1997). Indeed, one often finds efficiency evaluations without any other form of evaluation. This is unfortunate, as cost should be related to both process and outcome. Also, even with sophisticated techniques of data collection and storage, all the data is seldom available, and value assumptions continue to play a role (Rossi et al., 1979). Two of the most basic methods are unit costs and cost benefit. Another approach is to determine cost-effectiveness, which is presented as a case example of evaluating mental health services.

Unit Cost

Unit costs are determined by dividing the number of service units into the funds allocated for the service (Lewis et al., 1991). This requires decisions about segmentation and allocation of costs to a given service unit; that is, what amount of costs from marketing, administration, and maintenance can be allocated to a unit? A unit cost can be the basis for further evaluation and can be used for comparing costs to establish benchmarks. These measures do not necessarily result in a reduction or the elimination of a program, because that is often impossible. Food service, for example, at a nursing home will not be eliminated, for that is not an option. However, benchmarks exist for unit cost of meals, and deviations are a reason to make changes.

Cost-Benefit Analysis

This essentially is a systematic way to measure investments in a program; that is, in terms of outcome, what is the return on funds expended? The relationship can be expressed as a ratio when benefits (quantified) are divided by unit costs (Rossi et al., 1979). Benefits, such as improving communications between adult children and older adults, are difficult to quantify. Information to place a monetary value on benefits comes from research and other program evaluations. Depending on the program and values, the extent of benefits can reach from the individual to society.

Evaluating Mental Health Services for Older Adults

Goddard and Powell (1994) report on the use of naturalistic evaluation techniques (open-ended interviews) and cost-effective analysis used with a psychogeriatric service in the United Kingdom. The psychogeriatric program is a community-based service in a district health authority. It has multiple components and provides services to individuals in a variety of settings, using different teams of mental health providers operating from a district office. The effectiveness of each component was evaluated using interviews of service providers and administrators, and a sample of 50 clients and caretakers. Each service component's cost was determined, and the unit costs were calculated. Unit costs were also estimated for alternative strategies. A computer simulation model assisted with calculations.

The finding was that the services should be more community-based, consolidating services at a single site and integrating the service teams. The evaluation found it was more cost-effective to consolidate the referral and assessment aspects. This could be accomplished by reallocation of staff. These changes would result in earlier assessments and entry into service.

Effects, Influences, and Ethical Considerations

The role for the gerontologist administrator in evaluation will primarily be related to financial resources, selection of evaluators, complexity of design, dissemination of information, and determining influence of the results on decisions. Evaluations will also require continued cooperation from the administration and support for the integrity of the findings. Staff anxiety and resistance is a given. All evaluations have flaws and are open to criticism. The thoughtful administrator will have anticipated potential problems and be prepared to deal with them.

The administrator needs to be prepared to explain and defend the evaluation efforts (Hoefer, 1994). The administrator should participate in the reading and editing of evaluation reports, not to alter or manipulate the data, but to assure accuracy of basic information which lends to credibility. Careful description of undesirable findings, with mention of mitigating circumstances, will help prevent misinterpretations and misuse (Iutcovich, 1987). Additional factors that need to be taken into consideration are the use of outside evaluators, evaluation design, and political aspects of evaluations.

Evaluation Consultants

One of the key questions for the gerontologist administrator is whether to use an outside consultant to conduct an evaluation. Generally, this is more likely with outcome and effectiveness evaluations. Seldom do programs with small staffs have the expertise or time to conduct a meaningful evaluation. An external evaluator will counter criticism, concerns about objectivity, and ethics problems associated with evaluations that are internal (Lewis et al., 1991). The perceived status of the evaluation often will be linked to the evaluator's qualifications and experience. The other perspective is that the knowledge of the programs and older adults possessed by staff is important for meaningful evaluations. There are different degrees of involvement that can be selected in using a consultant. A shared effort by staff and consultant can overcome many of the criticisms of evaluation efforts.

Design Concerns

The importance of design must be emphasized. The literature is replete with articles reporting on program evaluations with weak or poor designs. Overly complex designs often do not result in a useful evaluation, as too much data is amassed and it becomes difficult to control variables. It is most important to construct a design that is appropriate to the essential elements of the actual program (Hoefer, 1994; Light, 1994). The influence of the design on the findings is extensive. Light (1994), commenting on the future of evaluation, said, "If you tell me how you will design your next evaluation, I think we can do a pretty good job of predicting what results you'll find" (p. 250).

Design also determines the appropriateness of generalizing findings. Program evaluations are primarily used to produce information about whether the program is being implemented as intended with the expected outcome (internal validity). Evaluative studies frequently focus on selected samples and may change program elements based on findings. Thus, most evaluations have poor external validity, and generalizations that go beyond the groups studied are not appropriate (Rossi et al., 1979). Further, it may be very difficult for anyone to replicate the program using precisely the same resources.

Evaluation Politics

The political ramifications of evaluations are not limited to politicians or even to the public. All of the stakeholders, clients, staff, volunteers, and funding sources are involved in the political process. Belief systems about programs generate a certain validity with or without data. If you believe you have a good program, why would you evaluate it and possibly find negative results? Of course, some programs are more political than others because of visibility to the community, like paratransit and housing for older adults. Given the political nature of evaluations, there are a number of dangerous assumptions:

- Positive results of an evaluation will be perceived as desirable.
- A carefully designed, scientific evaluation will result in acceptance and changes.
- Most people will understand the evaluative process or the basis on which the data was obtained.
- The definition of positive findings will be acceptable.
- The work and information produced by the evaluation will be used in the intended manner.

For those who hold views different from what the findings show, every aspect of an evaluation—its design, objectivity, purpose, and cost—will be criticized. The importance of the gerontologist administrator's commitment to improved programs, cost-effectiveness, and documented impact, as well as understanding the impact of findings on staff, must be continually emphasized and reinforced. One must keep in mind that the primary and ultimate purpose for conducting an evaluation is to make informed decisions about programs.

SUMMARY

Planning and evaluation are linked and are an intricate part of programs for older adults. While planning is a systematic and thoughtful process, flexibility and adaptability are essential ingredients in developing a plan. Likewise, evaluation may produce adjustments in the program to achieve the desired results of improving quality. Planning and evaluation require the establishment of goals and objectives. The trends in funding and the dictates of profit reinforce the use of goals and objectives.

Planning is the key to achieving efficiency and effectiveness by incorporating accountability measures and a willingness to consider alternative program models. Planning that seeks to involve staff, volunteers, and, when appropriate, stakeholders, is the most likely to be successful. A traditional, time-tested planning model includes a statement of purpose, establishment of objectives, forecasting, determining alternatives, choosing alternatives, and implementation. The final step is evaluation. The information from evaluations then stimulates and supports future planning efforts.

There are basically three levels of planning: strategic planning, which is long range and visionary; developmental planning, which is mid-range and focuses on the functions and the specific interventions of service organizations; and operational planning, which is short range and requires adjustment and adaption to known resources. Another kind of planning, which operates parallel to the other levels, is contingency planning. This involves making preliminary decisions about alternatives should certain circumstances arise, and developing a procedure for adjusting a plan to unanticipated circumstances. Successful planning is more likely when planners have knowledge of the clients, there is broad involvement, and planning is a concentrated and conscious process which follows a logical sequence.

Evaluation is primarily to assist in making decisions about programs. It also provides information for public relations, expectations of accountability, fundraising, and motivation of staff. The discussion of evaluation focused on four approaches: needs assessment, process evaluation, outcome evaluation, and efficiency evaluation. Needs assessment is often the first step in planning. It attempts to ascertain the characteristics and scope of particular concerns or problems. A constructive needs assessment uses several methods of data collection.

Process evaluation examines the way a program's methods and interventions are being implemented. Process evaluations are less rigorous than outcome evaluations and more oriented to documenting activities. This type of evaluation fosters alterations and improvements in program components.

Outcome evaluation, also known as impact evaluation, can be applied during the duration of a program or at some strategic end points, such as the end of the year. It involves more sophisticated designs but is seldom a traditional experimental design. Thus, non-experimental and quasi-experimental designs are more likely. A meaningful outcome evaluation must have a question or hypothesis, will use an established design, will seek to use reliable and valid measures in collecting data, and will utilize an external evaluator.

Efficiency evaluations, perhaps the most common and well-known, are procedures to relate cost to outcome. A basic component of efficiency evaluations is making decisions about assignment of cost and establishing a unit cost. Subsequently, cost-benefit analysis and cost-effectiveness can be determined. The primary rationale for effectiveness evaluation is the full and complete utilization of resources or the maximization of income.

Evaluation of service programs involves many parties that extend beyond the evaluation procedure itself, to the interpretation, dissemination, and use of the results. Careful preparation and presentation of evaluations must include the gerontologist administrator. Certain reactions and interpretations to evaluation information can be anticipated. Additionally, the gerontologist administrator has a responsibility to assure the integrity of an evaluation. This can be accomplished by selecting a meaningful design, using multiple evaluation methods, and demonstrating support for evaluation.

Planning an evaluation is an important part of administration, requiring the support of stakeholders and governance bodies. New programs that are based on prior evaluated models will increase the likelihood of success. However, it is ethically questionable to justify starting a program based on positive evaluation findings and then alter the essential elements of the program design. For the benefit of all parties, it is incumbent upon the gerontologist administrator to institutionalize planning and evaluation, integrating them into an organization's functions and programs.

LEARNING EXPERIENCE

The Logic Model of Planning and Evaluation

In the 1990s, United Way organizations across the country who were concerned about making changes in the community began to use a different approach to program planning. Many adopted the logic model of planning and evaluation. This is not a new technique, tool, or even a category of planning and evaluation. It is a framework that offers a paradigm for the relationship between perceived community needs, programs, immediate outcomes, and system impact.

This relatively simple framework conceptualizes components into four columns: community conditions, activities, outcomes, and impacts (Julian, 1997). Conditions, like problem statements, result from needs assessments using community volunteers and representatives who have concerns. Activities are funded programs or interventions related to conditions. Outcomes are the direct results of a program measured by a selected evaluative technique. Impact, in this model, requires an evaluation of the benefits to the community (system). For example, concerns about elder financial abuse would be depicted as follows:

Condition	Activities	Outcome	Impact
Financial abuse of the elderly in non-institution living circumstances	1. ACE educational program 2. Police prevention 3. Media awareness 4. Legal services	1. Pre/post-test scores 2. Workshop evaluations 3. Number of people reached 4. Number of cases, successes, and failures	Incidence of reported financial abuse cases compared for the past five years

With this model, the community impact can be used to make decisions about changes needed in activities, and to determine the need for new activities or expansion of some of the same activities. According to Julian, Jones, and Deyo (1995), the strength of this model is its ability to link the four components and adjust planning over time. Further, the model focuses on composite impact on the community. It could lead to attempts at system change rather than activities directed toward individuals or groups. Perhaps legislation is needed to ensure better protection of older adults from financial abuse.

Answer the following questions:

1. This model has been used by United Way organizations to determine funding for existing and new programs. What are the benefits and drawbacks?

2. What are the implications of finding that a long-standing, popular program (for example, police prevention) may not have an impact?

3. What are some of the limitations of this model?

4. Do you think this model would be useful for Area Agencies on Aging (AAA) and why?

5. How would you use this model to generate more resources for older adult programs?

REFERENCES

Agor, W. (1989). Intuition and strategic planning: How organizations can make predictive decisions. *The Futurist, 23*(6), 20–23.

Albanese, R. (1975). *Management: Toward accountability for performance.* Homewood, IL: Richard D. Irwin.

Brody, R. (1993). *Effectively managing human service organizations.* Newbury Park, CA: Sage.

Bryson, J. M. (1988). A strategic planning process for public and nonprofit organizations. *Long Range Planning, 21*(1), 73–81.

Campbell, D. T., & Stanley, J. C. (1963). *Experimental and quasi-experimental designs for research.* Chicago: Rand McNally College Publishing.

Crow, R. T., & Odewahn, C. A. (1987). *Management for the human services.* Englewood Cliffs, NJ: Prentice-Hall.

Edwards, R. L., & Eadie, D. C. (1994). Meeting the change challenge: Managing growth in the nonprofit and public human services sectors. *Administration in Social Work, 18*(2), 107–123.

Gatewood, R. D., Taylor, R. R., & Ferrell, O. C. (1995). *Management: Comprehension, analysis, and application.* Chicago: Austen.

Goddard, A., & Powell, J. (1994). Using naturalistic and economic evaluation to assist service planning: A case study in the United Kingdom. *Evaluation Review, 18*(4), 472–492.

Goldberg, G. S. (1995). Theory and practice in program development: A study of the planning and implementation of fourteen social programs. *Social Service Review, 69,* 614–655.

Hickson, L., Worrall, L., Yiu, E., & Barnett, H. (1996). Planning a communication education program for older people. *Educational Gerontology, 22*(3), 257–269.

Hirschhorn, L. (1980). Evaluation and administration: From experimental design to social planning. In F. D. Perlmutter & S. Slavin (Eds.), *Leadership in social administration: Perspectives for the 1980s* (pp. 173–194). Philadelphia: Temple University.

Hoefer, R. (1994). A good story, well told: Rules for evaluating human services programs. *Social Work, 39*(2), 233–236.

Iutcovich, J. M. (1987). The politics of evaluation research: A case study of community development block grant funding for human services. *Evaluation and Program Planning, 10,* 71–81.

Julian, D. A. (1997). The utilization of the logic model as a system level planning and evaluation device. *Evaluation and Program Planning, 20*(3), 251–257.

Julian, D. A., Jones, A., & Deyo, D. (1995). The utilization of open systems evaluation and the logic model as tools for defining program planning and evaluation outcomes. *Evaluation and Program Planning, 18,* 333–341.

Kuechler, C. F., Velasquez, J. J., & White, M. J. (1988). An assessment of human services program outcome measures: Are they credible, feasible, useful? *Administration in Social Work, 12*(3), 71–89.

Lewis, J. A., Lewis, M. D., & Soufleé, F. (1991). *Management of human service programs* (2nd ed.). Pacific Grove, CA: Brooks/Cole.

Light, R. J. (1994). The future for evaluation. *Evaluation Practice, 15*(3), 249–253.

Lohmann, N. (1991). Evaluating programs for older people. In P.K.H. Kim (Ed.), *Serving the elderly: Skills for practice* (pp. 259–277). New York: Aldine De Gruyter.

Longest, B. B. (1976). *Management practices for the health professional.* Reston, VA: Reston Publishing.

Meenaghan, T. M., Washington, R. O., & Ryan, R. M. (1982). The planning model: Content and phases. In T. M. Meenaghan, R. O. Washington, and R. M. Ryan, *Macro practice in the human services: An introduction to planning, administration, evaluation, and community organizing components of practice* (pp. 19–34). New York: Free Press.

Mintzberg, H. (1989). *Mintzberg on management: Inside our strange world of organizations.* New York: Free Press.

Miringoff, M. L. (1980). *Management in human service organizations.* New York: Macmillan.

Morgan, E. E., Jr., & Hiltner, J. (1992). *Managing aging and human service agencies.* New York: Springer.

Parsons, R., Higley, H. B., & Okerlund, V. W. (1995). Assessing the needs of our elders. *Public Management, 77*, 14–16.

Patchner, M. A., & Balgopal, P. R. (1993). *Excellence in nursing homes: Care, planning, quality assurance, and personnel management.* New York: Springer.

Rog, D. J., & Fournier, D. (1997). *Progress and future directions in evaluation: Perspectives on theory, practice, and methods.* San Francisco: Jossey-Bass.

Rossi, P. H., Freeman, H. E., & Wright, S. R. (1979). *Evaluation: A systematic approach.* Beverly Hills, CA: Sage.

Rubin, H. J., & Rubin, I. S. (1992). *Community organizing and development* (2nd ed.). Boston: Allyn & Bacon.

Rutman, L. (1977). Formative research and program evaluability. In L. Rutman (Ed.), *Evaluation research methods: A basic guide* (pp. 59–71). Beverly Hills, CA: Sage.

Simyar, F., & Lloyd-Jones, J. (1988). *Strategic management in the health care sector: Toward the year 2000.* Englewood Cliffs, NJ: Prentice-Hall.

Skidmore, R. A. (1995). *Social work administration: Dynamic management and human relationships* (3rd ed.). Boston: Allyn & Bacon.

Strang, V. R., & Pearson, J. (1995). Factors influencing the utilization of results: A case study of an evaluation of an adult day care program. *The Canadian Journal of Program Evaluation/La Revue Canadienne D'Evaluation de Programme, 10*(1), 73–87.

Chapter 12

Community Relations and Volunteers

Organizations that provide programs for older adults are deeply involved with and linked to the community. For the effective gerontologist administrator, community involvement offers opportunities to garnish resources, increase program impact, and demonstrate public accountability. Community relations extend beyond clients, stakeholders, staff, and volunteers to public interest, political circles, and the media. Further, other programs that produce different services are often directly or indirectly linked. For example, the city transportation system changes a route so that the day care center clients now have to walk three blocks and arrive 30 minutes after activities normally begin. Community involvement, both formal and informal, is an essential endeavor for the gerontologist administrator.

In our survey and discussions with gerontologist administrators, an area often identified was the responsibility for networking with other organizations. Networking is a pattern of linked relationships through which help and information flow on a particular issue or around a service (Rubin & Rubin, 1992). Many of the programs are uniquely structured in a system where networking is expected, with funding and coordination through the AAA. However, networking reaches far beyond those programs.

Public relations is about the image of the program, and it extends to the marketing of services, case findings, and, perhaps the most sensitive area, media relations. Few administrators possess skills in media relations, and the community program is rare that can afford a specialist. Organizations also demonstrate social responsibility, often through advocacy.

Not-for-profit and profit sectors generally have boards of directors. The board functions differ for each, with the not-for-profit sector having volunteer board members. Another area identified by gerontologist administrators that involves considerable time and effort is work with volunteers. Volunteers have tradition-ally been a mainstay of service organizations. In fact, many not-for-profit service organizations originated as completely voluntary agencies (Netting, Kettner, & McMurtry, 1993). The 1995 White House Conference on Aging recognized the contributions of volunteers as one of the top ten resolutions (Green, 1997). Older adults compose a large number of the volunteer force of America. In the early 1990s, 41 percent of all those age 60 and older were performing volunteer work (ICR Survey Research Group, 1991). Each of these areas of community rela-tions—networking, public relations, boards of directors, and volunteers—will be discussed in more detail.

NETWORKING

It is often difficult for programs to keep pace with the diverse needs of older adults, especially those who require multiple health and social services (Briar-Lawson, 1998; Wilber & Myrtle, 1998). Many older adults have a large number of different service providers. Formal and informal networks can help to coor-dinate and focus needed services. Networking can be formal when organizations are linked by representatives or when activities related to clients are articulated in a signed "cooperative agreement." Compared to hierarchical structures, net-works tend to be flexible, decentralized, and horizontal (Karuza, Calkins, Duf-fey, & Feather, 1988). The size of a network is determined by its mission, goals, and community needs. Other networks are informal and open-ended, with some common bond.

An example of the latter is the Sarasota County Aging Network (SCAN), which holds monthly breakfast meetings open to self-determined attendance. The organization produces an annual publication of all agencies and businesses re-lated to older adults in the county. Membership is broadly representative, in-cluding all sectors, with many product vendors. The purpose of SCAN is summarized in its mission: "The Sarasota County Aging Network is a not-for-profit, voluntary coalition of persons representing both profit and not-for-profit health, human, and social services, and other persons with aging issues. Its purpose is to identify services in the Sarasota County area and share that infor-mation; to provide information and referral; to analyze unmet needs and advo-cate solutions; and to increase public awareness of elderly services in the area" (Sarasota County Aging Network, 1997, p. 1).

Some relatively informal networks grow, becoming more formal with ex-panded missions, even to the point of having professional staff, bylaws, and incorporating as a not-for-profit corporation. However, these characteristics do not necessarily identify a formal network. There are actually two types of formal networks.

The first is organized around shared interests or an area of services, attracting individuals who are highly committed (Rubin & Rubin, 1992). An example might be a network that is developed around the need for better transportation for older adults in a given community. Second are networks where organizations seek to directly assist and complement one another and to mutually provide services to clients. These networks are based upon reciprocal relationships. One feature of these networks is written cooperative agreements that detail the services each organization will provide, resulting in greater continuity of health and social services for older adults. Such agreements extend beyond personal cooperative efforts tied to the individual.

Benefits of Networks

Networks of programs for older adults can be found in most communities and have both direct and indirect benefits. Indirectly, these collaborative and cooperative efforts reach beyond the narrow perspective of services by a particular agency to a common agenda of promoting system development (Wilber & Myrtle, 1998). System development means new, and hopefully improved, policies and norms for meeting the needs of older adults. More direct and immediate benefits of networking are:

- More effective use of resources and identification of service gaps
- Enhanced communications between programs and professionals
- Coordination of services and identification of unnecessary duplication
- Obtaining information about the external community and resources
- Opportunities for bartering exchanges
- Sharing of professional information and opportunity for interdisciplinary contact
- Facilitation of positive cooperative efforts that extend beyond the network
- Public relations and marketing

Planning and Programming

Ginsberg (1995) maintains that participation in networks provides early warning signs and other information for planning and redesigning programs. Information is provided for one's own organization, as well as the opportunity to plan programs together. In some instances, this could result in joint funding. Further, issues that relate to older adults and the agencies involved can be addressed more fully through networks. Networks have become involved in influencing local, state, and federal policy about older adults' quality of life and programs for older adults.

Planning and coordination of programs for older adults extends even beyond older adult program networks. As gerontologist administrators rise in the ranks to higher positions, they are less likely to be involved in networks specifically related to older adult programs and more likely to broaden their networks to business and community organizations, such as the chamber of commerce or relevant service clubs. Networking activities independent of formal networks are an essential ingredient and one that will occupy a considerable amount of the administrator's time (Mintzberg, 1980). This kind of networking requires considerable leadership skill. In general, the more extensively the gerontologist administrator can network, through both formal and informal arrangements, the more likely it is that opportunities and resources will be found to plan, expand, and fund programs.

Network Anxieties

Many administrators are skeptical about participation in networks. Networks are often a place where employees seek and find other positions. Losing good employees to another organization has a number of negative implications. Time spent in networking by staff is also a concern. This is time that may be taken away from direct services, services that can be billed, and collaboration within the organization. Certain individuals may use networking as a way of avoiding other work responsibilities.

While networking provides a great opportunity for public relations and marketing, it also becomes a forum for competition. Programs for older adults have strong competition in many areas, such as long-term care, assisted living, day care, home health, and mental health services. The concern is that the other programs will gain information from these networks about organizations in order to pursue a competitive advantage.

PUBLIC AND MEDIA RELATIONS

Community relations involve formal interaction with consumers, stakeholders, the media, and the general public. This interaction is realized through public relations and marketing. Media relations, for routine matters, are a significant aspect of public relations and marketing. Large grant awards, controversial issues like fraud of older adults, evaluation findings, and competition are all part of the public relations agenda, and frequently involve the media.

It is common for public relations and marketing to be thought of as one and the same (Sumariwalla, 1988). While they are closely related, it is constructive for the gerontologist administrator to understand both the relationship between public relations and marketing and the differences. These are technical areas, often requiring the assistance or involvement of appropriately trained staff or consultants. For the gerontologist administrator, it is most important to give attention to public relations and marketing concepts and practices, and to understand the relationship to decision-making and ethics.

Good public relations will contribute greatly to an organization's ability to avoid, or at least minimize, organizational conflict and controversy (Guth, 1995). Organizational problems or even daily circumstances can become a crisis simply because of media attention. Changes in media values and methods have forced a distinct area of media relations associated with controversial matters. Media relations, even with the assistance of qualified public relations staff, frequently will require the direct interaction of administrators with reporters. Administrators are perceived as the spokespersons for their organizations (Crow & Odewahn, 1987).

Public Relations

Public relations is the fostering of two-way communication between the organization and groups in the community. It is distinguished from marketing in that public relations promotes the organization's image and abilities. Public relations for service organizations is a service in itself, as it informs and educates the public not only about the services but about the issues and problems to which the organization is responding. First and foremost, when it comes to the image of the organization, every gerontologist administrator represents that image. Behaviors, appearance, conduct, and manner, both in formal public gatherings and in certain social activities, convey the image of the organization with which an administrator is affiliated.

The image of the organization is embodied in the promotion of the mission, the purpose, the programs, and the reasons that the organization was established. The public image should be clearly defined, consistent with the organization's mission, and ethically accurate. The image relates not only to the credibility of the services offered, but also to the ability of the organization to attract both personnel and financial resources.

For the gerontologist administrator or his representative, it is essential to have knowledge of the community; public relations, like politics, is, in part, influencing the influential. Key relationships need to be cultivated by phone calls, congratulatory notes, invitations to events, and appearances at community events. While large organizations have public relations staff, this still does not remove the responsibility or the effectiveness of the key administrator's participation in cultivating community goodwill. Also required is some in-depth knowledge of the programs and the older adult population being served. It was not just embarrassing, but unfortunate for the organization's image, when a visiting district administrator was asked, during a community service club presentation, whether an older adult with certain characteristics would be eligible for the home health program and he could not give a definitive answer.

Public relations activities will vary, depending on the sector, and the higher an administrator rises in the ranks of an organization the more time will be required (Crow & Odewahn, 1987). The director of a state agency on aging, for example, could spend 60 percent or more of his time traveling to various parts of the state to make presentations and appearances. Of course, the chief executive is not alone in representing an organization; staff, volunteers, especially board members, and even those outside the organization will contribute to the public image. Influential and recognized community leaders' communicated perceptions of an organization will also greatly influence the public perceptions.

Marketing

Marketing, in contrast to public relations, directs efforts at potential consumers and features information about the program of services. A modern definition of marketing that applies to all sectors is, "the process of planning and executing the conception, pricing, promotion, and distribution of ideas, goods, and services to create exchanges that satisfy individual's and organizational objectives" (Peterson, 1989, p. 4). This definition is distinguished from the traditional conception that emphasizes profit. With the public sector, marketing at times is discouraged, and efforts to dissuade or disqualify clients are made. In the other two sectors, not-for-profit and profit, marketing, although taking distinct forms, has grown to share a similar philosophy and approach.

Marketing research and needs assessment are used to construct a marketing approach or plan. Often this is part of a larger scheme known as a business plan. Skills and abilities to produce these plans will often require assistance from outside the organization. A good marketing plan will be based on data and have goals, objectives, and strategies (Simyar & Lloyd-Jones, 1988). Consequently, where substantial needs exist, the ability to pay for services or the availability of funding will determine whether programs are developed, expanded, or modified. However, here is an area where similarities dissolve. A not-for-profit might make the decision to develop or offer a program when the numbers are small or the ability to pay is low, even non-existent, based on service values and community responsibility (Weinbach, 1998). Further, unlike free enterprise, not-for-profits are not governed by the rules of supply and demand. Program development is frequently governed by availability of funds, government regulations, or pre-established mandates.

Emphasis on certain market techniques may differ. Whereas profit programs are more likely to have a budget to be able to advertise in the media, not-for-profit programs and government programs will be inclined to use outreach and case findings. At times, outreach is mandated by legislation. A community-based organization, targeting well older adults with the goal of preventing institutionalization, engaged in the following outreach strategies (Stven, 1985):

- Personal home visits to explain the program
- Phone contact to describe the program
- Letters and printed material
- Contact with non-consumers, such as indigenous leaders and human services professionals
- Contact with religious institutions and civic organizations

Table 12.1
The Four Ps of Marketing

1. **Product.** Description of the program and its abilities to meet a need or desire. This would include the criteria for service and the limits.

2. **Price.** Costs of service are always an issue in instances where minimal or no costs are required of the consumer. Pricing services may be governed by competition, government regulations, established standards, policy, or consumer income. Information as to how cost will be handled is important.

3. **Place.** Location, access, and variations in delivery methods need to be considered. Transportation for the elderly will be a major concern.

4. **Promotion.** Informing potential consumers about the services and convincing them to use the services is the responsibility of public relations and marketing. These activities could extend to sales promotions, creative advertising, and packaging of services.

Source: Adapted from Peterson (1989).

It is common to hear concerns expressed about the lack of funds for marketing. For certain kinds of marketing, especially the use of major media, this is accurate. However, successful marketing can be achieved with a multitude of other techniques and administrative decisions. Networking, described in the previous section, is a prime opportunity to achieve multiple objectives, among which is marketing. An illustration of marketing techniques, in the highly competitive area of home health care and home services for older adults, is reported by Brown (1987). The technique included sales calls, direct mailing, telemarketing, mass media advertising, arranging media coverage, speaking engagements, special projects, and use of advisory committee members.

Regardless of the technique, certain basic marketing principles compose an effective marketing approach. Table 12.1 describes the four Ps of marketing. With these principles in mind, it is equally critical to control and assure consistency of information and language using language that is consumer oriented. Information should ethically represent the program, not an ideal model. Furthermore, "overselling" a program builds unrealistic expectations and brings disappointment.

Media Relations

The wise gerontologist administrator will assure that organizations and programs have established policies and procedures for interaction with the news media (Guth, 1995; Netting et al., 1993). These procedures should distinguish between routine contact and crisis communications. Routine contact is generally proactive, initiated by the program. Crisis communications will necessitate training to understand the stages of crises. All crises have a warning stage with distinct signals. Controversy, crisis, and contradiction are the life blood of the news media. The major axiom of the news media is, "If it bleeds, it leads!"

Nevertheless, even with the growing public distrust, the news media continue to be a viable source of information.

In general, if conflicting information about a program exists, or a crisis is brewing, administrators need to be proactive in resolving the issues and, when appropriate, communicate with the news media. Timely decisions need to be made. Under no circumstances should the news media be a source of information about the program or circumstances surrounding the program. Recently, a not-for-profit board member was contacted by a news reporter. The conversation began with a discussion about some general community events of a non-controversial nature. Eventually, the reporter steered the conversation to the organization where the person was a member of the voluntary board. The reporter then provided the board member with information that one of the staff members had been arrested, and proceeded to question the board member about background information on this employee. The board member responded, and the next day the newspaper reported the board member's disapproval of this employee and of his behavior.

Getting the facts correct is merely a part of the problem in communicating with the news media, for accurate facts can be made to appear negative and be combined with unverified information, and communications can be distorted by tone and use of language. Executives who leave an organization by any means are seldom characterized as dismissed, asked to leave, or asked to resign. Rather, they are reported by the media to have been "fired" or "booted out." News reporters may be unfamiliar with the area of aging services, and their reports can be fraught with myths and misconceptions about older adults and programs for older adults.

For the reasons noted, and to protect programs from unfair and misleading news stories, follow these canons for media relations:

- Nothing is ever off the record.
- Promises that your name will not be used means controversy, and one should exercise extreme caution.
- When contacted about any non-routine item, notify a superior and/or the designated media contact person.
- Only the designated media contact person(s) should represent the organization on controversial issues. This is usually the chief executive.
- Provide information in written form whenever possible.
- Repeated contacts from a reporter indicate a controversy, even if none is apparent.
- Never use "no comment"; it will be portrayed as negative. Use "no further information is available," "that is confidential," or "I'll get back with you when I have more information."
- Do not be intimidated by demands to access information or for an interview.

The press is on no one's side permanently. Many reporters believe or profess that they have a civic responsibility to report on matters of public interest and concern. Moreover, the contemporary view of most journalists is that they must maintain independence and accept criticism in the interest of the free flow of information (Overholser, 1999). Media relations often force conflicts over rights and values. The free flow of information comes into conflict with rights to privacy, confidentiality, protection under the law, and maintaining the integrity of valuable programs for older adults.

BOARDS OF DIRECTORS

Direct involvement from the community occurs for organizations that have boards of directors (also called trustees or governing boards). Public programs do not have boards of directors but may have an advisory board. A large number of profit programs are private proprietorships or partnerships where a board is not required. Many small profit corporations have inactive boards of relatives or friends that are not a governing body except for selective decisions required by law. Boards of directors are found with large profit corporations and not-for-profit corporations. These organizations are legally incorporated with boards that meet on a regular basis, and authority is vested in the board of directors. Board authority and activities are described in the articles of incorporation and the bylaws.

There are marked differences in profit and not-for-profit boards. However, in recent years, these differences have dwindled as private corporations learned and adopted some of the characteristics of not-for-profit boards (Drucker, 1989). Profit boards frequently were vested with a broad range of authority but chose not to exercise it. The trend in profit corporate boards has been to reduce the employee executive membership, to become more directly involved in certain decisions, and to engage in policy and planning. Not-for-profit boards have also changed over the years. Since the mid-1980s, not-for-profit boards have reduced the number of service professionals, advocates, and consumers and added professionals from other areas, such as finance, public relations, real estate, and profit corporations (Miller, 1988).

Boards of Different Kinds

Perhaps the greatest distinction between profit and not-for-profit boards is that profit boards rarely are actively engaged in governance and are usually controlled by the top executive (Drucker, 1989; Gatewood, Taylor, & Ferrell, 1995). This lack of clarity of authority has great potential for conflicts of interest. Conversely, not-for-profit boards composed of volunteers only are deeply involved, and occasionally overinvolved, in the activities of the corporation. Often a dynamic tension exists between the professional administrator and the volunteer board. Advisory boards have no direct authority, often have members who are technically related to the service area, and are restricted to recommendations. A closer examination of these differences will guide the gerontologist administrator to appropriately adjusting management and leadership behavior.

Profit Corporate Boards

These boards are composed of part-time, paid members who are stockholders and bring prestige, influence, and business contacts to the corporation (Mintzberg, 1989). Board members from the community are called "outsiders," and members who are executive employees are called "insiders." The board represents the stockholders, and members are elected from this group, but this is superficial, as nominations made by the executives and existing board members are usually uncontested. Two types of profit corporate boards have evolved: the "traditional" and the "modern." The traditional profit board has a membership that includes insiders, typically is manipulated by the CEO, and tends to rubber stamp decisions made by administration. The board's primary function is to select or dismiss the CEO and make decisions about stock issues (Dale, 1978; Gatewood et al., 1995).

Insiders are reduced to only the president (CEO) or are non-existent in the modern private board. Directors are more involved in planning, oversight of operations, evaluation of the CEO (president), and financial liability issues. In actuality, modern profit boards have become more like not-for-profit boards. These changes were stimulated by a Supreme Court ruling in 1966 about representation of stockholders, the Court's tendency to hold board members more responsible for corporate activities, and crises (Dale, 1978; Gatewood et al., 1995).

Not-for-Profit Boards

Volunteers who derive satisfaction from their participation, who share common values, and who have been nominated by a committee of the board compose these governing bodies. Members are selected on the basis of their interests or expertise, status in the community, or they are consumers. These boards almost always have some members with backgrounds relevant to the service. For example, it is very common for university gerontology professors to hold voluntary board positions with an organization that has programs for older adults. There are two main types of not-for-profit boards: administrative and policy.

When an organization has been developed by leaders in the community, the board of directors has been selected primarily because of their expertise and skills; the board essentially runs the organization. This is an administrative board. These boards typically have no staff or very few staff members. Most of the services offered by these organizations are by volunteers or through contracts. These boards meet frequently, sometimes twice a month, and board meetings are used to make administrative decisions. It is difficult for an organization to remain in this status for long, as this is often a stage of development. Once staff are hired, there will be a (often rocky) transition to a policy board.

For programs that serve older adults, a policy board is the most common type of board. These boards have authority to hire one staff member, the chief executive, who hires all other staff members. The boards have responsibility for reviewing and establishing policy, which has usually been recommended by staff, and to be involved in long-range planning and fund-raising. With the policy board, it is inappropriate, unwise, and cumbersome for board members to be involved in daily operations.

Advisory Boards

Governing boards hold ultimate administrative authority, even though it may be delegated to executives, but advisory boards have no such authority (Duca, 1996; Rosenthal & Young, 1980). The advisory board draws upon the expertise and talents of the community to advise the governing board, administrators, or a particular program within an organization. Their authority is vested in wisdom and the ability to influence other parties. Advisory boards might include clients or consumers as well as prominent individuals. These boards, in addition to providing consumer feedback and technical expertise, may also be used as public relations vehicles and for fund-raising (Duca, 1996). Even though advisory boards do not require incorporation, for they are technically not boards, it is useful to have written guidelines for operations and at least one staff member assigned to work in cooperation with the board. In some instances, members who have served on advisory boards become candidates for membership on governing boards.

Primary Functions of Governing Boards

The modern profit corporation board and the not-for-profit policy board have many functions in common. The level of involvement of the board may vary, depending on the relationship with the chief executive, the bylaws, and the precedents within the organization. The primary responsibilities of these boards can be identified. First, it is necessary to clarify some terms, because many titles like chairperson and president are used for the top position on the board, while in other organizations president might be used as the top executive position. For the discussion here, the head of the board of directors will be referred to as the chairperson. The top executive, who in some organizations will be called president, administrator, or executive director, will be referred to as the chief executive. Eight major responsibilities are as follows:

- *Employ and Evaluate the Chief Executive.* Independent of the method used to search for a chief executive (board committee, outside consulting firm), the board makes the final decision, establishes the duties, fixes the salary, and delegates the management of the organization to the chief executive. Further, it is the responsibility of the board to conduct an annual performance evaluation of the chief executive.
- *Long-Range Planning.* Participation of the board or members of the board in long-range planning assures that the purpose, mission, and goals of the organization are firmly established and revised when necessary.

- *Ensure Financial Stability.* This is accomplished in many ways. The board, through its finance committee, should be involved in monitoring the financial situation. The board will participate in and approve the final budget, and will contract for an external audit.
- *Establish and Revise Policy.* The administration operates in accordance with policy that has been established and approved by the board. New policies will be recommended to the board by administration, and old policies will be revised and brought to the board for approval.
- *Oversight of Operations.* Through a variety of methods, reports, visits, and presentations, the board, sometimes through a special committee, selectively and periodically will examine operations.
- *Community Relations.* The board both represents the community and represents the organization in the community. Board members may be involved in generating funds for the organization, speaking about and for the organization, and marketing the organization's programs.
- *Ensuring the Integrity of the Legal Structure.* Although the requirements differ for different kinds of corporations, the board will be responsible for and perhaps have assistance in making sure there is compliance with local, state, and federal laws applicable to the corporation. This would also include attention to potential or actual conflicts of interest.
- *Maintenance of the Board.* Through the nominating committee, the board, in accordance with its bylaws, replaces board members as necessary. Additionally, a formal or informal self-evaluation of the board's performance and determination of what is needed to improve performance should be made at least annually.

Boards exercise these responsibilities partly through members' participation in key committees. The executive committee, usually made up of the officers and several at-large board members, is a universal component of an effective board. Certain committees, such as finance and nominating, are usually established by the bylaws, while other committees can be established by the chairperson. When committees meet regularly, deal with materials, and produce reports, this will contribute to an effective board. Many decisions are actually made in committees and are then ratified by the full board. Committees work most effectively when a staff member is assigned to each committee. To ensure effective board and committee meetings, the gerontologist administrator must take responsibility for coordinating activities.

Board–Chief Executive Relationship

The essential element of having a positive relationship between the board and the chief executive is to maintain the separation between governance and operations. Each entity has its appropriate sphere of responsibility. The chief executive is the administrator who has been delegated authority by the board and is responsible for the daily operations. The board, which represents the legal entity of the organization, like a legislative body, establishes the policies.

Trust is at the crux of the relationship between the chief executive and the board of directors. Frank and consistent dialogue between the chief executive and the chairperson will build the kind of relationship that will support the programs of the organization. To have a meaningful and effective relationship with the board of directors, the gerontologist administrator who is a chief executive needs to be actively involved with board members, taking time to meet with them as individuals and in groups. He should seek to find common values and visions, always keep the board informed on major issues, and demonstrate leadership abilities to board members (Duca, 1996). The most desirable circumstance is for the chief executive to exert significant influence without controlling the board.

The relationship will be positive when the board treats the chief executive as a partner, although recognizing its responsibility to supervise and evaluate him (Duca, 1996; O'Connell, 1981). It is essential that board members work through the administrator and not be engaged in communications with other staff members about the organization. Under no circumstances should board members be contacting staff members individually to gain information about the operations. Finally, it is important to recognize that disagreements are inherent, as board members and chief executives will not always share the same frame of reference or life circumstances.

It is possible and desirable to have a strong board and a strong chief executive. In these circumstances, the chief executive frequently holds an ex officio position on the board, meaning that, as a member of the board, he does not vote. With a strong board and a strong chief executive, the gerontologist administrator can consult board members on operational issues to receive advice without feeling compelled to comply. At the same time, board members and the chairperson can accept advice and counsel from the chief executive on how to achieve and maintain the effectiveness of the board.

Board Problems

Problems with boards of directors are legendary. Some boards have maintained a "hands-off" policy, turning over full authority or complying with, without any significant discussion, executive wishes. These circumstances beget abusive power, flawed decision-making, and often loss of direction for the organization. The converse of this situation is equally problematic. Boards that become too deeply involved in operations compromise the authority of the chief executives, cause additional conflict, and seriously jeopardize the efficiency and effectiveness of an organization. While there is no single formula, it is worth repeating that a guiding principle is to maintain a proper balance and a division between administration and governance. This will require constant diligence and, at times, external assistance.

Boards that have membership by category, that is, where members represent certain organizations and automatically become members of the board, are inherently weak. This is because existing board members are not permitted to select a member on the basis of established technical or value-oriented criteria. Frequently, changes in board members and officers also present a problem of continuity and consistency. Board membership should be staggered, and officers should serve multiyear terms with term limitations.

Board members frequently have divergent perspectives that will inevitably lead to controversy and conflict. An example of this is commonly found in not-for-profit board members with an entrepreneurial orientation, who seek systematic information, and are result oriented, interested in efficiency, and anxious to make quick decisions. This perspective is contrasted with those who embrace the values of the program, are program oriented, hold a strong commitment to the clients, and are cautious about making changes too quickly. These perspectives will often result in coalitions or factions within the board.

Widely varying perspectives of board members that are not compromised will produce contradictory expectations of the chief executive (Miller, 1988). Alliances by administrative staff with factions of the board are doomed to eventual disruption. Consistent with this situation are dominant members who control the board. These dominant board members also often seek to control administrative staff. Moreover, dominant board members will preclude valuable contributions of those who are less verbal and aggressive. Systematic and orderly board meetings, use of Robert's Rules, and adopting board policies and resolutions will contribute to a balanced contribution from board members.

VOLUNTEERS AND PROGRAMS FOR OLDER ADULTS

The involvement and management of volunteers is a major area of concern for the gerontologist administrator, because volunteers are a significant resource. To fully utilize these resources administrators must spend time and concentrate efforts to build a successful volunteer program. In the past, volunteers were most commonly found in the not-for-profit sector supporting direct service activities or as board members. Now volunteers are present in all sectors, performing a large range of activities; for example, a government agency that uses volunteers to gather information and research background for a policy issue. Another example, demonstrating creative use of volunteers, is offered by the Center of Applied Gerontology at the University of Birmingham in England. The Center assists in the development of new products for older adults by using a nationwide pool of older adult volunteers to advise manufacturers, test new products, and engage in discussions with manufacturer representatives ("Seniors Consult," 1995).

Volunteer opportunities for older adults are voluminous. In some programs, like the federally sponsored volunteer services for older adults, the work force is primarily volunteers. Among all three sectors that offer programs for older adults, volunteers can be found assisting with direct medical care; supporting medical care in hospitals, hospice, and nursing homes; as members of a team in social service agencies; providing transportation and offering direct service,

Table 12.2
National Programs for Adult Volunteers

- **RSVP.** The Retired Senior Volunteer Program places older adult volunteers in schools, hospitals, libraries, courts, day care centers, and a variety of other organizations. Programs are locally planned and sponsored and include transportation to and from the place of service. Volunteers can be reimbursed for out-of-pocket expenses.

- **SCORE.** The Service Corps of Retired Executives utilizes retired business people to help small businesses and voluntary organizations with problems. These volunteer activities can be one-time counseling sessions, ongoing consultation, or workshops. Volunteers are reimbursed for out-of-pocket expenses. This program has the additional benefit of increasing intergenerational contact.

- **The Senior Companion Program** provides a small stipend to older adults who help adults who are handicapped or disabled, with emphasis on helping older adults. The program emphasizes the involvement of low-income elderly.

- **Foster Grandparents Program** offers the opportunity for older adults to work with children who have special physical or psychological conditions. Volunteers receive a small, nontaxable stipend to cover reimbursement for transportation, meals, and insurance. To qualify for this program, there is a means test, so it is not available to all older adults. Thus, programs are most likely found in low income areas.

like telephone reassurance; as well as in administrative tasks such as data entry. To examine volunteers' involvement more closely, the focus will be primarily on community-based programs for older adults.

A vast number of older volunteers assist with community programs for older adults. Older volunteers are composed mostly of early retirees, partially retired, and the young-old (age 65–75). Volunteer participation declines with age during the last third of life (Atchley, 2000). However, a substantial number of volunteers can be found among the oldest-old (85 and older group). In addition to the broad range of volunteer opportunities referred to, older adults have been provided opportunities to volunteer in formal national programs authorized by the Older Americans Act (see Table 12.2.). Because of the significance of volunteer work and the role of volunteers in later life, a portion of the discussion will be dedicated specifically to older adult volunteers.

Volunteers in Community Programs for Older Adults

The availability of volunteers continues to grow, despite predictions that the volunteer force in America would shrink with women entering the marketplace in large numbers. Younger volunteers, often associated with college or high school projects, and early retirees have increased the ranks of volunteers. The use of volunteers by a program is more a matter of motivation, desire, and organization.

The occasional remark and often unspoken motivation for the use of volunteers is because they are "free labor." This is a common misconception that leads to misuse and disenchantment with volunteers. Volunteers are not free (Weinbach, 1998). Volunteers require time, energy, and effort, as well as physical space. Often expenses like travel and meals need to be reimbursed. In some instances, the organization will need to purchase insurance. To have viable volunteers, recognition is required. This recognition requires time to plan for events and costs. Problems with volunteers, which will surely arise, also require involvement of staff, administrators, and other resources. However, the benefits of volunteers far outweigh the burdens; consider the following:

- Increase in self-esteem for the older adult and the opportunity to fulfill altruistic needs.
- Volunteers can supplement and support the delivery of service programs and assist with administrative tasks.
- Often the activities of volunteers will free professional staff to concentrate on areas of higher technical skills.
- The presence of volunteers in an organization often increases the credibility.
- Volunteers represent a public relations and marketing opportunity.
- Often volunteers can give attention to older adults that may not be available from staff.
- The work of volunteers can be cited as in-kind contributions in developing grants.

An innovative fund-raising program for a multipurpose senior center using volunteers was reported by Jackson and Mathews (1995). Donations to the organization were increased through a program called "Coupons for Caring." Senior volunteers clipped grocery coupons from newspapers, sorted them, and attached them to respective products in local grocery stores. The customers had the option of donating the coupon to the senior center or redeeming it themselves. Signs were posted that provided visual and written instructions about how consumers, "at no expense to themselves," can donate to the senior center.

Maximizing Benefits

For the organization that wishes to use volunteers, this should be an established goal with objectives: a plan. The plan should identify specific areas where volunteers are needed, and descriptions of the functions of the volunteers should be formulated. Thus, recruitment can be aimed at fulfilling these functions. In many ways, volunteers should be treated like staff. They need to be screened, interviewed, oriented, and trained (Atchley, 2000; Lewis, Lewis, & Souflée, 1991). Orientation and training programs should include content on older adults, basic understanding of the organization's policies and practices, the significance of volunteer work to the organization, communication skills with older adults, and ethical considerations. Volunteers should not be put to work under any circumstances without an orientation.

Administering Volunteers

Every volunteer should have a supervisor. In larger organizations, the opportunity for a paid staff member who is a director of volunteers is the most desirable. In other circumstances, a volunteer director of volunteers who reports to a staff member is a workable structure. Staff and administrative support for volunteers should be concrete, consistent, and visible. This support can be demonstrated in the following ways:

- Include volunteers in the communication system of memoranda and information about the organization.
- Selected volunteers should attend staff meetings, planning sessions, and client-focused meetings.
- From time to time, hold meetings with groups of volunteers to disseminate information, answer questions, and obtain input into the operations of the organization.
- Establish policy on the use and care of volunteers.
- Offer credit and recognition to volunteers whenever possible.

To elaborate on the last point, the gerontologist administrator should seek every opportunity to give public recognition and credit to volunteers. These opportunities should go beyond simply mentioning the number of hours of volunteer service given to the organization, and should include mentioning specific names and projects in newsletters, newspapers, annual reports, public meetings, and presentations. To retain and manage volunteers effectively, organizations must provide a variety of placement options and attempt to match the volunteer's interest and skills with assigned tasks (Atchley, 2000).

Older Adult Volunteers

The number of older volunteers has increased considerably over the years. The majority of those over 65 are involved in some form of volunteer work (Atchley, 2000; Gelfand, 1993). By including care taking of family and friends as uncompensated work with community volunteer service and advocacy activities, the mean number of volunteer hours per week ranges from fourteen to twenty. About half of the older volunteers are involved with more than one kind of volunteer responsibility. Many older volunteers have a history of volunteerism throughout life.

Indeed, the older adult as a volunteer has been institutionalized and established as a role of choice for many. The AARP has established rights and responsibilities for AARP volunteers that also serve as a guide for other organizations (see Table 12.3).

Volunteer activity begins to increase in second adulthood (45–65 years of age). Volunteers are usually persons with a higher education and socioeconomic level, without disabilities, and married (Atchley, 2000; Fischer & Schaffer, 1993). Many volunteers are still engaged in the marketplace as employees. The federal government has attempted to expand volunteer activities into lower socioeconomic classes by using compensation and restricted recruitment, as noted

Table 12.3
Rights and Responsibilities of Volunteers

An AARP volunteer may expect...

- Equal opportunity and consideration throughout recruitment, appointment, training, and service.

- Information concerning volunteer opportunities and appointments based on the volunteer's interests and capabilities.

- A written position description, to be used for subsequent planning and review.

- An orientation to AARP and the program to which the volunteer is assigned, and the training needed to carry out the responsibilities of the position.

- Encouragement, guidance, and the resources necessary for successful productivity.

- Inclusion in the planning and decision making relevant to the volunteer's activities.

- Consideration of and responses to questions, suggestions and concerns.

- Assistance in resolving problems or conflict.

- Respect, recognition, and appreciation for the volunteer's efforts and contributions.

An AARP volunteer is expected...
- To be supportive of AARP, its mission, and goals.

- To encourage others to contribute to the work of the Association.

- To participate in the orientation and training required for the volunteer's position.

- To perform assignments to the best of the volunteer's abilities.

- To participate in the planning and reviews relevant to the volunteer's position.

- To be dependable, cooperative, and accountable.

- To communicate ideas, opinions, questions, and concerns to appropriate persons within the Association.

- To contribute constructively in the resolution of the problems and conflict.

- To value and express appreciation for the efforts and achievements of others.

- To accord all others respect, equal opportunity, and fair treatment.

Source: AARP Volunteer Policy Task Force (1991). Used with permission of AARP.

in two of the national programs in Table 12.2. These programs, particularly Senior Companion and Foster Grandparents, have experienced limited levels of funding. In the profit sector, a number of health maintenance organizations (HMOs) have enticed volunteers by creating a "service credit" program (Pallarito, 1996). In this program, volunteers, such as drivers, earn credit for every hour of work. These credits can then be redeemed for certain services or donated.

Older volunteers can be found in all facets of community social and health services. A distinction can be made between expressive and instrumental vol-

Table 12.4
Bob Is Retired and a Volunteer

   Bob retired at 62, after 30 years of practicing medicine in New York City. Several years after medical school, he opened a walk-in clinic in the Bronx, building the business to three locations and over 100 staff. When he retired, he sold the business to three young physicians and retained the lease on the building and a 10 percent interest as a silent partner. He is retired.

   Two mornings a week for an hour or so and once in a while in the afternoon, but not every week, he communicates with his business associates in New York from his home in Venice, Florida. He still, of course, receives a quarterly income at the age of 72. Three mornings a week, he goes to the "other job," arising at 7:00 A.M. to read the newspaper before he reports to work at 9:00 A.M. Bob is a volunteer physician at a community program where he performs general practitioner duties for older adults in the center's medical clinic. His boss is a paid clinical coordinator, a registered nurse. He takes vacations two or three times a year, has holidays off, and loves his work. He receives no compensation or reimbursement for expenses. Some of the medical services provided by Bob and his 30 fellow physician volunteers can be billed through Medicare or Medicaid. He holds a limited practitioner's license in the state of Florida. He has been heard to comment, "This is the most satisfying job of my career." Bob is retired.

unteer service. Ozawa and Morrow-Howell (1988) found that, consistent with previous studies, older adults prefer expressive activities, such as socializing and reassurance, versus more instrumental activities, such as transportation or help with physical care. They conclude further that these kinds of services are mutually beneficial.

   Older adult volunteers are motivated by seeking to assist others and satisfying their own needs (Morrow-Howell & Mui, 1989; Okum, 1994). This differs from younger adults, some of whom are motivated by making business contacts, interest in new careers, and status. The motivation of one older adult volunteer is illustrated in the scenario, "Bob is retired and a volunteer," presented in Table 12.4. Bob is a classic example of appropriate compensation for loss of the work role.

Problems Associated with Volunteers

   It would be misleading to suggest that the use of volunteers is always a positive experience for the organization and for the volunteer. Up to one-third of volunteers leave their positions after a relatively short time. Among the issues for these volunteers is a feeling that they were not accomplishing anything meaningful, a lack of support when there were problems, and not enough training (Morrow-Howell & Mui, 1989). This presents an interesting dilemma for the gerontologist administrator, because many paid staff view volunteers as economic competitors. Thus, when the administrator expands training so volunteers can be more competent and confident in handling problems, this exacerbates the problems with paid staff and possibly could interfere with the necessary cooperative relationship between paid staff and volunteers (Morris & Caro, 1995).

Yet another dilemma that faces the gerontologist administrator is, unless volunteers can provide the service, there is likely to be no service at all. This is contrasted with the reality that if you can provide the service with volunteers why would you need paid professional staff? The answer to that question is, realistically, volunteers are not paid staff and are difficult to control. Seldom do volunteers have the professional education, the values socialization, and the ethical orientation of paid professional staff. It is not unusual for a volunteer, with no intention of harm, to breach confidentiality.

Some activities may be more desirable for volunteers than others. Many of the needs of community services organizations are not necessarily in the area where volunteers have an interest. For example, in community centers, there is no difficulty in obtaining volunteers to help arrange programs. However, finding volunteers to assist with envelope stuffing and labeling is not nearly as easy. Thus, the administrator cannot just arbitrarily assign volunteers to tasks. Otherwise, there will be difficulty in retaining and eventually recruiting volunteers. In addition to providing screening, orientation, training, and supportive staff, there are a number of practices that will prevent problems with volunteers. Some of the items on the list below are commonly practiced by community agencies. This does not make them correct. The experience of the authors and reports in the literature substantiate that the following practices should be avoided:

- A commitment to volunteer work in your organization before screening and orientation are complete.
- A volunteer governing board member who also volunteers in the area of direct services; this produces a conflict between governance and administration.
- Replacement of professional staff on a permanent basis.
- Using relatives of professional staff and administrators as volunteers.
- Aside from reimbursing volunteers for expenses, paying volunteers contradicts the definition of volunteer work. Further, it is especially harmful to have certain volunteers who are compensated and others who are not.
- Leaving volunteers alone to do their "own thing," without supervision.
- Expecting volunteer problems to solve themselves. Corrective and decisive intervention should not be delayed.
- Treating volunteers as a homogeneous group, failing to account for differences in motivation based on stage of life, interests, education, and commitment.

SUMMARY

Community relations are an extension of the organization that includes involvement with stakeholders, the public, political circles, and other institutions of the community. Volunteers are part of community relations, both in the service offered to the organization and as representatives of the organization. Community relations for organizations that provide programs for older adults encompass formal and informal networking, public relations and marketing efforts, and the activities of board members.

Networking activities, sometimes mandated by funding programs, provide opportunities for continuity of care, shared responsibilities, public relations, and marketing. Participation in networks is important to help coordinate the diverse programs for older adults. In addition, particular networking activities of the gerontologist administrator will increase opportunities for expanding human and financial resources. Networking can be a drain on staff time, can be used inappropriately by staff, and can create problems related to competition.

Public relations incorporates general corporate image activities, specific marketing for clients, and media relations. Public relations and marketing are highly technical areas and frequently require specialized staff or assistance from external consultants. Through public relations, the organization attempts to inform the public of its purpose and mission. Regardless of the staff assigned to such activities, the chief executive is the foremost public relations representative. Marketing includes pricing, promotion, and distribution of ideas to attract more, and, in some cases, certain kinds of consumers. Overmarketing should be avoided, as it builds unrealistic expectations and is unethical.

Media relations need to be thought of as two categories: relations about routine involvement of the media with programs, and relations with media during crises. It is constructive for an organization to have a media policy to guide behavior for routine aspects and also for dealing with crises. For routine aspects of a program, considerable latitude can be provided to staff. However, for crisis situations, media relations will need to be restricted to identified individuals or the chief executive.

In the current media environment, crisis, controversy, and contradictions are what make desirable news. It is not uncommon for those associated with the mass media to angle crisis situations to enhance the story line. A variety of rules for media relations under crisis conditions are offered. It should be recalled that many journalists feel it is important to maintain independence and not take sides. Media relations under crisis conditions often force a clash between rights and values.

Boards of directors of profit corporations and not-for-profit corporations have become more similar over time. Not-for-profit boards have been praised for their development and appropriate levels of involvement with programs. Over the years, changes in board memberships in profit organizations resulted in fewer executives on the board. In not-for-profit organizations, recruitment of volunteers with specific skills in areas of business and technical expertise has increased. The general rule to follow with boards of directors is that a certain division must be maintained between the governance and administration of the organization. Advisory boards have a different purpose, as they are not involved with governance and serve to influence programs.

The critical component with boards, regardless of type and sector, is the relationship between the chief executive and the board. Mutual trust, support, and extensive communication are essential for good relations. Problems occur with boards when board members become inappropriately involved with the staff or divide into factions, and when board members hold unrealistic expectations of the chief executive and the staff.

Volunteers are an integral part of programs that serve older adults. Volunteer involvement in programs for older adults continues to increase, as does volunteer activity in the country as a whole. Older volunteers compose a significant proportion of the number of volunteers who work in programs for older adults. In some instances, federally funded programs have been established to attract older volunteers.

In many ways, volunteers should be treated the same as staff. Volunteers should fill out applications, be screened, have an orientation, and receive an assignment consistent with their talent and interest. All volunteers need support and recognition and to feel valued for their contribution. Volunteers, like staff, will bring problems to the organization. Volunteer personnel problems should be dealt with in a timely manner and may involve intervention by administrators. To prevent volunteer problems, a list of practices to avoid has been provided. There are financial and time expenses related to the use of volunteers. Generally, use of volunteers offers many more benefits than disadvantages.

LEARNING EXPERIENCE

The Administrator's Dilemma

Marty Levowitz awoke with a start. She glanced over at the illuminated clock on the bed stand that had been given to her for her forty-sixth birthday by her husband Tom. It said 3:30. Tom was sleeping peacefully with a slow, even snore. As she eased herself from the bed so as not to wake her husband, her thoughts turned to Sunrise Manor, where she is the administrator. Intending to get a cold glass of water or juice and return to bed, she found herself 30 minutes later driving to work. This had been the week from hell, she thought.

At 40, she had left her job as a public relations person to reduce stress and have more free time. Those goals had not been realized. While the career change was smooth as she followed her inner urge to work with older adults, she first made the transition by taking a marketing director's job at a nursing home. During those two years, she took gerontology classes at the local university and eventually became certified as an assisted living facility (ALF) administrator.

Four years ago, when she secured the administrator position at Sunrise Manor, things were different. The 80-bed ALF was not only full but had a long waiting list. The board of directors of the not-for-profit organization was eager to make improvements in the facility and accept proposals for additional staff. Now, recently, with the proliferation of ALFs and specialized facilities for Alzheimer's patients, the census is below 60, and the board is reluctant to make any major decisions.

On Monday, Marty noticed that Sophie Rucker, a 60-year-old resident who had been experiencing intermittent depression, remained in her room the whole day. When Marty entered the room in the afternoon, Sophie was crying and not willing to talk. Marty was pleased that the paperwork had been completed for Sophie to see the contract mental health therapist, a licensed clinical social worker, on Tuesday. Little did she know that the result of that session would dramatically change her life and the future of the facility.

During the session, Sophie told the therapist that she had been raped on Sunday coming home from the corner store. The rape had not occurred at the facility, but several blocks away. The therapist told Marty that she would return the next day to spend more time with Sophie, but in the meantime suggested a physical examination. Eventually, Sophie was able to talk to Marty about the incident. Marty assured Sophie that confidentiality would be maintained. By the end of Tuesday, everyone in the facility knew about it. The walls indeed have ears.

Perhaps that's why she's driving to work at 4:00 in the morning on Wednesday. This facility, because of its status, is required to have nurses on duty 24 hours. Marty immediately walked to the nurse's station where she found the certified nurse assistant (CNA) with his head down on his arms on the table top. He heard her appear and abruptly stood up. Marty asked for the nurse. He said, "I'll get her for you." Marty intuitively raised her hand and said, "No, don't do that. You come with me." It was the look on his face of slight panic and deception that caused her grave concern. She asked him when was the last time he saw the nurse. He didn't answer. As they walked the halls, the nurse was not in view. After about ten minutes, Marty opened the door to the conference room, and there was the nurse bedded down on the conference table, sheets, blankets, and a comfortable pillow laid out nicely. She was sleeping soundly.

The nurse finished her shift, but was told at the end of the shift that she would be on suspension. Further investigation by Marty found that the CNA on duty and other CNAs were paid ten dollars to cover for her while she slept. After consultation with the director of nursing, the nurse was called in for an interview, and despite the apologies and pronouncements that this "would not happen again," and that this "was the only time," she was dismissed. She left angry, glaring at the director of nursing and Marty over her shoulder as she went through the door.

Thursday, at about 10:00, Marty received a phone call from a reporter who introduced herself as being responsible for health beat for the local newspaper. This was a different person from the reporter she had had contact with over the past couple of years. The reporter stated over the phone, "We have an anonymous report that one of your residents has been raped."

Assume that you are in Marty's position and answer the following questions:

1. What preparation should you have made prior to the media involvement?

2. Once learning of the incident, what steps would you have taken?

3. How would you deal with the responsibility to keep the victim's name confidential?

4. Should you contact anyone from the board of directors? If yes, who, and what would you tell them?

5. What would be the implications of the publicity about a rape of a resident, even though it did not occur on the premises, for the marketing of ALF services?

6. Other than the board of directors and key staff members, who else might you contact about the situation?

7. Assuming that you choose not to resign and return to public relations, how would you be able to assure the board that you will overcome any negative publicity and maintain the viability of the program?

8. Sophie's son appears, having read the article in the paper, and although the name was not mentioned, he was able to ascertain from the description that it was his mother who had been raped, and wants to know what happened. What is your approach?

REFERENCES

AARP Volunteer Policy Task Force. (1991). *AARP Volunteer Expectations*. Washington, DC: AARP.

Atchley, R. C. (2000). *Social forces and aging: An introduction to social gerontology* (9th ed.). Belmont, CA: Wadsworth Thomson Learning.

Briar-Lawson, K. (1998). Community collaboration and service integration: Models and challenges. In J. McCroskey & S. D. Einbinder (Eds.), *Universities and communities: Remarking professionals and interprofessional education for the next century* (pp. 155–166). Westport, CT: Praeger.

Brown, S. R. (1987). Marketing home health care to the community. *Topics in Geriatric Rehabilitation, 2*(2), 55–65.

Crow, R. T., & Odewahn, C. A. (1987). *Management for the human services*. Englewood Cliffs, NJ: Prentice-Hall.

Dale, E. (1978). *Management: Theory and practice* (4th ed.). New York: McGraw-Hill.

Drucker, P. F. (1989, July–August). What business can learn from nonprofits. *Harvard Business Review*, 88–93.

Duca, D. J. (1996). *Nonprofit boards: Roles, responsibilities, and performance*. New York: John Wiley.

Fischer, L. R., & Schaffer, K. B. (1993). *Older volunteers: A guide to research and practice*. Newbury Park, CA: Sage.

Gatewood, R. D., Taylor, R. R., & Ferrell, O. C. (1995). *Management: Comprehension, analysis, and application*. Chicago: Austen.

Gelfand, D. E. (1993). *The aging network*. New York: Springer.

Ginsberg, L. (1995). Concepts of new management. In L. Ginsberg & P. R. Keys (Eds.), *New management in human services* (2nd ed., pp. 1–37). Washington, DC: National Association of Social Workers.

Green, R. R. (1997). Emerging issues for social workers in the field of aging: White House Conference themes. *Journal of Gerontological Social Work, 27*(3), 79–87.

Guth, D. W. (1995). Organizational crisis experience and public relations roles. *Public Relations Review, 21*(2), 123–127.

ICR Survey Research Group. (1991). *Marriott seniors volunteerism study.* Washington, DC: Marriott Senior Living Services and United States Administration on Aging.

Jackson, N. C., & Mathews, R. M. (1995). Using public feedback to increase contributions to a multipurpose senior center. *Journal of Applied Behavioral Analysis, 28*(4), 449–456.

Karuza, J., Calkins, E., Duffey, J., & Feather, J. (1988). Networking in aging: A challenge, model, and evaluation. *The Gerontological Society of America, 28*(2), 147–155.

Lewis, J. A., Lewis, M. D., & Soufleé, F. (1991). *Management of human service programs* (2nd ed.). Pacific Grove, CA: Brooks/Cole.

Miller, J. N. (1988). New management concept in family and children's services. In P. R. Keys & L. H. Ginsberg (Eds.), *New management in human services* (pp. 212–234). Silver Spring, MD: National Association of Social Workers.

Mintzberg, H. (1980). *The nature of managerial work.* Englewood Cliffs, NJ: Prentice-Hall.

Mintzberg, H. (1989). *Mintzberg on management: Inside our strange world of organizations.* New York: Free Press.

Morris, R., & Caro, F. G. (1995). The young-old, productive aging, and public policy. *Generations, 19,* 32–37.

Morrow-Howell, N., & Mui, A. (1989). Elderly volunteers: Reasons for initiating and terminating service. *Journal of Gerontological Social Work, 13*(3/4), 21–33.

Netting, E. F., Kettner, P. M., & McMurtry, S. L. (1993). *Social work macro practice.* New York: Longman.

O'Connell, B. (1981). *Effective leadership in voluntary organizations.* New York: Walker.

Okum, M. A. (1994). The relation between motives for organizational volunteers and frequency of volunteering by elders. *The Journal of Applied Gerontology, 13*(2), 115–126.

Overholser, G. (1999, September 1). The public's growing distrust of the media. *Chicago Tribune,* p. 21.

Ozawa, M. N., & Morrow-Howell, N. (1988). Services provided by elderly volunteers: An empirical study. *Journal of Gerontological Social Work, 13*(1/2), 65–80.

Pallarito, K. (1996, March). Finance: Assistance programs bank on volunteers. *Modern Healthcare,* p. 50.

Peterson, R. T. (1989). *Principles of marketing.* Orlando, FL: Books for Professionals.

Rosenthal, S. J., & Young, J. E. (1980). The governance of the social services. In F. D. Perlmutter & S. Slavin (Eds.), *Leadership in social administration: Perspectives for the 1980s* (pp. 86–104). Philadelphia: Temple University.

Rubin, H. J., & Rubin, I. S. (1992). *Community organizing and development* (2nd ed.). Boston: Allyn & Bacon.

Sarasota County Aging Network. (1997). Our Mission. *Directory of Sarasota County Senior Services* (p. 1). Sarasota, FL.

Seniors consult on products for the elderly. (1995). *The Futurist, 29*, 42.

Simyar, F., & Lloyd-Jones, J. (1988). *Strategic management in the health care sector: Toward the year 2000*. Englewood Cliffs, NJ: Prentice-Hall.

Stven, C. (1985). Outreach to the elderly: Community based services. *Journal of Gerontological Social Work, 8*(3/4), 85–96.

Sumariwalla, R. D. (1988). Modern management and the nonprofit sector. In P. R. Keys & L. H. Ginsberg (Eds.), *New management in human services* (pp. 184–211). Silver Spring, MD: National Association of Social Workers.

Weinbach, R. (1998). *The social worker as manager: A practical guide to success* (3rd ed.). Needham Heights, MA: Allyn & Bacon.

Wilber, K. H., & Myrtle, R. C. (1998). Developing community-based systems of care: Lessons from the field. In J. McCroskey & S. D. Einbinder (Eds.), *Universities and communities: Remarking professionals and interprofessional education for the next century* (pp. 119–138). Westport, CT: Praeger.

Chapter 13

Organizational Renewal and Change

Accurately envisioning the future of an organization with programs for older adults requires knowledge of older adults, knowledge of administration, understanding organizations and staff, as well as the ability to assess the internal and external forces of change. Furthermore, it inspires the administrator to plan for alternative futures. This requires motivation to depart from tradition, leaving the relative comfort of the status quo, and a willingness to deal with fear (Johnson, 1998; Oakley & Krug, 1991; Weiner, 1990). Changes can be relatively minor, such as alterations in policy or procedure, or substantial organizational changes that impact the goals, structure, and culture of an organization. This chapter is directed at substantial organizational change and improvement. The forces of change and the range of responses to those forces need to be considered.

Forces of change can be internal or external; when change occurs, it is usually the result of both. Figure 13.1 depicts forces and a continuum of responses. The internal and external forces listed in the figure are only a fraction of the possible complexities calling for change. Other internal forces include administrative succession, staff turnover, consumer feedback, organizational conflict, and technological needs (Champion, 1975; Robbins, 1995). External forces are numerous; for example, each time Congress changes the Older Americans Act or Medicare, an adjustment is required. Demographic changes that involve increasing numbers of older adults and changes in age groups, such as the oldest-old, impact programs. Additionally, competition, cooperation, or consolidation with other programs may require substantial changes.

Responses to these forces range from minimal, where the posture is usually reactive (making small adjustments to each incident), to a systematic, planned change. While organizations in maintenance states certainly require adjustments, often the acknowledgment of a need for substantial change is delayed. Small

Figure 13.1
Forces of Change and Range of Responses

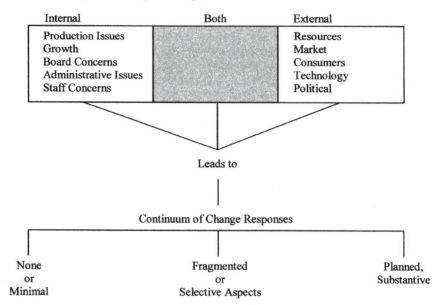

changes will accumulate but fail to impact the system as they become assimilated into the traditional practices and behaviors (Lynch & Kordis, 1988). With planned change, certain forces are anticipated and indicators of future needs are interpreted. Planned substantial organizational change, the focus of this chapter, increases the likelihood of success of change efforts (Gatewood, Taylor, & Ferrell, 1995). However, many systematic change efforts have fallen short of expectations (McCune, 1999; Oakley & Krug, 1991). Consequently, the perspective and technology of organizational change has undergone change itself.

CHANGING PERSPECTIVE ON ORGANIZATIONAL CHANGE

Organizational change strategies and methods, like management and leadership theory, have evolved from a highly directive orientation to a more participatory orientation. Most early organizational change efforts were characterized by either a power approach that involved coercion and manipulation or a rational educative orientation (Weiner, 1990). With the infusion of behavioral sciences and human relations into administration, a more person-oriented approach emerged, along with an extensive technology of people involvement known as organizational development (OD). In many instances, change was attempted with minimal planning but by instituting OD technology (described later in this chapter). The human relations perspective dominated change efforts in the 1960s and through the late 1980s, and continued to evolve as research provided new direction (Bargal & Schmid, 1992; Buller, Saxberg, & Smith, 1985). The human relations perspective and the emerging perspective deserve closer examination.

Human Relations Change Perspective

This perspective focuses on changing people's attitudes, values, relationships, skills, and competencies. Human relations change efforts clearly identify beginning and ending phases (Robbins, 1995). The dominant model for organizational change emerged from Kurt Lewin's field theory (see Buller et al., 1985; Robbins, 1995; Weinbach, 1998; Weiner, 1990). This model has three phases:

1. *Unfreezing* represents the current state of affairs that must be disrupted. This is accomplished by providing information about lack of efficiency and effectiveness or about the discrepancy between the organization's current position and a future desired point. The evaluation identifies forces that prevent the organization from moving forward.

2. *Moving* is a transition state, with behaviors and attitudes as well as structures and policies changing.

3. *Refreezing* is the stage of the new organization that uses feedback from the successive change, rewards, and support to stabilize the organization. The organization is seen to reach a new state of equilibrium.

Evaluations and organizational diagnoses are completed primarily by using pencil-and-paper surveys of attitudes, morale, management and leadership style, communications flow, and a plethora of other components of the organization. Interviews might also be conducted with key staff and executives. Many of these evaluations and surveys—often several are used—are extensive and costly. These instruments frequently produce results that identify issues and problems that are far greater than can be redressed by the resources available. Based on the results of these evaluations and the experience derived from other organizations, areas of change are identified (Oakley & Krug, 1991). There exists the risk of targeting too much or, when focusing change efforts, neglecting important areas of concern. Organizational development technology, such as seminars and team sessions, is used to re-educate staff and to deal with resistance while attempting to maintain control. In this approach, major efforts are made to control conflict and avoid chaos (Weinbach, 1998). Substantial change projects often take between three and five years.

Emerging Perspective on Change

The emerging change perspective is distinguished by three features: (1) a view that change is continuous and constant; (2) greater attention given to behavior; and (3) early involvement of staff in the future design.

Table 13.1
The Change Train

- Moving most of the time, often at high speed
- Changes must occur while in motion
- People get on and off often while moving
- Occasionally must stop briefly for repairs

Change Is Continuous and Constant

Unlike the view of the past, change has no beginning, middle, or end and is almost seamless. The notion of constant change is perceived as essential for survival. This picture of change is illustrated by the characteristics of a high-speed train; see Table 13.1. These change initiatives are superimposed on the continuous change and have a duration of a few months to one and a half years. Organizations are expected to maintain continuity with program commitments.

Attention to Behavior

The human relations perspective on change pays great attention to attitudes and dedicates considerable time to trying to change attitudes. The emerging perspective focuses on behavior, both as it relates to the change efforts and as it relates to performing duties. It is more suited to a diverse work force and the mobility of the work force. Emphasis is also placed on overcoming fear (Johnson, 1998). OD technologies that have survived over time, including coaching, are used to address fear of the unknown and fear about competencies necessary for the new organization.

Early Involvement of Staff in Future Design

In the previous model, staff were involved in providing information to help develop a report, making recommendations for organizational change, and participating in implementation of change elements. The emerging perspective's approach to staff involvement, in addition to evaluation of behaviors and management practices, includes eliciting from staff at all levels recommendations and suggestions for the changes that will contribute to the future organization (Bargal & Schmid, 1992). Expanded staff involvement recognizes the uniqueness of individuals and capitalizes on their in-depth knowledge of the workplace. This involvement also provides increased opportunity for leadership. A partnership between staff, administrators, and the consultants is a more likely composition for organizational change.

There are several other distinct characteristics of the emerging perspective. Rather than viewing conflict and chaos as needing to be mediated, conflict and chaos are expected and seen as functional. Without conflict, there is no indication of change. According to Tom Peters' (1987) book *Thriving on Chaos*, chaos provides opportunity for change. Also with this emerging model, evaluation and assessment are seen as continuously necessary, like checking the oil.

Evaluations are likely to use focus groups, observation, and interviews in replacement for, or in addition to, the traditional surveys. Furthermore, assessment takes into consideration the life cycle of the organization and its current situation (Oakley & Krug, 1991). Last, the essential role of top administration is not limited to showing commitment and support for change, but to demonstrating such by behavior and greater direct involvement.

An example of this approach to change is the emergency room of Harris Methodist Hospital in Fort Worth, Texas, which was given the 1996 Rochester Institute of Technology and USA Today Quality Cup Award for not-for-profit corporations (Wiseman, 1996). Patient satisfaction surveys had consistently showed dissatisfaction with the emergency room, even though the staff felt they had a good system. The emergency room medical director was encouraged by corporate staff to focus on improving customer satisfaction. Typically, the director started by using some OD training on how to be nicer to customers, but it did not significantly change the customer satisfaction scores. Eventually, the director reached the conclusion that the unit needed to replace the entire system and formed a team of staff to address the issue. After a period of self-examination and brainstorming, this team devised a way to redesign the emergency care system for patients' needs, rather than for the convenience of staff. As a result, waiting time to see the doctor dropped from 52 minutes to 10 minutes. The team established a quick care unit for patients with less serious injuries that reduced the time in the emergency room from 137 minutes to 55 minutes. Consequently, other associated units, such as lab and x-ray, were able to respond more quickly. These changes occurred in less than a year.

Demonstrating Commitment to Change

The vision-setting leader is associated with the new perspective, where the task master and supportive motivator are part of the other schools of change (Perlmutter, 1998; Shin & McClomb, 1998). Currently, the successful change effort is tied to the ability of the leader to operate in a chaotic environment and to be perceived as committed to change (Bargal & Schmid, 1992). The gerontologist administrator can support and participate in the change effort or be a reluctant leader who is part of the problem. The leader will need to deal with her own resistance and fears, while challenging her own beliefs and the conventional wisdom (Fitz-enz, 1990; London, 1988; Oakley & Krug, 1991; Perlmutter, 1998). Efficacious leader behaviors associated with facilitating change consistent with the emerging perspective are:

- Acknowledge that one's own behavior and that of others will be different with the pressures of change (Briscoe, 1977; Moore, 1988).
- Develop and use the skill to examine situations, events, and structures through the eyes of others (Briscoe, 1977).

- Relax some controls with associated authority to other leaders and staff (Oakley & Krug, 1991).
- Assume a fear of the future and pose the following questions to oneself and others (Doyle, 1985; Johnson, 1998; Lynch & Kordis, 1988):
  —What would I do if I was not afraid?
  —What is the worst thing that can happen?
  —What is the best thing that can happen?
  —What would happen if we do nothing?
- Embrace the vision or goal and repeat the essence of the vision constantly (Lynch & Kordis, 1988; McCune, 1999; Oakley & Krug, 1991).
- Incorporate the vision into daily life, correspondence, conversations, and presentations.
- Expect to be involved and instrumental in the change process, for with substantive change everyone is in the process together (McCune, 1999).
- Guard against over-reaction to surprises and mistakes. Such over-reactions are unnecessarily time-consuming and can cause deviations from the vision.

CHANGE FOCUS AND ORGANIZATIONAL ASSESSMENT

Every substantive change effort should have a primary focus. Recognizing the need for change is usually not that complex or radical, but forging a focus requires systematic inquiry into the nature of the organization. An organizational assessment will assist in establishing the focus and the details of a plan. This typically precedes implementation of substantive organizational change. Assessment, which generally has multiple components, is actually integrated with the beginning of the change process, as will be discussed later in this chapter.

Recognition must be given to a universal phenomenon of organizational change; regardless of the focus, every aspect of the organization will be affected. Establishing a focus directs energy and resources toward the main goals. Consideration of new computer technology in the service organization is rarely, and correctly, not the focus of change. Rather, new technology should be selected to support and enhance the new organizational plan. Three foci for change in organizations are the culture, structure, and service technology. Methods of organizational assessment and analysis used and available to formulate the plan will also be presented.

Changing the Culture

Certainly the most difficult and resistant area to change is the organizational culture, for this involves changing values, norms, habits, and long-established patterns of behavior. It often extends into belief systems and philosophy. The culture is mostly invisible with its own logic of survival that doggedly persists over time (Sluyter, 1998). To change the culture of an organization is to challenge the core identity, the status quo, and the history of behaviors (Beckhard

& Harris, 1977; Schein, 1987). New employees are quickly socialized to the rules and behaviors, and those who do not comply leave or become isolated. Simply replacing people will not change the culture. The culture is frequently so strong it can shape the administrators.

Cultural change is indicated when there is deterioration of the purpose of the organization and when the culture controls behavior, diverting energy from the intended efforts of the program. More precisely, change is needed when unwillingness to change with the times exists, when there is role confusion, or when an unfair reward distribution exists (Holloway & Brager, 1985).

Changing organizational culture is reconstructing the organizational vision, articulating that vision, and giving it meaning for the organization and the individual (Sluyter, 1998). Cultural change is directed toward people—their thoughts, views, opinions, and, ultimately, behavior. Therefore, change will need to occur in communications, reward systems, group interaction, social behavior, and self-perceptions. This change will need to penetrate the informal organization.

TQM, discussed in Chapter 3, represents such a change. A new culture cannot be instituted if one follows the methods and pathways of the old culture (Pritchett & Pound, 1993). In bringing about cultural change, if the administrator engages in behavior that feels right and does not become the subject of criticism and concern, it is unlikely that substantive change is occurring. Meaningful cultural change will seriously affect the structure of power and influence and often result in the loss of staff.

Changing the Structure

Structural change, unlike cultural change, is highly visible. It means redesigning the organizational chart to create or combine departments, change supervisory relationships, and redefine organizational authority. The purpose may be to "flatten" an organization, removing layers of administration and combining departments, or to add a layer of administration. Structural change also means a review of policies and procedures and altering those policies and procedures to correspond to the new structure. For example, when a human resources department in an AAA moved the employment interview process to the programs throughout the organization, it required a rewriting of the employment procedure and corresponding training for supervisors.

An organization that is structured according to functions could be changed, maintaining the functional orientation (finance, human resources, and programs, etc.), or seek to become structured along project or program lines (Beckhard & Harris, 1977). Project structure develops teams with greater autonomy. Structural change may also seek to shift responsibility and accountability to lower levels of the organization or to return responsibility and accountability to a centralized location. Organizational change to centralize or decentralize represents a major rationale for bringing about structural change. A closer examination of the notion of decentralization will serve to illustrate structural change.

Decentralization

When organizations grow in size, a decision may be made to decentralize. In a centralized structure, most authority is vested in administrative executives, and most major decisions are made by those executives (Allan, 1958). In a decentralized structure, authority is given to organizational subunits, like departments or divisions, for decisions that directly relate to activities performed by the staff (Champion, 1975). Decentralization of an organizational structure will achieve several goals. First, this structure reduces the number of decisions that need to be made by central administration, producing more rapid decision-making. Second, it allows subunits to adopt practices that can be adjusted to a given client mix or type of service. Third, decentralization along with emphasis on training helps to develop the strength of the middle management of an organization. Fourth, since decentralization facilitates participation, greater control over work environment, and delegation of decision-making, it frequently improves employee motivation (Allan, 1958; Gatewood et al., 1995; Mintzberg, 1989).

The most effective way to decentralize is by creating divisions or some similar units within the organizational structure. A typical feature of a decentralized organization occurs when personnel activities such as hiring, firing, and promoting employees have been delegated to a division or department level. Another strong indicator is the discretion that a department head, division chief, or unit supervisor may have in making expenditures.

An organization can be both decentralized and centralized. For example, in a large community center serving older adults, the top administration was located in a separate geographical location from the three service areas and had decentralized much of the decision-making. At the same time, each of the service areas, which have a designated administrator, is highly centralized. All hiring and other personnel activities and expenditure authorizations are the responsibility of the division administrator.

Regardless of the intent of the structural change, substantive change of the formal structure will also change the informal structure. This will represent a strong area of resistance as, unlike the formal structure, it cannot be directed to change. When the focus is on structural change, one must adopt a range of strategies that will change both the formal and informal structure.

Changing the Service Technology

Service technology changes can involve organizational philosophy and methodology or relate to a specific program or project. Of all the change efforts, once implemented, it is the least likely to be reversible (Holloway & Brager, 1985). Service technology change is particularly subject to external forces. Such changes may expand, retract, or open new markets (Gatewood et al., 1995).

Information from consumer surveys and evaluations of service effectiveness or judgments about the impact on the population often produce the impetus for such change. New funding sources based on allocations responding to pressure groups or evaluation findings will often require different approaches for areas of concern.

It is less common to find service technology change that encompasses the entire organization, but it does occur. A mental health center in a northern Alabama metropolis decided, after considerable study, to convert the entire organization to a behavioral orientation, so that the only kind of therapy that was offered to consumers was behavioral therapy. To implement this, an elaborate mechanism of monitoring therapy sessions was instituted. Only therapists with a background in behavioral therapy were hired. Consequently, all treatment technology must fit this adopted model.

An innovative service might be added to an organization so that existing employees would have to be retrained. For example, a state agency that provides adult protective services was provided the opportunity to change its service technology. Consequently, several of the caseworkers conducting investigative work were assigned to an educational unit with a mission of teaching and empowering older adults and caretakers to prevent abuse situations. This required retraining of certain caseworkers, as well as the formulation of a new team within the organizational unit. In other instances, the service technology change may be so radical that existing employees do not have the requisite qualifications or cannot be retrained.

Organizational Assessment and Analysis

To determine the primary focus of the change effort and, equally as important, the selection of change technology, an assessment of the organization's current state is essential. Assessment of the organization is much more complex and comprehensive than the traditional process that starts with "identifying the problem." Indeed, not only is simply identifying the problem insufficient, but it is not necessary to have a "problem" to engage in organizational change. Organizational improvement is most meaningful when the current picture of the organization can be contrasted with a desired or required future organization. To formulate a picture of the organization, a variety of methods can be used independently or together.

Traditionally, surveys, questionnaires, and interviews have been used to gather information. Surveys that are highly focused, such as the attitudes of staff toward administration, are of limited value for substantive organizational change. Surveys that examine a broad range of activities and a number of subsystems, such as the decision-making process, problem-solving approach, relationship to administration, or communication channels, are more valuable.

Recently, with the new approach to changing organizations, there is more extensive use of open-ended interviews with staff, stakeholders, former employees, and volunteers. Strategic observation of meetings, training sessions, and the delivery of services produces information about the real organization rather than the self-perceived organization. Further, analyses of budgets, audits, grant reports, and policies are used for cross-validation of information obtained from other methods. These organizational analysis techniques are more useful if conducted by external consultants. The methods for assessing an organization have limited value if they are primarily accomplished by internal staff. Consider the following:

• Internal staff rarely have the education or background to use or construct staff surveys properly.
• When assessments are conducted by staff, the analysis is seen as a project that would produce highly suspect results.
• Organizational surveys conducted by staff, especially the internally designed, often raise more issues than can be dealt with and have questionable reliability.
• Rarely do staff have adequate time to allocate to conducting a systematic, comprehensive survey or to analyze results properly.

An organizational analysis can also be achieved by using group interaction, either with one representative group or with several groups. For instance, an organizational scan, such as the one described in Chapter 11, can be used to identify strengths, weaknesses, and new opportunities for the organization. The result of the process is to establish a list of priorities for change. In a similar vein, a systematic set of questions can be posed to the group that will contribute to the genesis of a change plan. Brody (1993) suggests asking, at a minimum, four fundamental questions:

1. What business are we in?
2. What business should we be in now?
3. What business do we want to be in in future years down the road?
4. What will happen if we stay in the same business?

These two methods, the scan or standard questions for groups, will produce less depth of information than surveys and interviews. They can be successfully conducted by internal staff, provided that the leader has group facilitation skills and remains neutral during the group process. However, it is best to engage a professional organizational consultant for these methods as well.

An important consideration that should be factored into the change plan is the stage of the life cycle of the organization (Lynch & Kordis, 1988; Mintzberg, 1989). A well-established professional bureaucracy that has existed for some time certainly will present challenging contingencies for organizational change. Rogers and Hough (1995) argue that organizational evaluations must also assess the administrative style and assumptions that control the organization. Thus, determining the stage of development and the character of the organization are vital elements of the assessment process.

Paramount in conducting organizational change is the need to avoid the mistake of "analysis paralysis." This is by far the most commonly expressed complaint and reason for failure. When an organization expends most of its resources and energies in a prolonged effort to analyze the organization, it dampens the commitment to and interest in change. Often, these extensive analyses generate problems with and areas of concern about the organization that go far beyond the organization's ability to engage all of them in a reasonable period of time. Three-quarters of the effort and energy should be directed toward the implementation of the changes.

A CHANGE PROCESS FOR CONTINUAL RENEWAL

A systematic approach to change is offered as a change process for organizational renewal. This process offers a structure and is consistent with contemporary thinking on change. The process can be operationalized using administrative principles and guidelines presented throughout this text and selected organizational development technology presented in the next section of this chapter. This change process rejects the old notion that "change is a product of one minor adjustment after another, fueled by time and subtle environmental forces, largely outside the direct control of management" (Greiner, 1978, p. 336). Moreover, this process provides the gerontologist administrator with a proactive approach that anticipates change and guides a substantive change effort.

To highlight the contemporary view of change and delineate it from older models, we have cast this as organizational renewal, which means that, for organizations that offer programs for older adults, change efforts are viewed as a constant responsibility, with ongoing evaluation, in a continuous effort to improve (Johnson, 1998; Oakley & Krug, 1991; Robbins, 1995). This perspective on organizational change includes anticipating change, determining the focus of renewal, developing a plan, preparing for renewal, implementing change, and realizing renewal.

Anticipating Change

The gerontologist administrator must learn to read the natural indicators within the organization and in the greater environment that would suggest change. Noticing small changes, both the number and the kind, helps to recognize the need for organizational renewal (Johnson, 1998). There is considerable information available for the gerontologist administrator to review, such as consumer feedback, monthly budget statements, quality assurance information, safety information, and listening to the comments and concerns of staff. Testing the water with occasional open-ended questions provides valuable information.

In a more formal sense, systematic planning efforts, in particular strategic planning, will identify goals and strategies for the future of the organization which may require substantive change.

Determining the Focus of Renewal

The recognition of specific problems on an informal and casual basis, and the identification of future goals, should lead to a more systematic approach in assessing the organization. As we described earlier in this chapter, a variety of assessment methods can be used to achieve a focus. It is best if substantive change efforts have a primary focus, although it is recognized that they may not be categorized as changing the culture, the structure, or the service technology. In some instances, certain areas may have already changed, and the focus is on changing another area to coincide. For example, a multiprogram senior center adopted a new structure in response to federal funding changes, then adjusted the service technology, but the culture was lagging, requiring refocused efforts and external assistance to bring about complete change.

Development of a Plan

In the contemporary approach to change, the plan represents a vision of what the organization would like to achieve or become. Once a focus is established, the plan, which incorporates recommendations that have been made by staff, consultants, or others, based on the assessment process, is forged with broad participation. In formulating this plan, it may be necessary to engage in reassessment and perhaps adjustment of the focus. The plan should identify specific areas to be targeted for change and should incorporate technologies to deal with resistance to change. A systematic assessment of resistance will provide information about elements of the plan and about designing the implementation (Patti, 1983).

Preparing for Renewal

The most important preparation is to communicate the vision of the future, obtaining commitment to that vision from administration and staff. It must become part of the job to pursue the vision—ideally, with the fervor of a cause (London, 1988; Pritchett & Pound, 1993). The administrator should also appeal to staff's professional values, ethics, and logic in supporting the change effort. Many staff members, as has been discussed previously, work at organizations that serve older adults because of their strong commitments and advocacy for improving life circumstances.

It is necessary during this phase to enhance and/or create dissatisfaction with the existing state of affairs. This often requires information and feedback obtained from surveys, assessments, and other sources about negative aspects of a current situation, especially as compared to the possible vision. Creating dissat-isfaction and concern can also be achieved by relating present practices to es-tablished standards, benchmarks, or measurable organizational goals. This process is meant to be discomforting.

The sensitivity of this area is extensive, for communicating dissatisfaction with the current state of affairs must be couched as changing expectations and goals. It is not necessary to criticize the old ways or the old system, but rather to recognize the value of the new systems in relationship to the future organi-zation. Preparation for change that reaches into all corners of the organization and touches most of the employees will contribute greatly to constructive im-plementation and assimilation of the changes.

Implementing Change

Substantive change efforts need to have direct guidance and continued mon-itoring. This is often accomplished by appointing a change committee that sys-tematically implements the elements of the change plan and monitors the effect. In other instances, an internal change agent is identified; this person oversees the implementation of the elements of the plan. The most common mechanism is using an external consultant to assist the organization by working with the leadership and the staff to adjust implementation methodologies and to maintain focus.

The implementation stage is essentially a transition state which is uncom-fortable, disruptive, and often unpleasant. Administrators frequently feel that they are in charge of a mess and that "things are getting out of hand." This is normal; in fact, it is how you know that you are in the midst of a change process. In the words of one organizational improvement consultant, who is one of the authors of this text, "If you have no crises, resignations, or conflicts, you are not changing."

During this phase, the organization learns behaviors needed to realize the future organization (Greiner, 1978). Often this is done by trial and error and reality testing. It is generally not a smooth and even process. As soon as major changes are implemented, other related decisions will need to be made through-out the organization. It is critical that information and feedback be continuous so that these smaller changes can be assessed in terms of the relevance to the overall goals.

Increased communication is absolutely necessary during the implementation; this communication should not follow only the regular channels (Pritchett & Pound, 1993). For example, the organization's leadership and the consultant can conduct change-oriented meetings that focus discussion on the implementation of the changes, the impact, the barriers, and, equally as important, the rumors. Increased communication is especially important in dealing with rumors. When-ever a rumor of any proportion surfaces, administration needs to formally clarify the issues related to the rumor, orally and in writing.

During implementation, there is the opportunity to bring in new staff, for some staff will "jump off" the moving train. To facilitate the transition and realize the new organization, administrators must select people who will be strong enough to resist conforming to the old culture and can demonstrate enthusiastic commitment to the vision (Pritchett & Pound, 1993).

Resistance to Change

The most discussed aspect of organizational change is resistance. Indeed, in the literature on organizational change, discussions of resistance, and especially the reasons for resistance, consume a major part of most narratives. In our discussion we will not dwell on reasons for resistance, as resistance is overemphasized for many reasons. Resistance, although present during other steps in the change process, truly becomes a factor during implementation. Resistance is most profound and difficult when organizational change is implemented using a highly directive, coercive approach. Such an approach is in marked contrast to the guidance presented in this text. Further, resistance to change is reduced considerably by early involvement of staff in identification of the need for change and assisting with the nature of the change. That involvement begins with anticipating changes. Generally, the earlier and more extensive the staff involvement, the less resistance.

Some resistance is beneficial and, at times, could be the most appropriate response. Resistance should be examined closely. A revealing phenomenon about resistance is that the strongest resistors are often people who initially were the apparent supporters of change. As soon as implementation occurs, thereby affecting their work, a change of mind or heart brings resistance. Resistance distills to such fears as not having the skills to accomplish the tasks of the new organization, the loss of relationships, the loss of power and status, and changes in the rewards and recognition (Crow & Odewahn, 1987; Robbins, 1995; Weinbach, 1998).

Recognition and Reduction of Resistance

Most of the time, it is advisable to reduce resistance to change, and these strategies should be part of the overall change plan. Resistance may be subtle, such as production slowdown or increased absenteeism, or openly defiant, and even conspiratorial where staff agree on certain resistive activities. Strategies that can be employed to deal with resistance to change are described in Table 13.2.

When the gerontologist administrator finds herself willing to accept expressed barriers, proposed impossibilities, and challenges to the change goals, then it is time for self-examination. If a systematic change process has been followed, most of these contingencies were anticipated and decided upon prior to implementation. When the administrator accepts this kind of resistance, which is a test of commitment, there is the need to examine her own resistance by speaking with a superior or a consultant.

Table 13.2
Dealing with Resistance to Change

- Change-oriented group sessions that are informative about the changes, the process of change, and the part group members play. These group sessions can be conducted by administrators at all levels or by consultants.

- Training and education which should be done internally and should always incorporate the vision of the new organization. Such training can clarify information and often provide staff with new knowledge and skills.

- Build trust and credibility with the change leaders and the consultants. This is accomplished in part by visibility, expression of commitment, and one-on-one interaction. This is especially difficult in organizations that are faltering, or where authoritative, coercive administration is present.

- Involvement of staff in all aspects of the change process should strive to bring about investment. It is important to express repeatedly what the benefits will be for the individual, and to be willing to negotiate some of the methods for achieving the goals, but not the goals themselves.

- Forceful directives, both oral and written, that provide a rationale and specific elements that need to be changed help to clarify information, reduce rumors, and provide direction.

- Recognition of all movement in the desired direction. This would include visual indicators of increased productivity, content and extent of staff training, and reward of innovative approaches to accomplishing the goals of change.

- Administrators at all levels should be role models demonstrating a positive attitude and refraining from public expression of fear and doubt.

- Acknowledge all expressed barriers and be prepared to look for alternatives to overcome or go around those barriers. Most barriers can be overcome no matter how difficult it looks initially. Be unwilling to buy into such statements as "the software won't allow us to do that" as the final word.

Realizing Renewal

Organizational renewal will be realized gradually (Mintzberg, 1989). In this stage, the main tasks are to remain focused on the goals and to sustain the change process. The pace of change will increase as staff recognize accomplishments that reinforce the changes in relation to the vision. Refinement of change strategies also contributes to remaining focused. Refinement of strategies results from determining on a continuous basis what works, and engaging in systematic adjustment of change efforts.

If renewal is not realized, there will be a clear return to old behaviors while maintaining a façade of change. Assuming that renewal is realized, a growing acceptance of the change strategies and the new organization will be demonstrated (Greiner, 1978), often by testimonials of personal revitalization and evidence of improved productivity. Training and group discussions during this stage will be most constructive if they provide opportunity for reflection on old behaviors, and refinement of new behaviors and values, as well as the use of rituals (Fitz-enz, 1990). A ritual might be the chief gerontologist administrator appearing at the end of a workshop to offer recognition to the team and to express confidence. On a larger scale, the organization could celebrate a period, say six months, of change efforts and visually list accomplishments. These and other methods are used to sustain the momentum of change (Gatewood et al., 1995; Johnson, 1998).

It is often useful to formally measure the extent of the changes. The most formal method is to administer instruments randomly. For example, Sluyter (1998) offers the "Performance Improvement Progress and Cultural Change Scale," which evaluates change in values, leadership practices, and eight other dimensions, including a global rating. Another method, somewhat less formal, is to use focus groups drawn from different parts of the organization. The same set of questions can be used with all groups, although the discussion may vary greatly once the questions are answered; this can include such questions as, "What is new about your job since . . . ?" or "What have you observed about the clients in the past six months?" Data from both of these techniques needs to be considered by the change team or the management team and followed with appropriate acknowledgment of changes, refinement of strategies, or both.

ORGANIZATIONAL DEVELOPMENT TECHNOLOGY

Organizational development (OD) technologies, which focus primarily on the thoughts, feelings, and attitudes of people, are used extensively to assist with planning, implementing, and sustaining change. OD, as an organization-wide planned change effort to increase organizational effectiveness, in practice rarely encompasses the entire organization (Beckhard & Harris, 1977). For the most part, OD technologies are used in different parts of the organization undergoing changes. OD has its roots in the long-term change efforts of the 1960s.

In its most systematic and comprehensive form, OD as a change approach was characterized as action research (French, 1978). However, OD is not presented here in that context. We have sought to extract from the OD literature those techniques that have survived over time and are considered useful for modern organizations.

- *Team Building*. Use of structured group experiences to help work teams improve performance and achieve greater satisfaction with work (French, 1978; Gatewood et al., 1995; Weiner, 1990).

- *Inter-group Team Building*. These are attempts to build better relationships between departments and teams in an organization. They seek to resolve conflict, establish common ground, and understand the mutual interdependence (Gatewood et al., 1995).

- *Conflict Management*. Systematic attempts either to reduce or to stimulate conflict to improve organizational effectiveness (Weiner, 1990).

- *Professional Development Training*. Training experiences using instruments and structured learning in understanding and developing interpersonal skills, administrative techniques, supervisory skills, and communications. Such training usually involves self-assessment and new skill training.

- *Job Redesign.* This encompasses adjustments to one's job, often called job enrichment or job enlargement, in which additional tasks are assigned that are of interest to the employee. At times, it also involves job rotation, especially where cross-training of jobs is important. This is used to develop and motivate employees (Weiner, 1990; Gatewood et al., 1995).

- *Quality of Work Life.* Administrative activities that improve the physical and social environment in the work organization; for example, reorganization or expansion of work space (Weiner, 1990).

- *Career Planning.* The administrator or human resources staff work with the employee to achieve career goals. These goals, then, in part determine selection of educational and training experiences that will be mutually beneficial to the employee and the organization.

These technologies are selectively used to facilitate perpetual change, increase organizational effectiveness, and to assist with substantive renewal. Many of these technologies and tools, such as supervisor skills training, have become integrated into the operations of modern organizations that provide programs for older adults. Some of these technologies have been previously explained in greater detail in this textbook. For the gerontologist administrator, OD technology is an integral part of the activities of most modern organizations.

NOTE ON ORGANIZATIONAL RENEWAL AND CONSULTATION

As a final discussion in this text, it seems constructive to offer a perspective on the use of consultation, particularly as it relates to organizational renewal. For these OD technologies, and many other technologies not mentioned here, it is common to use outside consultants and trainers on a selective basis (Bennis, 1969; French, 1978; Gatewood et al., 1995; Weiner, 1990). Consultation is considered by many to be one of the OD technologies. Consultation directed toward implementing a change plan is called process consultation (Gatewood et al., 1995; London, 1988; Weiner, 1990). In this role, the consultant assists in implementing the goals associated with the plan and monitors the implementation through observations and interactions with staff. The consultant provides systematic feedback to staff and administration on observations of progress and difficulties and is involved in the problem-solving process with staff to overcome barriers and facilitate change.

Consultants can also be used to determine the focus by using the assessment techniques mentioned in this text and by facilitating group discussion to develop a change plan. Clearly, the consultant can be used throughout all phases of the change process. The advantages of using consultants are that they are not part of the established administrative structure, not emotionally attached to any aspects of the organization, and can provide a different perspective, bringing examples and experiences from other organizational change efforts (Fitz-enz, 1990; London, 1988). It is wise to have a formal contract or agreement with an outside consultant. Such agreements generally have a mutually agreed-upon scope of work and are voluntary, temporary, and collaborative.

SUMMARY

Organizational renewal and change require a departure from the status quo and a willingness to envision and embark upon a change process, as well as the recognition that modern organizations are constantly changing. This chapter focuses on substantial organizational change and renewal. The stimuli to change organizations are both external and internal. Internal indicators for change may come from consumer feedback, organizational conflict, or measure of efficiency; external indicators are driven by competition, funding sources, or changes in the client population.

Both the literature and the practice of organizational change have, like management approaches and leadership, evolved over the years. The human relations perspective of organizational change which incorporated many OD technologies is best characterized by the three-phased notions of unfreezing the organization, moving the organization through transition, and then refreezing the new organization to establish a state of equilibrium.

The emerging perspective on change for contemporary organizations has been influenced by greater demand for change, the desire to remain productive during the change, and research on change efforts. This new perspective views change as continuous, gives greater attention to behavior and less to attitudes, and involves staff much earlier in the change design. The emerging perspective on change is depicted as a "change train," which is moving at high speeds, brings about change while in motion, adds and loses people while continuing to change, and may stop briefly to make repairs.

Successful change efforts are greatly dependent upon administrative leadership. Leaders need to be introspective with regard to their own issues about change and be able to review the organization from several perspectives. They also need to articulate the vision of the desired organization, and be deeply involved in the change process. Organizational assessment has moved more toward comprehensive organizational analysis that combines pencil-and-paper instruments, group sessions, individual interviews, observations of meetings, and measures of productivity.

Most substantial change efforts are anticipated with the focus documented in the strategic plan or an organizational renewal plan. It is useful to prepare the organization for renewal by identifying the necessity to change and the dissatisfaction with continuing practices of the past. It is not necessary to criticize the past; it will be more productive to illustrate how current practices are irrelevant and unable to meet future needs and demands. The transition state of change requires increased communications, specifically around change efforts and dealing with resistance. Resistance to change is most prominent during the implementation phase. Using OD technology and early staff involvement in the change process will help minimize resistance.

In the renewal phase, the pace of the change will increase with reinforcement and recognition of accomplishments. Continued group sessions are necessary to assist with reinforcement. Actual measures of progress using hard data, when available, to present to the group will help the organization realize the new vision.

OD technology, which is consistent with much of the information presented in this text, has been institutionalized into modern organizations that serve older adults. The effective gerontologist administrator will be participating in and encouraging selective use of this technology on a continual basis. The literature on OD and on organizational change supports the use of organizational consultants to assist with change and renewal.

LEARNING EXPERIENCE

This final learning experience presents an actual organizational change (renewal) as presented at the American Association of Aging Annual Conference, 1999. The presenter was also the leader in the change process (Maxwell, 1999), holding the position of System Gerontology Business Leader at Lee Memorial Health Systems, Ft. Myers, Florida. An overview of the change model used, "idealized design," is presented below (Bright, 1996). The overview will be followed by the actual planning process that brought change to the Geriatric Service Program.

Idealized Design

This is a change process that identifies the desired program elements wanted here and now, rather than at some point in the future. It is based on an approach developed by Russell Ackoff, Professor Emeritus of the Walton School at the University of Pennsylvania (Ackoff, 1981). According to Bright (1996), the ideal design has five phases:

- *Formulating the Mess.* This involves an organizational and environmental scan that extends beyond the typical scan process. It seeks to analyze the interactions between the various identified forces both within the organization and in the outside environment.
- *Idealized Design.* This is the essence of the model where the preferred state of how the organization should look now is formulated. The preferred state will continue to evolve throughout the planning and implementation process.

- *Means Planning.* This is identifying the alternative approaches (strategies) that will be strong enough to implement the desired state. These strategies must be strong enough to avoid absorption and to establish new elements.
- *Resource Planning.* Determination of human and fiscal resources to implement the desired state; this means both available resources and those that are likely to be acquired.
- *Design of Implementation and Control.* Changes are implemented. Individuals are identified to oversee and report on the progress of change. At some point during this stage, the entire "mess" will need to be re-analyzed.

The assessment (formulating the mess) and planning activities are to be accomplished using a collaborative group process with emphasis on creative development. The process can be used to begin a program or to renew a program.

Renewing the Geriatric Program

The change process was stimulated by recognition of a growing market of older adults and the fragmentation of programs that existed at the hospital. Further motivation came from strategic, planned goals that sought to increase access to services and to develop new and existing resources. Prior to the planning process, the hospital was operating a number of independent, semi-autonomous services: a memory clinic, a fall clinic, a wellness program, caregiver support, geriatric care management, and a parish nurse program.

The Path to Change

A group of older adults, community leaders, and hospital staff conducted four meetings of approximately three hours in duration, using the "idealized design" phases to establish a coordinated, interrelated set of programs for older adults. However, administrative concerns about cost and validation of the process produced a repetition of the phases with a newly constituted group of hospital administrators and staff. This group was named the Geriatric Process Management Team. From the various planning processes associated with this approach, an improved, integrated service system emerged.

This account has combined the products that resulted from the two planning groups. Such issues as patients not served as a whole, cost of government controls, changes in Medicare, issues with loss of control, and expected resistance to change were identified. The design that emerged was not a centralized set of services but a concept of coordinated, interrelated seamless services. The services would exist on a wellness to sick continuum, with a major focus on prevention. This design required the hospital staff to think differently about care of the older adult population. Thus, consideration was given to how to address that determination.

Components of the Change

The change was guided by a gerontology charter "to establish a three-year Gerontology Business Plan that responds to the integrated delivery system design, providing for seamless care delivery and value-added service to older adults across the Lee Memorial Health System where quality, cost, and access are in balance." The design repositions older adult services within the organizational design of the hospital and establishes a new leadership position. The service components reorganized or to be established were placed in three categories: increased access, coordination, and early intervention.

Increased Access

- Group care (insurance) offered to older adults
- Primary care by telephone offered by nurses
- A conveniently located 24-hour immediate care center with group-level access
- Specialist medical care at a central location to minimize the necessity of travel
- Direct older adult access to in-house (hospital) specialists

Coordination

- Social work to organize non-medical services
- Community case management provided to high-risk patients
- Terminally ill management program that provides coordinated legal, social, and behavioral services to dying patients
- To position internists, who will maintain a dedicated geriatric practice
- An ambulatory care pathway specifically for chronic conditions
- Pharmacy committee to provide advice to physicians on senior medication protocols

Earlier Intervention

- Comprehensive welcome and telephone screening provided to all new inquiries by older adults
- Psychosocial geriatric assessment provided to at-risk seniors
- Chronic disease management and wellness classes offered to develop older adult self-care abilities
- Transportation provided to clinics and physicians' offices

The new design also instituted "sensitivity training" for staff throughout the hospital to understand the developmental process of aging and the needs of older adults. Community committees were established to obtain continued feedback of the newly integrated and coordinated services.

Questions:

1. What elements of this change experience are consistent with the emerging approach to renewal described in this chapter?

2. What are the advantages or disadvantages of the "idealized design" process?

3. What measures were taken to deal with the organizational system that lacked knowledge of older adults and older adult medical issues?

4. Of all the changes that are proposed or have taken place, which one do you think would be the most difficult for the hospital staff, and why?

5. What do you think is the greatest challenge for the Geriatric Business Manager who is the leader of this newly designed complex of integrated services?

6. What is your reaction to the goals of this approach and the results of the change process?

REFERENCES

Ackoff, R. L. (1981). *Creating the corporate future: Plan or be planned for.* New York: John Wiley.

Allan, L. A. (1958). *Management and organization.* New York: McGraw-Hill.

Bargal, D., & Schmid, H. (1992). Organizational change and development in human service organizations: A prefatory essay. *Administration in Social Work, 16*(3/4), 1–13.

Beckhard, R., & Harris, R. T. (1977). *Organizational transitions: Managing complex change.* Reading, MA: Addison-Wesley.

Bennis, W. G. (1969). *Organizational development: Its nature, origins, and prospects.* Reading, MA: Addison-Wesley.

Bright. S. L. (1996). Idealized design. In R. G. Gift & C. F. Kinney (Eds.), *Today's management methods* (pp. 139–152). Chicago: American Hospital Publishing.

Briscoe, D. R. (1977). Toward an individual strategy for coping with change. *The Personnel Administrator, 22*(7), 45–48.

Brody, R. (1993). *Effectively managing human service organizations.* Newbury Park, CA: Sage.

Buller, P. F., Saxberg, B. O., & Smith, H. L. (1985). Institutionalization of planned organizational change: A model and review of the literature. In L. D. Goodstein & J. W. Pfeiffer (Eds.), *The 1985 annual: Developing human resources* (pp. 189–199). San Diego, CA: University Associates.

Champion, D. (1975). *The sociology of organizations.* New York: McGraw-Hill.

Crow, R. T., & Odewahn, C. A. (1987). *Management for the human services.* Englewood Cliffs, NJ: Prentice-Hall.

Doyle, P. (1985). Considerations for managers in implementing change. In L. D. Goodstein & J. W. Pfeiffer (Eds.), *The 1985 annual: Developing human resources* (pp. 183–188). San Diego, CA: University Associates.

Fitz-enz, J. (1990). *Human value management: The value-adding human resource management strategy for the 1990s.* San Francisco: Jossey-Bass.

French, W. (1978). Organizational development: Objectives, assumptions and strategies. In W. E. Natemeyer (Ed.), *Classics of organizational behavior* (pp. 348–362). Oak Park, IL: Moore.

Gatewood, R. D., Taylor, R. R., & Ferrell, O. C. (1995). *Management: Comprehension, analysis, and application*. Chicago: Austen.

Greiner, L. E. (1978). Patterns of organization change. In W. E. Natemeyer (Ed.), *Classics of organizational behavior* (pp. 336–347). Oak Park, IL: Moore.

Holloway, S., & Brager, G. (1985). Some considerations in planning organizational change. In S. Slavin (Ed.), *An introduction to human services management. Volume I of Social administration: The management of the social services* (2nd ed., pp. 309–318). London: Haworth.

Johnson, S. (1998). *Who moved my cheese?* New York: G. P. Putnam's Sons.

London, M. (1988). *Change agents: New role and innovation strategies for human resource professionals*. San Francisco: Jossey-Bass.

Lynch, D., & Kordis, P. L. (1988). *Strategy of the dolphin: Scoring a win in a chaotic world*. New York: William Morrow.

Maxwell, S. (1999, March). *How to gain control of your organization's future*. Presented at the American Society on Aging: 45th Annual Meeting, Orlando, FL.

McCune, J. C. (1999). The change makers. *Management Review, 88*(5), 16–22.

Mintzberg, H. (1989). *Mintzberg on management: Inside our strange world of organizations*. New York: Free Press.

Moore, R. (1988). *Personnel profile training*. Seminar presented in Tampa, FL. Sponsored by Portermill, Inc., Minneapolis, MN.

Oakley, E., & Krug, D. (1991). *Enlightened leadership: Getting to the heart of change*. New York: Simon & Schuster.

Patti, R. J. (1983). *Social welfare administration: Managing social programs in a developmental context*. Englewood Cliffs, NJ: Prentice-Hall.

Perlmutter, S. (1998). Self-efficacy and organizational change leadership. *Administration in Social Work, 22*(3), 23–38.

Peters, T. (1987). *Thriving on chaos: Handbook for a management revolution*. New York: Harper & Row.

Pritchett, P., & Pound, R. (1993). *High velocity culture change: A handbook for managers*. Dallas, TX: Pritchett.

Robbins, S. P. (1995). *Supervision today!* Englewood Cliffs, NJ: Prentice-Hall.

Rogers, P. J., & Hough, G. (1995). Improving the effectiveness of evaluations: Making the link to organizational theory. *Evaluation and Program Planning, 18*(4), 321–332.

Schein, E. H. (1987). Defining organizational culture. In J. M. Shafritz & J. S. Ott (Eds.), *Classics of organization theory* (2nd ed., pp. 381–395). Chicago: Dorsey.

Shin, J., & McClomb, G. E. (1998). Top executive leadership and organization innovation: An empirical investigation of nonprofit human service organizations (HSOs). *Administration in Social Work, 22*(3), 1–21.

Sluyter, G. V. (1998). *Improving organizational performance: A practical guidebook for the human services field*. Thousand Oaks, CA: Sage.

Weinbach, R. (1998). *The social worker as manager: A practical guide to success* (3rd ed.). Needham Heights, MA: Allyn & Bacon.

Weiner, M. E. (1990). *Human services management: Analysis and applications* (2nd ed.). Belmont, CA: Wadsworth.

Wiseman, P. (1996, May 3). ER workers help patients lose the wait: Others will copy Harris Methodist. *USA Today*, p. 6B.

Appendix: Professional Associations

The American Geriatrics Society
770 Lexington Ave., Suite 300
New York, NY 10021
Telephone: (212) 308–1414
Fax: (212) 832–8646
E-mail: info.amger@americangeriatrics.org
Web Page: http://www.americangeriatrics.org

American Management Association
1501 Broadway
New York, NY 10019
Telephone: (212) 586–8100
Fax: (212) 903–8168
E-mail: cust_serv@amanet.org
Web Page: http://www.amanet.org

American Nurses Association
600 Maryland Ave., S.W., Suite 100 West
Washington, DC 20024
Telephone: (800) 274–4262
Fax: (202) 651–7001
E-mail: ana.org
Web Page: http://www.nursingworld.org

American Psychological Association (APA)
750 First St., N.E.
Washington, DC 20002
Telephone: (202) 336–5500
Fax: (202) 336–5502

E-mail: executiveoffice@apa.org
Web Page: http://www.apa.org

American Society for Public Administration
1120 G Street, N. W., Suite 700
Washington, DC 20005
Telephone: (202) 393–7878
Fax: (202) 638–4952
E-mail: info@aspanet.org
Web Page: http://www.aspanet.org

American Society on Aging (ASA)
833 Market St., Suite 511
San Francisco, CA 94103
Telephone: (415) 974–9600
Fax: (415) 974–0300
E-mail: info@asa.asaging.org
Web Page: http://www.asaging.org

American Sociological Association
1307 New York Avenue, N. W., Suite 700
Washington, DC 20005
Telephone: (202) 383–9005 Ext 316
Fax: (202) 638–0882
E-mail: executive.office@asanet.org
Web Page: http://www.asanet.org

Association for Gerontology in Higher Education (AGHE)
1030 15th Street, N.W., Suite 240
Washington, DC 20005
Telephone: (202) 289–9806
Fax: (202) 289–9824
E-mail: aghetemp@aghe.org
Web Page: http://www.aghe.org

The Gerontological Society of America (GSA)
1030 15th Street, N.W., Suite 250
Washington, DC 20005
Telephone: (202) 842–1275
Fax: (202) 842–1150
E-mail: geron@geron.org
Web Page: http://www.geron.org

The National Association of Social Workers (NASW)
750 First Street, N.E., Suite 700
Washington, DC 20002
Telephone: (202) 408–8600
Fax: (202) 336–8311
E-mail: info@naswdc.org
Web Page: http://www.socialworkers.org

Southern Gerontological Society (SGS)
Suite 110, Box C-5
1018 Thomasville Road
Tallahassee, FL 32303
Telephone: (850) 222–3524
Fax: (850) 222–2575
E-mail: SGS111@aol.com
Web Page: http://www.wfu.edu/Academic-departments/Gerontology/sgs

Bibliography

AARP Volunteer Policy Task Force. (1991). *AARP Volunteer Expectations*. Washington, DC: AARP.

Ackoff, R. L. (1981). *Creating the corporate future: Plan or be planned for*. New York: John Wiley.

Administration on Aging. (1998). Assistant Secretary for Aging stresses need to prepare for global aging. *Administration on Aging Update, 3*(6) [On-line serial]. Available FTP: Hostname: aoa.dhhs.gov   Directory:update/default.htm

Agor, W. (1989). Intuition and strategic planning: How organizations can make predictive decisions. *The Futurist, 23*(6), 20–23.

Albanese, R. (1975). *Management: Toward accountability for performance*. Homewood, IL: Richard D. Irwin.

Albrecht, K. (1978). *Successful management by objectives*. Englewood Cliffs, NJ: Prentice-Hall.

Alderson, W. T., & McDonnell, N. A. (1994). *Theory of management*. Atlanta, GA: Thomas Nelson.

Allan, L. A. (1958). *Management and organization*. New York: McGraw-Hill.

Alter, C. F. (1988). The changing structure of elderly services delivery systems. *The Gerontologist, 28*(1), 91–98.

American Society for Public Administration. (1994). *Code of Ethics*. Washington, DC: Author.

Anthony, R. N., & Herzlinger, R. E. (1975). *Management control in nonprofit organizations*. Homewood, IL: Richard D. Irwin.

Appelbaum, S. (1975). A model of managerial motivation. *Training and Development Journal, 29*(3), 46–49.

Atchley, R. (1996). Are we preparing gerontology students for the real world? *AGHE Exchange, 20*(2), 1–9.

Atchley, R. C. (1995). Gerontology and business: Getting the right people for the job. *Generations, 19*(2), 43–45.

Atchley, R. C. (2000). *Social forces and aging: An introduction to social gerontology* (9th ed.). Belmont, CA: Wadsworth Thomson Learning.

Austin, D. M. (1995). Management overview. In R. L. Edwards & J. G. Hopps (Eds.), *Encyclopedia of social work* (Vol. 2, 19th ed., pp. 1642–1658). Washington, DC: National Association of Social Workers.

Bargal, D., & Schmid, H. (1989). Recent themes in theory and research on leadership and their implications for management of the human services. In Y. Hasenfeld (Ed.), *Administrative leadership in the social services: The next challenge* (pp. 37–54). New York: Haworth.

Bargal, D., & Schmid, H. (1992). Organizational change and development in human service organizations: A prefatory essay. *Administration in Social Work, 16*(3/4), 1–13.

Barnard, C. (1978). Informal organizations and their relation to formal organizations. In W. E. Natemeyer (Ed.), *Classics of organizational theory* (pp. 239–243). Oak Park, IL: Moore.

Bass, B. (1985). *Leadership and performance beyond expectations.* New York: Free Press; Macmillan.

Beauchamp, T. L., & Childress, J. F. (1989). *Principles of biomedical ethics.* New York: Oxford University.

Beckhard, R., & Harris, R. T. (1977). *Organizational transitions: Managing complex change.* Reading, MA: Addison-Wesley.

Benham, P. (1999). Supervisory selection: The Supervisory Assessment Instrument. In Jossey-Bass/Pfeiffer (Ed.), *The 1999 annual: Vol. 1. Training* (pp. 93–105). San Francisco: Jossey-Bass/Pfeiffer.

Bennis, W., & Nanus, B. (1985). *Leaders: The strategies for taking charge.* New York: Harper & Row.

Bennis, W. G. (1969). *Organizational development: Its nature, origins, and prospects.* Reading, MA: Addison-Wesley.

Berk, J., & Berk, S. (1993). *Total quality management: Implementing continuous improvement.* New York: Sterling.

Bevilacqua, J. (1995). The imperative of professional leadership in public service management. In L. Ginsberg & P. R. Keys, (Eds.), *New management in human services* (2nd ed., pp. 283–289). Washington, DC: National Association of Social Workers.

Blackmon, T., Mdir, M., Craig, T., Jackson, D., Urquhart, P., & Noel, M. (1997). Case study: Utilization of a bioethics consultation team in the nursing home setting. *Nursing Home Medicine, 5*(1), 21–23.

Blair, J. D., & Fottler, M. D. (1990). *Challenges in health care management: Strategic perspectives for managing key stakeholders.* San Francisco: Jossey-Bass.

Blake, R. R., & Mouton, J. S. (1978). *The new managerial grid.* Houston, TX: Gulf.

Blancato, B. (1999). Prospects brighten for action on Older Americans Act. *Southern Gerontologist, 7*(5), 1.

Blanchard, K., & Johnson, S. (1982). *The one minute manager.* New York: William Morrow.

Blanchard, K., & Lorber, R. (1985). *Putting the one minute manager to work.* New York: Berkley.

Blanchard, K., & Peale, N. (1988). *The power of ethical management.* New York: William Morrow.

Blanchard, K., Zigarmi, P., & Zigarmi, D. (1985). *Leadership and the one minute manager*. New York: William Morrow.

Bluford, V. (1994). Working with older people. *Occupational Outlook Quarterly, 38*, 28–31.

Bradsher, J. E., Estes, C. L., & Stuart, M. H. (1995). Adult day care: A fragmented system of policy and funding streams. *Journal of Aging and Social Policy, 7*(1), 17–38.

Brammer, L. M., & MacDonald, G. (1999). *The helping relationship*. Boston: Allyn & Bacon.

Brauchle, P., & Wright, D. (1993). Training work teams. *Training & Development, 47*(3), 65–68.

Briar-Lawson, K. (1998). Community collaboration and service integration: Models and challenges. In J. McCroskey & S. D. Einbinder (Eds.), *Universities and communities: Remarking professionals and interprofessional education for the next century* (pp. 155–166). Westport, CT: Praeger.

Bright, S. L. (1996). Idealized design. In R. G. Gift & C. F. Kinney (Eds.), *Today's management methods* (pp. 139–152). Chicago: American Hospital Publishing.

Brill, N. J. (1976). *Team work: Working together in the human services*. Philadelphia: Lippincott.

Brilliant, E. L. (1986). Social work leadership: A missing ingredient? *Social Work, 31*(5), 325–331.

Briscoe, D. R. (1977). Toward an individual strategy for coping with change. *The Personnel Administrator, 22*(7), 45–48.

Brody, R. (1991). Preparing effective proposals. In R. L. Edwards & J. A. Yankey (Eds.), *Skills for effective human services management* (pp. 44–61). Washington, DC: National Association of Social Workers.

Brody, R. (1993). *Effectively managing human service organizations*. Newbury Park, CA: Sage.

Brown, S. R. (1987). Marketing home health care to the community. *Topics in Geriatric Rehabilitation, 2*(2), 55–65.

Brunk, D. (1996, October). A rising star: Adult day services find a place in the constellation of services. *Contemporary Long Term Care, 19*(10), pp. 38–46.

Bryson, J. M. (1988). A strategic planning process for public and nonprofit organizations. *Long Range Planning, 21*(1), 73–81.

Bucher, R., & Stelling, J. (1969). Characteristics of professional organizations. *Journal of Health and Social Behavior, 10*(1), 3–15.

Buller, P. F., Saxberg, B. O., & Smith, H. L. (1985). Institutionalization of planned organizational change: A model and review of the literature. In L. D. Goodstein & J. W. Pfeiffer (Eds.), *The 1985 annual: Developing human resources* (pp. 189–199). San Diego, CA: University Associates.

Burke, W. W. (1982). Leaders: Their behavior and development. In D. A. Nadler, M. L. Tushman, & N. G. Hatvany (Eds.), *Managing organizations: Readings and cases* (pp. 237–245). Boston: Little, Brown.

Buzan, T. (1974). *Use both sides of your brain*. New York: E. P. Dutton.

Campbell, D. T., & Stanley, J. C. (1963). *Experimental and quasi-experimental designs for research*. Chicago: Rand McNally College Publishing.

Campbell, J. P., & Pritchard, R. D. (1976). Motivation theory in industrial and organizational psychology. In M. D. Dunnete (Ed.), *Handbook of industrial and orga-nizational psychology* (pp. 63–130). Chicago: Rand McNally College Publishing.

Cannon, N. (1993). Older Americans Act reauthorization targets more services to mi-norities; funding for low-income aged. *Aging, 365*, 58.

Capitman, J. A. (1986). Community based long-term care models, target groups, and impacts on service use. *The Gerontologist, 26*(4), 389–397.

Caudron, S. (1994). Diversity ignites effective work teams. *Personnel Journal, 73*(9), 54–63.

Caudron, S., & Laabs, J. J. (1997). It's taken 75 years to say . . . here's to you! *Workforce, 76*, 70–82.

Champagne, P., & McAfee, R. B. (1989). *Motivating strategies for performance and productivity*. New York: Quorum.

Champion, D. (1975). *The sociology of organizations*. New York: McGraw-Hill.

Cohen, E., & Tichy, N. (1998). Teaching: The heart of leadership. *The Healthcare Forum Journal, 41*(2), 20–22, 24, 75.

Cohen, S. G., & Ledford, G. E. (1994). The effectiveness of self-managing teams: A quasi-experiment. *Human Relations, 47*(1), 13–43.

Cole-Gomolski, B. (1998). HR pros take steps to keep up on issues. *Computerworld, 32*(27), 35.

Computers in human services [Journal]. New York: Haworth.

Congress, E. (1997). Is the code of ethics as applicable to agency executives as it is to direct service providers? In E. Gambrill & R. Pruger (Eds.), *Controversial issues in social work ethics, values, and obligations* (pp. 138–142). Boston: Allyn & Bacon.

Cormier, K. A. (1996). Outsourcing accounts receivable and other, serendipitous, bene-fits. *Management Accounting, 78*, 16–17.

Crosby, B. (1986). Employee involvement: Why it fails, what it takes to succeed. *Per-sonnel Administrator, 31*(2), 95–96, 98–106.

Crow, R. T., & Odewahn, C. A. (1987). *Management for the human services*. Englewood Cliffs, NJ: Prentice-Hall.

Dale, E. (1978). *Management: Theory and practice* (4th ed.). New York: McGraw-Hill.

Davidson, J. (1978). *Effective time management*. New York: Human Sciences.

Dellinger, S., & Deane, B. (1980). *Communicating effectively: A complete guide for better managing*. Radnor, PA: Chiton.

Deming, W. E. (1986). *Out of the crisis*. Cambridge, MA: Massachusetts Institute of Technology.

De Vries, R. E., Roe, R. A., & Taillieu, T.C.B. (1998). Need for supervision: Its impact on leadership effectiveness. *Journal of Applied Behavioral Science, 34*(4), 486–501.

Doyle, M., & Straus, D. (1982). *How to make meetings work*. New York: Jove.

Doyle, P. (1985). Considerations for managers in implementing change. In L. D. Good-stein & J. W. Pfeiffer (Eds.), *The 1985 annual: Developing human resources* (pp. 183–188). San Diego, CA: University Associates.

Dreilinger, C. (1998). Get real (and ethics will follow). *Workforce, 77*(8), 101–102.

Drucker, P. (1985). *The effective executive*. New York: Harper & Row.

Drucker, P. F. (1982). *The practice of management*. New York: Harper & Row.

Drucker, P. F. (1989, July–August). What business can learn from nonprofits. *Harvard Business Review*, 88–93.

Duca, D. J. (1996). *Nonprofit boards: Roles, responsibilities, and performance*. New York: John Wiley.

Eberhardt, B. J., & Shani, A. B. (1984). The effects of full-time versus part-time employment status on attitudes toward specific organizational characteristics and overall job satisfaction. *Academy of Management Journal, 27*(4), 893–900.

Edwards, R. L., & Eadie, D. C. (1994). Meeting the change challenge: Managing growth in the nonprofit and public human services sectors. *Administration in Social Work, 18*(2), 107–123.

Egan, G. (1975). *The skilled helper: A model for systematic helping and interpersonal relating*. Monterey, CA: Brooks/Cole.

Ehlers, W. H., Austin, M. J., & Prothero, J. C. (Eds.). (1976). *Administration for the human services*. New York: Harper & Row.

Elkin, R. (1985). Paying the piper and calling the tune: Accountability and the human services. In S. Slavin (Ed.), *Managing finances, personnel, and information in human services. Vol. II of Social administration: The management of the social services* (2nd ed., pp. 138–153). New York: Haworth.

Ellis, L., & Roe, D. A. (1993). Home-delivered meals programs for the elderly: Distribution of services in New York State. *The American Journal of Public Health, 83*(7), 1034–1037.

Elloy, D. F., & Randolph, A. (1997). The effect of superleader behavior on autonomous work groups in a government operated railway service. *Public Personnel Management, 26*(2), 257–270.

Emmerich, R. (1998). Motivation at work. *Executive Excellence, 15*(6), 20.

Etzioni, A. (1964). *Modern organizations*. Englewood Cliffs, NJ: Prentice-Hall.

Evered, R. D., & Selman, J. C. (1989). Coaching and the art of management. *Organizational Dynamics, 18*(2), 16–27.

Ezell, M. (1991). Administrators as advocates. *Administration in Social Work, 15*(4), 1–18.

Famularo, J. J. (Ed.). (1986). *Handbook of human resources administration* (2nd ed.). New York: McGraw-Hill.

Fayol, H. (1949). *General and industrial management*. London: Sir Isaac Pitman.

Fiedler, F. E. (1967). *A theory of leadership effectiveness*. St. Louis, MO: McGraw-Hill.

Fiedler, F. E., & Chemers, M. M. (1974). *Leadership and effective management*. Glenview, IL: Scott, Foresman.

Fischer, L. R., & Schaffer, K. B. (1993). *Older volunteers: A guide to research and practice*. Newbury Park, CA: Sage.

Fitz-enz, J. (1990). *Human value management: The value-adding human resource management strategy for the 1990s*. San Francisco: Jossey-Bass.

Follett, M. P. (1986). Management as a profession. In M. T. Matteson & J. M. Ivancevich (Eds.), *Management classics* (3rd ed., pp. 7–17). Plano, TX: Business Publications.

Ford, D. L. (1975). Nominal group technique: An applied group problem-solving activity. In J. E. Jones & J. W. Pfeiffer (Eds.), *The 1975 annual handbook for group facilitators* (pp. 35–37). La Jolla, CA: University Associates.

Frease, M., & Zawacki, R. (1979). Job-sharing: An answer to productivity problems? *The Personnel Administrator, 24*(10), 35–38, 56.

French, W. (1978). Organizational development: Objectives, assumptions and strategies.

In W. E. Natemeyer (Ed.), *Classics of organizational behavior* (pp. 348–362). Oak Park, IL: Moore.

French, W. L. (1982). *The personnel management process: Human resources administration and development.* Boston: Houghton Mifflin.

Friedsman, H. J. (1995). Professional education and the invention of social gerontology. *Generations, 19,* 46–50.

Gandy, J., & Tepperman, L. (1990). *False alarm: The computerization of eight social welfare organizations.* Ontario, Canada: Wilfrid Laurier University.

Gates, B. (1998, April 21). *Bill Gates outlines Windows principles.* [On-line]. Available: www.microsoft.com/ntworkstation/news/newsarchive/Apr98/BillGkeynote.asp

Gatewood, R. D., Taylor, R. R., & Ferrell, O. C. (1995). *Management: Comprehension, analysis, and application.* Chicago: Austen.

Gelfand, D. E. (1993). *The aging network.* New York: Springer.

George, C. (1972). *The history of management thought.* Englewood Cliffs, NJ: Prentice-Hall.

George, S., & Weimerskirch, A. (1994). *Total quality management: Strategies and techniques proven at today's most successful companies.* New York: John Wiley.

Gewirth, A. (1978). *Reason and morality.* Chicago: University of Chicago.

Ginsberg, L. (1995). Concepts of new management. In L. Ginsberg & P. R. Keys (Eds.), *New management in human services* (2nd ed., pp. 1–37). Washington, DC: National Association of Social Workers.

Ginsberg, L., & Keys, P. R. (Eds.). (1995). *New management in human services* (2nd ed.). Washington, DC: National Association of Social Workers.

Giordano, J. A. (1996, October). *Management skills.* Intensive presented at Professional Proficiency: It Takes a Whole Network, a regional training conference, Area Agencies on Aging, Tampa, FL.

Giordano, J. A. (2000). Communications and counseling with older adults. *International Journal of Aging and Human Development, 51*(4), 71–80.

Gitterman, A. (1972). Comparison of educational models and their influences on supervision. In F. W. Kaslow and Associates (Eds.), *Issues in human services* (pp. 18–38). San Francisco: Jossey-Bass/Pfeiffer.

Glisson, C. (1989). The effect of leadership on workers in human service organizations. *Administration in Social Work, 13*(3/4), 99–116.

Goddard, A., & Powell, J. (1994). Using naturalistic and economic evaluation to assist service planning: A case study in the United Kingdom. *Evaluation Review, 18*(4), 472–492.

Goldberg, A. C. (1997). Top 8 legal issues affecting HR. *HR Focus, 74*(12), 1–4.

Goldberg, G. S. (1995). Theory and practice in program development: A study of the planning and implementation of fourteen social programs. *Social Service Review, 69,* 614–655.

Golden, R. L., & Sonneborn, S. (1998). Ethics in clinical practice with older adults: Recognizing biases and respecting boundaries. *Generations, 22*(3), 82–86.

Green, R. R. (1997). Emerging issues for social workers in the field of aging: White House Conference themes. *Journal of Gerontological Social Work, 27*(3), 79–87.

Greenberg, J. (1996). *The quest for justice on the job: Essays and experiments.* Thousand Oaks, CA: Sage.

Gregoire, T. K., Propp, J., & Poertner, J. (1998). The supervisor's role in the transfer of training. *Administration in Social Work, 22*(1), 1–18.

Greiner, L. (1973). What managers think of participative leadership. *Harvard Business Review, 51*(2), 111–117.

Greiner, L. E. (1978). Patterns of organization change. In W. E. Natemeyer (Ed.), *Classics of organizational behavior* (pp. 336–347). Oak Park, IL: Moore.

Gross, M. J. (1985). The importance of budgeting. In S. Slavin (Ed.), *Managing finances, personnel, and information in human services. Vol. II of Social administration: The management of the social services* (pp. 11–25). New York: Haworth.

Guth, D. W. (1995). Organizational crisis experience and public relations roles. *Public Relations Review, 21*(2), 123–127.

Gutiérrez, L., Glen Maye, L., & DeLois, K. (1995). The organizational context of empowerment practice: Implications for social work administration. *Social Work, 40*(2), 249–258.

Hage, J., & Aiken, M. (1970). Organizational alienation: A comparative analysis. In O. Grusky & G. Miller (Eds.), *The sociology of organizations* (pp. 517–526). New York: Free Press.

Hansen, K. A. (1998). Cybercruiting changes HR. *HR Focus, 7*(9), 13–15.

Harcourt, J., Richerson, V., & Wattier, M. (1991). A national study of middle managers' assessment of organization communication quality. *Journal of Business Communication, 28*(4), 348–365.

Harlow, K. S. (1993). Proxy measures, formula funding, and location: Implications for delivery of services for the aging. *Journal of Urban Affairs, 15*(5), 427–444.

Harrington-Mackin, D. (1996). *Keeping the team going.* New York: Amacom.

Harshman, C. L., & Philips, S. L. (1994). *Teaming up.* San Diego, CA: Pfeiffer.

Havassy, H. M. (1990). Effective second story bureaucrats: Mastering the paradox of diversity. *Journal of the National Association of Social Workers, 35*(2), 103–109.

Herzberg, F. (1986). One more time: How do you motivate employees? In M. T. Matteson & J. M. Ivancevich (Eds.), *Management classics* (3rd ed., pp. 282–297). Plano, TX: Business Publications.

Hickson, L., Worrall, L., Yiu, E., & Barnett, H. (1996). Planning a communication education program for older people. *Educational Gerontology, 22*(3), 257–269.

Hirschhorn, L. (1980). Evaluation and administration: From experimental design to social planning. In F. D. Perlmutter & S. Slavin (Eds.), *Leadership in social administration: Perspectives for the 1980s* (pp. 173–194). Philadelphia: Temple University.

Hoefer, R. (1994). A good story, well told: Rules for evaluating human services programs. *Social Work, 39*(2), 233–236.

Holland, J. E., & George, B. W. (1986). Orientation of new employees. In J. J. Famularo (Ed.), *Handbook of human resources administration* (2nd ed., pp. 24-1–24-35). New York: McGraw-Hill.

Holloway, S., & Brager, G. (1985). Some considerations in planning organizational change. In S. Slavin (Ed.), *An introduction to human services management. Volume I of Social administration: The management of the social services* (2nd ed., pp. 309–318). London: Haworth.

Holt, B. J. (1994). Targeting in federal grant programs: The case of the Older Americans Act. *Public Administration Review, 54*(5), 444–449.

Hooyman, N. R., & Kiyak, H. A. (1993). *Social gerontology: A multidisciplinary perspective* (3rd ed.). Boston: Allyn & Bacon.

Hooyman, N. R., & Kiyak, H. A. (1999). *Social gerontology: A multidisciplinary perspective* (5th ed.). Boston: Allyn & Bacon.

Hopkins, K. M. (1997). Supervisor intervention with troubled workers: A social identity perspective. *Human Relations 50*(10), 1215–1231.

House, R. J., & Mitchell, T. R. (1978). Path-goal theory of leadership. In W. E. Natemeyer (Ed.), *Classics of organizational theory* (pp. 226–236). Oak Park, IL: Moore.

Hoy, W. K., & Miskel, C. G. (1978). *Educational administration: Theory, research, and practice.* New York: Random House.

ICR Survey Research Group. (1991). *Marriott seniors volunteerism study.* Washington, DC: Marriott Senior Living Services and United States Administration on Aging.

Iutcovich, J. M. (1987). The politics of evaluation research: A case study of community development block grant funding for human services. *Evaluation and Program Planning, 10,* 71–81.

Jackson, N. C., & Mathews, R. M. (1995). Using public feedback to increase contributions to a multipurpose senior center. *Journal of Applied Behavioral Analysis, 28*(4), 449–456.

Jamieson, D., & O'Mara, J. (1991). *Managing work force 2000.* San Francisco: Jossey-Bass.

Janis, I. (1982). *Groupthink.* Boston: Houghton Mifflin.

Jansson, B. S. (1990). *Social welfare policy: From theory to practice.* Belmont, CA: Wadsworth.

Jessup, H. (1992). The road to results for teams. *Training & Development, 46*(9), 65–68.

Johnson, S. (1998). *Who moved my cheese?* New York: G. P. Putnam's Sons.

Julian, D. A. (1997). The utilization of the logic model as a system level planning and evaluation device. *Evaluation and Program Planning, 20*(3), 251–257.

Julian, D. A., Jones, A., & Deyo, D. (1995). The utilization of open systems evaluation and the logic model as tools for defining program planning and evaluation outcomes. *Evaluation and Program Planning, 18,* 333–341.

Kadushin, A. (1976). *Supervision in social work.* New York: Columbia University.

Kantz, M., & Mercer, K. (1991). Writing effectively: A key task for managers. In R. L. Edwards & J. A. Yankey (Eds.), *Skills for effective human service management* (pp. 221–257). Washington, DC: National Association of Social Workers.

Karuza, J., Calkins, E., Duffey, J., & Feather, J. (1988). Networking in aging: A challenge, model, and evaluation. *The Gerontological Society of America, 28*(2), 147–155.

Kaslow, F. W. (1972). Group supervision. In F. W. Kaslow & Associates (Eds.), *Issues in human services* (pp. 115–141). San Francisco: Jossey-Bass.

Kast, F. E., & Rosenzwig, J. E. (1986). General systems theory: Applications for organizations and management. In M. T. Matteson & J. M. Ivancevich (Eds.), *Management classics* (3rd ed., pp. 44–62). Plano, TX: Business Publications.

Katz, D., & Kahn, R. (1978). *The social psychology of organizations* (2nd ed.). New York: John Wiley.

Katz, R. L. (1982). Skills of an effective administrator. In D. A. Nadler, M. L. Tushman, & N. G. Hatvany (Eds.), *Managing organizations: Readings and cases* (pp. 7–19). Boston: Little, Brown.

Kennedy, P. W. (1995). Performance pay, productivity and morale. *Economic Record, 71*(214), 240–248.

Keys, P. R. (1995). Japanese quality management techniques. In L. Ginsberg & P. R. Keys (Eds.), *New management in human services* (2nd ed., pp. 162–170). Washington, DC: National Association of Social Workers.

Kidder, R. M. (1989). *Agenda for the 21st century*. Cambridge, MA: Massachusetts Institute of Technology.

Kindler, H. S. (1999). Risk taking for leaders. In E. Birch (Ed.), *The 1999 annual* (pp. 169–178). San Francisco: Jossey-Bass/Pfeiffer.

Koontz, H. (1990). *Essentials of management* (5th ed.). New York: McGraw-Hill.

Kotter, J. P. (1986). Why power and influence issues are at the very core of executive work. In S. Srivastva (Ed.), *Executive power* (pp. 20–32). San Francisco: Jossey-Bass.

Kouzes, J. M., & Posner, B. Z. (1988). *The leadership challenge*. San Francisco: Jossey-Bass.

Kovner, A., & Neuhauser, D. (1997). *Health services management: Readings and commentary* (6th ed.). Chicago: Health Administration.

Kuechler, C. F., Velasquez, J. J., & White, M. J. (1988). An assessment of human services program outcome measures: Are they credible, feasible, useful? *Administration in Social Work, 12*(3), 71–89.

Laabs, J. J. (1998). Targeted rewards jump-start motivation. *Workforce, 77*(2), 88–94.

Lakein, A. (1974). *How to get control of your time and your life*. New York: New American Library.

Larue, G. (1992). *Geroethics: A new vision of growing old in America*. Buffalo, NY: Prometheus.

Latham, G. P., & Locke, E. A. (1991). Self-regulation through goal setting. *Organizational Behavior and Human Decision Processes, 50*, 212–247.

Lavelle, M. (1998, July). The new rules of sexual harassment: The Supreme Court defines what harassment is and who can be held responsible. *U.S. News & World Report*, pp. 30–31.

Lawler, E. E., Mohrman, S. A., & Ledford, G. E. (1992). *Employee involvement and total quality management: Practice and results in Fortune 1000 companies*. San Francisco: Jossey-Bass.

Legnini, M. (1994). Developing leaders vs. training administrators in the health services. *American Journal of Public Health, 84*(10), 1569–1572.

Levy, A. (1982). *The art of effective presentations*. St. Petersburg, FL: Hazlett.

Levy, C. (1985). The ethics of management. In S. Slavin (Ed.), *Managing finances, personnel, and information in human services. Vol. 11 of Social administration: The management of the social services* (2nd ed., pp. 283–293). New York: Hawthorn.

Lewis, B. (1997). Praising the right people at the right time and place can be a powerful tool. *InfoWorld, 19*(42), 116–117.

Lewis, H. (1987). Ethics and the managing of service effectiveness in social welfare. *Administration in Social Work, 11*(3/4), 271–284.

Lewis, J. A., Lewis, M. D., & Souflée, F. (1991). *Management of human service programs* (2nd ed.). Pacific Grove, CA: Brooks/Cole.

Liebig, P. S. (1996). Area Agencies on Aging and the National Affordable Housing Act:

Opportunities and challenges. *The Journal of Applied Gerontology, 15*(4), 471–485.

Light, R. J. (1994). The future for evaluation. *Evaluation Practice, 15*(3), 249–253.

Likert, R. (1967). *The human organization: Its management and value.* New York: McGraw-Hill.

Locke, E. A. (1975). Personnel attitudes and motivation. In M. R. Rosenzweig & L. W. Porter (Eds.), *Annual Review of Psychology,* Vol. 26 (pp. 457–480). Palo Alto, CA: Annual Reviews.

Loen, R. O. (1994). *Superior supervision: The 10% solution.* New York: Lexington Books.

Loewenberg, F. M., & Dolgoff, R. (1992). *Ethical decisions for social work practice.* Itasca, IL: F. E. Peacock.

Lohmann, N. (1991). Evaluating programs for older people. In P.K.H. Kim (Ed.), *Serving the elderly: Skills for practice* (pp. 259–277). New York: Aldine De Gruyter.

Lohmann, R. A. (1980). Financial management and social administration. In F. D. Perlmutter & S. Slavin (Eds.), *Leadership in social administration: Perspectives for the 1980s* (pp. 123–141). Philadelphia: Temple University.

London, M. (1988). *Change agents: New role and innovation strategies for human resource professionals.* San Francisco: Jossey-Bass.

Longest, B. B. (1976). *Management practices for the health professional.* Reston, VA: Reston Publishing.

Lynch, D., & Kordis, P. L. (1988). *Strategy of the dolphin: Scoring a win in a chaotic world.* New York: William Morrow.

Mali, P. (1986). Testing and the employment procedure. In J. J. Famularo (Ed.), *Handbook of human resources administration* (pp. 15-1–15-20). New York: McGraw-Hill.

Manning, S. (1997). The social worker as moral citizen: Ethics in action. *Social Work, 42*(3), 223–230.

Marion, D. J. (1975). Open systems. In J. Jones & J. W. Pfeiffer (Eds.), *Annual handbook for group facilitators* (pp. 132–134). La Jolla, CA: University Associates.

Martin, L. (1993). *Total quality management in human service organizations.* Newbury Park, CA: Sage.

Martin, L. L., & Kettner, P. M. (1997). Performance measurement: The new accountability. *Administration in Social Work, 21*(1), 17–29.

Maslow, A. H. (1986). A theory of human motivation. In M. T. Matteson & J. M. Ivancevich (Eds.), *Management classics* (3rd ed., pp. 251–272). Plano, TX: Business Publications.

Maurer, R. (1997). Transforming resistance. *HR Focus, 74*(10), 9–11.

Maxwell, S. (1999, March). *How to gain control of your organization's future.* Presented at the American Society on Aging: 45th Annual Meeting, Orlando, FL.

McClelland, D. (1986). The urge to achieve. In M. T. Matteson & J. M. Ivancevich (Eds.), *Management classics* (3rd ed., pp. 273–281). Plano, TX: Business Publications.

McConnell, C. R., & Brue, S. L. (1996). *Economics: Principles, problems, and policies* (13th ed.). New York: McGraw-Hill.

McCune, J. C. (1999). The change makers. *Management Review, 88*(5), 16–22.

McNeely, R. L. (1988). Five morale enhancing innovations for human services settings. *Social Casework, 69*(4), 204–213.

Meenaghan, T. M., Washington, R. O., & Ryan, R. M. (1982). The planning model: Content and phases. In T. M. Meenaghan, R. O. Washington, and R. M. Ryan, *Macro practice in the human services: An introduction to planning, administration, evaluation, and community organizing components of practice* (pp. 19–34). New York: Free Press.

Miller, D., & Friesen, P. (1984). A longitudinal study of the corporate life cycle. *Management Science, 30,* 1161–1183.

Miller, J. N. (1988). New management concept in family and children's services. In P. R. Keys & L. H. Ginsberg (Eds.), *New management in human services* (pp. 212–234). Silver Spring, MD: National Association of Social Workers.

Mintzberg, H. (1979). *The structure of organizations.* Englewood Cliffs, NJ: Prentice-Hall.

Mintzberg, H. (1980). *The nature of managerial work.* Englewood Cliffs, NJ: Prentice-Hall.

Mintzberg, H. (1989). *Mintzberg on management: Inside our strange world of organizations.* New York: Free Press.

Miranda, R., & Keefe, T. (1998). Integrated financial management systems: Assessing the state of the art. *Government Finance Review, 14*(2), 9–15.

Miringoff, M. L. (1980). *Management in human service organizations.* New York: Macmillan.

Moniz-Cook, E., Millington, D., & Silver, M. (1997). Residential care for older people: Job satisfaction and psychological health in care staff. *Health and Social Care in the Community, 5*(2), 124–133.

Moody, H. (1982). Ethical dilemmas in long term health care. *Journal of Gerontological Social Work, 5*(1/2), 97–111.

Moody, H. (1992). *Ethics in an aging society.* Baltimore, MD: Johns Hopkins University.

Moore, R. (1988). *Personnel profile training.* Seminar presented in Tampa, FL. Sponsored by Portermill, Inc., Minneapolis, MN.

Morgan, E. E., Jr., & Hiltner, J. (1992). *Managing aging and human service agencies.* New York: Springer.

Morris, R., & Caro, F. G. (1995). The young-old, productive aging, and public policy. *Generations, 19,* 32–37.

Morrow-Howell, N., & Mui, A. (1989). Elderly volunteers: Reasons for initiating and terminating service. *Journal of Gerontological Social Work, 13*(3/4), 21–33.

Morse, J. J., & Lorsch, J. W. (1970). Beyond theory Y. *Harvard Business Review, 48*(3), 61–68.

Mueller, N. V. (1999). The professional pairing program: A new way to mentor. In Jossey-Bass/Pfeiffer (Ed.), *The 1999 annual: Vol. 2. Consulting* (pp. 187–198). San Francisco: Jossey-Bass/Pfeiffer.

Musick, J. L. (1997). A helping hand on personnel. *Nation's Business, 85*(8), 38–41.

Nadler, D. A., & Lawler, E. E. (1977). Motivation and performance. In D. A. Nadler, M. L. Tushman, & N. G. Hatvany (Eds.), *Managing organizations: Readings and cases* (pp. 101–113). Boston: Little, Brown.

Natemeyer, W. E. (Ed.). (1978). *Classics of organizational behavior.* Oak Park, IL: Moore.

Netting, E. F., Kettner, P. M., & McMurtry, S. L. (1993). *Social work macro practice*. New York: Longman.

Nicole, D. R. (1981). Meeting management. In J. E. Jones & J. W. Pfeiffer (Eds.), *The 1981 annual handbook for group facilitators* (pp. 183–187). San Diego, CA: University Associates.

Nixon, R., & Spearman, M. (1991). Building a pluralistic workplace. In R. L. Edwards & J. A. Yankey (Eds.), *Skills for effective human services management* (pp. 155–170). Washington, DC: National Association of Social Workers.

Nobile, R. J. (1997). HR's top 10 legal issues. *HR Focus, 74*(4), 19–21.

Norton, R. (1983). *Communicator style, theory, application and measures*. Beverly Hills, CA: Sage.

Nye, Robert D. (1992). *Three psychologies: Perspectives from Freud, Skinner, and Rogers* (4th ed.). Pacific Grove, CA: Brooks/Cole.

Oakley, E., & Krug, D. (1991). *Enlightened leadership: Getting to the heart of change*. New York: Simon & Schuster.

O'Brien, J. A. (1999). *Introduction to information systems: Essentials for the internetworked enterprise* (9th ed.). New York: McGraw-Hill.

O'Connell, B. (1981). *Effective leadership in voluntary organizations*. New York: Walker.

Odiorne, G. S. (1987). *The human side of management: Management by integration and self-control*. Lexington, MA: Lexington Books.

Okum, M. A. (1994). The relation between motives for organizational volunteers and frequency of volunteering by elders. *The Journal of Applied Gerontology, 13*(2), 115–126.

Olson, L. K. (1982). *The political economy of aging: The state, private power, and social welfare*. New York: Columbia University.

O'Neill, M. (1989). *The third America*. San Francisco: Jossey-Bass.

Orpen, C. (1997). The interactive effects of communication quality and job involvement on managerial job satisfaction and work motivation. *The Journal of Psychology, 131*(5), 519–523.

Osgood, D. (1992). Developing a new kind of motivation. *Supervisory Management, 37*(8), 6–7.

Ouchi, W., & Jaeger, A. (1978). Theory Z organizations: Stability in the midst of mobility. *Academy of Management Review, 3*, 305–314.

Overholser, G. (1999, September 1). The public's growing distrust of the media. *Chicago Tribune*, p. 21.

Ozawa, M. N., & Morrow-Howell, N. (1988). Services provided by elderly volunteers: An empirical study. *Journal of Gerontological Social Work, 13*(1/2), 65–80.

Pallarito, K. (1996, March). Finance: Assistance programs bank on volunteers. *Modern Healthcare*, p. 50.

Pareek, U., & Rao, T. V. (1990). Performance coaching. In J. W. Pfeiffer (Ed.), *The 1990 annual: Developing human resources* (pp. 249–263). San Diego, CA: University Associates.

Parsons, R., Higley, H. B., & Okerlund, V. W. (1995). Assessing the needs of our elders. *Public Management, 77*, 14–16.

Patchner, M. A., & Balgopal, P. R. (1993). *Excellence in nursing homes: Care, planning, quality assurance, and personnel management*. New York: Springer.

Patti, R. J. (1983). *Social welfare administration: Managing social programs in a developmental context.* Englewood Cliffs, NJ: Prentice-Hall.

Patti, R. J. (1987). Managing for service effectiveness in social welfare: Toward a performance model. *Administration in Social Work, 11*(3/4), 7–22.

Pearlman, S. (1996). Dignity and respect for all. *CA Magazine, 129*(8), 29–32.

Penley, L., Alexander, E., Jernigan, I., & Henwood, C. (1991). Communication abilities of managers: The relationship to performance. *Journal of Management, 17*(1), 57–76.

Perle, A. (1997). Have an attitude of gratitude. *Workforce, 76*(11), 77–79.

Perlmutter, F. D. (1995). Administering alternative social programs. In L. Ginsberg & P. R. Keys (Eds.), *New management in human services* (pp. 203–218). Washington, DC: National Association of Social Workers.

Perlmutter, S. (1998). Self-efficacy and organizational change leadership. *Administration in Social Work, 22*(3), 23–38.

Peters, T. (1987). *Thriving on chaos: Handbook for a management revolution.* New York: Harper & Row.

Peters, T., & Austin, N. (1985). *A passion for excellence: The leadership difference.* New York: Warner.

Peterson, R. T. (1989). *Principles of marketing.* Orlando, FL: Books for Professionals.

Pfeiffer, J., & Jones, J. (1973). Force-field analysis inventory. In J. Pfeiffer & J. Jones (Eds.), *A handbook of structural experiences for human relations training* (Vol. II, pp. 79–84). La Jolla, CA: University Associates.

Pincus, J. D. (1986). Communication satisfaction and job performance. *Human Communication Research, 12*(3), 395–419.

Pinderhughes, E. (1989). *Race, ethnicity, and power.* New York: Free Press.

Polak, R. J. (1999, March). *How to hire good employees—how to fire bad ones.* Workshop conducted at the American Society of Aging Annual Meeting, Orlando, Florida.

Pritchett, P., & Pound, R. (1993). *High velocity culture change: A handbook for managers.* Dallas, TX: Pritchett.

Ralston, P. A. (1986). Senior centers in rural communities: A qualitative study. *The Journal of Applied Gerontology, 5*(1), 76–92.

Rantz, M. J., Scott, J., & Porter, R. (1996). Employee motivation: New perspectives of the age-old challenge of work motivation. *Nursing Forum, 31*(3), 29–37.

Rauktis, M. E., & Koeske, G. F. (1994). Maintaining social worker morale: When supportive supervision is not enough. *Administration in Social Work, 18*(1), 39–60.

Raymond, F. B. (1991). Management of services for the elderly. In P.K.H. Kim (Ed.), *Serving the elderly: Skills for practice* (pp. 233–258). New York: Aldine De Gruyter.

Rees, F. (1991). *How to lead work teams.* San Diego, CA: Pfeiffer.

Richer, S. F., & Vallerand, R. J. (1995). Supervisor's interactional style on subordinates' intrinsic and extrinsic motivation. *The Journal of Social Psychology, 135*(6), 707–723.

Robbins, S. P. (1995). *Supervision today!* Englewood Cliffs, NJ: Prentice-Hall.

Rog, D. J., & Fournier, D. (1997). *Progress and future directions in evaluation: Perspectives on theory, practice, and methods.* San Francisco: Jossey-Bass.

Rogers, P. J., & Hough, G. (1995). Improving the effectiveness of evaluations: Making the link to organizational theory. *Evaluation and Program Planning, 18*(4), 321–332.

Rosengren, W. R. (1974). Structure, policy, and style: Strategies of organizational control. In Y. Hasenfeld and R. A. English (Eds.), *Human service organizations: A book of readings* (pp. 391–412). Ann Arbor, MI: University of Michigan.

Rosenthal, S. J., & Young, J. E. (1980). The governance of the social services. In F. D. Perlmutter & S. Slavin (Eds.), *Leadership in social administration: Perspectives for the 1980s* (pp. 86–104). Philadelphia: Temple University.

Rosenzweig, E. P. (1995). Trends in home care entitlements and benefits. *Journal of Gerontological Social Work, 24*(3/4), 9–30.

Rossi, P. H., Freeman, H. E., & Wright, S. R. (1979). *Evaluation: A systematic approach.* Beverly Hills, CA: Sage.

Royster, E. C. (1972). Black supervisors: Problems of race and role. In F. W. Kaslow and Associates (Eds.), *Issues in human services* (pp. 72–84). San Francisco: Jossey-Bass.

Rubin, H. J., & Rubin, I. S. (1992). *Community organizing and development* (2nd ed.). Boston: Allyn & Bacon.

Russell, P. A., Lankford, M. W., & Grinnell, R. M. (1985). Administrative styles of social work supervisors in a human service agency. In S. Slavin (Ed.), *Social administration: The management of the social services: Vol. 1 of An introduction to human services management* (2nd ed., pp. 150–167). Binghamton, NY: Haworth.

Rutman, L. (1977). Formative research and program evaluability. In L. Rutman (Ed.), *Evaluation research methods: A basic guide* (pp. 59–71). Beverly Hills, CA: Sage.

Ryan, E., Hamilton, T., & See, S. (1994). Patronizing the old: How do younger and older adults respond to baby talk in the nursing home? *International Journal on Aging and Human Development, 39*(1), 21–32.

Ryder, R., & Hepworth, J. (1990). AAMFT ethical code: "Dual relationships." *Journal of Marital and Family Therapy, 16*(2), 127–131.

Sarasota County Aging Network. (1997). Our Mission. *Directory of Sarasota County Senior Services* (p. 1). Sarasota, FL.

Schein, E. H. (1987). Defining organizational culture. In J. M. Shafritz & J. S. Ott (Eds.), *Classics of organization theory* (2nd ed., pp. 381–395). Chicago: Dorsey.

Schick, J., & Schick, T. (1989). In the market for ethics: Marketing begins with values. *Health Progress, 70*(8), 72–76.

Schmid, H. (1990). Staff and line relationships revisited: The case of community service agencies. *Public Personnel Management, 19*(1), 71–83.

Schoonover, P. (1996). Forced fit: Like a glove. *Think: The magazine on critical and creative thinking, 7*(2), 18–21.

Schuler, R. S. (1981). *Personnel and human resource management.* St. Paul, MN: West.

Schulz, J. H. (1995). *The economics of aging* (6th ed.). Westport, CT: Auburn House.

Scott, W. (1978). Organization theory: An overview and an appraisal. In J. Shafritz & P. Whitbeck (Eds.), *Classics of organization theory* (pp. 274–290). Oak Park, IL: Moore.

Seijts, G. H. (1998). The importance of future time perspective in theories of work motivation. *The Journal of Psychology, 132*, 154–168.

Seniors consult on products for the elderly. (1995). *The Futurist, 29*, 42.

Shera, W., & Page, J. (1995). Creating more effective human service organizations through strategies of empowerment. *Administration in Social Work, 19*(4), 1–15.

Shin, J., & McClomb, G. E. (1998). Top executive leadership and organization innovation: An empirical investigation of nonprofit human service organizations (HSOs). *Administration in Social Work, 22*(3), 1–21.

Sifonis, J. G., & Goldberg, B. (1996). *Corporation on a tightrope: Balancing leadership, governance, and technology in an age of complexity.* New York: Oxford University.

Simyar, F., & Lloyd-Jones, J. (1988). *Strategic management in the health care sector: Toward the year 2000.* Englewood Cliffs, NJ: Prentice-Hall.

Skidmore, R. A. (1995). *Social work administration: Dynamic management and human relationships* (3rd ed.). Boston: Allyn & Bacon.

Slavin, S. (1980). A theoretical framework for social administration. In F. D. Perlmutter & S. Slavin (Eds.), *Leadership in social administration: Perspectives for the 1980s* (pp. 3–21). Philadelphia: Temple University.

Slavin, S. (Ed.). (1985). *Managing finances, personnel, and information in human services. Vol. II of Social administration: The management of the social services* (2nd ed.). New York: Haworth.

Sluyter, G. V. (1998). *Improving organizational performance: A practical guidebook for the human services field.* Thousand Oaks, CA: Sage.

Smith, M., Buckwalter, K. C., Zevenbergen, P. W., & Kudart, P. (1993). An administrator's dilemma: Keeping the innovative mental health and aging programs alive after the grant funds end. *Journal of Mental Health Administration, 20*(3), 212–222.

Sonnenberg, F. (1994). *Managing with a conscience: How to improve performance through integrity, trust, and commitment.* New York: McGraw-Hill.

Sonnenstuhl, W., & Trice, H. (1990). *Strategies for employee assistance programs: The crucial balance.* Ithaca, NY: ILR Press.

Sontz, A.H.L. (1989). *Philanthropy and gerontology.* Westport, CT: Greenwood.

Spier, M. (1973). Kurt Lewin's force field analysis. In J. Jones & J. Pfeiffer (Eds.), *Annual handbook for group facilitators* (pp. 111–113). La Jolla, CA: University Associates.

Stein, H. (1970). Social work administration. In H. Schatz (Ed.), *Social work administration: A resource book* (p. 7). New York: New York Council on Social Work Education.

Strang, V. R., & Pearson, J. (1995). Factors influencing the utilization of results: A case study of an evaluation of an adult day care program. *The Canadian Journal of Program Evaluation/La Revue Canadienne D'Evaluation de Programme, 10*(1), 73–87.

Stven, C. (1985). Outreach to the elderly: Community based services. *Journal of Gerontological Social Work, 8*(3/4), 85–96.

Sumariwalla, R. D. (1988). Modern management and the nonprofit sector. In P. R. Keys & L. H. Ginsberg (Eds.), *New management in human services* (pp. 184–211). Silver Spring, MD: National Association of Social Workers.

Tan, D., Morris, L., & Romero, J. (1996). Changes in attitude after diversity training. *Training and Development Journal, 50*(9), 54–55.

Tannenbaum, R., & Schmidt, W. (1986). How to choose a leadership pattern. In M. T.

Matteson & J. M. Ivancevich (Eds.), *Management classics* (3rd ed., pp. 325–341). Plano, TX: Business Publications.

Thorson, J. A. (2000). *Aging in a changing society* (2nd ed.). Philadelphia: Brunner/ Mazel.

Torres-Gil, F. (1992). *The new aging: Politics and change in America*. Westport, CT: Auburn House.

Toseland, R. T., & Rivas, R. T. (1984). Structured methods for working with task groups. *Administration in Social Work, 8*(2), 49–58.

Townsend, P. L. (1986). *Commit to quality*. New York: John Wiley.

Ulrich, D. (1998). A new mandate for human resources. *Harvard Business Review, 76*(1), 124–135.

Umiker, W. (1988). *Management skills for the new health care supervisor*. Gaithersburg, MD: Aspen.

Wallsten, K. (1998). Targeted rewards have greater value—and bigger impact. *Workforce, 77*(11), 66–71.

Walsh, J. A. (1990). From clinician to supervisor: Essential ingredients for training. *Families in Society, 71*(2), 82–87.

Ward, P., & Preziosi, R. (1994). Fostering the effectiveness of groups at work. In J. W. Pfeiffer (Ed.), *The 1994 annual: Developing human resources* (pp. 213–226). San Diego, CA: Pfeiffer & Pfeiffer.

Webb, L. D., Montello, P. A., & Norton, M. S. (1994). *Human resources administration: Personnel issues and needs in education* (2nd ed.). New York: Macmillan.

Weber, M. (1986). The ideal bureaucracy. In M. T. Matteson & J. M. Ivancevich (Eds.), *Management classics* (3rd ed., pp. 220–226). Plano, TX: Business Publications.

Weinbach, R. (1990). *The social worker as manager: Theory and practice*. New York: Longman.

Weinbach, R. (1998). *The social worker as manager: A practical guide to success* (3rd ed.). Needham Heights, MA: Allyn & Bacon.

Weiner, M. E. (1990). *Human services management: Analysis and applications* (2nd ed.). Belmont, CA: Wadsworth.

Weiner, M. E. (1991). Motivating employees to achieve. In R. L. Edwards & J. A. Yankey (Eds.), *Skills for effective human service management* (pp. 302–316). Washington, DC: National Association of Social Workers.

Wendt, P. F., & Peterson, D. A. (1992). National survey of professionals in aging network supports need for formal training in gerontology. *AGHE Exchange, 15*, 1–4.

Wilber, K. H., & Myrtle, R. C. (1998). Developing community-based systems of care: Lessons from the field. In J. McCroskey & S. D. Einbinder (Eds.), *Universities and communities: Remarking professionals and interprofessional education for the next century* (pp. 119–138). Westport, CT: Praeger.

Wiley, C. (1992). Create an environment for employee motivation. *HR Focus, 69*, 14–15.

Wilkerson, A. E. (1980). A framework for project development. In F. D. Perlmutter & S. Slavin (Eds.), *Leadership in social administration: Perspectives for the 1980s* (pp. 157–172). Philadelphia: Temple University.

Wiseman, P. (1996, May 3). ER workers help patients lose the wait: Others will copy Harris Methodist. *USA Today*, p. 6B.

Wren, D. (1979). *The evolution of management thought*. New York: John Wiley.

Yeatts, D. E., Ray, S., List, N., and Duggar, B. (1991). Financing geriatric programs in community health centers. *Public Health Reports, 106*(4), 375–384.

Zaleznik, A. (1977). Managers and leaders: Are they different? *Harvard Business Review, 55*(3), 67–78.

Zaleznik, A. (1989). *The managerial mystique: Restoring leadership in business.* New York: Harper & Row.

Zaleznik, A. (1990). The leadership gap. *Academy of Management Executives, 4*(1), 7–22.

Zastrow, C., & Kirst-Ashman, K. (1997). *Understanding human behavior and the social environment* (4th ed.). Chicago: Nelson-Hall.

Zimmerman, M. A. (1990). Toward a theory of learned hopefulness: A structural model analysis of participation and empowerment. *Journal of Research in Personality, 24,* 71–86.

Zunin, L., & Zunin, N. (1972). *Contact: The first four minutes.* New York: Ballantine.

Index

AAA, 13–14, 121–22, 193, 217, 219
AARP, 283
Accountability, 213, 231–32, 237, 255; problems, 232; public, 267; and supervision, 185–86, 193, 195; for teams, 132
Action research. *See* OD
Administration, 5, 7; challenges of, 1, 9; definition of, 3; and ethical behavior, 85; functions of, 5–6; in human services, 3; a model of, 5–7
Administration on Aging (AOA), 13, 33
Administrative: decision-making, 4; jobs for gerontologists, 2; practices, 76; relationships related to ethical considerations, 78–80; transitions, 38
Adult day care, 111; evaluation of, 257
Advocacy by leaders, 33–34
Affirmative action, 148
Aging network, 13–14
Aging services, 13–15
American Association of Retired Persons (AARP), 283
American Society for Public Administration, 73, 78; code of ethics for, 79
Americans with Disabilities Act, 144, 151
AOA, 13, 33

Area Agencies on Aging (AAA), 13–14, 121–22, 193, 217, 219

Behavior modification, 174; dimensions of, 169, 174–76. *See also* Learning theory
Behavioral contract, 177
Bennis, W., 23, 30, 31, 36, 37
Blake, R., 197, 198, 199
Blanchard, K., 25, 82, 83, 84, 161, 173, 174, 175, 176
Boards: advisory, 277; not-for-profit, 276–77; primary functions, 277–78; problems, 279–80; profit corporate, 276; relationship with chief executive, 278–79
Boards of directors, 12, 275; and fund-raising, 221, 224
Budget: adjustments, 230; formats, 228; monitoring of, 229–30; planning, 228–29; reductions, 230; types, 225–28
Bureaucracy, professional, 113
Bureaucratic management, 47–48
Bureaucratic structure, 112; and communication, 91–92

Career development, 159
Chain of command, 127–28

About the Authors

JEFFREY A. GIORDANO was an Associate Professor and a member of the Department of Gerontology at the University of South Florida. He was also an organizational improvement consultant and seminar leader. Giordano's research and teaching in gerontology focused on administration, social policy, economics, families, and mental health issues. His management consulting experiences included long-term care, hospitals, community health services, and independent living communities. He had authored 15 scholarly journal articles, numerous articles on administrative processes in trade journals, and a book chapter, "The Aged within a Family Context," in *The Handbook of Family Psychology and Therapy* (1985).

THOMAS A. RICH was formerly Professor and Chair of Gerontology at the University of South Florida at Tampa (USF). While at USF he also served as Dean of the College of Social and Behavioral Sciences and Director of the Center for Applied Gerontology. After retiring from USF, he was Professor of Gerontology and Sociology and Director of the Gerontology Program at the University of West Georgia. His research and teaching interests include gerontology, community health, and cross-cultural studies. He is the author or editor of six other books, including *Old and Homeless—Double Jeopardy: An Overview of Current Practices and Policies* (1995).